Debbie
KAREN
and special love from your
horsey friend Luv,
Jennifer.

DOG DIGEST

Edited by Susan Bernstein

FOLLETT PUBLISHING COMPANY

CHICAGO
T-0271

ABOUT THE AUTHOR

A busy suburban mother of three pre-schoolers, Susan Bernstein, editor of Dog Digest, is very involved with the dog fancy. At the moment there are two West Highland White Terriers in the Bernstein household, Cream Puff and a new puppy, Snowflake. Formerly a high school teacher of English and history and a guidance counselor, Susan now devotes herself to her family, dogs (showing, grooming, training and breeding) and a variety of special projects such as writing, pottery, sculpture and travel. This is her first book.

CONTENTS

INTRODUCTION

I SET OUT with genuine enthusiasm on my quest to learn as much as possible about the various breeds, puppy care and dog ownership when it was time for our family to acquire a dog. Indeed there were a large number of books available on dogs, on particular breeds, on training, and on many specific dog subjects. To my surprise I could find no general book covering all the areas in which I was interested.

As I have become more involved in the dog fancy I have frequently needed an information source and all too often this was not readily available. Going to my first dog show was a confusing and overwhelming experience and I didn't know what was really happening. How much I would have appreciated an introduction to this complex adventure. Breeding our female for the first time involved reading many books which never really told it "as it was."

As the years passed it became a stronger and stronger conviction that a general all-encompassing dog book would truly be of benefit to the dog owner as well as the prospective dog owner. Thus, when the opportunity to prepare such a book arose it was with real joy that the task was undertaken.

In the process of gathering material, a tremendous amount of informative and interesting data was covered. I have tried to select the most helpful and interesting portions. Preparing a book of this magnitude proved to be quite an undertaking and although as many subjects as possible have been covered, at times there just wasn't space or time to probe them all. The subjects have been treated as fairly and as objectively as possible. The information given is based on personal experience as well as extensive research. The most recent research findings have been used and the very latest American Kennel Club information has been incorporated.

This book has two functions—first as a book which is enjoyable and informative to read and secondly, as a good referral source to use over the years. It is *not* a training manual—hints are given but I suggest you use them as a stepping stone to further training. It is *not* a grooming manual—the advice is sound as far as it goes but for trimming a specific breed you should obtain additional information. It is *not* a breeding manual—even though a tremendous amount of information on the various aspects of breeding is included, more than in the majority of dog books, it wouldn't hurt to read more on genetics and difficulties that might arise in your specific breed. The amount of information given on each breed has been severely edited because of space limitations. Thus, once you have selected a specific breed we would recommend your reading about it further in a book limiting itself just to that breed.

Some of what has been said in reference to selecting and training a dog is actually common sense for many individuals. I have restated it though to alleviate the anxiety and uncertainty many people have expressed. Having someone confirm your own beliefs is most encouraging when setting forth on a new endeavor.

The chapter on diet is quite scientific and was included primarily for reference, however, reading it will probably help the dog owner to become a wiser consumer and to select his dog's food with care.

Every dog owner, new or old, should read the health chapter. An awareness of the diseases and problems to which dogs are susceptible can be of utmost importance as far as having a healthmaintenance program. Giving your dog the proper medical care in terms of preventative medicine (shots and vaccines) as well as treatment whenever necessary will mean a healthy and happy animal.

Also found in this volume, are the excerpts from the rules and regulations for registering, showing, and participating in field trials. This has been included specifically so that the dog owner will have necessary and vital information readily available at his finger tips, whenever it is required. All too often it has been our frustrating experience to suddenly have an important question arise only to discover that the answer must come from the official regulations.

So now, happy reading toward a richer and fuller enjoyment of one of the great pleasures of life—dog ownership.

Susan Bernstein

CHAPTER I
YOUR FIRST DOG

WHY OWN A DOG?

THAT'S really a good question. Why own a dog? Who needs it? Why take on another responsibility, another mouth to feed, another complication, another source of concern, another burden? Life is complex enough, why add another element to an already over-taxed situation? A dog may create spots on your carpeting, possibly tear your drapes, chew your furniture, scratch up your woodwork, ruin your lawn, disrupt your peace and quiet, and occasionally cause friction with your neighbors. So who needs that? Or what about those sudden urgent outings in the midst of a blizzard or late at night when you would rather go directly to sleep or at ten in the morning when you intended to sleep until noon? All those expenses too—vet, license, shots, stitches after a dog fight, X-rays for that swallowed bone, kennel fees while you're away—and on and on. Who needs it? What about all the extra work—brushing, bathing, feeding, and walking? Non-dog owners ask these kinds of questions and they do so in all sincerity for they truly cannot understand the whole bit.

We, who keep and love dogs, often merely smile knowingly and don't try to refute such arguments. Others, who are patient and understanding, may try

---

REASONS FOR THE PET BOOM

- More leisure time and an affluent society are the reasons most often given for the growth of interest in pets. Certainly the increase in the number of registered, pure-bred dogs (about 7 per cent a year since 1958) substantiates this theory.
- Parents perennially give children pets for their educational value.
- Many people these days are acquiring dogs for protection as well as companionship.
- New thinking among psychologists offers the theory that *people need pets*. A leading exponent of this theory, Dr. Boris Levinson, Professor of Psychology at Yeshiva University and a clinical psychotherapist, says this in his new book *Pet-Oriented Child Psychotherapy*.
  Pet Food Institute

---

to explain to the non-believer what we, in the dog fancy, know so well: that the love and companionship of a dog is one of the truly satisfying, rewarding, enjoyable, enriching, fulfilling, and unforgettable relationships one can have in life. Picture what a marvelous experience it is to be always welcomed by an excited, loving, tail-wagging friend. It's incredibly emotionally uplifting to be greeted with such warmth and love when returning home from the alien outside world. What a rare situation to have someone give you lifelong, non-diminishing, unaltered love; with so little demanded in return. Once a dog's confidence and affection is won, it is for life. The loyalty dogs display is quite remarkable. Innumerable stories have been told which illustrate the tremendous loyalty and love of dogs. We know of dogs who traveled hundreds of miles to find their master, or those who sacrificed their lives to remain with or to rescue their master. The news media regularly recounts tales of dog heroism—rescuing a drowning person, saving someone from a flaming building, warning of danger and attacking an intruder.

In this highly computerized, mechanized, data processed, and impersonal world, there is a comforting sensation in sharing your abode with something that is still very natural. This need felt by modern man has resulted in the tremendous growth of pet ownership. Man apparently needs and appreciates this type of relationship—providing for an animal's existence in return for its love. The animal pet which is capable of actually offering the most in return is the dog.

Dogs have been man's companion and helper since ancient times. Art and literature testifies to this fact. Through the ages, dogs have remained with man during good times as well as bad. Dogs were the first domesticated animals and originally won man over by proving their usefulness. Scientists believe that dogs served first as scavengers, thus keeping their masters' camping site clean. Later, they proved themselves by herding, being beasts of burden, and assistants in hunting. Even today, numerous breeds of dogs serve man. Yet most dogs, even though they may have a definite working role, will also be a faithful companion to the one they serve.

Love, loyalty, companionship are the basic ingredients in the man-dog relationship, as well as the dog's unquestioning subservience. When you have your dog at your side you need never feel alone. In fact, this truth is being more fully realized today than

ever before. Many institutions have come to realize the positive value of dogs and have begun utilizing them for therapy. Institutions for the mentally disturbed have discovered the beneficial aspects of dogs through controlled experiments and found that their patients responded well to these pets. Some psychiatrists are using animals, dogs in particular, in working with disturbed children. Senior citizens find tremendous comfort in their dogs and some keep going because of them.

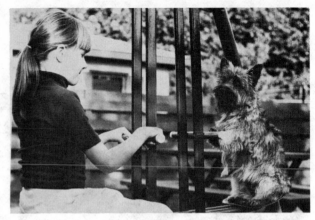

Photo by Tom Morrissette

Probably the only real disappointment experienced by the dog owner is the loss of this close, beloved companion. Since the dog's life span is shorter, man outlives his canine friend. However, since replacement is quite easy, this loss can become the opportunity for making a new relationship. Each animal is unique in its own way, but yet they can all provide the love and companionship, fun and frolic, that we all desire.

In today's crime ridden society, dog ownership is growing because people wish to use them as a deterrent. Research has shown that a large dog, for example, will do a good job of guarding since its presence alone scares off undesirable characters. Even a small dog can serve a valuable guarding function by merely being alert enough to bark at an intruder, since noise will often discourage them.

Why own a dog? Has the question been answered? Perhaps words cannot truly explain this phenomenon. But, if you are willing to take some chances, overlook some little "accidents," devote a little time and effort, you will be amazed by the rewards to be reaped. To our knowledge, there have been few real regrets by those who make the final plunge and adopt a dog. Errors in selection and judgment do occur, but these can be corrected. Therefore, don't let fear of a mistake be a deterrent. Dog ownership isn't like marriage or like having a child. Should you be unhappy with your new dog and it's something that can't be worked out, then do exchange him for another. Amazingly, such a problem is rather infrequent. Most people are delighted with their four-footed, furry selection.

Photo by Tom Morrissette

HOW TO CHOOSE YOUR DOG

ONCE you have decided to get a dog, the obvious question that follows is—what kind to purchase? Some people will adopt the first cute mutt available. Others prefer to do some investigating of the 116 different pure breeds and make a careful choice in terms of personal taste, needs, and desires.

Both ways can result in a satisfactory choice, however, the latter has a distinct advantage. When you select a pure bred puppy, you can be fairly certain of what the full grown dog will be like in appearance, size, personality, etc. With a mixed breed, you never can tell.

When trying to select a breed, it might be helpful to go to an American Kennel Club sanctioned all-breed dog show. At such a show, you will have the opportunity to both observe some of the best specimens of each breed and note how the various breeds behave in a stress situation—a real bonus if temperament and personality are important to you.

Male or Female?

Generally, a female dog (bitch) is a more affectionate pet. She is often better with children, doesn't tend to wander and is more sedate than the male. She is quieter and cleaner—and more easily house broken. Since the female squats to urinate, there is less damage to gardens and furniture. The female comes into season twice a year unless she is spayed (altered). Thus, should your bitch be of breeding quality, you have an opportunity to expand your hobby. The heat period (more thoroughly discussed in Chapter VI) does present added considerations, so if breeding is not desirable, a female may be spayed. A spayed female is really quite perfect for a family pet.

A male (dog) is the more aggressive specimen and should be selected if you want a dog for protective purposes. Males love to roam and are livelier. They lift a leg to urinate, which results in urine burns on bushes, trees, and buildings. They are often more difficult to housebreak and have more frequent "accidents" in the house.

Young males can be problems "sexually." They will often mount and pump on furniture legs, people's legs, and make an embarrassing nuisance of themselves. With training, this form of unacceptable behavior can be stopped. Males do like to roam often in search of a female in heat or just for fun. Since

other males are also looking for that female in heat, dog fights may result, thus male dogs are involved in more fights than females. However, the male usually develops into the larger and more impressive animal and, if showing is a main consideration, this must be kept in mind.

Puppy or Grown?

If you are getting a family pet, you naturally want it to build its affection, loyalties, and behavior patterns to please you. Training a puppy is no simple

---

POINTS TO CONSIDER IN CHOOSING A DOG

- ☐ MALE OR FEMALE?
- ☐ PUPPY OR GROWN?
- ☐ LARGE OR SMALL?
- ☐ LONG OR SHORT HAIRED?
- ☐ COST?
- ☐ FUNCTION AND PURPOSE?
- ☐ PERSONALITY AND CHARACTERISTICS
- ☐ PURCHASE OR ACCEPT AS A GIFT?
- ☐ PET QUALITY OR TOP QUALITY?

---

chore, but it is easier than retraining a dog with habits which are unsuitable to you. Your best bet is to get a puppy from eight weeks to six months of age. However, if it is completely impossible for you to be available to train a puppy, and it comes down to choosing between a mature dog or none at all, then try to remember to investigate these points:

Why is this dog being sold?

Is there a health or personality problem? Never be misled into feeling that you can correct a bad situation which the first owner couldn't handle. Naturally, there are circumstances which sometimes make it necessary for a very fine, well-trained and well-adjusted dog to be given away or sold; someone else's misfortune might be your good luck. Before you grab a mature dog, have it checked by your vet, and be sure it is housebroken, as it is quite difficult to housebreak a grown dog.

When acquiring a mature dog, you can tell exactly what you are getting. Beware of either aggressive or timid dogs. These undesirable features are often indicative of neglected animals with little human contact and are very difficult to alter.

Again, your best bet is a puppy.

Large or Small?

The size the dog attains when fully grown is an important consideration. What function will it serve and what accommodations are available? If your dog is to be a true house pet, confined to an apartment or home with a small yard, a toy or small terrier is quite appropriate. The larger breeds and sporting breeds need space in which to run. Unless you can provide such space, don't penalize your dog and yourself by subjecting him to an unsuitable environment.

Small dogs are most appropriate for apartments, small homes, and small yards. They cost very little to feed and, normally, have a longer life span than large dogs. However, if you are getting a dog and have small children you should be aware of the fact that small dogs are fearful of children and rightfully so. They will not tolerate being abused and their response will be either escape or defense. While a larger dog who feels less endangered by the antics of little children will be more tolerant and playful.

A large dog is best suited to living in its own quarters rather than in your home. A friendly wave of the tail by a Saint Bernard can knock over that favorite jar on your coffee table. Now please understand, there are many large dogs living happily in their masters' homes. But, hopefully, they are exceedingly well trained and the mistress of the house is happy with this arrangement.

Long or Short-Haired?

The amount of time and energy you have to devote to your dog's grooming will influence this decision. A long-haired dog needs daily, time consuming grooming. If the environment subjects him to thorns, burrs, thistle and twigs, then your job becomes a more difficult one. Your dog should be appropriate to your life style. For example, a short-legged, long-haired dog would be quite a chore to take care of in a woodsy type setting. Shedding can also be a house keeping problem. Be sure the one who has to keep house has a "say" in this decision.

The climate you live in should also be considered. In a cold climate a short-haired dog might need special apparel. In a very warm climate a heavy, long-haired dog might suffer from the heat.

Cost?

The initial purchase price is only a small fraction of the total cost of dog ownership. Therefore, it would seem to make good sense to get the very best dog you can afford. Over the lifetime of your dog, the $25, $50, or even $100 difference between the breed you really want and perhaps a "cheaper" one won't really make a difference. So get the dog you truly want and feel is right for you. The pleasure you receive from owning the dog you have set your heart on will make it all worthwhile.

The other cost factors to keep in mind are food, grooming, and health. Quantity and quality will give you some idea of the feeding cost. Some owners spend a fortune feeding their tiny dogs choice bits of meat. Some farm dogs get only scraps which cost nothing. To get a correct estimate, see Chapter IV. Some breeds require special grooming and unless you learn to do this yourself, these regular visits to the canine

or Grown?

Large or Small?

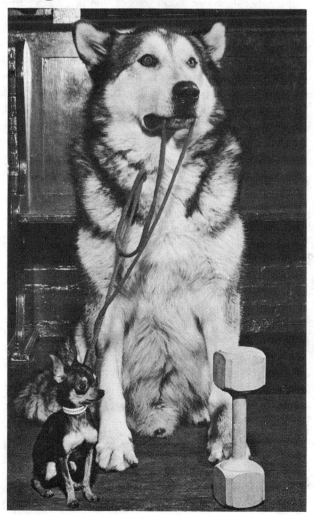

Long or Short-Haired?

POPULARITY OF VARIOUS BREEDS

Dog breeds vary in popularity as the years go by. But the shift is gradual and changes among the more popular breeds occur only every five to ten years. Since the American Kennel Club is the largest of the registration agencies, their annual tables are fairly accurate for the entire dog fancy.

Breed	Rank
Poodles	1
German Shepherd Dogs	2
Dachshunds	3
Beagles	4
Miniature Schnauzers	5
Chihuahuas	6
Pekingese	7
Collies	8
Labrador Retrievers	9
Cocker Spaniels	10
St. Bernards	11
Basset Hounds	12
Irish Setters	13
Pomeranians	14
Shetland Sheepdogs	15
Doberman Pinschers	16
Boston Terriers	17
German Shorthaired Pointers	18
Fox Terriers	19
Brittany Spaniels	20

beauty parlors can be quite an expensive item in your dog budget. Certain breeds are more prone to health problems and thus veterinarian bills can be quite high.

When the dog is first purchased, you'll need to know what point of immunization has been reached. Shots and other procedures which may still have to be handled such as spaying, cropping the ears, and docking the tail should be figured into the cost of the dog.

In calculating your expenses, don't forget you'll need some equipment, and many communities require yearly licenses and yearly rabies shots.

Function and Purpose?

To avoid eventual disappointment, be certain that you have thought out this question carefully and honestly. One dog cannot fulfill an infinite number of roles. Decide the main and most important function you wish your dog to serve and, then, perhaps if you are lucky, you can select a breed that also satisfies some of your minor requirements. For example, you could find a lovable pet that is a good watch dog; a beautiful dog can also be a fine companion and a good sporting dog can often help build responsibility in a boy. However, don't expect one dog to be tops in all areas.

Personality and Characteristics

To a fairly great extent, the personality and characteristics of a pure bred dog can be predicted, so select one that meets your needs. If you desire quiet and peace, you will be quite irritated by a high strung,

active, energetic dog. Choose one that enjoys curling up by his master's feet, and one who doesn't bark at each falling leaf. If you want a dog who will run and frisk with you for hours, you will have to pick accordingly. There are breeds that tend to be identified as being more masculine or feminine—you may want to consider this in your decision as well. Do you want a friendly companion or a watch dog? Do you want a beautiful dog or an affectionate one? Analyze yourself and choose wisely.

Purchase or Accept as a Gift?

Except for special circumstances, a dog of real quality is rarely given away. So, unless you fully know the situation, always be suspicious of a "gift" puppy or full grown dog. It would be most unusual for someone to be giving away exactly the type and breed of dog which you had carefully chosen. The opposite case is more likely. A dog is being offered—it isn't exactly what you wanted but you decide to take it anyway. It *can* work out. However, more often than not, you are not completely happy, and, deep down, acknowledge that you made a mistake. You may have ended up with a problem dog: who can't be trained, or is deaf, nearly blind, bites children, has serious digestive disturbances, or is a roamer. In other words,

your best bet is to purchase the breed and quality you've decided on and avoid so-called gifts.

Pet Quality or Top Quality?

When you are buying a pure bred dog, there will often be an opportunity to purchase a "pet." What this implies is that the breeder feels this animal is an inferior specimen in some way, or does not conform to the breed standards. Perhaps it is small, or the hind legs are cow hocked, or its coat isn't of the proper color or many other reasons. What the breeder is saying is that this dog would probably make a fine house pet but that it should not be bred or shown. So, if you are quite certain that you have no aspirations in the show or breeding line, then do consider getting a pet. A saving of perhaps 25 per cent can be realized by doing this. Often when first purchasing a pure bred dog, one really doesn't know if one will want to show or breed. Once you purchase a dog of pet quality, this decision has already been made for you. Therefore, give careful consideration to the quality you want, and, unless your budget is very tight or your plans are definite, don't settle for anything but the best. Now, that doesn't necessarily mean the highest price—it means the best quality. Shop around a little!

THINGS TO KNOW BEFORE BUYING A DOG

The Papers

WHEN purchasing a pure bred dog, be certain that you are getting the dog's "papers." These are registration papers from one of the three major accrediting organizations, the American Kennel Club, the United Kennel Club, or the Field Dog Stud Book. The litter should be registered with one of these to qualify as pure bred, and each puppy should have his own certificate. When you purchase the dog, you will be given this certificate. As soon as you select a name, fill in the application certificate correctly, enclose the specified fee, and send it to the club. You will then be sent an official registration for your dog, which bears the registration number needed when showing and breeding your dog. Be sure to keep this certificate in a safe place.

The Pedigree

The pedigree is merely the dog's family tree which tells you the ancestry from both the mother's and

The A.K.C. Registration Form

16

father's side. It is nice to have and quite necessary should you decide to breed. A completed pedigree should be presented to you by the seller when you purchase the dog.

The Dog's Health

The dog you are selecting should appear healthy. Its eyes should be clear and clean, the nose wet, its coat shiny. The dog should be alert, and its body nicely filled out as a fat puppy is usually a healthy one. If you are observing an entire litter, you can get a general idea which pups are frisky, which are withdrawn, and which one is the friendliest. Check the dog's mouth and teeth; the teeth should be white and the gums pink. Examine his skin for patches which may mean eczema, mange, or ringworm, and be sure to test for deafness. *Don't accept a dog that is obviously sick.*

Make an agreement with the owner that you will have the dog checked by your veterinarian by the next day, and, if there is any problem, that he may be returned. Your vet can check the puppy for any congenital defects and for existing conditions. Of course, he can't tell if the dog has been exposed to anything or what illness may be incubating.

At the time of purchase, find out what shots the puppy has already received and which are still required. (For a more complete discussion of shots, see Chapter V.)

The Panic Button

All too often, once the decision to get a dog is made, the prospective buyer rushes out too quickly to get his new "best friend." Take your time, look around, see a number of litters, find out what the price range is for the type of dog you are seeking. This can be a fun project for a few days or a few weeks. Don't feel you have to buy the first dog you see.

How to Purchase a Dog

After thoughtful and careful evaluation which included reading about, actually seeing, and being with the various breeds, you decided which one is right for your family. Hopefully, everyone who will be involved in caring for and living with this pet agrees with the selection. Now comes the question of where

A typical pedigree.

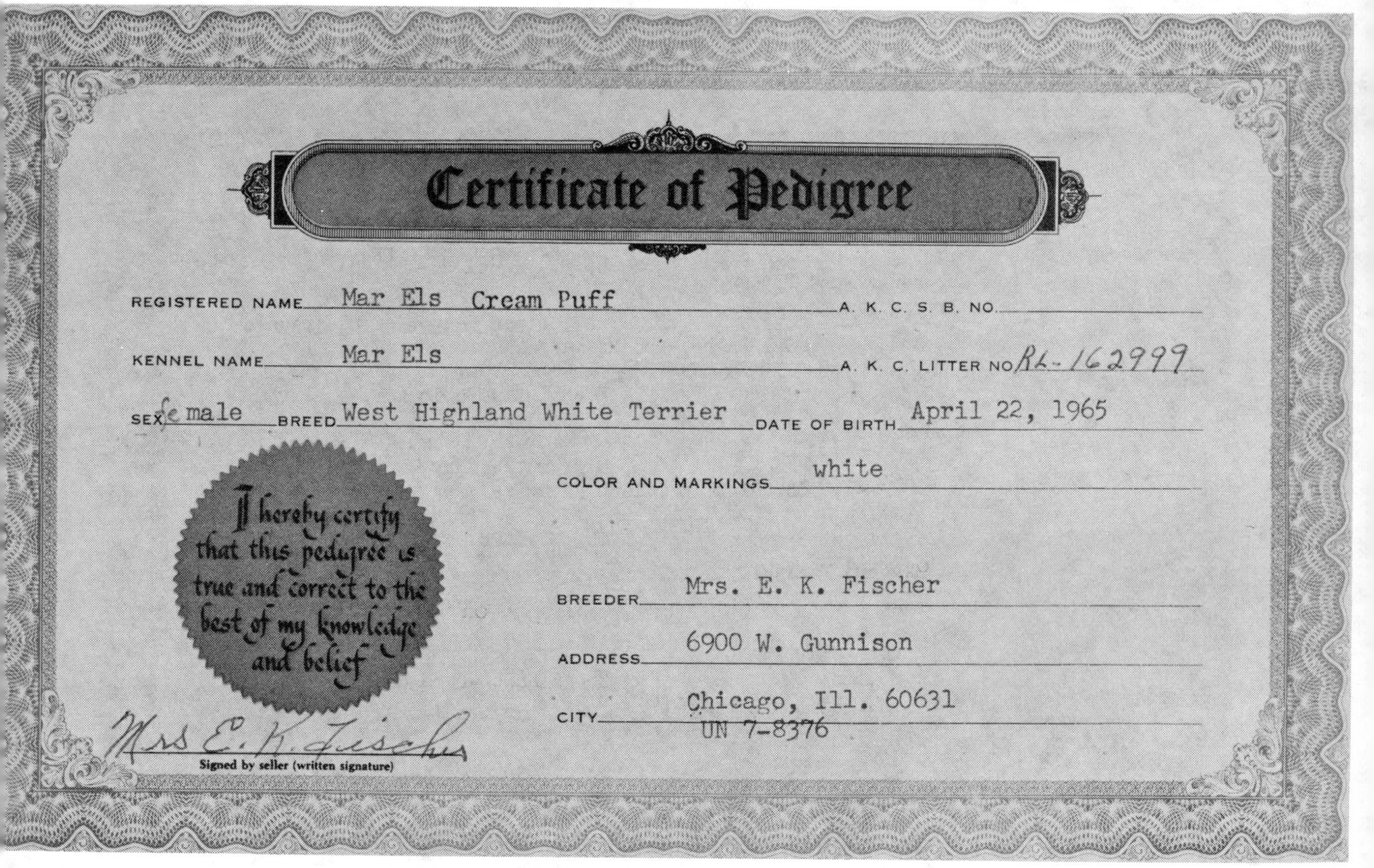

Certificate of Pedigree

REGISTERED NAME Mar Els Cream Puff A. K. C. S. B. NO.

KENNEL NAME Mar Els A. K. C. LITTER NO. RL-162999

SEX female BREED West Highland White Terrier DATE OF BIRTH April 22, 1965

COLOR AND MARKINGS white

I hereby certify that this pedigree is true and correct to the best of my knowledge and belief

BREEDER Mrs. E. K. Fischer

ADDRESS 6900 W. Gunnison

CITY Chicago, Ill. 60631
UN 7-8376

Mrs E. K. Fischer
Signed by seller (written signature)

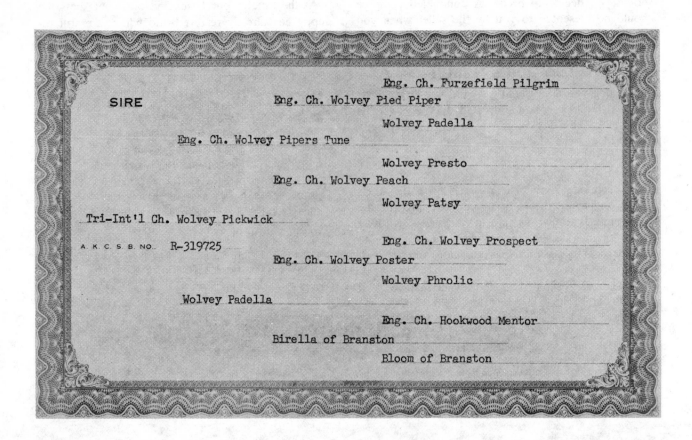

SIRE

Eng. Ch. Wolvey Pipers Tune

Eng. Ch. Wolvey Pied Piper

Eng. Ch. Furzefield Pilgrim

Wolvey Padella

Eng. Ch. Wolvey Peach

Wolvey Presto

Wolvey Patsy

Tri-Int'l Ch. Wolvey Pickwick

A. K. C. S. B. NO.   R-319725

Eng. Ch. Wolvey Poster

Eng. Ch. Wolvey Prospect

Wolvey Phrolic

Wolvey Padella

Birella of Branston

Eng. Ch. Hookwood Mentor

Bloom of Branston

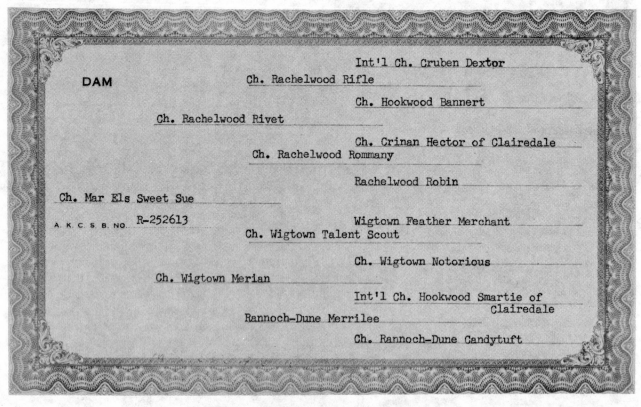

DAM

Ch. Rachelwood Rivet

Ch. Rachelwood Rifle

Int'l Ch. Cruben Dextor

Ch. Hookwood Bannert

Ch. Rachelwood Rommany

Ch. Crinan Hector of Clairedale

Rachelwood Robin

Ch. Mar Els Sweet Sue

A. K. C. S. B. NO.   R-252613

Ch. Wigtown Talent Scout

Wigtown Feather Merchant

Ch. Wigtown Notorious

Ch. Wigtown Merian

Rannoch-Dune Merrilee

Int'l Ch. Hookwood Smartie of
                        Clairedale

Ch. Rannoch-Dune Candytuft

*The pedigree includes a dog's family tree—giving
ancestry from both mother's and father's side.*

A healthy dog is alert, frisky, with clear eyes, a wet cold nose, and a shiny coat. Be certain the dog you purchase is a healthy one.

to get the dog. A dog can be purchased from a pet store, a large breeder, a "home" breeder, and through the mails. The proper steps for buying a dog are these: (1) you select the dog; (2) you and the seller agree on a purchase price; (3) you pay for the dog; (4) you receive the dog, the A.K.C. (American Kennel Club) registration and pedigree—if it is pure bred.

The Pet Shop

In most larger cities there are pet stores that offer puppies for sale. They usually only have a few litters at any one time and do not offer all breeds. There is a possibility that the one type you have selected may not be available. There are some pet shops that only offer dogs from the finest breeders. They will guarantee the puppy's health and will have all the necessary "papers." However, one should exercise care in buying a puppy from a shop, because the best dogs are usually not sold in this manner. Puppy mills—breeders producing puppies merely for large profit and not to maintain and better the breed—

sometimes use pet stores as their outlet. The price you pay for a given degree of quality can, sometimes, be higher in a pet store.

Mail Order

More and more dogs are being bought in this manner. Write to the American Kennel Club and request information about the breed which interests you. Large breeders advertise in the dog magazines. In the ad, they will often describe the dogs and give you their prices. You can order by writing or calling and the dog will be sent to you, usually by air. If you have no direct access to a certain breed, this method can be a fine solution. The breeder will give you a few days to evaluate the dog and the option to return it if it isn't suitable, but make sure these details are clearly spelled out. Most breeders who advertise in well-known dog magazines have fine reputations and will send exactly what you have requested. Since you do not have the advantage of seeing the dog in the flesh, try to be as specific as possible in your correspondence. Give exact details of what you want in

Typical mail order advertisements.

your initial inquiry, such as, sex, age, size, coloring, pet or show quality, training desired, and all other useful information. Clarity will avoid disappointment. Pictures are also valuable in helping you select and they often will be provided upon request. Consider this method of buying if you can't find the breed you want in your community.

The Large Breeder

Breeding the more popular dogs has become big business. Large breeders maintain their dogs in well kept kennels and often have a good-sized selection of dogs. Here you can usually choose from a very

The Right Dog For City Living

Very large dogs, such at Great Danes, St. Bernards, Irish Wolfhounds; and sport dogs like Irish and English Setters, Pointers and Retrievers are not recommended for city living. Both types need plenty of space and exercise, usually more than the average city dweller can or will give them.

Boxers, German Shepherds, Doberman Pinschers, Collies and mixtures of these breeds are popular and seem to adapt to city living, providing they receive enough exercise and are trained to get along in their cramped quarters.

The small, medium and toy dogs make the best city pets. These dogs take up less space and don't need lengthy and vigorous exercise periods required by larger dogs. They can be paper-trained.

young puppy (8 weeks) to a more mature pup. Occasionally there has already been some training in terms of housebreaking and special training for the sporting dogs. These breeders can discuss the puppy quite thoroughly. They should be familiar with the bitch and stud and be able to give you interesting background information as to championships won, history of other litters, characteristics of these puppies, and specific details about this particular litter and this puppy. The large breeder of one or two breeds is often well-informed about happenings in the specialty clubs. They can tell you how to join and what the meetings are like. At this time you should inquire about the dog's diet, shots that may still be needed, and what terms have been used for training.

Since the large breeder is probably a good businessman, he will have all your papers ready for you when you purchase the dog and a written health guarantee. Perhaps even time payments will also be possible. Breeders often provide other services, such as grooming and boarding.

The Small "At Home" Breeder

The name and location of small breeders can usually be found in the newspaper and in dog magazines. It may be a true dog enthusiast who shows, grooms, boards, and breeds dogs. Many of these small breeders are located all over the country. Very often they have litters available most times of the year, although there are times when you may have to wait a few weeks until puppies are available. These breeders are generally dog lovers and can be of real help to you in selecting a pup and starting his training at home.

Non professional breeders often expose their puppies to children and get the dogs used to a family atmosphere.

The Non-Professional

Thousands of non-professional breeders who have mated their bitches often wish to sell their pups. Newspaper ads, your local vet, or friends can help you locate these pups. Home raised dogs are fine, as they have often been handled more than kennel raised dogs and may already be used to children and to home living. These breeders are usually looking for good homes for their puppies and will give you much help and advice.

The Anti-Cruelty Society, Humane Society, or Dog Pound

Most communities have agencies offering dogs whose original owners, for some reason, were unable to keep them. It *is* possible to find a nice dog in this manner. Sometimes, even pure bred dogs are available. Sometimes for a very small fee or for a contribution, a good dog can be obtained. Having such a dog carefully checked by your veterinarian is of utmost importance. It is wise to see how the dog behaves and adjusts before getting attached. If unsatisfactory he can and should be returned.

Pedigrees for Pure Bred Dogs

A pedigree is the dog's "family tree." It will trace back the ancestry for several generations on both sides. The dog's owner should have this pedigree available for you at time of purchase. It is necessary for you to have this so that you can know your dog's background. This information is needed if you show your dog and if you should decide to breed. Do not forget it. A pedigree is important. However, if for some reason you have not received the pedigree and yours is an A.K.C. registered dog you can still get one. This is done by writing to the American Kennel Club and asking for the pedigree—including the dog's full registered name, his registration number, and a check. At present, the fee is $2 for a three generation pedigree and $5 for a four generation pedigree.

REVIEW OF POINTS TO REMEMBER

(1) Pure bred dog must be registered with A.K.C. (or another club). Club registration papers must be provided at time of purchase, as well as the complete pedigree.

(2) Price of the puppy is determined by:

  A. going general rate for the breed which is affected by availability and popularity.

  B. whether the pup has both mother and father who are champions or just one champ parent. If neither parent is a champ, a lower price should be charged. With some breeds, the female demands a higher price while in others it is the male. Check around as to the practice in the breed which interests you. "Pet quality" costs less.

  C. the age of the pup. If a pup has all its shots, dew claws removed, ears cropped (if necessary), the price will be higher than a dog that still needs to have these matters taken care of.

(3) Beware—sire and dam must be pure breds of the same breed.

(4) Learn how to read a newspaper advertisement:

A. Here you are told that both parents are champions and that these pups are already housebroken:

  BEDLINGTONS—Outstanding blue puppies from champion sire and dam. Housebroken . . .

B. Both qualities of pups are available. Probably only the sire was a champ:

  BEDLINGTONS—Blue puppies, pet/show. Champion stud . . .

C. Sire, a champ. X-Rayed parents to check for hip problem (see Chapter V):

  OLD ENGLISH SHEEPDOG—Ch. (Group 1st & sire of 6 champions) has sired another beautiful litter now available to good homes. Healthy, happy country-raised pups. X-Rayed parents. Also older male . . .

D. Sire, a champ. Three qualities available—undoubtedly with three price ranges. Fully guaranteed:

  LHASA APSO—Nice healthy puppies. Golden, particolors, grizzle and black from champion and pointed studs. Pet, show and breeding quality. Conformation and health guaranteed . . .

E. They feel these dogs are so fine that they will only sell them if you promise to show:

  IRISH SETTERS Select Show Puppies — SHOW HOMES ONLY —

F. Temperament stressed:

  BULLMASTIFF—Raised with children for temperament. Champion bloodline bred for size . . .

G. Field trial winners rather than bench:

  OUTSTANDING BRITTANIES FOR FIELD or show from dual champion and National Field champion sires. Unconditional guarantee . . .

H. Note—this breed is not registered by the A.K.C. Breeder guarantees working qualities:

  AUSTRALIAN CATTLE DOG Purebred, though not AKC registerable. Shown in Misc. Class. **AUSTRALIAN CATTLE DOG PUPS, AIR** shipment. Guaranteed to heel and work stock. Excellent watchdogs . . .

REGISTERING YOUR DOG

The official information you need to know about registering your pure bred dog with the American Kennel Club—

The American Kennel Club
Incorporated

Rules and Regulations
and

Extracts from By-Laws

CHAPTER 1
GENERAL EXPLANATIONS

SECTION 1. The word "dog" wherever used in these Rules and Regulations includes both sexes.

SECTION 2. The words "United States of America" wherever used in these Rules and Regulations shall be construed to include all territories and possessions of the United States of America and all vessels sailing under the American Flag.

CHAPTER 2
REGISTRABLE BREEDS BY GROUPS

The following breeds divided by groups shall be all the breeds now recognized by The American Kennel Club as being distinct breeds of pure-bred dogs eligible for registration in the Stud Book of The American Kennel Club.

GROUP 1
SPORTING DOGS

GRIFFONS (WIREHAIRED POINTING)
POINTERS
POINTERS (GERMAN SHORTHAIRED)
POINTERS (GERMAN WIREHAIRED)
RETRIEVERS (CHESAPEAKE BAY)
RETRIEVERS (CURLY-COATED)
RETRIEVERS (FLAT-COATED)
RETRIEVERS (GOLDEN)
RETRIEVERS (LABRADOR)
SETTERS (ENGLISH)
SETTERS (GORDON)
SETTERS (IRISH)
SPANIELS (AMERICAN WATER)
SPANIELS (BRITTANY)
SPANIELS (CLUMBER)
SPANIELS (COCKER)
SPANIELS (ENGLISH COCKER)
SPANIELS (ENGLISH SPRINGER)
SPANIELS (FIELD)
SPANIELS (IRISH WATER)

GROUP 1—SPORTING DOGS: White and Orange English Setter, Regent, owned by Henry H. Townshend. (Photo courtesy American Field.)

SPANIELS (SUSSEX)
SPANIELS (WELSH SPRINGER)
VIZSLAS
WEIMARANERS

GROUP 2—HOUNDS

AFGHAN HOUNDS
BASENJIS
BASSET HOUNDS
BEAGLES
BLOODHOUNDS
BORZOIS
COONHOUNDS (BLACK AND TAN)
DACHSHUNDS
DEERHOUNDS (SCOTTISH)
FOXHOUNDS (AMERICAN)
FOXHOUNDS (ENGLISH)
GREYHOUNDS
HARRIERS
IRISH WOLFHOUNDS
NORWEGIAN ELKHOUNDS
OTTER HOUNDS
RHODESIAN RIDGEBACKS
SALUKIS
WHIPPETS

GROUP 3—WORKING DOGS

ALASKAN MALAMUTES
BELGIAN MALINOIS
BELGIAN SHEEPDOGS
BELGIAN TERVUREN
BERNESE MOUNTAIN DOGS
BOUVIERS DES FLANDRES
BOXERS

BRIARDS
BULLMASTIFFS
COLLIES
DOBERMAN PINSCHERS
GERMAN SHEPHERD DOGS
GIANT SCHNAUZERS
GREAT DANES
GREAT PYRENEES
KOMONDOROK
KUVASZOK
MASTIFFS
NEWFOUNDLANDS
OLD ENGLISH SHEEPDOGS
PULIK
ROTTWEILERS
SAMOYEDS
SCHNAUZERS (STANDARD)
SHETLAND SHEEPDOGS
SIBERIAN HUSKIES
ST. BERNARDS
WELSH CORGIS (CARDIGAN)
WELSH CORGIS (PEMBROKE)

GROUP 4—TERRIERS

AIREDALE TERRIERS
AUSTRALIAN TERRIERS
BEDLINGTON TERRIERS
BORDER TERRIERS
BULL TERRIERS
CAIRN TERRIERS
DANDIE DINMONT TERRIERS
FOX TERRIERS
IRISH TERRIERS

GROUP 2—HOUNDS: Afghan Hound, American and Canadian Champion Tajmirs Redstone Rocket, owned by Joan Fantl and Patricia Sinden.

KERRY BLUE TERRIERS
LAKELAND TERRIERS
MANCHESTER TERRIERS
NORWICH TERRIERS
SCHNAUZERS (MINIATURE)
SCOTTISH TERRIERS
SEALYHAM TERRIERS
SKYE TERRIERS
STAFFORDSHIRE TERRIERS
WELSH TERRIERS
WEST HIGHLAND WHITE TERRIERS

GROUP 5—TOYS

AFFENPINSCHERS
CHIHUAHUAS
ENGLISH TOY SPANIELS
GRIFFONS (BRUSSELS)
ITALIAN GREYHOUNDS
JAPANESE SPANIELS
MALTESE
PAPILLONS
PEKINGESE
PINSCHERS (MINIATURE)
POMERANIANS
PUGS
SHIH TZU
SILKY TERRIERS
YORKSHIRE TERRIERS

GROUP 6—NON-SPORTING DOGS

BOSTON TERRIERS
BULLDOGS
CHOW CHOWS
DALMATIANS
FRENCH BULLDOGS

KEESHONDEN
LHASA APSOS
POODLES
SCHIPPERKES

The Board of Directors of The American Kennel Club may add other breeds to the foregoing list whenever in its opinion sufficient evidence is presented to said Board to justify its belief that such other breeds have been in existence as distinct breeds for such length of time as to justify being designated pure breeds. The Board of Directors also may remove any breed from the foregoing list or may transfer any breed from one group to another group whenever in its opinion sufficient evidence is presented to the Board to justify such removal or transfer.

CHAPTER 3

REGISTRATION

SECTION 1. The breeder of a dog is the person who owned the dam of that dog when the dam was bred; except that if the dam was leased at the time of breeding, the breeder is the lessee.

SECTION 2. An American-bred dog is a dog whelped in the United States of America by reason of a mating which took place in the United States of America.

SECTION 3. Any person in good standing with The American Kennel Club may apply for the registration of any pure-bred dog or litter of pure-bred dogs owned by him, by supplying The American Kennel Club with such information and complying with such conditions as it shall require.

SECTION 4. No individual dog from a litter whelped in the United States of America of which both parents are registered with The American Kennel Club shall be eligible for registration unless the litter has first been registered by the person who owned the dam at time of whelping; except that

GROUP 3 — WORKING DOGS: Collie, Champion Ruflane's Sire Nonrine, owned by Mrs. Hans Borringer, Valparaiso, Ind. (Photo by William H. Oskay, SeeSharp Photography, Muncie, Ind.)

if the dam was leased at time of whelping, the litter may be registered only by the lessee.

SECTION 5. No dog or litter out of a dam under eight (8) months or over twelve (12) years of age at time of mating, or by a sire under seven (7) months or over twelve (12) years of age at time of mating, will be registered unless the application for registration shall be accompanied by an affidavit or evidence which shall prove the fact to the satisfaction of The American Kennel Club.

SECTION 6. No litter of pure-bred dogs and/or no single pure-bred dog which shall be determined by The American Kennel Club to be acceptable in all other respects for registration, shall be barred from registration because of the failure, by the legal owner of all or part of said litter, or said single dog to obtain some one or more of the signatures needed to complete the applicant's chain of title to the litter or dog sought to be registered, unless that person who, when requested, refuses so to sign the application form shall furnish a reason therefor satisfactory to The American Kennel Club, such as the fact that at the time of service an agreement in writing was made between the owner or lessee of the sire and the owner or lessee of the dam to the effect that no application for registration should be made and/or that the produce of such union should not be registered. In all cases where such an agreement in writing has been made, any person disposing of any of the produce of such union must secure from the new owner a statement in writing that he receives such produce upon the understanding that it shall not be registered. For the purpose of registering or refusing to register pure-bred dogs The American Kennel Club will recognize only such conditional sale or conditional stud agreements affecting the registration of pure-bred dogs as are in writing and are shown to have been brought to the attention of the applicant for registration. The American Kennel Club cannot recognize alleged conditional sale, conditional stud or other agreements not in writing which affect the registration of pure-bred dogs, until after the existence, construction and/or effect of the same shall have been determined by an action at law.

The owner or owners of a stud dog pure-bred and eligible for registration who in print or otherwise asserts or assert it to be pure-bred and eligible for registration and on the strength of such assertion secures or permits its use at stud, must pay the cost of its registration. The owner or owners of a brood bitch pure-bred and eligible for registration who in print or otherwise asserts or assert it to be pure-bred and eligible for registration and on the strength of such assertion leases it or sells its produce or secures the use of a stud by promising a puppy or puppies as payment of the stud fee in lieu of cash, must pay the cost of its registration.

That person or those persons refusing without cause to sign the application form or forms necessary for the registration of a litter of pure-bred dogs or of a single pure-bred dog and that person or those persons refusing without cause to pay the necessary fees due from him, her or them to be paid in order to complete the chain of title to a pure-bred litter or a pure-bred single dog sought to be registered, when requested by The American Kennel Club, may be suspended from the privileges of The American Kennel Club or fined as the Board of Directors of The American Kennel Club may elect.

The registration of a single pure-bred dog out of a litter eligible for registration may be secured by its legal owner as a one-dog litter registration and the balance of the litter may be refused registration where the breeder or the owner or lessee of the dam at the date of whelping wrongfully has refused to register the litter and that person or those persons so wrongfully refusing shall be suspended from the privileges of The American Kennel Club or fined as the Board of Direc-

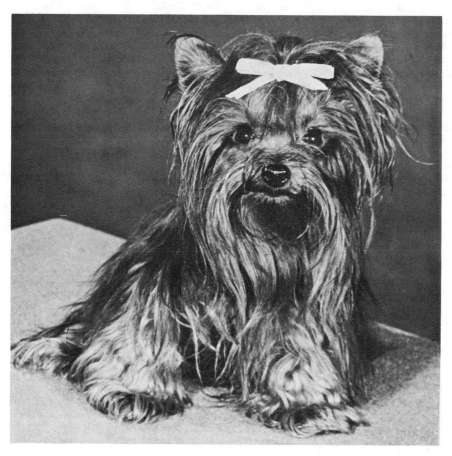

GROUP 4—TERRIERS: Yorkshire Terrier, owned by Mrs. Lawrence Lattomous, Muncie, Ind. (Photo by William H. Oskay, SeeSharp Photography, Muncie, Ind.)

GROUP 5—TOYS: Maltese, Champion Mike-Mar Maji Puff,
owned by Rena Martin, Highland Park, Ill. (Photo by Ritter.)

tors of The American Kennel Club may elect.

SECTION 7. No change in the name of a dog registered with The American Kennel Club will be allowed to be made.

SECTION 8. Any person in good standing with The American Kennel Club may apply for transfer of ownership to him of any registered dog acquired by him by supplying The American Kennel Club with such information and complying with such conditions as it shall require.

SECTION 9. The American Kennel Club will not protect any person against the use by any other person of a kennel name in the registration of dogs with The American Kennel Club or in the entry of registered dogs in shows held under The American Kennel Club rules, unless the kennel name has been registered with The American Kennel Club.

SECTION 10. On and after October 1, 1948, applications for the use of a kennel name as a prefix in the registering and showing of dogs shall be made to The American Kennel Club on a form which will be supplied by said Club upon request, and said application must be accompanied by a fee, the amount of which shall be determined by the Board of Directors of The American Kennel Club. The Board will then consider such application and if it approves of the name selected will grant the right to the use of such name only as a prefix for a period of five (5) years.

SECTION 11. The recorded owner shall have first consideration of the grant to use said kennel name for additional consecutive five (5) year terms upon receipt of the application for renewal accompanied by the renewal fee, the amount of which shall be determined by the Board of Directors, when received before the date of expiration of the original grant but the grant for any five (5) year renewal term will be made only at the expiration of the previous term.

In the event of the death of a recorded owner of a regis-

tered kennel name, his executors, administrators or legal heirs, upon submission of proper proof of their status may use the name as a prefix during the remainder of the five (5) year term of use and the legal heir of the deceased recorded owner, or the executors or administrators acting in his behalf, shall have first consideration of the grant to the use of said name for additional terms, as provided heretofore in this section.

SECTION 12. If the recorded owner of a registered kennel name granted after October 1, 1948, desires to transfer ownership of or an interest in said kennel name to a new owner, application to transfer such name for the unexpired term must be made to The American Kennel Club on a form which will be supplied by said Club upon request. The application must be submitted for the approval of the Board of Directors of The American Kennel Club and accompanied by a fee, the amount of which shall be determined by the Board of Directors of The American Kennel Club.

Any kennel name granted by The American Kennel Club prior to October 1, 1948 may be transferred by its present owner or owners to another only by consent and on certain conditions and payment of fee as determined by the Board of Directors of The American Kennel Club.

SECTION 13. In the case of any registered kennel name which is recorded as jointly owned by two or more persons, application to transfer the interest of one co-owner to another co-owner, may be made to The American Kennel Club on a form which will be supplied by said Club upon request. The application must be submitted for the approval of the Board of Directors of The American Kennel Club but no fee will be charged for such a transfer.

SECTION 14. The protection of all kennel names registered between March 1, 1934 and October 1, 1948 shall depend upon their continuous use by registered owners. Neglect by the recorded owner of a registered kennel name to use such name in the registration of dogs for a continuous period of six years or more shall be considered such an abandonment of the name as to justify The American Kennel Club in refusing to protect its use unless the owner or owners thereof prior to the expiration of such six-year period shall notify The American Kennel Club of his, her or their desire to retain the same.

CHAPTER 3-A
IDENTIFICATION AND RECORDS

SECTION 1. The word "person" as used in this chapter includes any individual, partnership, firm, corporation, association or organization of any kind.

The word "dog" as used in this chapter includes a dog or puppy of any age and either sex.

SECTION 2. Each person who breeds, keeps, transfers ownership or possession of, or deals in dogs which are registered or to be registered with The American Kennel Club, whether he acts as principal or agent or sells on consignment, must make in connection therewith and preserve for five years adequate and accurate records. The Board of Directors shall by regulation designate the specific information which must be included in such records.

SECTION 3. Each person who breeds, keeps, transfers ownership or possession of, or deals in dogs that are registered or to be registered with The American Kennel Club, whether he acts as principal or agent or sells on consignment, must follow such practices as, consistent with the number of dogs involved, will preclude any possibility of error in identification of any individual dog or doubt as to the parentage of any particular dog or litter.

SECTION 4. The American Kennel Club or its duly authorized representative shall have the right to inspect the records required to be kept and the practices required to be followed by these rules and by any regulations adopted under them, and to examine any dog registered or to be registered with The American Kennel Club.

SECTION 5. Each person who transfers ownership or possession of a dog that is registered or to be registered with The American Kennel Club must describe the dog in the records of The American Kennel Club in writing to the person acquiring the dog at the time of transfer, either on a bill of sale or otherwise. The Board of Directors shall by regulation designate the descriptive information required.

SECTION 6. The American Kennel Club may refuse to register any dog or litter or to record the transfer of any dog, for the sole reason that the application is not supported by the records required by these rules and the regulations adopted under them.

SECTION 7. Any person who is required to keep records and who fails to do so or who fails or refuses when requested to make such records available for inspection by The American Kennel Club or its duly authorized representatives, may be suspended from all privileges of The American Kennel Club by the Board of Directors.

Any person who fails to follow such practices as will preclude any possibility of error in identification of an individual dog or doubt as to the parentage of a particular dog or litter, or who fails or refuses to permit The American Kennel Club or its duly authorized representatives to examine such practices, or to examine a dog that is registered or to be registered with The American Kennel Club, may be suspended from all privileges of The American Kennel Club by the Board of Directors.

Reprinted by permission of The American Kennel Club.

GROUP 6—NON-SPORTING DOGS: Black Poodle (Miniature), owned by Mr. Del Dahl, Champagne, Ill. (Photo by William H. Oskay SeeSharp Photography, Muncie, Ind.)

WHEN IS THE BEST TIME TO ADOPT A DOG?

VIRTUALLY any time is a good time to adopt a dog. Puppies are available all year around, so, there should never be any real difficulty in finding the kind you want. Sometimes, you may have to wait a few weeks until the desired pup is old enough to leave the litter, or you may have to check in another nearby city or town. But, once you've decided on a particular breed you'll find that some inconvenience like this is well worth the trouble.

Actually the ideal time to adopt is when you have ample time to devote to this new and fun-filled experience. It should be a time when you are able to take the dog outside so he can learn to be housebroken correctly. If you live in an area which has pleasant weather all year around this is no problem. However, if you live in a section which has some very bad seasons, you may want to plan accordingly. Remember, if it's so bad outside that you don't want to go out—neither does the puppy who is just learning. So, get the new addition when the weather is

---

CHRISTMAS GIFT PUPPY

Christmas time is a very popular season for dog giving. Make certain that the recipient of your doggy present has the brains, heart and time to take sane care of it. Also, make sure there are suitable quarters for its housing before you give a Christmas dog. First, try to find out what dog is suitable for the available quarters. If the recipient lives in a city apartment, don't give a large dog. The average big dog is terribly out of place in a cooped-up city flat. If the beneficiary lives in the country or has a home in the suburbs with ample grounds, then a large breed can be considered.

Nothing else can form and develop certain gloriously needful traits in a child as can having a dog of its own. On the other hand, there is nothing else which can develop a child's latent traits of cruelty and bullying as can the possession of a helpless puppy. It depends on the parents whether their child learns patience, common sense, kindliness, and consideration towards the dog, or whether the dog is to be tortured, neglected, and ill treated. In the latter case, the poor puppy is not the ultimate loser, but the child itself.

The Christmas dog can be made a joy or a tragedy, according to the instincts of the recipient. It may be the most ideal gift or the worst gift in Santa's bag.

mild and when you have sufficient time to devote to this very important early training.

If you are employed but want a dog, it can be done. Plan to get the dog at the beginning of your vacation and then spend your vacation on the training project. Before returning to work make arrangements to have someone come in to take the dog out while you are away until it is old enough to wait for your return. Many people feel that it is unfair to have a dog when they spend eight hours a day away from home. This doesn't have to be unfair if you really care about the dog and make up for your absence by giving him the exercise, affection and attention he needs when you are home. An early morning romp in the outdoors can be just as stimulating and fun as one at mid-day; and week-end activity can also make up for those quiet week days. If the dog's needs, as far as food, water, exercise, and love, are met, having someone constantly at home is not necessary. Good sense and consideration must be used. No animal should suffer! A dog left alone should have adequate, cool, clean water for the duration of your absence; he should have been fed and exercised; and, he should have space in which to move comfortably in an area which is neither too hot nor too cold. If such conditions cannot be provided, then the dog should not be left. These are minimum standards and dog ownership requires these basic care considerations.

Should one get a dog when one has very young children; will the children hurt the puppy? This question is asked frequently. The answer depends on the circumstances of each family. If there is sufficient time to supervise their activities, then the answer is yes. However, if it is a busy home and a puppy would be at the mercy of young children who do not understand how to handle it, then the answer would have to be a strict NO! Serious injuries can be done to the dog by improper handling and dropping. Children can also be cruel by hurting and teasing a puppy, which can result in future personailty problems in the dog. This can mean a fearful dog or one that snaps at or bites children. That is why it is so important to treat a pup correctly and to avoid problem situations. So, if you feel that you can't have close supervision of the pup and the children, then wait until the children are older and can understand the importance of careful handling and considerate behavior.

Best Age to Adopt a Puppy

Research shows that socialization begins between six and eight weeks of age. Removing the puppy from its litter at this time means that this social relationship will be transferred from the littermates to human beings. If the removal is done much later, then the puppy has developed stronger attachments to other dogs rather than people. It is helpful for a pup to be introduced early to the type of environment that will be its future home. Those puppies which remain in a kennel well beyond 12 weeks of age may develop into shy and timid dogs. Professional dog people feel that sometime between the age of eight and 12 weeks is the best time to place a dog in its home environment.

Summary—When to get a dog...
(1) when your desired breed is available.
(2) when the weather is good for housebreaking.
(3) when you have time to devote to training.

Naming Your Dog

Usually the naming of the dog is the joyous duty of the new owner. The breeder will often supply the kennel prefix which is used when applying for registration to the American Kennel Club or to another registry, and when showing the dog. But, the real "name" that you call your dog is your responsibility. When you get your puppy don't be in too much of a hurry to name him. Get acquainted first and familiarize yourself with its temperament and personality. Visualize it as a full grown dog; then try to select a name that is appropriate. Try to avoid long and cumbersome names, or those that are overly ostentatious. If you have children, you will want a name they can pronounce. Avoid trite common names as well as giving your dog the same name as another dog living nearby. We know of a case where a homeowner bought the same breed of dog as the neighbors only one house away, and then gave it the same name. The poor dogs didn't know which way to turn when they heard their names being called. Show at least a small amount of thoughtfulness and originality in your selection.

VAL

LONE DOG

I'm a lean dog, a keen dog, a wild dog and lone;
I'm a rough dog, a tough dog, a howling on my own;
I'm a bad dog, a mad dog, teasing silly sheep,
I love to set and howl by the moon to keep
  fat souls from sleep.

I'll never be a lap dog, licking dirty feet,
A sleek dog, a meek dog, cringing for my meat.
Not for me the fireside, the well filled plate.
But shut door, and sharp stone, and cuff,
  and kick, and hate.

Not for me the other dogs, running by my side,
Some have run a short while but none of them
  would bide.
O mine is still the lone-trail, the hard trail, the best,
Wide wind, and wild stars, and the hunger
  of the quest!

from *Songs to Save a Soul* by Irene Rutherford McLeod
Reprinted by permission of the Viking Press, Inc.

CHAPTER II
DAY-TO-DAY CARE

PREPARING FOR THE NEW ARRIVAL

For housebreaking purposes keep the puppy confined to an area that is easy to keep clean and yet where "socialization" is possible as well. (Ericonji Basenjis, Northbrook, Illinois.)

A dog needs to have his own bed and a spot he can consider his own. The bed need not be fancy, just suitable in size and easy to keep clean. (Photo by Maria Coven.)

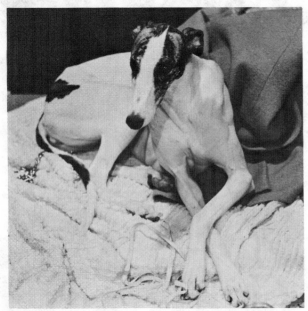

WHAT an exciting moment it is when you've made your selection and that darling, warm, lovable new dog is ready and waiting to enter your home and your life. A young puppy will need certain essentials, and pre-planning should make it an enjoyable rather than a hectic experience. *A small box,* lined with newspapers, is needed for transporting your new possession. Place the box on the back floor of the car so that the dog will be secure. If you have a long ride home from the breeder, stop occasionally so the puppy can relieve himself. Since this is undoubtedly his first car ride, he may be nervous and need reassurance. Allow him to have water only if the trip is long or very hot. Normally, it is best not to feed a puppy just prior to, or during, an automobile ride as this can induce car sickness.

Once you arrive home, get the dog settled with a minimum of fuss and excitement. His living "area" should have been selected and readied in advance. In most homes or apartments, the kitchen is the ideal spot to confine the puppy until housebreaking is completed. We recommend an area which is both easy to keep clean and where the puppy will be near you and have "human contact." *Socialization is most important, so the puppy should not be isolated.* Some dog trainers recommend a wire cage but if there is an alternative which would give the dog somewhat more freedom and yet keep it confined to a specific area, this is ideal.

Don't give your puppy free run of the house. Training cannot be accomplished if this is done.

The Bed

Provide your dog with his own bed and place it in one corner of his area. The bed should be appropriate to the dog's size—cozy enough to cuddle in. Most breeds will outgrow their first bed, so it should be

---

Puppy Training Tip

Keeping a new puppy in a playpen for a few days will protect him from overenthusiastic hugging by the children and may also save rugs and furniture from accidents. Chicken wire stapled to the outside of playpen frame will keep a small dog inside. With a blanket for his bed, some toys, and newspapers over the playpen floor, he'll soon begin to paper-train himself.

BEFORE THE DOG ARRIVES

When a dog enters the family circle for the first time, certain adjustments and plans need to be made beforehand. Responsibilities must be clearly defined. The dog's feeding, grooming, and training must be provided for. Who will do these chores and when they will do them must be spelled out. Remember, the well being of an animal is too important to be entrusted solely to a youngster; close adult supervision is necessary.

If family members are going to be away, arrangements for the care of the puppy must be made. The dog cannot be left alone for an extended period, especially when it is still on three meals per day. Someone must be able to come in and care for the pup. Arranging for a "puppy sitter" is a good idea. That way, the dog can be fed and taken out and a regular schedule maintained.

inexpensive. A small washable rug or blanket can be used. Frequent washing of the bedding is necessary.

Newspaper

Stock up on newspapers since you will be using large quantities if you "paper train" your puppy.

Dishes

Your dog will need two dishes, one for his food and one for water. Dishes which are unbreakable, weighted and rustproof are best. You will find a weighted dish is worth the extra cost in order to avoid spilled water and food. Puppies love to play and will run around and frolic with an aluminum or small plastic container. And it's amazing, but, until the family members are fully adjusted to the new addition and all his equipment, they will accidentally tip over the water dish—unless it is weighted. The size and shape of the dishes should be determined by the size and shape of the dog's head and ears. Dogs with long ears should have a dish with a narrow opening so that their ears stay out of the food. Flat-faced dogs need a shallow dish and long-nosed dogs need a deep bowl.

The shape of the dog's feeding dish is determined by the shape of the nose and length of the ears. This long nosed Pointer would enjoy a deep bowl. (Photo courtesy of American Field.*)*

A Reminder

Don't forget to purchase a dog license promptly or to comply immediately with local rules on rabies innoculation and other shots.

Grooming Materials

To keep your puppy looking neat and clean, you will need a suitable brush, comb, and nail clippers. The type of comb and brush required will depend on the dog's coat and even his size, so discuss this at time of purchase. Don't get carried away with enthusiasm and purchase large amounts of grooming equipment and aids. Comb, brush, and nail clippers are the basic essentials. A mild dog shampoo is also needed. Other items can be purchased when you discover a real need.

Diet

Since moving to a new home is quite traumatic for a dog and just this change can cause digestive disturbances, it is wise to maintain the dog's former diet. Once your puppy has adjusted to your home and his digestion is normal, you may wish to start a different diet. We would recommend discussing the maintenance diet with your vet and planning one that is suitable to the breed, the activity level of your dog, and one that will help him attain optimum growth and development.

An active dog has different dietary requirements than a house pet. Temperature also changes dietary needs. More "fuel" is needed in cold weather. (Picture courtesy of American Field.)

Puppies love to play and chew. Provide them with something suitable. (Ericonji Basenjis)

Health

Visit your veterinarian and have him give the puppy a complete checkup. Be certain the dog is healthy and sound, because, if something is wrong, it would be best to return him now before getting attached. Bring a stool sample to the vet so he can check for worms. Any innoculations needed can be given at this time.

Other Essentials

A small collar and a leash will have to be purchased. The size and shape should be suitable to the dog. For example, a rounded collar is used for a long haired dog so that it won't rub off the fur. Again, as this item also will soon be outgrown, an inexpensive one is best.

Puppies love to chew and unless you provide them with something to gnaw on, they will help themselves. Don't ever allow them to chew an old shoe or sock, because a dog can't discriminate between one of your "good" shoes and an old one. Do provide your puppy with rawhide bones which are made specifically for this chewing purpose. They can be purchased at pet stores or wherever dog food is sold. Avoid rubber or plastic toys as these can be chewed to pieces and can lodge in the dog's throat or digestive tract, causing severe damage and even death.

The First Nights

The first few nights the puppy spends in his new home are the most difficult. He misses the warmth and companionship of his brothers, sisters, and mother. Most puppies will cry, but comforting words, a little petting, a hot water bottle, and a ticking clock will ease the anxious baby. Remember a puppy is a baby dog, and he will often require nearly as much attention as a new infant. You should plan to devote a few days to this baby and to making him feel at home; however, don't spoil him and start bad habits. It is a sad mistake to let him sleep in your room and bed. Once this is started, your privacy is over. The dog should have his own bed in a cozy nook in another part of the house and sleep there without exception. This procedure should be followed from the beginning.

Let the puppy sleep when he wants to. Don't start off by having numerous visitors come over to see him and pick him up. A gradual introduction to the family members is wise. Small puppies must be handled with utmost care. Children and many adults must be taught how to pick them up, hold them, carry them, and put them down. Injuring a small pup by careless treatment is cruel and needless.

Until the puppy has had all his shots and innoculations, it is best to keep him away from other dogs in order to avoid unnecessary exposure to disease.

Children and Dogs—Some Do's and Don'ts

CHILDREN AND DOGS

Here are a few do's and don'ts to teach your children about getting along with dogs:

1. Never approach a strange dog. Most dogs are friendly, but it's not worth taking a chance.
2. Don't allow small children to be rough with a pet. Always supervise young children and pets.
3. Train your child how to pick up and carry the puppy or dog, so that it is supported, secure, and comfortable.
4. Dogs should be approached gradually and slowly. After some sniffing, a dog likes to be stroked and scratched behind the ears.
5. Dogs should not be teased or annoyed while eating, or startled while sleeping.

Never entrust a dog's well-being to a youngster. Adult supervision of feeding, grooming, play and exercise is essential.

Children and Dogs—A Fine Way to Teach Responsibility

Children can be taught the responsibilities of dog care at an early age. Once respect and consideration for an animal is developed, it is life-long. These youngsters are learning how to groom the family dog (under supervision, of course).

TRAINING YOUR DOG FOR HOME LIVING

Psychology of Dog Care

AS you will soon discover, a dog that is intended as a house pet quickly becomes a family member. Since he will, hopefully, be living happily with you for a number of years, it is a wise and necessary thing for you to guide him into acceptable behavior. A dog must learn to conform to your life style and not vice versa, thus standards should be set from the very beginning. Be certain that all the members of the family understand what these standards are, and that all abide by them. It is most important to be consistent so that the dog will not be confused.

Virtually all dogs like to please their master and once they fully understand what is required of them, and how to do it, they will. Therefore, it is most desirable to develop a sense of affection and companionship between master and dog. Training is easier and more fun once this relationship is established. The dog is truly man's best friend—he will be loyal and faithful. It's nice to be able to feel deserving of this devotion.

Training for Everyday Living

When bringing home a new dog, be he young or old, you must begin training immediately. Show him what he can and cannot do—where he can go and cannot go—and sometimes when and with whom things are or are not permissable. If there is a room or even parts of the house that you don't want him to enter, then establish that from the beginning and be firm about it. Be consistent, don't allow him to enter the room on one day and then punish him the next. The first lesson to teach a dog is what you mean by saying "NO." Make this your first training lesson. Once he learns this, all other lessons become easier. How can this be done? Put a special tidbit down and when he goes for it, yell "No" and slap him away. Keep repeating this procedure until the pup stops approaching the tidbit. When you put down his food dish, say "No" and make him wait until you are ready for him to eat. *Repetition, firmness,* and *reward* will do the trick. Try to always reward your dog when he responds correctly by giving him a dog treat or something special he likes and training will be easier and faster.

Your dog can be taught to do the following:

(1) To Behave While You Are Eating
No "begging at the table" can be accomplished simply by never giving the dog anything to eat from the table. And if he should beg, firmly say "no" and push or send him away. Keeping him away from your eating area until he gets the message will also help. Dogs that beg at the table frequently do so because, at first, they were allowed to or even encouraged. When the owner later decides that this is annoying and should stop, it is very difficult to "unlearn" this bad behavior.

(2) To Stay off Furniture
From earliest puppyhood, teach your dog his restrictions. You may enjoy having your St. Bernard puppy on the couch, but consider what this will mean when he grows up. So, don't allow your pup to do anything you wouldn't allow your fully grown

---

THE DO'S AND DON'TS OF DOG OWNERSHIP

DON'T . . .
- let your dog roam the neighborhood
- let your dog bark excessively
- let your dog soil your neighbor's shrubbery or lawn, or tear up his flower garden
- let your dog chase cars or bicycles
- let your dog frighten or bite the postman, milkman, or other service people
- let your leashed dog lunge at or jump on passers-by
- let your dog howl for hours while you are gone

DO . . .
- teach your dog to be obedient and well-behaved
- walk your dog on a leash and curb him when necessary
- teach him to stay in your yard
- train your dog to stay quietly within his kennel or crate while you are away
- train your dog to walk quietly at heel on a loose leash

All dogs like to please their master. (Welsh Corgi owned by Mrs. R. Ayers. Photo by William H. Oskay, SeeSharp Photography, Muncie, Indiana.)

Don't ever allow your puppy on the furniture unless you want him to be there when he grows up.

Your puppy needs to be trained to walk on the leash. This is not instinctive.

dog. If you don't want him on your furniture, **never** allow him to be on it!

(3) Not to Run Out the Door

For city and suburban dwellers this is a most important lesson. Too many dogs are lost or run over and injured or killed by automobiles. Make this lesson one of your first and most important ones and be sure it is learned well. Even if your yard is fenced in or if you live far from the road, train your dog to go out only when you give your permission. If your facilities are not enclosed, train your dog never to go out the door without the leash and you. This training is best accomplished while the puppy is still small. Running out at mailmen and delivery men is a very popular canine sport but this very disturbing behavior should not be permitted to become a habit.

(4) To Walk on the Leash

Have your new puppy wear a small collar. When he becomes accustomed to having it on—this may take several days — attach a leash and let him walk around with it on. Then, gradually begin holding it and walking with him. Don't pull or drag him, just gently guide him until he becomes accustomed to responding to the lead. Don't allow the pup to bite the leash or to tangle himself around your legs. Speak to him, be friendly but firm, and reward him with praising and petting when he does it correctly.

(5) Not to Bark Unnecessarily

Most people want their dog to bark when a stranger is around or in case of some danger. However, too many dogs bark constantly at people or events, and this becomes annoying and bothersome. So, if your dog barks when you leave the house, you must return and scold him. Barking at mailmen, delivery men, and garbage men must also be curtailed early. Shout "No," clamp the mouth shut with your hand, and swat the behind with a rolled-up newspaper. Splashing them with cold water or picking them up and shaking them soundly while scolding has also been suggested. Be persistent and consistent.

It is most disturbing to your neighbors if your dog barks while outside; don't allow this. If he persists in barking, act firmly. Some authorities suggest throwing a bucket of water on the dog that barks in the yard, while others suggest using a spray attachment on the garden hose. Punish him immediately when he barks and he will soon understand that this is unacceptable behavior.

(6) Not to Chew and Tear Clothes or Furniture
Never give the puppy an old shoe, sock, or piece of clothing with which to play for it is impossible for him to distinguish between a shoe he may chew and one he isn't allowed to touch. A pup has a strong natural chewing instinct. He needs to chew to ease some of the discomfort of teething and to keep himself occupied. Give him rawhide bones to chew— these are healthy and won't cause you any damage. For safety, once the pieces get small, take them away as a small piece of rawhide can be swallowed and get stuck in the puppy's throat.

If junior chews at furniture punish him immediately with a good hard slap and tie him up or confine him to a place where he can't do any harm. Chewing can be a very expensive and destructive habit if allowed to continue. Remember that a small destructive dog will mature and become even more destructive. If you find you can't control the situation, don't delay —call a professional trainer for assistance.

(7) Not to Snap, Growl, or Bite
Instinctively, most dogs will growl if anyone approaches them while they are eating or gnawing on a bone. Some will snap and even bite if their food is touched. Such behavior must not be tolerated. Demonstrate to your dog that you can and will take his food dish or bone away from him and don't tolerate any signs of anger from him. You may have to do some punishing, but it's easier to do this with a young puppy than to have a mean, full grown dog who can't be approached while eating.

Dog License

In most parts of the United States, it is required that you get your dog licensed. These license fees are an excise tax levied upon the dogs of the community or county. License-issuing agencies are required to keep dog records and to supply the dog owner with a license tag. This tag is designed to be placed on a dog's collar. It serves to identify the dog if he is picked up by police. But it also identifies him if he gets lost. So a dog license tag is good insurance for you. Remember, the tag is no good to you unless it is securely fastened to the dog's collar, and the dog must be wearing that collar.

Unnecessary barking is very annoying — train your dog in proper canine behavior.

A vicious dog is a frightening thing—from earliest puppyhood your dog must be taught not to snap, growl, or bite.

41

ROUTINE HEALTH CARE

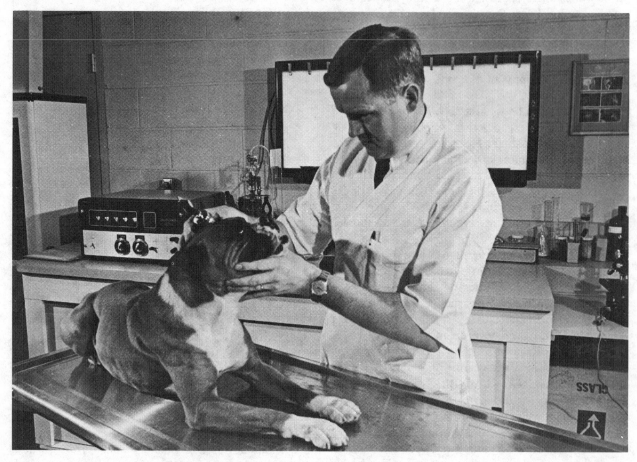

Your veterinarian uses all the knowledge and tools of modern medicine to keep your pet in good health. (Dr. Tom Keefe—Purina Pet Care Center.)

AN integral part of the care of your family dog is regular veterinary visits. During puppyhood, the visits will be quite frequent as all the necessary innoculations must be taken promptly. Distemper, leptospirosis and hepatitis can now be practically prevented by the proper administration of vaccines. Although they are not 100 per cent effective, the incidence of these dread diseases has been significantly reduced. Your veterinarian will work out a schedule of innoculations for your new puppy and will advise you about yearly booster shots. Since there is now a triple booster covering these diseases, one booster injection is all that is necessary. The innoculation for rabies should also be given during the first year and then repeated yearly. Many communities make this yearly rabies vaccination mandatory.

It is good preventative medicine to have the vet check your dog at least once a year—when you go in for boosters. Ask him to check your dog's teeth and gums and to remove tartar accumulations. If you have the slightest suspicion that your dog may have worms, then have the vet examine a stool specimen.

There are many things which should be done at home as part of your routine health care program:

(1) **Maintain a clean environment:** wash the dog's bedding frequently, wash the eating utensils scrupulously after each meal, provide fresh water daily.

(2) **Protect your pet from unnecessary dangers:** train him to stay off the street, keep your garbage cans covered, remove him when insecticides and other poisons are being used.

(3) **Be perceptive:** take note of changes in your

dog's appetite, digestion, and personality.

(4) Examine your dog at every grooming: observe any skin lesions and treat accordingly; check eyes, ears and feet. Run your hands over the body checking for tumors.

Should your dog be ill and require treatment, be sure you follow the vet's directions carefully and administer medication only as directed. Provide as quiet and restful an environment for your sick pet as possible. Your care and love will help to speed his recovery.

Care of the Bitch

The ownership of an unspayed female presents certain responsibilities. When your dog goes into heat, this information is announced to all eligible males in the vicinity at large by a telltale odor emitted by her urine. Usually before you are even suspicious of this event, the appearance of males at your doorstep will herald its arrival. All too often these ever-anxious suitors will camp themselves around your premises creating a nuisance for you and most probably for your neighbors as well. Action is required before you alienate your entire neighborhood. Either have your dog put into a kennel until the end of her cycle or use special measures such as taking her far from the house to urinate and using a no-odor medication. If you keep your bitch at home, take extreme precautions to protect her from any indiscriminate alliance. Cleanliness is also vital at this time. If she is unable to keep the vulvar area clean, then you must wash this area with warm water.

Care of the Male

The male presents other considerations to his master. Instinctively, most males like to roam—either in search of a female or a companion or just for fun. Those dog owners who live in an area where this is permissible and does not annoy others, are most fortunate. Most dog owners though cannot allow their pets a free reign either because of the danger to the dog himself, or because of the nuisance such freedom causes to the community as reflected in local legal ordinances. A dog running loose is in danger of being hit by a car, of ingesting something poisonous, and even of becoming lost or stolen. All people hate having a neighbor's dog wander onto their property, making deposits which burn their grass, bushes, and soiling and ripping up chunks of their lawn. Thus, out of consideration for others no dog should be allowed to roam. Unfortunately many dog owners are far from considerate which has resulted in "leash laws" being enacted in many communities around the country. These laws prohibit

the dog's uninhibited wanderings and enforce this regulation with fines levied against the owner.

The male dog can also become a sex offender by masturbating on furniture and people's legs. So far, there seems to be no real cure for stopping such offensive behavior. Firm correction of this misbehavior seems to be the only remedy although it is far from effective.

A bitch must be protected while in heat, otherwise the result can be an undesired litter of puppies.

Most males like to roam, unfortunately many communities can not tolerate this. (Photo courtesy of American Field.)

Many communities have leash laws, so if your dog is out "visiting" a fine can result!

Mental Health

Believe it or not, dogs too can have mental health problems. Thus, the best thing to do is try and raise a normal healthy puppy into a well-adjusted dog. This can best be accomplished by providing a happy, relaxed, home environment. The effects of early experiences should not be underestimated. Frightening experiences can do permanent damage to a dog's mode of behavior and personality development. For example, allowing a pup to be mistreated by a child can have the unfortunate consequence of creating a dog who is fearful of children. Fear biters are a menace and are usually too dangerous to keep. *A puppy should never be harshly or cruelly handled.* A calm tension-free environment is best for raising dogs that are not high strung and nervous. Only with love and patience can you expect to create an adult dog that is affectionate and well-tempered.

There are instances when even with the best of environment and care a dog develops unacceptable behavior patterns which do not yield to any form of correction or training. Should you encounter such a difficult animal—one that bites, or attacks and menaces, or one that barks uncontrollably—and you have exhausted all your methods, then by all means seek the services of a professional trainer for remedy. If in spite of professional attention, these traits cannot be eliminated, then seriously consider disposing of the dog. Don't hang on to a potentially hazardous animal until damage has occurred. However, only if the animal is dangerous should it be destroyed. If it has behavior that is unacceptable in your area, remember, it may be tolerated elsewhere. Be honest when disposing of it so that an unfortunate situation isn't perpetuated.

The nature-nurture controversy exists in dogdom just as in humans. One may well question how much a dog's personality is affected by nature (its genetic make-up) and by nurture (its upbringing). Presently, scientists are studying this dilemma. Studies indicate that both aspects play a significant part. Breeding for good temperament is essential and possible. Repeatedly, studies show that nervous, high-strung bitches have a high percentage of nervous, high-strung pups. Well-tempered, calm bitches have a high percentage of pups with these traits. It, therefore, behooves the breeder to be mindful of their bitches' and studs' personality and not to breed those dogs that display personality problems.

Breeding for good temperament is essential. (Photo courtesy of American Field.)

EXERCISE, ACTIVITIES, ELIMINATION

IN order to keep your dog happy and healthy, a regular daily exercise period is essential. Hunting and working dogs normally receive this vital exercise as a natural part of their existence, however, the house pet is all too often neglected in this area of care. A good brisk walk in the fresh air at least once a day is a minimum standard. Ideally, a one-hour walk is good for keeping the body toned, appetite stimulated, and weight down. Two half-hour walks are also suitable. Unfortunately, there are occasions when neither time nor weather will permit this type of activity. So, some substitutions should be made—a vigorous game of catch, a brief romp in the snow, etc.

The activity must be suitable to the weather since dogs cannot tolerate extremes of temperature. Excess heat can result in heat prostration and undue cold may lead to frostbite. Never leave your dog confined in a car on a hot day because many dogs die needlessly when they are thoughtlessly left in a parked car. The sun beats down on the roof creating a stifling situation and with no escape possible, heat prostration and death can occur rapidly. On a hot day, a dog is best off left at home with adequate ventilation or outside if there is shade and water available. If your dog lives outdoors in a dog house, make certain that it is so situated that it is protected by shade.

Only those animals born and bred for extremely cold weather and outdoor living can be left outside on sub-zero days. Large, heavy-coated dogs prefer living outside in their own house, but even these breeds must have protection during very inclement conditions. All other dogs cannot tolerate extreme

The weather should be suitable for long outings. Snow and ice are hard on dog's feet and cause them to cramp and freeze.

cold and should only be allowed out to relieve themselves. Ideally, an outdoor living setup should provide a means to protect the dog from rain, sun, cold, or danger from theft and injury.

Dogs allowed to exercise independently should have a fenced area such as a yard or dog run of adequate dimensions. If this isn't feasible, a long, nontangle chain device should be used. These special chains can be purchased at pet stores or even made by the "do it yourselfer."

It is generally agreed that any dog of value, be it either monetary or personal, should not be left outside even in a fenced enclosure without any type of supervision available. Our society today contains many "sick" individuals who have been known to maliciously harm unprotected animals or to steal them for monetary gain. Don't invite trouble, always insure your dog's safety by taking all necessary precautions.

How often should a dog be taken out for the purpose of elimination? During puppyhood, even after being housebroken, the pup is not physiologically able to concentrate its urine and will therefore need to go out more frequently than the adult animal. Once a dog is mature enough to concentrate its urine it will have to go out only about three times each day. It is certainly most convenient and pleasurable for our canine friend to be able to come and go at will. Since this is not always possible, training is necessary. Have regular times for these bodily functions and within the short period of a few weeks your dog will have adjusted to this routine. Once in the morning, during the afternoon, and before bed

WALKING YOUR DOG: SENSE AND NONSENSE

How often have you heard someone say that dogs need lots of exercise, or that the city is no place for a dog because dogs need lots of space to roam in, or that a dog needs to wander wherever he wishes in order to be happy?

Good sense? Sheer nonsense! Dogs don't need a lot of exercise. They don't need to be outdoors all day, nor do they want to be. Your dog likes to be with you. If you want to walk, your dog will go along joyously. But if you prefer to sit and read, your dog will be happy to lie beside you.

Dogs who roam the neighborhood usually do so because they are ignored by their owners. They get bored and form the habit of roaming about. And once the habit is formed, it is hard to break. So don't let your dog begin.

make a good minimum schedule. There is usually no reason why your dog should disturb you at an unreasonable early morning hour. Poor training is often the cause for such an irritating habit. Naturally, illness, certain medication, a change in diet, the female's "heat" period, and other such logical reasons can change even the best habits; thus, flexibility is essential.

Dogs of special value should not be left unsupervised even in a fenced area. Dog theft is amazingly popular. (Shipperke owned by Virginia Phillips.)

REGULAR GROOMING

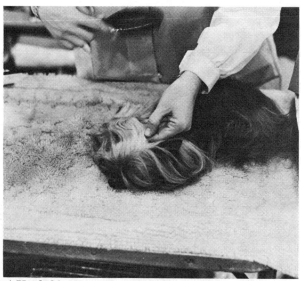

A Yorkshire Terrier requires a great deal of grooming. (Kajimonor Sissy Seymour owned by D. Creeden, Glen Ellyn, Illinois.)

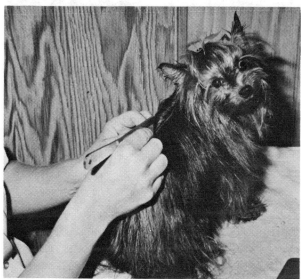

Correct combing involves parting the hair and combing a small section at a time working all the way down to the skin.

GROOMING can be one of the pleasurable experiences you can enjoy with your pet or it can be a trial for you both. Make it a joy from earliest puppyhood and it will be an activity bringing you both great satisfaction. Training your dog to co-operate during the grooming process is the first step. Insist that the young pup lies or stands still while you perform your combing and brushing rites. Speaking softly while tending to his coat will do much to reassure him. Praise him for his good behavior and he will try to please you at each subsequent session. Teach him exactly how you want him to turn and how you wish his head held. Placing him on a table will help make the job easier for you and will encourage his correct attitude. Ideally your dog should learn to jump up on the "grooming" table at your request and to stand as you desire until dismissed. Of course, not all dog owners reach this degree of training, but it's a goal for which to aim. A specially constructed grooming table, such as those used in dog grooming salons, is not necessary. Any table which can be covered with paper and which places the dog at a height comfortable for you is quite adequate. We have even used the top of our washing machine successfully for this job. A large dog may need only a crate, or, if there is nothing else avail-

A steel comb is best for this type of work. Long-haired breeds such as this do best with a daily combing and brushing.

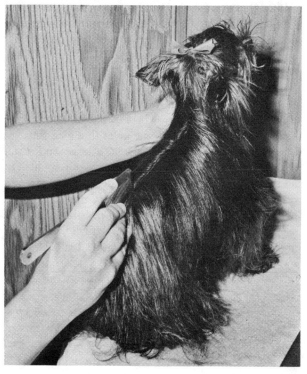

Left—Under all that hair is a Standard Poodle.

Below and right—These dogs are easy to groom because of their smooth coats.

able, there is always the floor. Regular grooming is the important thing—not the equipment.

Equipment

One only needs a few items for the regular, routine grooming which is so essential for your dog's appearance and health. A brush with a good sturdy handle and firm, but not hard, bristles is essential. Although nylon brushes are quite popular, you'll find that a genuine bristle brush lasts longer and seems to do a better job. Such a brush need not necessarily be purchased in the pet department—a "human" one will serve the purpose.

A metal comb is most helpful and you will find a large selection from which to choose. A wide toothed one is used for working out mats and tangles, and the fine toothed one gives that nice finished appearance. One comb having both large and small teeth may be satisfactory for your requirements. In addition to the basic comb and brush, there are other articles you may need or you may think you need. Before buying numerous—possibly unnecessary—items, determine what you actually need. Ask about this when you purchase your dog; ask your

---

Start Grooming Early

Dogs taught to stand for grooming, toe nail clipping, eye cleaning, burr removal, and similar things, while young, learn at that time that they cannot growl at or bite the person working on them.

vet or your local professional dog groomer. If you are doing "special" grooming for a show or if you are doing clipping, then you will need additional equipment.

Short-Haired vs Long-Haired

Smooth-coated or short-haired dogs are the easiest to groom and require the least amount of time. A thorough brushing once a week will keep the coat clean and shiny. Take care not to scrape the skin when combing a smooth-haired dog. Those dogs having long hair or undercoats require more attention. They must be combed with a wide toothed comb and then brushed thoroughly. This procedure will undo mats and tangles as well as removing dead hair, dirt, and stimulating new growth. Correct combing is done by parting the hair and combing a small section at a time working all the way down to the skin. Stroking first in one direction and then in the other makes it possible to get at all of the hairs. Since regular combing and brushing removes dead hairs, you will have less shed hair on your floors and carpets. The really long-haired breeds should be groomed daily to prevent any difficult mats and tangles from forming. A little neglect can have disastrous consequences for when mats are too thick to be coaxed out with a comb, then they must be cut out. As you can well imagine such cutting can result in an unsightly hole in the dog's coat. On occasion, even the frequently groomed pooch can develop a serious tangle which must be cut. Try to work it out

to the smallest possible area and then cut as little as necessary.

Novice dog owners are frequently surprised how much appearance affects their dog. A freshly groomed pet practically struts around like a proud peacock while a neglected or temporarily unsightly hound will slink around and hide whenever possible.

As part of their regular grooming care, some breeds require a little trimming here and there. Hair growing around the anus should be kept short so that excretia doesn't become lodged in it. You may want to trim hair which grows into the eyes and hinders clear vision. Use a blunt round-tipped scissors to prevent accidental injury. Uneven and long hair around the edge of the ear should be cut off neatly in most breeds.

Bathing

Generally, a dog should be bathed only when necessary. Frequent combing and brushing should keep him quite clean and the bath should be reserved for special occasions. When Rover rolls in the mud, or even worse, and the smell is enough to stop anyone at ten paces, then the time has come. Why not bathe more frequently — what harm can it do? Plenty! The typical dog will suffer from dry skin and hair if bathed too often. The natural oils are removed and the coat will lose its shine and luster. Dogs washed too frequently will display a thin soft coat. Unnecessary bathing also needlessly exposes the dog to possible chilling, and eye or ear irritations.

The Bath: Before the bath your dog should be completely brushed and combed since bathing will increase any mats and tangles which exist. The actual mechanics of the bath are quite simple. Have all your necessary equipment and bathing materials at hand before you start since you want to proceed quickly to avoid chilling the dog. Using a laundry tub is ideal because pup won't jump out. Protect the ears and eyes and then wet down the dog thoroughly. The water temperature should be lukewarm, like you would use to bathe a baby. Apply a rich lanolin or protein dog shampoo and rub vigorously through the fur to work up a lather. If there are problems such as dandruff or external parasites, then you will need to use a special shampoo. Several complete and thorough rinses are of utmost importance. A hose with a spray attachment simplifies the procedure. Rinsing is of utmost importance as shampoo remaining on the coat may irritate the skin and will dull the fur. Be certain that the feet are washed and rinsed carefully.

Now comes the drying. With a long-haired dog you should pat off the excess moisture, others can just be towel dried. Vigorous rubbing with several turkish towels should get your soppy friend damp dry. If he will then submit to being dried by an electric hair dryer, your job is much easier. Many dogs are deathly afraid of a dryer though and it isn't worth creating a problem. Continue drying until your dog feels practically dry. Pay special attention to the ears to be certain that they are completely dry. Wipe them clean with cotton dipped in a little oil.

Now you may brush and comb your clean and fresh smelling companion. If his coat has a tendency to be unusually dry and brittle, you may wish to use a special spray for this condition. Or if your purpose in bathing the dog was to combat external parasites, then apply whatever powder was prescribed as treatment. While you are drying and grooming during this clean stage you can most easily observe your dog's skin. Check it for any problems; investigate those areas that he's been scratching. This is too good an opportunity to miss.

It's generally advised to keep the dog in for at least six to 12 hours after a bath if the weather is cool or wet.

The Nails

A dog's nails should be kept cut quite short to keep his feet feeling comfortable and neat in appearance. Walking on long nails will spread the toes, thus adversely affecting the dog's gait, as well as presenting the danger of their being caught and torn accidentally which can cause great pain.

Cutting the nails regularly is recommended. Special pet nail cutting scissors are available for this purpose. Proceed with this task most cautiously as the quick above nail bed is highly sensitive and will bleed and cause extreme pain if cut. Once a dog has been hurt he will usually resent having his nails cut. Some dogs are so terrified of have their nails touched, often because of some previous injury, that only a vet or professional can handle them.

In white nailed dogs, the quick, which is pink, is visible and cutting too short can be avoided. However, black nails are difficult to judge and the novice should not attempt it. Using a file may be preferable at first until you learn to gauge correctly. Frequent cutting helps the quick to recede. The section to cut is the hook which curves downward.

City dogs that walk on sidewalks a great deal keep their nails filed down and need cutting infrequently. By filing the nails with a regular canine file, they can be kept shortened without frequent cutting.

The Teeth

Tartar deposits may form on your dog's teeth if his diet contains inadequate amounts of hard biscuits or rawhide bones. These black tartar deposits should be removed since they cause recession and irritation of the gums. Have your veterinarian show you how this is done and then you can handle this chore should deposits continue to form. If you wish, you can brush his teeth with baking soda, salt, or a mild pumice. The best care though is providing chewable material which will clean the teeth.

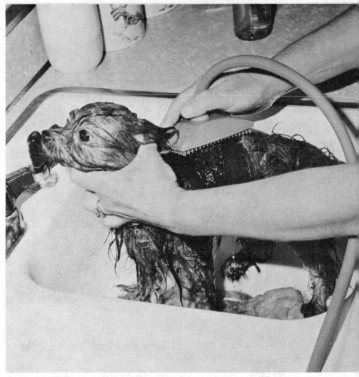

A small dog can be washed in the sink and a spray simplifies the procedure.

Rinsing thoroughly is essential. A long haired dog may require eight to ten minutes of rinsing.

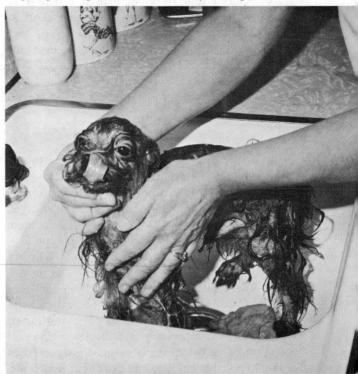

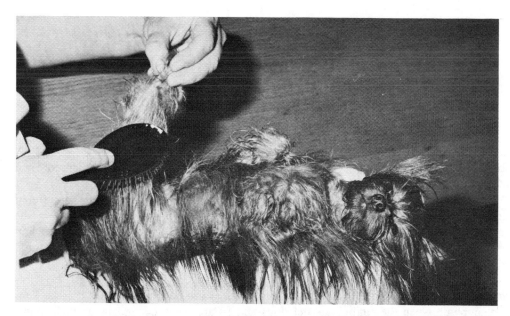

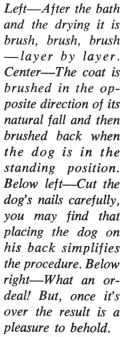

Left—After the bath and the drying it is brush, brush, brush—layer by layer. Center—The coat is brushed in the opposite direction of its natural fall and then brushed back when the dog is in the standing position. Below left—Cut the dog's nails carefully, you may find that placing the dog on his back simplifies the procedure. Below right—What an ordeal! But, once it's over the result is a pleasure to behold.

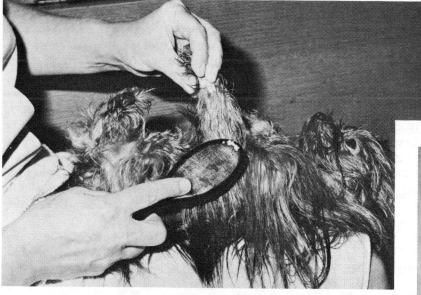

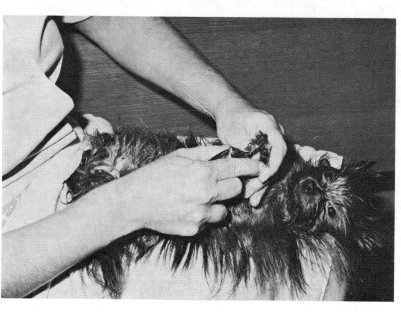

SUMMERTIME DOG CARE

THE good old summertime is a season of suffering for a lot of dogs. It shouldn't be.

Anyone who assumes the responsibility of dog ownership should make provisions to see that his dog (or dogs) comes through the hot weather in good shape and with a minimum of discomfort.

This responsibility applies to the gun-dog breeds in particular. Purely from the owner's standpoint— that is, aside from consideration for the animal itself —a hunting dog that has been cared for properly in summer will be easier to shape up when the hunting season rolls around.

In a time that is probably still fresh in the memory of anyone past 40 years of age, dog care was a much more casual thing than it is today. Perhaps many dogs were better off in those days, than they are today, when close supervision and confinement, to protect a valuable investment or to comply with local ordinances, is the general practice.

Prior to World War II many homes had yards. Today, even where space is no problem, homes have lawns. Lawns are fussed over, carefully tended. Yards weren't; they were places where kids and dogs played, and their appearance suffered accordingly.

The family dog, unless he was a complete bum, had free run of the yard. And, as dogs will do, he and the other canines in the neighborhood exchanged "calling cards." It was an accepted fact of canine life that no decent dog would squat or lift a leg on his own property, and things evened out.

Today? Let a dog run across a manicured lawn and a neighborhood feud develops.

The free-roaming dog saw to it that he suffered as little as possible from the heat. He'd lie in the shade of a tree or outbuilding, dig in the cool damp earth, and if the water pail went dry slake his thirst in a creek or puddle.

Times have changed. Few "yard dogs" exist today. Most canines are now either house dogs or kennel dogs and so are more dependent upon humans.

Dog care at any time of year is mostly a common-sense matter. Yet many persons who acquire dogs today have had little or no experience with animals in their youth, so a lot of dog owners lack this basis of common sense and may unknowingly neglect their pets.

So it doesn't seem out of place to suggest some tips for the inexperienced—tips that may also serve as reminders to those who know what should be done but forget to do it.

Dogs are tough, resilient animals and do not have to be pampered. But there is no reason for them to suffer unnecessarily because of the lack of a little planning and a few minutes' effort each day. A dog owner owes at least that to his dog.

Whether a dog is kept in the house, out in a kennel run, chained to a doghouse, or free in the yard, he needs water. In the home, it can be in a dish in

*The free-roaming dog sees to it that he
suffers as little as possible from the heat.*

any convenient place, usually on a floor surface that's easily wiped up. In the kennel, a pailful should be placed in a shady spot where it can be easily reached by a chained or loose dog and yet won't be tipped and spilled.

A dog can get by on some pretty scummy, dirty, stale water. But he shouldn't have to. Someone in the family should be able to find time to change the water at least once a day. Some dogs play in their water buckets and spill them. If constant refilling is too much of a nuisance, buy one of the nonspillable containers.

Plenty of fresh water, a must at all times, is of even higher priority if the dog is "dry fed," getting his ration just as it comes out of the bag. Dry feeding is a highly acceptable and convenient procedure. But a dog must drink more when so fed, to furnish the moisture that he'd get if fed canned dog food or meal or kibble mixed with water, gravy, milk, or what have you.

You'll do your dog a favor by reducing his food intake in the hot months. We've reached such a state of affluence today and know so much about canine nutrition that there are as many overfed dogs waddling around today as there were underfed ones in the lean years.

However, overfed dogs can be undernourished. Good-quality table scraps *probably* will sustain nine dogs out of ten. But a commercial dog food of high quality will turn the probability of proper nutrition into a certainty. On table scraps consisting largely of potatoes, bread, vegetables, and other plate scrapings, a dog may get fat and yet be woefully lacking in stamina, subject to skin and virus diseases, and just not up to snuff.

Even if enough meat, fat, and bone scraps were available to supply all your dog can eat—which is very unlikely—a straight-meat diet is not an adequate ration either. By all means, give him table leftovers, either as a treat or to supplement the balanced commercial dog food, particularly if you are feeding more than one dog and when dogs are being worked hard. But commercial dog food, proven safe and adequate for most dogs through intensive testing and research, as the "main course" is wisest and cheapest in the long run.

In hot weather most dogs voluntarily cut down on food intake. But some won't, and if yours is one of those, give him a little less food, maybe as much as one-third less than his cooler-weather ration.

Fat on a dog is uncomfortable in the summer, and shedding it may take most of the hunting season. The larding up is likely to start in late spring and early summer. A dog must eat heavily to keep going in the fall and winter hunting seasons, and if he's kept outside in an unheated kennel he needs additional calories to keep warm. He carries the heavy-eating habit into Spring but no longer uses the energy furnished by the food. If he doesn't cut down on food himself, you'd better make the change for him.

I couldn't prove it, but I'd bet that many of the skin troubles that can afflict dogs in the summer have as one of their causes a too-rich diet during the transition from the work and chill of fall and winter to the idleness and warmth of spring and summer.

Summer skin troubles can be reduced or eliminated if owners practice good kennel sanitation and promptly treat any outbreak of fleas, mange, eczema, "hot spots," or what have you.

Powders, dips, soaps—even a medicated collar and medicine that can be mixed with the dog's food —will rid the dog of fleas. But you can't stop there. Doghouse, bedding, kennel yard, and the rug or blanket that he sleeps on in the house must all be fumigated.

Fleas can contribute to the outbreak of various skin disorders. They seem to come out in force about the time a dog starts shedding his winter coat. By combing and brushing him, you'll cut down on the scratching a dog does to help rid himself of dead hair. But if it's flea bites he's scratching, he may dig at them until he breaks the skin and infection can set in.

Few dog owners can correctly diagnose a skin disorder or know the cause of it. So consult your veterinarian if your dog exhibits sores, runny spots, exposed patches of skin, and so on. Follow the vet's advice. Some skin troubles clear up without treatment, but most are hard to diagnose and tough to eradicate. Prevent when possible; seek professional

Dogs pant in order to cool themselves off. They do not sweat which makes it difficult for them to cool off in a hurry when overheated.

treatment if skin problems do crop up.

A dog kept outside in a small town or rural area will just have to make his own peace with flies and mosquitoes. Check him for wood ticks. These three pests can bother city dogs, too.

Ticks should be pulled off and then burned or squashed. You can cut down on the fly nuisance by picking up excrement and washing surfaced runs daily, which will also reduce odor and keep your dog clean.

I don't like insecticides around dogs. This stuff is poisonous and can be dangerous to dogs. And except in the South, where mosquitoes are heartworm carriers, the insects are less hazardous than the treatment. Some commercial kennels are screened—a fine idea but hardly practical for the one-dog owner. If your dog is a house pet, let him share the screened porch, basement, recreation room, or wherever you go for relief from heat and mosquitoes.

If the dog is confined outside, be sure that he can find shade, particularly after 9 or 10 a.m. He may like the early-morning sun, but if he's to avoid discomfort, heat exhaustion, or sunstroke he must be able to find shade when it heats up.

Most doghouses, unless specially constructed with a breezeway or something similar, become stuffy ovens on hot days. There should be a tree, building, solid fence, wall, matting, or some other structure to provide shade through the day. A doghouse that's up off the ground and properly placed will throw shade and provide crawl space underneath. There the dog can lie and benefit from air movement.

The doghouse should provide a dry shelter from hard summer rains and should be comfortable to curl up in during damp, chill nights.

Traveling with a dog in summer is complicated by the heat. Many a good dog, left in the car while the family frolicked in the sun and sand or went shopping, has died a horrible death from heat build-up in a closed auto.

Don't ever leave a dog alone in a closed car. Even if you have found a parking place in the shade, you may not get back before the sun shifts. And cracking the windows slightly so that the dog can't get out or to prevent break-ins doesn't provide adequate ventilation. Maybe your dog won't die under those conditions, but he will suffer.

The best investment that can be made by any dog owner who takes his dog or dogs on trips, summer or any other time, is a commercially manufactured travel crate. If you're handy and like making things, you can build your own. But for anyone else, the ready-made models are a bargain.

I prefer all-wire models to the solid plywood or aluminum crates. They can be ordered in different sizes and shapes, provide ventilation that is as good as if the dog were loose in the vehicle, and don't seriously obstruct the driver's rear vision.

It's easy to train a dog to ride in a travel crate. He can see what's going on about him, and once accustomed to it he is contented and much safer than if he were rattling around all over the car, being a threat to safe driving and a hairy, panting, muddy-footed, drooling nuisance to passengers.

If a crated dog must be left in the car for a time, all windows in the vehicle can be left open since the dog can't get out of the crate. Water can be provided in a small can hooked to the wire mesh so that it doesn't spill.

If you're on a trip and you don't want to leave the dog overnight in the car, you may get around objections to dogs at motels and campsites by moving the easily carried crate into your room or tent.

On a trip, don't let a dog overeat or overdrink. If he's prone to carsickness, let him lick ice cubes to slake his thirst en route, thus reducing the chance that a bellyful of sloshing water will contribute to an upset stomach. Feed him only in the evening when you're through traveling.

If you can afford it, while you are traveling feed him hamburger or meat scraps from your plate when you dine out. A straight-meat diet for a short period of time won't hurt your dog. Since meat is a low-residue dog food, it will lengthen the time between "relief" stops and reduce the quantity of excrement deposited. Avoid bones, which cause excessive flatulence and can "bind up" a dog.

Allow your dog a free run, letting him relieve himself, before you embark on each day's travel. After one to two hours, stop and "exercise" him again. Dogs can usually defecate again after a ride of this length if given a few minutes to loosen up. Activity makes a dog "go." Inactivity — enforced by the travel crate—slows down the digestion processes, and after this stop your dog will probably be content, or at least be able to "hold it," for the rest of the day.

When you pull in for the night, get the dog out,

All wire crates are fine for travel. They come in a variety of sizes and are easy to maneuver.

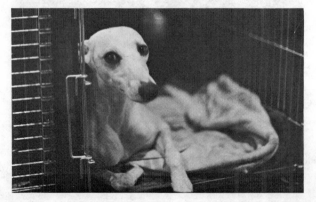

feed him, and then let him run again just before you turn in yourself. He should then be able to put in a quiet night until his morning run.

Try to plan things so that you won't be on a toll road or freeway two hours after you've gotten underway—that is, be sure you can find a side road on which to park while you exercise him in midmorning.

Play it safe, even if the dog minds well, by using a leash or long cord. Traffic, even on a byroad, can cause a tragedy. And don't give all dogs a bad name by making his relief stop at a park or other place frequented by large numbers of people.

Take along a stack of newspapers, and line the crate's floor with them. They will make cleaning up and disposing of a mess immeasurably easier if you are caught on a superhighway with a dog that can't hold it or is sick.

The breeze blowing through the car's open windows won't harm your dog. And if he's crated, you won't have to worry about his jumping out an open window.

If you use a station wagon, don't drive with the tailgate window open. Exhaust fumes sucked in can sicken a dog.

If you're caught without a water dish or food pan, a hub cap will serve the purpose.

Other problems may arise and solutions occur to you. The suggestions I've given are more or less basics that will provide a more enjoyable summer for your dog—rewards in advance for what he'll do for you when the air gets nippy and there's game in the cover.

With that in mind, don't forget exercise. Hours of hard running are out of the question in summer. And besides, you don't want to run your dog in game cover when birds and other animals of the year are just learning their way around.

But regular exercise during summer will keep your dog contented with his lot and will cut down on the conditioning time and discomfort that he'll go through in those early days of hunting season. Summer's the time to yard-train him and brush up his obedience. But do it in the cool of morning or evening when he's feeling frisky and alert, rather than under a broiling sun.

Retrieving lessons will make him run and will provide maximum exercise in a confined area; water work is easy and enjoyable in warm weather, and swimming is an excellent conditioner. Ramming around with the kids, another good idea, is easy on you and good for the dog.

Don't ignore your hunting buddy just because he's a bit of bother in the hot weather. He'll benefit as much from the human attention as from anything else and will be less likely to bark, chew, and dig when left to his own devices.

Give him some consideration in the summertime, and it'll pay off for you in the fall. *David Michael Duffey.*

Reprinted from *Outdoor Life*: Copyright © 1969 Poular Science Publishing Company, Inc.

If you travel with your dog or dogs, having your car properly equipped will be of tremendous help. (Photos courtesy of Kennel-Aire.)

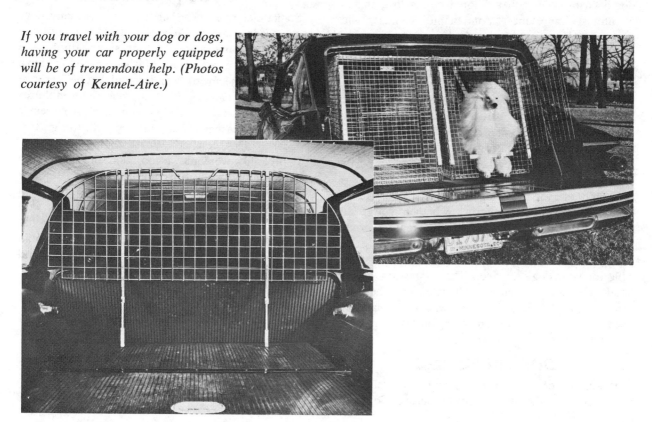

TRAVELING WITH YOUR DOG

MOST vacationing and moving families are confronted with the dilemma of what to do with their dog. Going on a vacation—should you take him or leave him? Think through the pros and cons. As a member of the family, your pet would enjoy the fun of traveling with you. On the other hand, some dogs can take all the pleasure out of a vacation.

A dog should be accustomed to riding in a car before you consider taking him on a long automobile trip. If your dog does not travel well, and he either gets sick or restless, consider a well-run boarding kennel instead.

Should you decide to take him along, you will have to accept certain responsibilities. Write ahead to hotels and motels for reservations advising them that you will have a dog with you. Automobile clubs and motel guides often list hotels and motels which accept dogs.

Take your dog's bowl and food along. He will feel more secure having his own dish and regular diet. Provide him with his sleeping pad so he will have "his own place" in the car and in the hotel.

Be certain your dog has an identification tag and dog license on his collar. Should he get lost, this is of utmost importance. Your name, address, and phone number should be on the identification tag.

Taking a can of flea powder along is a good idea. En route, he may pick up fleas, and you don't want these in your car or in the hotel.

Don't allow your dog to hang his head out the window while you are driving. Dust or grit may be blown into the eyes. The dog could get nasal and eye inflammation just from the wind. Discourage him from doing this by keeping the window partly closed.

Should you be traveling between several states, check with your veterinarian whether you need health certificates. Many states do require some form of health certificate.

Remember that wherever you go, you are responsible for your dog's conduct. The impression left on hotel and motel managers will determine their attitude toward all dogs and dog owners. By planning ahead and observing the rules of courtesy, you can take your dog with you anywhere.

DOGS IN EUROPE

It was a pleasant surprise to find how well dogs are accepted in the major cities of Europe. So many restrictions which are common in the United States seemed to be non-existent. In Paris, nearly every outside cafe has its own dog. This "chaperone" often greets the customers, waits for a friendly pat, and generally circulates around. When business is quiet, he snoozes in the sun. It is not at all unusual to find people taking their own dog with them to the restaurant and even to see them seated in a chair at the table. We observed this in Paris and Vienna. Dogs can be seen walking with their masters in department stores in London, in grocery stores in Switzerland, and in virtually all public places.

Many Americans who have witnessed this relaxed attitude toward dogs in Europe are now bringing theirs along. However, good doggy manners are required everywhere. Fines are quite stiff for their infringement; for example in London, one sees signs threatening a £20 fine for soiling the foot path. So, if you wish to travel with your dog, you'll find it quite enjoyable; but follow all the foreign travel requirements and have a well-behaved and well-trained dog.

DOGS IN MEXICO

Sometimes one feels that there are as many dogs as people in Mexico. They seem to be mainly muts who roam around and take long siestas during the afternoon. Although most of them probably have homes, they seem to wander and probe garbage wherever they can find it. What interesting mixtures of breeds can be seen! It's quite fantastic. Apparently licenses and leashes haven't arrived with too great a vengeance. Dog catcher? What's that?

It probably wouldn't be too good an idea to take your dog along while traveling in Mexico. Although dogs seem welcome everywhere, it might present a problem health-wise. Tourists have difficulties with water, food, and altitude. A dog traveling here would probably experience these same problems. It would be necessary to provide bottled, purified water and to have adequate supplies of his regular food. Special precautions to avoid overheating would also be necessary. Remember though, taking along a pet is a real responsibility, and, unless you are willing and eager to expend the necessary effort and time required, don't do it!

TATTOO YOUR DOG

Even the most determined dognapper is going to think twice before he tries to peddle a permanently marked pup; such marks will make his "buyers" balk too.

NO hotter or more important issue exists in all of dogdom than that of the theft of dogs. Accurate figures are hard to come by, but it seems conservative to say that almost a million dogs a year are stolen. The vast majority of these canines go to laboratories; the rest are sold as pets and hunting dogs.

The dog seems to be the most desirable animal for research work. Medical schools use them; food research institutes, chemical labs, psychological and reaction labs, dog food companies, all use them. The list is endless, the total numbers in the hundreds of thousands. The research is valuable and necessary. Most medical teams of doctors working on transplants learn to coordinate teamwork by performing a highly complicated operation several times on dogs before turning to humans. The research generally is conducted under clean conditions, for this is necessary for the accurate gathering of knowledge. That the experiments be humane has been provided for by recent public law. All this is fine and commendable, but for dog owners the existence of so much research increases the danger that their animal may be stolen in order to be sold to a lab. Hunters are especially vulnerable because their dogs tend to run loose more and often they live in rural areas where it is easier to steal a dog. Furthermore, the market value of hunting dogs is better, either as working or research animals, because they are usually strong and healthy.

I lost a dog this way about eight years ago. The dog that was stolen was a bitch I had already paid the stud fee on to breed to the National Pheasant Champion that year. I took her out to Long Island for an afternoon hunt. She got away from me, became lost, then looped back toward the car. Before she got there, somebody drove up, opened his door, whistled her inside and drove off. I could see it all from a distance, but I couldn't get there in time.

I rushed to the police. They were sympathetic but un-cooperative. "Mister, we get a dozen complaints a week on stolen or lost dogs. We've got more important things to do than chase around on them."

I got mad because this was pretty important to me, but later I could see their point.

"Well," I said, "I'm going to drive around until I see the guy, then get you to come arrest him."

"Can't do that unless you have positive identification of your dog," said the officer.

"What are you talking about?"

"You've got to be able to prove it before we'll make an arrest."

"I know my dog when I see it."

"That's not enough legally. If his collar's still on him, that's helpful, but the thief undoubtedly tore it off and threw it away within the first hundred feet. Markings don't stand up under a court of law. Tattoos are the best thing. Your dog tattooed?"

"No."

"Too bad. The only other thing is scars that a vet can positively identify."

"What about witnesses to verify the identity of the dog?"

"Not much," he shrugged, "especially if you've got a Weimaraner that looks like a thousand others. A room full of witnesses can't prove it then. Tattoo's the best thing."

Recently I spoke with a uniformed dog warden in Pennsylvania who told me some hair-raising stories of dog theft in his area. Pets were stolen from backyards, houses, parked cars. Whole kennels were cleaned out by dognappers who waited until the owner and family left home for a while. One amateur Beagle fancier who had spent a lifetime developing his own strain for hunting and field trials lost his entire kennel, including three field champions, though the thieves had to scale a fence and break a locked gate.

How to stop this black market in dogs?

The Congress of the U. S. tried with Public Law 89-544, known as The Laboratory Animal Welfare Act. Under the rules of this act, which appeared in the Federal Register of December 15, 1966, the Department of Agriculture issues licenses to dog and cat dealers, inspects laboratory facilities, and so on. All of this is helpful, but dog theft continues. Consider the following experiences of Mr. M. A. Jones from Mena, Arkansas, who is a three-time dog loser:

". . . Thieves have been stealing us blind here in

this part of the state. It goes on all year but starts in a big way in August and goes on until after the first of the year."

Or the following excerpt from an Associated Press story dated June 19, 1968:

"Three men . . . were arrested here [East Windsor, N. J.] Sunday as they were transporting 210 dogs to a Princeton Laboratory and charged with carrying animals in a cruel way. . . . One of the dogs was dead and another died soon after the arrest, police said."

In my opinion, tattooing is the only easy way to protect your dog from theft. A registered tattoo clearly identifies him as your personal property beyond any legal doubt. Because a tattoo will stand up in any court of law in the country, the chances are good that when a dognapper discovers a tattooed dog among those he has nabbed, he'll pull it out of the bunch and turn it loose rather than run the risk of a serious fine or a jail sentence.

Another restraining influence which the tattoo exerts is on the research lab as a buyer. As a result of the House hearings and PL 89-544, enough attention has been focused on the situation so the labs don't want to cause any unnecessary disturbance. Obviously, the discovery of a tattooed dog in a laboratory would create the kind of trouble no laboratory could afford, and the use of such dogs would surely be discovered. The result is that the labs refuse to buy them. Furthermore, it is a Federal crime to transport or sell stolen domestic animals in interstate or foreign commerce—another reason why all dealers and labs shy away from tattooed dogs, which can be positively identified by police or owners. Law provides for penalties of up to a year in prison or a fine of up to $1,000 or both.

This is why I urge you to tattoo your dog.

The process of tattooing is very simple. Two methods are available, one superior to the other, in my opinion. The oldest and poorest way is called the clamp method, and it is used to mark the inside of the dog's ear. The clamp is a gadget similar to a pair of pliers into which four numerals or letters formed by tiny, needle-sharp nails are inserted. The underside of the animal's ear is cleaned with alcohol, then two people hold the dog down on his back, one grasping his hind legs, the other his front legs and head. A third person works the tattoo pliers, breaking the skin of the ear with a quick squeeze, then thoroughly wiping the area with the tattoo ink which works into the perforations and becomes permanent when healed.

When my dog was stolen, I ran out and bought one of these sets and tattooed the remaining dogs in my kennel. This was in the days before any tattoo registry existed, so the problem was what to use in the way of a number. I finally settled on the dog's Field Dog Stud Book registration number, which

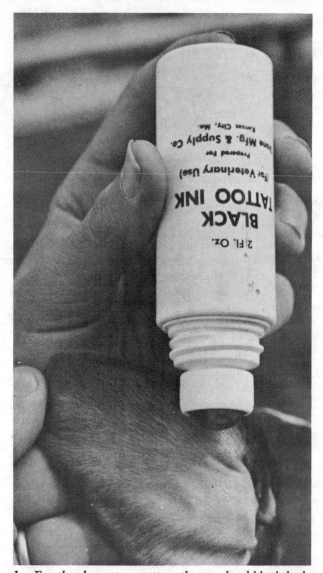

1—For the clamp-type tattoo, the ear should be inked.

2—The ear after it is inked.

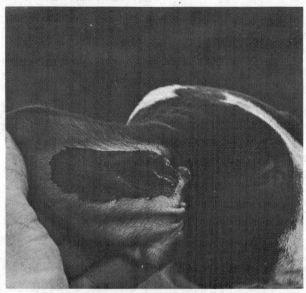

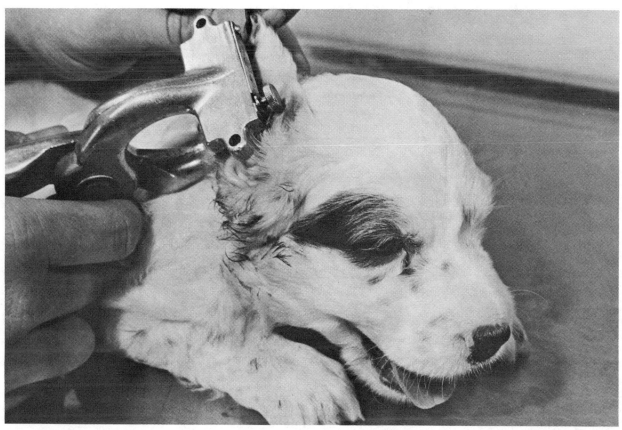

3—The clamp-type tattoo is applied.

4—After the clamp is used the ink is rubbed well into the perforations.

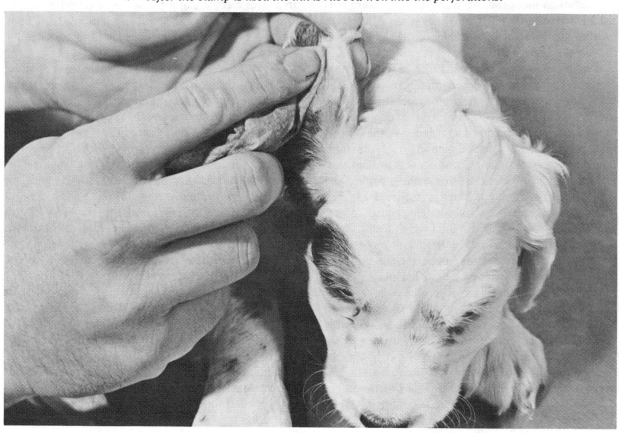

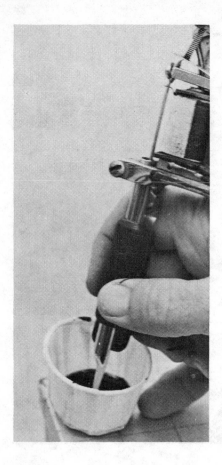

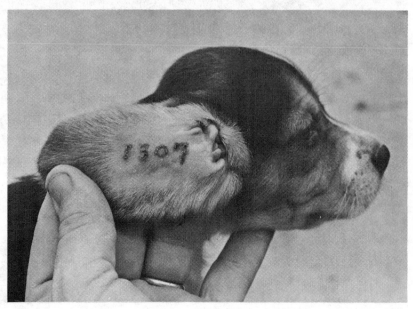

5—The vibrator-type of tattoo pen.

6—A tattoo produced by vibrator. (Photos courtesy of Purina Pet Care Center.)

involved tattooing FDSE 492844. Theoretically, this meant that if the dog were lost, a finder could get in touch with me through the registry if he were persistent and wanted to. It also meant three squeezes on the pliers—a lot of punching on the ear, which proved the biggest drawback.

Clamp tattooing is somewhat like having your ear pierced, but you're supposed merely to break the skin, not go deep into it or through it. The first squeeze comes as a surprise to the dog, for he doesn't realize quite what happened, but the second time he is ready to defend himself, and the third time he'll probably bite. A muzzle gets around this.

The biggest problem is that unless you're just plain lucky, you'll hit a blood vessel and cause a hematoma, which is exactly what happened to me. This is like a big bubble of blood which forms under the skin, and it is hard and bothersome to treat, particularly in field dogs who knock their ears a lot. The clamp method leaves a neat, clear marking, but the risk of hematoma is too much for me.

The second marking system makes use of a small portable pen like the ones in tattoo parlors. With this you can write any place on the dog with almost no trouble at all. Generally the tattoo is put on the inside of the leg groin where the blood vessels are deep, so there is little or no chance of hematoma.

To tattoo by the needle also requires three people. Two people hold the dog down on a table on its back so that the inside of the right leg is easily accessible. The third man first shaves the hair from the tattoo area with electric clippers, swabs it off with alcohol to disinfect, then rubs petroleum jelly over the spot. He now picks up his tattoo pen and handwrites the assigned number on the dog.

The whole process takes less than three minutes and is practically painless. The only problem is that the chattering of the tattoo needle upsets certain dogs the same way an aerosol spray will drive some dogs nuts. It is best to tranquilize this type of animal.

Making the tattoo is actually the final step in protecting your dog from theft or loss. First comes the matter of registration.

Because many people have seen the merit of tattoos as a means of identification, it is now possible to have your dog's tattoo listed in a registry. The trouble is that there are several registries to choose from, perhaps more than half a dozen. Unfortunately this leads to confusion, for if you or the police or the local pound find a tattooed dog, which registry do you get in touch with? To date, neither the American Kennel Club (all breeds), the Field Dog Stud Book (bird dogs), nor the United Kennel Club (hounds) has seen fit to come forward and say "This is our system."

I checked into two registries, and here's how they work.

The National Dog Registry, 227 Stebbins Rd., Carmel, N.Y. 10512, (phone: 914-277-4485) was started in early 1966 by Dr. David H. Timrud, a physician at Princeton University's infirmary, who had his beloved house dog stolen and went to no end of time, trouble, and expense to recover it. When all proved fruitless, he spoke to several veterinarians who encouraged him to start a national tattoo registry. This he did. The system he used is based on your social security number. Since everybody in the country has one, this is what is tattooed on your dog's right groin. The number is then registered for the lifetime of the owner upon payment of $15. Permanent registration permits you to tattoo all the dogs you will ever own with your social security number without any additional cost. The number is rather long, nine digits, and in the case of transfer or sale it becomes more complicated, although provisions are made for this.

Most of the tattooing for the NDR is done through clinics—women's civic groups, Humane Societies, dog clubs, field trial clubs, dog shows. NDR is strongest in the East, in the megapolis from Boston to Virginia. At these clinics, one pays for the registry of his social security number with NDR (fees above), and for the tattoo, usually a $5 fee which goes to the person who does the job—sometimes a veterinarian, more often someone handy with the tattoo pen.

Dr. Timrod claims that his NDR has made some remarkable returns, including dogs dumped out along the road, apparently from groups of stolen dogs. The discovery by the dognapper of the tattoo was undoubtedly the reason for the release of the animals.

The other registry, Canine Bureau of Identification, Inc., 17 Battery Place, New York, N.Y. (phone: 212-269-1200; Western Union Telex 12-5139) was begun by Harry Miller, former director of the Gaines Dog Research Center, and is based on the Telex system of the Marine Registration Bureau in conjunction with Western Union. This system consists of an Identa-Mark (combination letter-number never larger than four digits) which is tattooed on your dog's groin by a veterinarian. This group urges that you go to your vet for the tattoo to insure that a professional and sanitary job is done.

You also receive a metal tag for your dog's collar which reads: "Warning: Registered dog. If found, telegraph collect tattoo number on flank or ear to: Canine Bureau of Identification, N. Y. 10004."

If your dog is lost, the finder simply contacts the nearest Western Union office and gives them the Identa-Mark number. At no cost to the owner or finder, Western Union notifies the CBI over special teletype hookup. Within minutes the CBI will contact the owner with the news as to where his dog is being held. The cost is $5 for the special tag which is good for the lifetime of the owner. There is also the veterinarian's fee. If you happen to neglect to keep your number paid up, CBI will always notify you of your lost dog and you can update your account.

CBI is strongest in the East Coast area, Florida, and California. On the West Coast it operates under the name of Animal Identification Service, and has full veterinary approval. As I said earlier, it sees the Veterinary Medical Association as having the primary role in tattooing. It expects to begin conducting clinics for mass tattooing under veterinary supervision.

Mr. Miller and Dr. Westley Young, former director of the Los Angeles zoo, operate the West Coast AIS. Bruno Agenti, Bradford Mitchell, and J. Kilbourne King operate the New York office where all the records are kept.

The big problem with having two systems is, of course, who do you call when you find a tattooed dog. The registries tend to work together for the cause and make referrals to aid in the return of lost dogs to owners.

What the future will bring out of all this remains to be seen. My own feeling is that sooner or later the AKC, FDSB, UKC and other dog registries will require tattooing for permanent positive identification. At this point AKC has gone only so far as to recommend the groin tattoo in preference to ear tattoo.

There is another interesting aspect to this problem of dog theft. Connecticut seems to have solved it pretty well by legislation. In that state a law was passed that all dogs in a pound after two weeks, unclaimed by the owner or not placed, can be sold to research laboratories and medical schools. There was a great hullabaloo over this law—humane societies and anti-vivisectionists opposed it—but in practice it has eliminated just about all theft of dogs for sale to laboratories in a state which used to have a high rate of such crimes because of its many research institutions and medical schools.

The general public has little idea of the vast number of dogs put away by pounds because they are unwanted or are problem cases. If other states passed legislation similar to that in Connecticut, the vast majority of dog thefts would stop overnight. Want an ax to grind? Here's one for you.

This still does not eliminate the need for tattooing. It is a positive system for identifying dogs and having them returned when lost. All seeing-eye dogs are automatically tattooed, which speaks for itself. On the financial side, a tattoo clinic offers a fine way for your hunting or field trial club to raise some money for its treasury and at the same time accomplish a most worthwhile purpose. *Jeff Griffen*

Reprinted through the courtesy of Field & Stream

BECOMING A TWO-DOG FAMILY

For those dog lovers considering breeding their bitch and then becoming a two-dog family, here is one family's experiences which should provide food for thought.

WHEN my obstetrician confirmed our suspicions that it was indeed time to begin thinking about a name for our second child, Tom, my husband, also began thinking about a pet for Steven or Karin—whoever the child might turn out to be. Since Brian, our two-year-old, had no choice but to share his parents, Tom believed we should spare him the difficulties of sharing Mamie, his Miniature Schnauzer, as well. By the time I packed my suitcase, I had accepted the fact that the addition of our baby to the family would also mean the addition of another dog; and by the time Karin cut her first tooth, we had agreed that the best way of finding the perfect puppy for her would be to breed Mamie.

Our veterinarian suggested a champion Schnauzer who lived nearby as a suitable mate. To our surprise, Mamie had to pass inspection before terms of the contract were even discussed. Her family background and physical condition passed the test, so Mamie was squeezed into Rob Roy's busy schedule. As we began our nine-week wait, I decided that I might consider living my next life as a pampered Miniature Schnauzer. This was undoubtedly the easiest pregnancy I had ever been associated with—the biggest problem was to correctly alternate her calcium and vitamin pills! During the final trimester (three weeks are much more tolerable than three months), her veterinarian assured me that the delivery of her offspring would be no big deal and I needed no special training. His only instructions were to be there in case she got nervous. Unconvinced, we combed the local pet shops for the book with the most complete section on breeding Miniature Schnauzers and set about memorizing the information under "Whelping." Having no basement, we decided that one of the bedrooms would afford Mamie the most privacy. Karin moved into Brian's room, and we installed the whelping box in the nursery. I assembled all the equipment recommended in the book—iodine, scissors, alcohol, newspapers, hot water bottle, old towels, an eyedropper and ingredients for a formula in case the puppies needed supplemental feedings.

Whelping day approached and Mamie's temperature began dropping on Sunday. By Monday night she was below 100 deg. and our trusty book informed us that in about 12 hours we would witness the blessed event. Mamie didn't sleep that night and, of course, neither did I. She nested furiously everywhere but in her whelping box, and at one point I nearly crawled under our bed with her, just in case. Tuesday came and went (another sleepless night for Mamie and me), so Wednesday morning we went to see our veterinarian. He assured me there was no problem, that she probably would whelp by Thursday morning, and, once again, there was nothing I would have to do but "be there."

Tom took over the watch Wednesday night while I tucked in the children and for the third time told them when they woke up we might have our puppies. I opened the door of the nursery just in time to hear Mamie cry out in an almost human voice. We could see her abdomen contract, and with each contraction she cried out. Unable to reach the vet, we watched helplessly for nearly an hour aware that something was not right. Finally the bag of waters broke, but another hour went by, the hard contractions returned, and there were still no puppies. Suddenly we saw the first puppy emerging. It came out about two inches, but as Mamie relaxed, it was drawn back into her body about half way. Mamie contracted again, but it emerged no further and again withdrew. We tried to discover the cause (this obviously did not follow the book), and I thought I saw the tip of a tail within the membrane. After several more contractions with no more progress, we decided this must be a breech presentation and proceeded to deliver the puppy. Tom held Mamie while I tried desperately to follow the directions in our book. Before we knew it, the puppy —still in its sack—was in my hands, and Mamie jumped out of the box and ran to the opposite corner of the room. While Tom checked her, I quickly cut open the sack with the sterile scissors. The puppy did not appear to be breathing, so I massaged his chest with a towel. His head jerked and he began to breathe. I removed the rest of the membrane, cut the cord and dipped the end in the iodine according to the directions in the book.

Mamie rested for nearly an hour, and we dried her son and placed him in a separate box with a hot water bottle as a substitute mother. With very little warning and just a few contractions, Mamie delivered a second son, but again retreated to let me open the sack, cut the cord and dry him. Within ten minutes the contractions started again and Mamie's third puppy briefly appeared. Apparently it was another breech, but by this time we were so experienced we handled the delivery without a hitch. As I cut open the membrane and examined the puppy, I saw that Karin had her pet, for it was a female. On the spot, we named her Topsy Turvy, since that was how she entered the world.

Mamie now seemed more interested in sleeping than in her new family. She refused to allow them to nurse, so we mixed up a formula and fed them with an eyedropper. Several hours went by and Tom finally decided if Mamie could sleep, he would too. I promised to call him if she had any more puppies and fixed up a temporary bed for myself on the floor next to my new charges. I fed them whenever they cried during the night, and as I watched Mamie sleeping soundly, I decided to be reincarnated as a Schnauzer!

In the morning I took Mamie and her brood—which she still refused to acknowledge as hers—to our unconcerned veterinarian. As I related our experience of the night before, he examined the puppies and assured me they were beautiful specimens and we had proceeded correctly under the circumstances. He felt Mamie's rejection of the puppies was due to her inexperience and suggested I hold Mamie in the box to allow the puppies to nurse and leave the room open so that she could go into them whenever she liked.

I was amazed how much like babies our three little puppies were. They cried when they were hungry, nursed vigorously (while I held Mamie captive), and then fell asleep for another two or three hours. Mamie would jump out of the box and disappear until the next time I heard the puppies cry and carried her back to assume her motherly duties. I slept in the nursery and Mamie slept with Tom except for interruptions for middle-of-the-night feedings. Saturday night after a 2 a.m. feeding, she didn't jump out as soon as the puppies finished nursing. I fell asleep and was surprised to find Mamie and her family sleeping peacefully in the morning. From then on I was completely relieved of my duties, and we found it difficult to get Mamie out of the box for any reason. She turned out to be a perfect mother, and the next five weeks were a real pleasure for all of us. We excitedly noticed the puppies' eyes opening, and within a few days they not only walked but were learning to climb out of the box. The children laughed as Topsy and her brothers, affectionately called George and Herman, learned to lap up cereal while strolling through the bowl. Gradually they became independent of their mother, and I forgot what it was like not to have to watch for puppies underfoot—which is where

they usually could be found!

Sooner than we would have wished, the day arrived when it was time to send George and Herman on their way. We had long ago promised a puppy to one of our neighbors and to Tom's sister, at bargain prices. When Mamie's litter turned out to be only three puppies, we realized that we'd be lucky to meet our expenses! Nevertheless, Herman moved down the block and George went to live in St. Louis, and Mamie and Topsy began in earnest their life together.

I think the most important lesson to be learned about owning two dogs was one we learned the first night after George and Herman's departure. Ever since Mamie, as a seven-week-old puppy, had escaped from the barricaded kitchen and made her way up the stairs to our bedroom, she has slept with Tom and me, in our bed, often curled up between us like a fur-covered hot water bottle! We have long been aware of the less desirable aspects of this sleeping arrangement, but we've never had the heart to banish her to the hard, cold floor. We had decided, however, that we would never start the habit with Topsy. Things were going to be very different the second time around. Topsy spent the better part of that first evening alone looking for her brothers in all their favorite sleeping spots. By the time we turned in for the night, she was a lonely puppy indeed. When Mamie jumped up on our bed, Topsy's heart broke, and our resolve lasted about 20 seconds. Topsy has slept with us ever since. The moral? Admit the fact that you are you, with an already established system of dealing with a pet. That system will be as difficult to change as any other personality trait you might wish to alter. In our case, where we were indulgent with Mamie, we have been more so now that we have two dogs to indulge. We don't mind crowded sleeping quarters too much, but if we did, we would have been wiser not to get the second dog as any other solutions are practically impossible for us to enforce! Instead, we are now considering buying a king-sized bed!

The other lesson we have learned is really just a realization of a previously known but little heeded fact—owning two dogs means at least double the cost,

---

Here are a few things you can learn from your dog:
To keep clean.
To love children.
To keep your place.
To size up an enemy.
To drink plenty of water.
To be a dependable friend.
To express pleasure when favored.
To guard faithfully the interests of those who care
*   for and protect you.*
To be faithful unto death.

the time, the trouble, as well as the pleasure of owning one.

We gave hardly a thought to the fact that adding Topsy to the family would add a lot of bills! We knew we would be buying twice as much dog food, but we have since realized that dog food is only one expense of owning a dog. Yearly booster shots and rabies vaccinations are now double, as are dog licenses. There are now two dogs to get ear infections or skin rashes requiring visits to the veterinarian. Boarding one dog during a vacation is expensive, but the cost of boarding two can be actually prohibitive. Since we happen to have dogs that require professional grooming, we have another double expense. While I thought nothing of paying $10 every three months to have Mamie groomed, I have now found a new shop where I pay only $8 for each dog and I usually try to stretch the interval between haircuts to four months. If prices go up, I'm sure I will invest in my own clippers and learn to do the job myself—a time consuming task I would never consider if we had only one dog.

One rarely thinks of the time involved in owning and caring for a pet, but much of that time is doubled when the pets double. Mamie has always enjoyed a bath, and since she has a persistent skin rash which requires special medication, Tom spends a good hour every few weeks bathing, drying, and brushing her. Now it is often two hours, as Topsy doesn't like to be neglected! Ever since Topsy was a puppy, I have tried to get her and Mamie on the same calendar for their yearly shots. I have been unsuccessful so far, which means I make four trips (instead of two) to the vet every year—each visit involving at least an hour and a half.

When our dogs are taken out on a leash together, they are more interested in each other than in the purpose of their walk. Rather than take the time to walk each one separately several times each day, we allow them to run loose in our yard. Though we have no fence, they seem to have a sense of their own territory, which at least gives me enough time to vacuum and dust.

In the trouble category, the biggest problem we have had is housebreaking, and our experience is apparently quite common in two-dog homes. Mamie was beautifully trained and we naturally assumed that she would take the lead in introducing her daughter to the rules of the house. Instead, Topsy showed her mother that there were other, more convenient places besides the back yard. Mamie saw she had a good thing going when she realized that Topsy, as the puppy, got blamed for all the accidents. The result is two rather poorly trained dogs; Mamie has gotten careless and Topsy has never been truly conscientious. Two or three times a week I face the dilemma of which dog to punish—should I punish both or try to guess which is the culprit and run the risk of confusing an innocent dog with an unearned scolding? Neither way has solved the problem yet.

Another problem we have encountered has a similar origin. Mamie, following Topsy's example, has reverted to that marvelous stage of puppyhood during which shoes are chewed, wastebaskets are emptied, stuffed toys are unstuffed, and throw pillows are often thrown! Topsy's puppyhood and Mamie's second one are even more fun—for them! What one doesn't think of, the other will; and while one pup might tire after unstuffing one or two teddy bears, two dogs can—and on occasion have—unstuffed a whole menagerie. Fortunately, once this problem was evident we took steps to avoid it. No stuffed toys are easily accessible (unless Karin chooses differently), closet doors are firmly shut (unless Brian forgets), and whenever we go out, Mamie and Topsy are incarcerated in the utility room (unless I am too hurried and take a chance on trusting them). Perhaps when Topsy gets older they will both grow up, but after seeing the pure abandon with which they recently destroyed Raggedy Ann, I have my doubts!

Mamie and Topsy look very much alike, and there have been times when one or the other has spent the afternoon outside without my knowledge. Seeing a Schnauzer curled up in the family room, I don't even think about whether the other is accounted for; and ever since Karin learned to open the back door, I often find that one dog is mysteriously missing. A neighbor who owns two Yorkshire Terriers has the same problem complicated by the fact that her dogs run away whenever they get out. Chasing one dog who has been set free by a three-year-old is bad enough, but try catching two who go in opposite directions. It goes without saying that if you have two dogs, the three-year-old has twice the opportunities to set one free!

Having two females, we have twice the seasonal watches and, of course, our house is the neighborhood hangout for wandering Romeos about 12 weeks out of every year. This is another bit of scheduling that ideally would be coordinated!

Anyone familiar with Miniature Schnauzers knows that they are inveterate barkers. Mamie's high-pitched

---

THE FEMALE DOG

1. A female dog is instinctively more protective than a male.

2. Bitches aren't as aggressive as males.

3. A spayed dog isn't interested in sex.

4. Other dogs aren't as likely to attack a female.

5. Female dogs don't have to urinate as often as males.

yipe has always been her least attractive trait, but since Tom travels, I have been able to relax in the knowledge that no one can possibly sneak up on our house. In fact, no one can sneak up on the neighbors' houses either, and even any unusual movement across the street brings forth Mamie's shrill alarm. We learned to live with Mamie and her bark, but we were really unprepared for how much worse two yipers in the house would be. What Mamie might miss during an afternoon snooze, Topsy sees and announces. This, of course, wakes Mamie and together the two dogs try to frighten away the intruder. Even after they forget the cause of the alarm, they will continue howling at each other until I interrupt their chorus with my own version of a shrill yipe! I would almost welcome a burglar rather than face such an alarm at the approach of every delivery man, the garbage men, the milk man, cleaner, paperboy, and every child going to and from school. On days when someone in the visible vicinity has visitors, I nearly lose my mind. This is perhaps the one aspect of owning two dogs which I would consider most likely to discourage me from repeating our experience. With a quieter breed it would not be a problem, but with vocal dogs it can be a very real one. Any day I expect to be served with a ticket for creating noise pollution!

As I mentioned before, boarding Mamie and Topsy has gotten to be a costly venture, so whenever we travel by car, we take them along. Descending on relatives with one baby and a dog was acceptable, but I sometimes think since our family has grown our

"Somehow or other I've a feeling that there's something that she wants to tell us . . . !"

visits are less welcome! Fortunately, Mamie and Topsy get along quite well with our parents' dogs, so at least we have no dog fights to contend with.

Occasionally one encounters a babysitter who doesn't care to sit for a family with a dog. I learned long ago to warn prospective sitters that we have two. Taking care of our family can be like sitting for four preschoolers! The children, of course, don't intend to hurt their dogs, but they have twice as many ears to pull, eyes to poke, and necks to hug a bit too tightly. This means extra surveillance on the sitter's part in our absence.

At this point, owning two dogs sounds impossible and idiotic, and you must be wondering what kind of tranquilizers I take! But besides doubling the expense, time and trouble, we really do believe that all the pleasures of owning a pet are also increased twofold. Anyone who has been greeted at the end of the day by an affectionate pet can imagine Tom's very real pleasure at being met at the door by his two "girls." And while each one very carefully watches to see that the other doesn't get an extra scratch behind the ears, we have two lovable and loving dogs who enjoy snuggling up with us. I firmly believe that a pet returns the love it is shown, thus evoking even more love on the part of the master. Having two dogs to love and return that love is very fulfilling.

Our original reason for getting a second dog was ostensibly so that each child could—in a sense—have his own pet. This has made me a firm advocate of the two-child family, but beyond that I'm convinced there actually is some logic to it. While we live with almost constant bickering and haggling over other playthings —we seem to have only one red crayon, one Misterogers record, one blue hotwheels car—Brian and Karin can share their pets with hardly any effort. There are always two dogs to hug, two dogs to brush, two dogs to feed, two dogs to let out, two dogs to let in, and even two dogs to take for a walk on special days. The fun and pleasure of having a dog is doubled, in this case with the added bonus of each child always being able to be a participant.

Brian and Karin are at the age where they enjoy making up and dramatizing stories, and they nearly always include Mamie and Topsy in their cast of characters. Not too long ago, the entire family participated in Brian's version of Peter Pan, rewritten to include two crocodiles, portrayed by Mamie and Topsy, who had to be prodded into "attacking" Captain Hook (Daddy). When I asked Brian what he likes best about having two dogs, his answer amused me for what he was really saying. "The best part? That's easy. I can have two lions in my circus!" Most of us accept the fact that it is a wonderful experience for a child to have the opportunity to grow up with one "lion" for his circus. How especially lucky are the children who can have two! *Doe Hentschel*

CHAPTER III
TRAINING

HOUSEBREAKING

MANY puppies start their housebreaking training while they are still with their mother in the whelping box. Since dogs instinctively like to sleep in a clean area, they will usually relieve themselves away from where they want to lie. By having newspaper covering most of the whelping box floor, they begin to identify the paper as a good place to "go." With this background already in existence, the new owner has a good start with paper training.

Three months of age is when housebreaking is started, and the kitchen is a fine spot. Here, the pup is apt to have lots of company, and it is a location which normally has a washable floor covering and makes confinement possible. Spread several layers of newspaper over most of the floor and barricade the puppy so that he is confined to this area. Puppy's bed, food dish, and water pan should also be in this spot. The little pup will generally select one corner in which to relieve himself. Praise him, and reduce the size of the paper covered area. Always remove the soiled newspaper, but leave a sheet on

---

Puppy Training Tip

Some pups can be house-broken in a day; some not for long weeks. (Even as some children can learn to read in a day, while others take an interminable time over the task.) In house-breaking, more than in anything and everything else in his training, patience and common sense — especially the latter — must come into action.

top which still has the special odor. The odor will tell him that this is the spot, and he will use it again.

Praise and patience are the key ingredients in housebreaking a puppy. When he relieves himself on the newspaper, praise him lavishly. If he makes a mistake, scold him gently, pick him up, and put him on the paper. Remember, this must be done at the time of the "accident," not later. During this period, it is so important for someone to be able to devote a great deal of time to training. Unless you are present and able to indicate to the puppy exactly what you expect, learning will be very slow.

Allow nature to help you in this housebreaking procedure. Puppies relieve themselves immediately on waking in the morning and when awakening from naps, as well as after meals. Place the puppy on the paper at these times and you will be nicely rewarded.

During these first few weeks of serious paper training, restrict your punishment to a stern "No" and a shake of the finger. Show the dog what you expect rather than punishing him for his errors. Don't slap him, hit him with a newspaper, or stick his nose in his mistake. Since he is only a baby, these methods are much too severe.

By the age of four months, you can begin the real outdoor housebreaking. Transfer the paper to where you want him to go. Observe the puppy closely and when he heads to where the paper was located previously, pick him up and carry him outside to the new location. Continue to anticipate and

When housebreaking one puppy or an entire litter remember to keep your instructions simple and to always use the same terms. Until fully house-broken a dog should not be given the run of the house. (Crown Jewel Puppies.)

take the pup out first thing in the morning, after eating, at noon, after nap, and before going to bed for the night. Until housebreaking is really going quite successfully, continue to keep the pup confined. If he is given the run of the house, accidents are bound to happen. Once he really has the message, try to develop a good schedule. Remember, a young dog is not physically able to hold his urine for a long span of time. The schedule will probably be at least six times a day. Mistakes will occur, correct them immediately — take him to the place he made the error, show it to him, and then lead him outside. Keep your instructions simple and always use the same terms.

Until the puppy is well housebroken and old enough to control himself, put newspapers down whenever you must leave the house. This way your baby can be "good" and you won't have to clean up any accidents and do any scolding.

Some breeds train very easily and others are more difficult. Don't get discouraged if you find training isn't progressing as rapidly as you expected, and don't allow bad habits to develop. Firmness and consistency will pay off at the end. *Until the dog is fully trained, don't give him the run of the house.* If a relapse occurs after training, confine him again until he can be trusted. Since housebreaking is really one of the most important lessons to be learned, insist on complete compliance before you relax. There is nothing more annoying than a dog that cannot be trusted in the house.

Think twice about trying to housebreak a puppy of one of the large breeds. When they have an accident, it is quite a mess. Professionals recommend that you have it trained elsewhere, and bring it home after it is able to function on a four times a day exercise schedule.

REVIEW OF HOUSEBREAKING

- Enclose the dog in a small area. The kitchen is good.
- Begin by paper training.
- Use praise. Be patient. Correct mistakes immediately.
- When paper is mastered transfer outdoors.
- Keep at it until 100 per cent consistency is attained.

YARDBREAKING

While you are housebreaking your dog, you ought also to yard break him. You are already taking him to the same spot which may be behind or beside the garage. You can—and should—teach him not to use other sections of your yard.

Some fully trained dogs will leave a puddle to show resentment.

Special Problems

Believe it or not, some fully trained dogs seem to use anti-housebreaking behavior to display their anger or resentment. They will leave a puddle or deposit to show their disappointment when left home alone or in response to some punishment. Needless to say, such behavior cannot be tolerated, and a firm stand must be taken.

Training and Consideration

Now a special word about a special problem— where to exercise your dog. It is amazing how many dog owners are apparently oblivious to the resentment that they create in their neighbors by allowing their dogs to use the neighbor's property as a bathroom. In fact, some dog owners will actually walk their dog over to a neighbor's rather than allow him to use their own lawn. This type of behavior is definitely anti-social and most obnoxious. Dog owners should have more sense and consideration. By all means, give your dog a walk. However, don't allow him to make a mess on other people's lawns, walks, or gardens. Keep him on a lead and take him to an empty lot to relieve himself. City dogs must be curb trained—that is trained to make in the roadway. If you have a yard, the dog can be taught to use a special section for this purpose, and you can clean it up regularly. Should your dog make a mistake and use the neighbor's lawn, scold him and train him *not* to repeat this act. Your pet should not become a nuisance to anyone else.

SPECIAL TRAINING

MOST pet owners get great satisfaction from having their dogs display ability in doing some tricks.

BEGGING — OR — "SIT UP"

The young puppy often begs instinctively when some tidbit is held up in front of him. Should "junior" try to jump for the morsel, just scold him gently and push him back down. Begging can be learned rapidly so just repeat this exercise several times, giving a reward for the correct response and you'll have a little pup with one trick mastered.

SPEAKING

Having a dog that will bark on command is not only fun, but it can also be helpful at times. The easiest way to teach this trick is to initially say "Speak" when the dog barks voluntarily in order to help him associate the word with the act. Then, offer him a treat and command him to "Speak." When he finally barks, reward him with much praise and the treat. Repeat this lesson until he readily gives a loud bark when given the command.

"FETCH"

There are many other tricks that a dog can be taught, such as shaking hands, rolling over, jumping through a hoop, playing dead, and fetching. Undoubtedly, fetching is the most important as it can become part of a regular training program for advanced obedience or for field work, or it can be just for fun so that the dog can participate in a game of catch. Puppyhood is an ideal time to teach this trick since these youngsters love to put everything in their mouth. Tempt Rover with a ball or dumbbell or toy, then throw it and shout "Fetch." When the pup retrieves the object, he may stop and play and chew it. Encourage him to return directly to you and to give the ball back. A long lead will be helpful when training for this trick. Having fun, giving praise, and repetition will speed learning. You'll find this trick will give you, your family, and your dog a great deal of enjoyment.

"SHAKE HANDS"

A dog should be taught not to jump on people. Shaking hands is a more pleasant way for him to greet guests. It's an easy trick to teach. Put your dog in a normal sitting position and kneel in front of him. Tap the back of his foreleg with your hand. When he lifts his paw, take it gently in your hand and say "Shake" or "Shake hands." Smile and tell him he's a good dog.

"JUMP"

Jumping is fun for a long-legged dog and good exercise, too. Build a low bar—a long straight stick

Teaching your dog to "Fetch" can lead to bigger and better things, such as retrieving.

A GENERAL TRAINING RULE!

YOUR DOG MUST ALWAYS THINK HE IS A SUCCESS—this is the *sine qua non* of dog training. According to research, lack of success is the most common reason why some dogs fail to learn. Even if your dog gives a seemingly inadequate performance, it is essential that he feels he has done something right —something to merit your praise. Your praise is what he wants more than anything else.

When your dog has difficulty learning a new lesson, go back and repeat one that he has already mastered. Then you can honestly praise his performance, giving his ego a boost. He'll be ready to try the new lesson again.

Keeping a dog well-behaved requires continuous training. Photo by William H. Oskay, SeeSharp Photography, Muncie, Indiana.

OWNER'S VOICE SETS TONE FOR TRAINING

Tone of voice is one of the keys to successful dog training. In fact, some professional trainers name it as the most important factor in training.

Do dogs understand words? Animal behavior experts have differing opinions, comments the Gaines Dog Research Center. Some behaviorists hold that dogs do not comprehend the actual meaning of words. Others believe the average dog has a 30-50 word vocabulary; exceptional animals, up to 1,000-word vocabulary.

However, the experts generally agree it's not what you say that counts, but how you say it.

Do you react favorably to a shrill nagging voice? No? Neither does your dog. You're much more inclined to respond to a pleasant tone and so is the dog.

Training commands should be delivered in a well-modulated voice that's warm but decisive.

Of course the basic tone changes with the situation. The "come" command, for example, lends itself to an eager voice, encouraging the dog to come quickly and directly to you.

On the other hand, a reprimand, "no!" or "bad dog!" needs a firm, disapproving tone. Effectively delivered, it's often scolding enough without being reinforced with a slap or shaking.

No command should be given in hesitant or unsure tones. The dog senses your lack of conviction. This tone of voice doesn't urge obedience. Instead, it invites a let's-see-what-can-be-gotten-away-with reaction.

Nor should commands be shouted unless the dog is outdoors and not within normal hearing range. Shouting is not necessary under ordinary circumstances. Don't forget the dog's hearing is acute. A loud voice is painful to him and won't make him more clearly understand your wishes.

Raising your voice in anger also is poor training procedure. You may frighten the dog into obeying but probably only will frighten him, period, and confuse him.

Know what you want the dog to do and tell him. Use a tone of voice that makes the command clear, and encourges his cheerful, obedient response.

or broom handle laid across two or three piled up bricks. Put a training collar and lead on your dog. Walk him quickly toward the bar. When you want him to jump, give a quick, upward jerk on the collar and say "Jump." Practice this trick with the stick raised higher and higher until he can jump twice his shoulder height.

Training the Biter

It is not unusual for a dog to snap or bite if you try to take something away which he has and wants. Training to avoid this form of behavior is essential. When the dog refuses to surrender what he has, don't grab it! Firmly command "Drop it" or "Give me," and, if he lets go of the object, praise him. When it's something that he can have, return it. If he won't surrender his booty, quickly and quietly without growling, then follow one of these techniques:

1—**If he is a small dog, pick him up by the collar, and hold him until he releases the bone or whatever.**

2—**With a larger dog, slap him across the rump with a rolled up newspaper.**

3—**Or, slap him across the nose with a rolled up paper.**

Never put your hand out to take something if the dog growls menacingly at you. Be firm and speak strictly until the item is dropped. Even the best pet has been known to bite his master's hand if he tries to remove a favorite bone.

Conclusion

Training and education is *not* a once in a lifetime event. Puppies and young dogs are not the only ones that can profit from this type of attention. All dogs need to have their training refreshed and their education expanded. It isn't true that you can't teach an old dog new tricks—you can. You can also help Fido review those he learned before. Just because the course in obedience training is over doesn't mean that review must stop. On the contrary, maintaining a training program of some kind can bring you and your dog a great deal of pleasure. Remember a *well-behaved* dog is most satisfying and in the final analysis it is the dog owner's responsibility to train and maintain his dog in this manner.

The "Fear Biter"

In the man-shy dog we frequently have the "fear biter" and the one that ducks from your hand, whether he's ever been hit or not. Such an animal is difficult and often impossible to train. The sound-shy dog hides when thunder booms, scuttles under cover when a car backfires, and is almost always gun-shy.

DOG TRAINING TIPS

The dog training tips presented here outline the exact methods which the average dog owner can use to teach his dog the five basic obedience commands which every housedog should know and obey.

Diligent application of these step-by-step instructions will result not only in a well-trained dog, but also in a happier, more satisfying relationship between dog and master.

This material was compiled by Pet Food Institute with the assistance of Willy Necker, famous trainer of thousands of dogs. Mr. Necker was head of War Dog Training for the U. S. Coast Guard during World War II, and also trained many U. S. Army men and dogs.

GENERAL
TRAINING SUGGESTIONS

1. Conduct short, business-like training sessions, twice a day, if possible.

2. Give the dog exercise before each lesson begins, with ample opportunity to relieve himself.

3. Begin each lesson with a review of one or more previous lessons so that the dog can earn praise right from the start, putting you both in a good mood.

4. Make all commands definite and clear. Be firm.

5. Never let yourself become impatient with your dog. One quality you must exercise is patience.

6. Never let your dog disregard even one of your commands. From the first lesson on, once you give an order, see that it is obeyed. Stick with it. If you let a dog disobey you once, ignore one single command, he will feel that he can do it again. Your goal is to see that your dog never even suspects that he can do anything other than mind you. Your command must be law to him.

7. Always end each lesson with some improvement. If you are working on one of harder subjects, you may ease up a little if necessary in order to let the dog be successful. The dog must always succeed; if he fails to merit praise, keep on with it until he does accomplish his goal, even though slowly and clumsily. Quitting on a note of success, and meriting profuse praise, does wonders for the dog's morale.

8. If at all possible, conduct the lessons in strict privacy, without distractions. You should be able to obtain the dog's complete attention.

9. If any particular lesson is not going well, and relations between you and your pupil are becoming a bit strained, it is a good idea to switch to a review lesson for a few minutes to give you an excuse to praise and pet the dog, before resuming the tougher task. You will both feel a lot better for the interlude.

EQUIPMENT FOR TRAINING

A welded chain choke collar

Leash— six feet long

Leash— 25 to 35 feet long

HEEL

When a dog is commanded to HEEL, he walks without force or urging, at his handler's side with his right shoulder about even with the handler's left knee. If on leash, the leash hangs loose. If off leash, the dog walks equally well in the same position.

How to hold the leash: Snap the short leash on the collar with your dog at your left, pass the leash through a circle formed by your thumb and first and second fingers of your left hand. The end of the leash is held in your right hand. Hold your left hand and arm at your side in your usual walking position. Your dog can walk comfortably with a slack leash, and you can easily check him quickly if you hold him in this manner. Get the dog on your left side, give the command "HEEL" and walk forward. For the first lesson, don't pay much attention to the manner in which he goes —it is enough that he goes with you. Use the word "HEEL" often. During succeeding lessons keep him fairly well in the correct position. When he gets ahead of you, bring him back, commanding "HEEL" and at the same time make him mind by giving him quick, sharp jerks on the leash. DO NOT BRING HIM TO YOU BY SUSTAINED PULLING ON THE LEASH. Give him a little slack in the leash when he is heeling as he should. Then, if he drops behind or forges ahead, correct him with the vocal command and jerking on the leash. Keep at this, lesson after lesson, until your dog heels in the correct position without tugging at the leash. The dog must adapt himself to your changes of pace and direction. When you step backward or sideward, walk fast or slow, the dog must instantly do the same. As you make right or left turns, your dog must maintain his position at your left side, speeding his gait when you turn to the right or slowing it when you make a left turn. When you turn to walk in the opposite direction, it will make it easier for the dog to understand if you will hesitate a moment or step backward one step before reversing your direction.

DOWN

When a dog is commanded DOWN, he must immediately drop to a lying position. He must do this whether, at the moment of command, he is heeling, sitting, standing, running or walking.

Have the dog SIT at your left side. Drop to your left knee. With your left hand gripping the leash close to his collar, give it short, sharp jerks downward. Say "DOWN" "DOWN" "DOWN." Repeat this procedure again and again.

Some dogs will fight this lesson, and the trainer must persevere, with a great many repetitions. If your dog is stubborn, refusing to go down, use your right hand to pull his forefeet out from under him while giving him the verbal command and jerking downwards on the leash.

It helps to give the verbal command repeatedly, even during the time the dog actually is DOWN! He can't hear it too often while he is learning.

With this command, as well as with the command SIT, unless you order him to STAY, he must instantly get up and HEEL when you start to walk away.

This exercise has a depressing effect on most dogs, so it is well not to keep at it very long at a time. Be sure to give your pet plenty of praise and encouragement when he does a good job of it—not, however, when he is in the DOWN position. Then he should not be petted by anyone. If you do, he'll want to get right back up.

In teaching this command, vary your routine and don't always give various commands in the same order. As soon as he knows DOWN, give him the command at times other than when he is heeling. You want this command to be obeyed instantly no matter where the dog is or what he is doing.

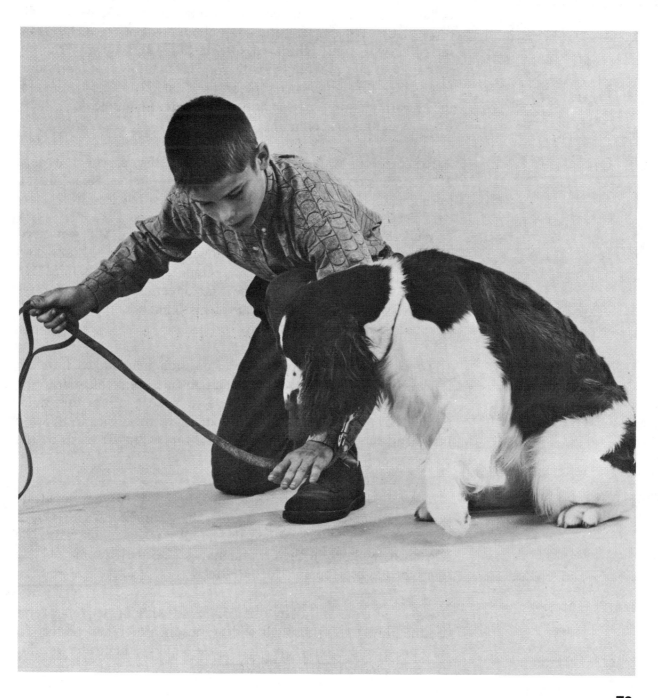

SIT

When commanded to SIT, the dog must promptly assume the sitting posture, squarely on both hips. He must SIT at once, whether, at the moment of command, he is heeling, running or lying down.

Put the dog's choke collar and short leash on him. Arrange the collar so that it is up rather close behind his ears. Walk with the dog at HEEL. Stop, grasp the leash about eight or ten inches from the collar with your right hand. Order "SIT." Jerk upward sharply on the leash and press down with your left hand on his hind quarters. All of this action takes place simultaneously: the command, the upward jerk on the leash, the downward push on the dog's back. Keep repeating the command, "SIT."

Resume your walk, telling the dog to HEEL as you start out. Take a few steps and repeat the whole performance. Keep this up for about 15 minutes, long enough for the first few lessons.

While he is learning what is meant by the word SIT, you need not be very much concerned about how he sits. After he knows and obeys the command, however, you should always have him SIT in the proper position—facing in the same direction as his handler, his head even with or slightly ahead of his handler's knees and with about six inches separating them.

To teach him to SIT in the proper position, help him each time it is necessary. As he assumes the sitting posture, swing his rear to the correct spot as he is going down. Use your left hand for this, holding his leash near the collar with your right. If he tries to SIT too far ahead of you or behind you, jerk him with the leash to the correct spot.

When he has mastered this routine, he must assume the sitting position promptly whenever you give the command, whether he is walking or lying down. When the handler resumes his walk, the dog must, without further command, get up and resume heeling unless he has been commanded to stay.

As soon as he will obey this command without help, the same routine must be run through with a loose leash. When perfect results are obtained on a loose leash, the pupil graduates to working this command off leash entirely.

STAY

The command STAY may be given while the dog is standing, sitting or lying down. At the command he should remain in the position he held when it was given.

Put your dog on his short leash. Command him to go DOWN. Tell him to STAY. Walk around him, keeping the end of the leash in hand, but do not tighten up on it. When he starts to get up, say "No, STAY." Back away from him; go sideways from him; step over him. Each time he starts to get up, repeat "No, STAY." Each time he tries to follow you when you walk away from him, you must command him to go DOWN again·

Soon he will STAY while you walk to the end of the short leash, while you walk around him, or even while you jump over him. You will have to try all of these if you want to make a good "stayer" out of him.

After he has made considerable progress, vary the routine by having him SIT while you repeat the procedure. When you feel that he is proficient when worked on the short leash, start work with the long one. Put the dog DOWN at your side. Wad up the surplus length of leash in your hand and throw it out away from you. Command him to STAY, repeating the word several times. Turn and walk to the free end of the leash. If he rises, rush right back and make him go DOWN again. Repeat the command STAY and walk away once more. Your immediate objective is to be able to walk to the end of the long leash, pick it up, turn and face the dog for a few minutes, while he remains quietly in position until you call him to you. Work on this until he will STAY in this way.

To have him STAY while you are completely out of sight, pick a quiet room and put the dog DOWN. Order him to STAY and leave the room. Watch him, if possible, through a crack in the door and, if he shows signs of getting up, go to him and repeat the command. Don't hesitate to use the word STAY again and again.

At first, leave him for only about one minute. Then, as he improves, gradually increase the time you stay away to around ten minutes. Each time that you come back and find that he has obeyed your order, have him SIT and then praise and pet him. (Praise the dog for good work in obeying the STAY command only after he has been released from it.)

To continue these lessons, take him out of doors, put him on his long leash and fasten this to a tree or post, restraining him from wandering away. Tell him to STAY, then go out of his sight and find a spot where you can observe his actions. Repeat the same procedure you used indoors. Take care that he does not chew the leash or otherwise misbehave while he is alone. If he does, it calls for a very sharp reprimand.

This exercise, making your dog obey you even though you are apparently not around to enforce your will upon him, is very important. The effect it has on the dog is to make him more obedient to all commands. He will get to feel that you know everything he does and that he must obey every order.

COME

When the dog is called, he must immediately COME to you, running or trotting, and when he reaches you he must SIT in front of and facing you, awaiting your further orders.

Have the dog on his long leash. Command him to DOWN, STAY. Toss the free end of the leash away, walk over to the end, pick it up, turn around and face your dog. Call him to you. Use his name in connection with the command "Duke, COME." The tone of your voice should be serious, commanding, not coaxing or wheedling. If he doesn't COME, reel him in hand over hand. Practice the lesson until he begins to obey and shows that he understands the words. Then you can change the routine a little. Leave the long leash stretched along the ground but not actually attached to his collar. Call him as before. If he is slightly hesitant, go so far as to pull in the leash. Even though it isn't attached to the dog he will think it is.

Next step is to work without using the leash at all. If he continues to COME the moment he is called, continue to work him off-leash. If, however, he ignores the command, get the leash out again for a little concentrated review.

When your dog reaches you, have him SIT in front of you for a few seconds before you pet him. This obviates any tendency he might develop to jump on you. If he does not SIT directly in front of you or close enough, seize the leash close to his collar and back away from him repeating the command, "COME, COME." After he has been sitting properly for a few seconds, command him to HEEL. Then you are free to, and should, praise and pet him.

Your dog should COME to you without delay, head up, on the double when you call him. If he takes his time, pull and jerk him on the long leash.

Never punish or scold your dog after he has COME to you even though he has not done it the way he should. If you punish him when he arrives in front of you, he will be confused, thinking the punishment was for coming to you, not for the manner in which he came.

AN INTRODUCTION TO DOGS

The dog is man's best friend
He has a tail on one end.
Up in front he has teeth
And four legs underneath.

Dogs like to bark.
They like it best after dark
They not only frighten prowlers away
But also hold the sandman at bay.

A dog that is indoors
To be let out implores
You let him out and what then?
He wants back in again.

Dogs display reluctance and wrath
If you try to give them a bath
They bury bones in hideaways
And half the time they trot sideways.

Dogs in the country have fun.
They run and run and run.
But in the city this species
Is dragged around on leashes.

Dogs are upright as a steeple
And much more loyal than people.
Well people may be reprehensibiler
But that's probably because they are sensibler.

—*Ogden Nash*
from *The Face is Familiar*
Copyright 1938 by Ogden Nash

CHAPTER IV
FEEDING

CANINE NUTRITION*

NUTRITION involves more than merely keeping a dog alive; it means maintaining clear, sparkling eyes, strong teeth, firm gums, a shining coat, healthy skin, and other manifestations of an optimal condition.

Optimum nutrition has been described as the supply of all elements necessary for the dog's entire bodily functions. A dog secures this from a complete, balanced, food supply, which provides all the nutrients needed by his body in the proper ratio, and enables him to receive maximum benefit from his diet.

Proper feeding consists of supplying nutrients in adequate amounts and in proper proportions. To maintain good health, the dog requires carbohydrates, fats, proteins, minerals, vitamins, and a continuous supply of water. The vitamins required by the dog are A, D, E, thiamine (B_1), riboflavin (B_2), pyredoxine (B_6), folic acid, panlothenic acid, niacin, and choline.

---

*Excerpts from *Basic Guide to Canine Nutrition*. Gaines Dog Research Center. New York, 1965.

Essential Nutrients and Their Role

CARBOHYDRATES

Carbohydrates are essential energy producing foods, consisting principally of cellulose, starch, and sugars. As a class carbohydrates are capable of supplying energy, furnishing heat, saving protein and forming fat. No specific requirement for carbohydrates has been demonstrated in the dog. However, carbohydrates have an important role in canine nutrition as a source of calories.

PROTEINS

Proteins that contain all the essential amino acids are called complete. Eggs, meat, milk, soybeans, peanuts, and yeast contain these complete proteins.

Complete proteins should contribute a minimum of 12 per cent of the calories required daily by the adult dog. However, most diets include both plant and animal proteins, some with relatively low biological

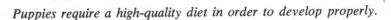

Puppies require a high-quality diet in order to develop properly.

values. For this reason, practical feeds usually include sufficient protein to supply 20 per cent to 25 per cent of the calories.

Since it has been demonstrated that high protein feeding favorably influences milk secretion, protein requirements during pregnancy and lactation are well above recommended maintenance levels. As a rule, the lactating bitch will require double the maintenance quantity of protein.

The need for dietary protein, as for caloric intake, is also high during growth. The National Research Council recommends that a ration deriving 20 per cent of its calories from protein should be considered a minimum for practical mixed diets in growing dogs.

FATS

Fats furnish a concentrated source of energy. In the diet of dogs, some fat is essential for normal health, but the minimum requirement has not been established. High fat diets pose one danger — they reduce food intake and thereby may retard growth.

A source of linoleic and arachidonic acid is required by dogs; deficiency of these "essential" fatty acids leads to defective growth, dry hair, scaly skin, and susceptibility to skin infections. Such symptoms usually are resistant to topical therapy, but they will respond well to dietary supplement. Lard or bacon fat is preferred in treatment of acute fat deficiency states.

MINERALS

Minerals are chemical elements used by the body in many ways and in varying amounts. They yield no energy to the body, yet many have a known or possible role in metabolism and nutrition.

Calcium/Phosphorus Ratio

Calcium and phosphorus constitute the greater part of the mineral matter of the body and are found in greatest amounts in the bones.

The metabolism of calcium and phosphorus and that of vitamin D are closely interrelated. A calcium to phosphorus ratio of 1.2:1 is considered optimum for maximum utilization. Well-formulated, high quality prepared dog foods provide adequate amounts in the necessary ratio.

Calcium has several well-known functions within the body. It is essential for ossification of bone and teeth and is an important ingredient of intercellular cement. Vitamin D appears to play a part in the deposition of calcium as well as in its absorption.

In the growing animal, a disturbance of normal calcium and phosphorus metabolism is characterized by inadequate retention of minerals which can lead to rickets in the immature animal.

Exposure to sunlight, whenever possible, is an aid in the treatment and prevention of rickets, particularly in short-haired dogs. (Photo courtesy of The American Field.*)*

Rapid growth in large breeds of dogs (Great Danes, St. Bernards) predisposes to rickets. The soft tissues also require and retain phosphorus. In cases of deficiency, the bone may be depleted in order to supply the proper amount of phosphorus for the soft tissues. The ration of the heavier breeds must contain proportionately larger amounts of minerals and vitamin D on a weight basis than are provided for smaller breeds .

In larger breeds, it may be necessary to administer extra doses of a combination of vitamins A and D. Exposure to sunlight, whenever possible, is an aid in the treatment and prevention of rickets, particularly in short-haired dogs.

Iron

Iron plays an essential role in the prevention and treatment of anemia. About two-thirds of the total iron in the body is present in the blood.

Assimilation of iron from foods is more efficient during growth, pregnancy, and periods of need. Iron deficiency can develop as a result of increased requirements, decreased assimilation, or a combination of both.

Various studies in dogs indicate that 0.600mg. of dietary iron per pound of body weight should supply adequately the needs of the growing puppy or the dog which is rebuilding blood, as well as of the normal animal.

Copper

Like iron, copper has been shown to be essential in the diet for prevention of anemia. Dogs presumably require small amounts of copper which are supplied in food.

Copper deficiency is related to the appearance of bone defects. Abnormalities in bone formation with frequent broken bones and enlarged joints have been observed in dogs. Lack of pigmentation has generally been associated with copper deficiency in the dog. Decreased copper also causes faulty keratinization in the skin and hair follicles so that changes in the growth and nature of the hair are observed in copper deficient dogs — that is, the hair of dogs becomes rough and dull.

Cobalt

Cobalt has been recognized as an essential dietary mineral for dogs. It appears to stimulate and provide for more efficient hemoglobin production.

Dogs Differ in Feeding Needs

Dogs are individuals just as humans are. Puppies from the same litter will differ in both their feed and water requirements. Some will be more difficult to keep in condition while others will tend to get too fat if not watched carefully.

Potassium

Potassium is another vital but poorly understood element that is required for proper metabolism of muscle and other body tissues. Potassium is present in all plant material in many times the concentration of sodium. Practical rations, therefore, contain an excess of potassium. Research shows that prolonged potassium deficiency produces kidney disease.

Magnesium

Magnesium appears important to a number of processes essential in metabolism. Little information is available on the quantitative requirements of dogs for magnesium; however, since this mineral plays a role in catalyzing certain metabolic reactions, it is common practice to include small amounts in the diet. The recommended amount is 5mg. per pound of body weight for adult maintenance and double that amount for growing puppies.

Sodium Chloride

Sodium and chlorine, along with potassium, are essential for normal physiological performance and must be supplied either in foodstuffs or as sodium chloride (salt).

In the dog, sodium deficiency causes weight loss, severe hair loss, dryness of the skin, and death within eight weeks.

Iodine

Small amounts of iodine are required by dogs for prevention of goiter. This requirement is met by the complete, balanced commercial dog foods.

Zinc

Research on dogs shows that zinc deficiency manifests itself in the form of marked emaciation, vomiting, conjunctivitis, keratitis, and retardation of growth.

Trace Elements

Little known about, the trace elements—manganese, molybdenum, fluorine, sulfur, selenium — are included in small amounts in the practical ration. The absolute requirements of these elements are unknown.

VITAMINS

Vitamin A

Vitamin A serves at least three important functions in the body:
(1) It is essential in the production of visual pigments in the eye.
(2) Proper functioning of the kidneys seems to depend on this vitamin.
(3) It is essential for growth of bony structures.
Data indicate that provision of 90 International Units of vitamin A per pound of body weight per day is adequate for the growing dog. Adult dogs appear

Just like humans, dogs need carbohydrates, proteins, fats, minerals, vitamins, and water to maintain their well-being. (Photo by Maia Coven.)

to have a lower requirement as indicated by various studies. Thus, 45 I.U. of vitamin A per pound of body weight daily is the recommended minimum.

Vitamin D

Vitamin D appears to be related to the following:
(1) absorption of minerals from the intestine,
(2) calcium, phosphorus, and phosphatase levels in the blood,
(3) growth rate,
(4) bone formation,
(5) efficiency of food utilization,
(6) reproduction.

Deficiencies of vitamin D are most common in rapidly growing puppies which develop rickets readily. Vitamin D deprivation impairs calcium transport.

Nine I.U. of vitamin D per pound of body weight daily appears adequate for growth. Much lower amounts — 3 I.U. per pound of body weight daily — are believed adequate for adult maintenance, but not for pregnancy or lactation.

Vitamin E

It is stated that vitamin E is required for normal reproduction and lactation. In its absence, researchers have observed that puppies were born dead or weak and that survivors suffered from muscular dystrophy.

Favorable results from vitamin therapy have been reported in cases of endocarditis and myocarditis in dogs.

For the average healthy dog, commercial dog foods are compounded to supply adequate amounts of vitamin E.

Vitamin K

Vitamin K is considered the anti-hemorrhagic vitamin. Normally, the dog requires no dietary vitamin K since sufficient amounts are synthesized in the intestinal tract to meet all needs.

Thiamine (Vitamin B₁)

Thiamine, a B complex vitamin, plays a fundamental role in the intermediate carbohydrate metabolism of all living cells.

The need for vitamin B₁ increases in proportion to the carbohydrates burned in the body. Thus, a hunting dog subjected to hard exercise needs two to three times as much as the normal daily requirements. Dogs kept in cold kennels also may need more thiamine.

Puppy Feeding Hint

Most people have found it a good idea to feed their dogs in the evening before their own supper. This helps to keep the dog from begging. If you're having housebreaking troubles, try feeding your puppy in the morning and earlier than usual in the afternoon.

Conditions caused by a deficiency of thiamine may occur on diets consisting largely of refined carbohydrates. Characteristic deficiency symptoms include decreased appetite, constipation, weight loss, weakness, and sometimes drowsiness, paralytic symptoms, tonic convulsions, spasticity of respiratory disturbances, impaired gastric secretion, and decreased ability to respond to conditioned reflexes.

Riboflavin (Vitamin B₂)

Riboflavin is involved primarily in protein metabolism. It is essential for normal growth and in maintaining a healthy condition of the skin.

Riboflavin is present in most foods. Liver and yeast are the natural foods richest in this compound. The average dog fed a well-balanced complete dog food gets a sufficient amount of riboflavin.

Niacin (Nicotinac Acid)

Severe niacin deficiency will result in the blacktongue syndrome in dogs. Blacktongue ordinarily occurs only in areas where corn forms the major part of the dog's diet. In the early stages, deficiency symptoms include poor appetite and progressive weight loss. In more advanced cases, the symptoms include vermilion bands on upper lips, general reddening of the mouth, and, occasionally, persistent diarrhea. Emaciation results, and, eventually, this leads to death unless niacin or high quality proteins are supplied.

In general, meats and poultry constitute the important food sources of niacin, although yeast and peanuts are rich sources. Cereals contribute a significant amount.

Dogs fed a good commercial diet usually are supplied with adequate amounts of niacin. Most diets containing meat are probably adequate in this essential vitamin.

Pyridoxine (Vitamin B₆)

Pyridoxine is a widely distributed vitamin important in the intermediary metabolism of proteins and fats. Vitamin B₆ is required in the diet of all animals. It is necessary for blood regeneration and normal growth in young puppies. Degenerative changes have been observed in the nerves of dogs suffering from a deficiency of B₆. Without this vitamin, growing puppies become very anemic. Iron will not cure this anemia, but a concentrate of this vitamin will.

Vitamin B₆ is supplied in the diet by wheat germ, yeast, and egg yolk. Good sources are fish, liver, legumes, milk, and whole wheat.

Pantothenic Acid

Pantothenic acid is essential for growth and for the maintenance of hair and skin. Deficiency of this vitamin in pups results in diminished food intake followed by growth retardation. Inflammation of the gut may be observed. Convulsions, collapse, and coma are symptomatic in severe cases. Liver damage may be extensive. Older dogs are less affected possibly indicating a lower requirement for maintenance than for growth. Organ meats, eggs, certain vegetables, and cereals are a good source of Pantothenic acid.

Biotin

Biotin is a dietary essential in the dog, but little is known of its minimum requirement. Dogs develop a progressive paralysis on a biotin-free diet that can be alleviated with low levels of this vitamin.

Excessive amounts of raw egg white can lead to biotin deficiency. Biotin is widely distributed in foods so its deficiency is rare.

Folic Acid

Folic acid appears essential for the formation of blood cells. A deficiency of this factor results in a lack of red and white blood cells of varying intensity.

Present knowledge indicates that regular rations provide adequately for this vitamin without supplementation.

Choline

Choline is required in the body. When choline is lacking, fat accumulates in the liver. Rich supplies of choline exist in meats, such as liver, and in eggs and plant foods.

Vitamin B$_{12}$

Vitamin B$_{12}$ is involved in protein metabolism in the dog, particularly as it relates to blood regeneration.

Vitamin B$_{12}$ is necessary for growth and blood regeneration, but it is believed that under ordinary circumstances the diet contains this vitamin or permits sufficient intestinal synthesis to prevent deficiencies.

Vitamin C (Ascorbic Acid)

Vitamin C is used by the body to form and maintain intercellular material to form the normal epthelial cement substance of the vascular tissues, especially the capillaries.

If the diet is adequate, sufficient vitamin C is normally synthesized by the dog to meet all needs. Greater than normal amounts of vitamin C may be required by the tissues in pregnancy, lactation, and disease states which require extensive tissue repair. Vitamin C also plays an important role in wound healing.

Low ascorbic acid blood levels have been reported in some dogs with nonparasitic dermatitis and these, as a rule, responded to vitamin C therapy. The survival rate in newborn pups has been reported to improve slightly with a daily supplement of 50mg. of ascorbic acid during pregnancy.

Anti-Vitamins

They interfere with vitamin function by competing with the vitamins in bodily biochemical reactions. An example is a thermolabile enzyme found in raw fish and raw meat which destroys thiamine. The action of aviden in raw egg white upon biotin has already been mentioned.

WATER

The physiological importance of water cannot be minimized. No living cell exists devoid of water and every cell requires a continuous supply in order to function.

Water gain is balanced by water loss principally through the urine, lungs, skin, and feces.

The inability of young puppies to cope with a high concentration of salt in their diet is probably due to their more limited reserves of body water available for salt elimination. Therefore, young puppies require more water intake per pound of body weight than adult dogs.

Deficiency of Pantothenic Acid in pups results in diminished food intake followed by growth retardation. Organ meats, eggs, certain vegetables and cereals are a good source of Pantothenic Acid.

BASIC DIETARY NEEDS OF DOGS*

SMALL dogs require more food per pound of body weight than large ones. The usual adult house dog weighing 12 to 14 pounds needs approximately one-third of a pound of dry food, 6 oz. of some moist food, or one can of complete dog food per day.

Growing puppies need about twice as many calories as the adult dog.

One generous meal of well-balanced, nourishing complete dog food is sufficient for the normal adult dog. If the owner prefers, there is no harm in feeding twice a day, just as long as the dog is not overfed. Frequent tidbits between meals are apt to reduce the appetite and may develop finicky eating habits.

Any food left at mealtime should be removed and discarded within a reasonable time after the dog loses interest; no other food should be provided until the next regular feeding time. If the dog becomes obese, the volume of food should be reduced even though he may beg for more. Mature spayed or castrated animals, old or very inactive dogs, may retain large appetites, but they require 25 to 50 per cent less food than younger more active dogs.

Ideally, dogs should be fed at the same time each day. Dogs appreciate regularity. Regular feeding often helps maintain steady appetites.

Provision for sufficient water is important. The requirement is self-regulated, depending on such factors as the type of food, environmental temperature, amount of exercise, and the temperament of the dog. The need can be satisfied by permitting the dog free access to water at all times. A dog should not be allowed large amounts of cold water immediately following violent exercise.

A sudden change of diet may upset the digestive system of a dog. If a new type of food is to be fed, it is advisable to make the change gradually by replacing some of the original diet with the new food over a period of a week or more before the latter becomes the total diet. By making a change in foods a gradual process, digestive upsets causing diarrhea or other temporary conditions can be avoided.

Dogs seem to thrive on monotony. Scientific tests indicate that the average dog prefers the food to which he has become accustomed the earliest and longest.

Numerous studies have established that a diet con-taining a sufficient amount of bulk to induce stool elimination is more beneficial to the dog than one producing hard stools and constipation. This is the reason all well-balanced prepared dog foods supply a small amount of fiber in the ration.

Dog foods represent a unique concept. Unlike foods prepared for human beings, the high quality commercially prepared dog food must be a complete diet. The commercial dog food manufacturer starts with the premise that the dog food being prepared is to be the sole diet of the animal; no other food will be required. Thus, the food plus water represents a complete, well-balanced diet.

COMMERCIAL DOG FOODS

Dry Dog Foods

Meals, either in flakes or pellet-type foods, usually are quite complete nutritionally; the *best* of them *may* be adequate for the lifelong activities of dogs.

Biscuits and Kibbles

Biscuit-type foods are *not* usually fed as a complete diet, even though some brands are nutritionally complete. These foods may be used as snacks or training treats.

Semi-Moist Dog Foods

Nutritionally complete, semi-moist dog food supplies adequate amounts of the essential nutrients for bitches in gestation and lactation, as well as growing puppies, old dogs, and normal adult dogs.

Canned Dog Foods

A complete dog food which is a blend of meat or meat by-products with the addition of cereals, other plant products, vitamins, minerals, and fats can be found in canned dog food.

Canned Meats

Canned meats are *not* considered complete diets but are intended for mixing with complete dog foods for palatability.

Because the dog is classed as a carnivore, many persons assume that his ideal diet should consist solely of meat. *The fact is that a dog fed entirely on meat would soon be undernourished and in poor condition.*

Self Feeding

Self feeding is one of the newer practices that is gaining in popularity. The puppy or adult dog feeds himself from a container in which dry meal is always

---

*Excerpts from *Basic Guide to Canine Nutrition*. Gaines Dog Research Center. New York, 1965.

available. He can eat as much as he wants whenever he wants it. An available supply of fresh water is essential is a self-feeding program.

A dog maintains an even level of nutrients in his bloodstream by eating when he is hungry. A self feeding program minimizes boredom and reduces the damage dogs will do to furniture and rugs. If the owner is away from home during the scheduled feeding time, the dog can satisfy his hunger.

Some puppies or dogs may overeat and become fat on a self-feeding regimen, but most animals will eat the amount needed for appropriate weight gain and growth, particularly if this system is begun as soon as a pup is old enough to chew dry foods easily, rather than long after his feeding habits have become well established.

Partial self feeding is an alternative plan. With this method, puppies are fed one or even two regular feedings a day which are supplemented by self feeding.

Feeding Animals with Specific Diseases

Dogs that have medical problems require special consideration in their nutrition.

KIDNEY DISEASE

Foods given the animal with kidney disease must be nutritious, palatable, and of the highest quality. Proteins in the diet of the dog with kidney disease should consist of high quality commercial canned foods or semi-moist rations to which ground glandular organs of liver, kidney, pancreas, ground muscle meat, cottage cheese, and hard boiled eggs are added. Additional carbohydrates in the form of cooked cereals may also be advantageous. Cooked prepared

Above—A good, well-balanced diet keeps a dog in top condition. Below—Growing puppies require twice as many calories as the adult dog.

cereals, such as oatmeal, farina, and boiled rice are energy-laden and helpful. Small amounts of polyunsaturated oils are useful as fat.

During a 24 hour period, it is desirable that these animals be given frequent small meals rather than one or two large meals. The food should be well salted; not only do these patients need sodium, but salt will stimulate water turnover in the body which is desirable.

Commercially prepared diets for the dog with kidney disease are available and can be obtained from your veterinarian.

GASTROINTESTINAL DISEASES

These dogs are not only unable to digest many foods properly, but also are somewhat nutritionally depleted because of vomiting or diarrhea. Foods given animals in this category must be bland, low in fiber, appetizing, nutritious, and well-supplemented with water-soluble vitamins.

Animals with gastrointestinal diseases should be fed small, frequent meals. In addition, only small amounts of water should be given at a time. Of course, the water ration may be given at fairly frequent intervals.

Canned special diets fulfilling the requirements of this category are commercially available to veterinarians. These are very convenient and efficient.

PANCREATIC INSUFFICIENCY

These dogs require very special dietary consideration. In general, the diet should contain minimal amounts of fat, most of the caloric intake being supplied by moderate amounts of carbohydrate and protein. In addition, pancreatic enzymes must be administered as replacement therapy.

DIABETES

Dogs suffering from diabetes require very close supervision of their nutritional needs. A balance must be struck between quantity and character of food ingested, activity that the animal is allowed, and the amount of insulin to be administered.

At the onset, the dog must be hospitalized to establish the proper insulin dosage, as well as the amount of food and energy expenditure.

A Puppy's Schedule

You can avoid almost all house accidents if you'll remember that the times when puppy has to relieve himself are immediately on waking in the morning, when awakening from naps, after meals, and during the excitement of play. If you want to play in the house with your puppy, then take him out to his spot first, and again immediately when he shows signs of losing interest in the game.

OBESITY

Obesity is a common canine disease and represents a serious health hazard.

The reducing diet given to an obese dog should be low in fat, high in protein and moderate in carbohydrate with adequate amounts of vitamins and minerals. It is wise to give two or more feedings per day so that the animal will have minimum hunger problems. A reducing diet consists of less than the dog's normal basal requirements. (See feeding chart.)

"SANITATION PROBLEMS"

A low-residue diet resulting in minimum bowel evacuation is desirable for animals with special problems such as fracture of the pelvis, abscess of the anal sacs and surgery in the anal area.

Foods that are rather completely digested should be used to produce a low-residue evacuation. Ground, glandular, or muscle meat, cottage cheese, boiled eggs and cooked cereals will fulfill the need under these circumstances.

SEVERE CARDIOVASCULAR DISTURBANCES

Dogs suffering from severe cardiovascular disturbances require a diet low in sodium (salt) and moderately high in protein and carbohydrates.

There is a commercially available low-salt dog food.

SKIN PROBLEMS

Nutritional problems will often be manifested by skin lesions. Internal parasites can cause skin problems by interfering with normal absorption of nutrients. Any animal with a skin problem should receive a high level, high quality, protein diet. Moderate amounts of fat in the form of polyunsaturated fats should be available, and carbohydrates in adequate amounts for energy are necessary. In addition, the diet should be very adequate in vitamins and minerals. Possible supplementation of a standard commercial diet is quite effective if the cause of the skin problem is definitely nutritional.

LIVER DISEASE

Fat and protein metabolism are greatly influenced by liver function. For this reason, diet consideration as well as other therapy is very important in these dogs.

The diet fed to an animal with liver disease should contain minimal amounts of fat, only enough protein to replace normal loss and high amounts of carbohydrate, to supply energy requirements. In addition, therapeutic amounts of the B group of vitamins and required doses of the fat soluble group of vitamins should be given.

DIGESTIVE PROBLEMS*

IF your dog has regular or continuous problems, such as vomiting or diarrhea, unthriftiness or not holding his weight, seek the help of your veterinarian. Worms or infectious disease are sometimes responsible but your veterinarian is the best authority on the cause and what to do. You can do severe damage to your dog by experimenting on your own diagnosis and using do-it-yourself "cures." For example, there are many types of internal parasites and these must be controlled by more than one worming compound. Your veterinarian can make the diagnosis and prescribe the proper treatment.

VOMITING

The dog can vomit at will much easier than humans, to which anyone who has tried to give a dog a foul-tasting medicine can attest. Therefore, vomiting may merely show dislike. Grass, which dogs often like to eat, may cause the same thing.

A drastic change in diet may cause vomiting (or diarrhea). Whenever you anticipate a change, go slowly. Mix a small amount of the new food in with the former food. At each feeding, add a bit more of the new, decreasing the same amount of the old, until, within a couple of weeks, you have changed the diet gradually, and with no problems. Persistent vomiting, however, can be a symptom of some disorder. In that case, be sure to consult your veterinarian.

CONSTIPATION

An annoying and worrisome problem in dogs is constipation. This may be caused by an unbalanced diet, not enough water in the diet or by feeding too

*Feeding Research from the Purina Pet Center reprinted by permission.

Left—A drastic change in diet may cause vomiting or diarrhea. Dietary changes should be made gradually. Below—A German Shepherd puppy usually wants to know when chow time is coming. (Photo by Tom Morrissette.)

many bones, causing impaction. Older dogs commonly suffer from constipation, due to reduced activity and because their whole system is slowing down. Natural foods, such as liver, may be useful in relieving constipation or a dose of milk of magnesia will often be enough to take care of the problem. Here, again, if it continues, if the dog appears to be in pain or has other symptoms, he should be examined by your veterinarian. Don't experiment.

DIARRHEA

Although diarrhea is one of the symptoms of a number of disorders, it may be of temporary nature, and caused by improper feeding or diet. Many people neglect to follow feeding instructions on the labels of commercially produced foods and add excess milk, rich gravies or fats to the dog's food, causing diarrhea. Cow's milk, because of the lactose is not always easily digested by certain puppies and will cause diarrhea. The dry or evaporated milks, diluted with water, can usually be digested more easily. Raw eggs can also cause diarrhea.

If the diarrhea is only a slight occurrence, withhold food for awhile. It may be nothing more than an intestinal upset, caused by a change in diet, a change in drinking water (as when traveling), nervousness or fright. But if it continues, a dog soon becomes dehydrated. Any persistent case of diarrhea should be diagnosed by your veterinarian.

FLATULENCE

Indigestion is not always to blame when your dog passes foul-smelling gases. Usually the cause is feeding too much meat or too many eggs in the diet. Cut down on such foods and keep your dog on a complete diet. A charcoal tablet given every day or so may help until the condition clears up.

FEEDING FALLACIES

There are many "old-wives" tales about various foods being helpful or harmful. Here are just a few:

"Meat is dog's natural food."

False: In the wild state, the dog not only eats the flesh of the animal he kills for food but the mineral rich organs, and the grain and vegetable matter in the animal's digestive tract. He balances his own diet. In the home it is up to the owner to supply a balanced diet.

"Dogs need bones."

False: There is little in a bone that a dog's system needs, as long as he derives calcium from his regular food. While a puppy is teething (around 4 months of age) a large, tough bone with some meat on it is useful in getting rid of baby teeth. It relieves the puppy's urge to chew on everything in sight and keeps him pleasantly occupied. But, only large bones, such as beef knuckle or shank, should be given to dogs. The small, sharp bones of poultry or chops can splinter, damage the mouth and when swallowed may puncture the intestinal tract. An occasional bone of the right kind is all right and will help prevent tartar formation on the teeth but so will dry dog foods or biscuits. Too much bone chewing will wear the enamel off the teeth and too many hunks of bone in the digestive tract can cause constipation or serious impaction.

"Garlic will cure worms."

False: Generally the only effect garlic has on dogs is the same one it has on people. It practically insures privacy.

"Raw eggs will make the dog's coat shiny."

False: On the contrary, raw egg white interferes with the absorption of biotin, a vitamin needed for proper digestion. Eggs should be soft-boiled or otherwise cooked, if fed to dogs.

"A dog should chew his food."

False: "Wolfing" his food without chewing it is natural for the dog whose teeth are designed for tearing, not masticating, food. Almost all digestion takes place in the dog's stomach.

"Sugar causes worms."

False: Sugar or any other food does not "cause" worms. All digestible forms of carbohydrate are converted to simple sugars in the digestive tract. These are the dietary sugars that provide energy.

FEEDING CHART

AGE No. Feedings per day	SIZE	Weight in lbs.	Calories Per Day	AMOUNT PER FEEDING*			
				Meal (nugget)	Meal (chunk)	Soft-Moist 1 burger = ½ pkg.	Canned
Weaning to 3 Months Four feedings per day or Self-feeding	Very Small Breeds	1-3	130-256	1½-3 tbsp.	1¾-3½ tbsp.	1⅔-3 tbsp.	2-4 tbsp.
	Small Breeds	3-6	348-520	¼-½ cup	⅓-½ cup	¼-⅓ pkg.	¼-⅓ can
	Medium Breeds	6-12	600-902	½-⅔ cup	½-¾ cup	⅓-½ pkg.	⅓-½ can
	Large Breeds	12-20	960-1368	¾-1 cup	¾-1¼ cups	½-¾ pkg.	½-¾ can
	Very Large Breeds	15-25	1140-1584	¾-1¼ cups	1-1½ cups	⅔-¾ pkg.	⅔-¾ can
3-5 Months Three feedings per day or Self-feeding	Very Small Breeds	3-10	348-792	⅓-¾ cup	½-1 cup	¼-½ pkg.	¼-½ can
	Small Breeds	5-15	520-1092	½-1 cup	⅔-1¼ cups	⅓-¾ pkg.	⅓-¾ can
	Medium Breeds	12-25	960-1584	1-1½ cups	1-1¾ cups	⅔-1 pkg.	⅔-1 can
	Large Breeds	15-35	1140-2148	1-2 cups	1⅓-2½ cups	¾-1½ pkg.	¾-1½ cans
	Very Large Breeds	25-50	1650-2744	1½-2½ cups	2-3 cups	1-1¾ pkg.	1-1¾ cans
5-7 Months Two feedings per day or Self-feeding	Very Small Breeds	4-12	424-902	⅔-1¼ cups	¾-1½ cups	½-1 pkg.	½-1 can
	Small Breeds	12-24	960-1518	1⅓-2 cups	1⅔-2⅔ cups	1-1½ pkg.	1-1½ cans
	Medium Breeds	20-35	1400-2148	2-3 cups	2½-3¾ cups	1½-2¼ pkg.	1½-2½ cans
	Large Breeds	35-50	2170-2744	3-3¾ cups	3¾-4¾ cups	2¼-2¾ pkg.	2½-2¾ cans
	Very Large Breeds	50-90	2700-4094	3¾-5⅔ cups	4⅔-7 cups	2¾-4 pkg.	2¾-4 cans
7-10 Months Two feedings per day or Self-feeding	Very Small Breeds	5-15	520-1092	¾-1½ cups	1-2 cups	½-1 pkg.	½-1 can
	Small Breeds	15-30	1140-1850	1⅔-2⅔ cups	2-3¼ cups	1¼-2 pkg.	1¼-2 cans
	Medium Breeds	30-45	1920-2464	2⅔-3½ cups	3⅓-4¼ cups	2-2½ pkg.	2-2½ cans
	Large Breeds	45-70	2520-3312	3½-4½ cups	4⅓-5⅔ cups	2½-3⅓ pkg.	2½-3⅓ cans
	Very Large Breeds	70-100	3360-4554	4⅔-6¼ cups	5¾-7¾ cups	3⅓-4⅔ pkg.	3⅓-4⅔ cans
Adult † One feeding per day or Self-feeding	Very Small Breeds	6-15	300-546	¾-1½ cups	1-1¾ cups	⅔-1 pkg.	⅔-1 can
	Small Breeds	15-30	570-928	1⅔-2½ cups	2-3 cups	1-2 pkg.	1-2 cans
	Medium Breeds	30-50	960-1372	2⅔-3¾ cups	3¼-4⅔ cups	2-2¾ pkg.	2-2¾ cans
	Large Breeds	50-90	1350-2047	3¾-5⅔ cups	4⅔-7 cups	2¾-4 pkg.	2¾-4 cans
	Very Large Breeds	90-175	2070-3654	5⅔-10 cups	7-12⅓ cups	4-7⅓ pkg.	4-7⅓ cans

* The total daily intake is the amount shown times the number of recommended feedings.

† The reduction in the number of calories required per lb. of body weight takes place gradually, not abruptly, as the dog approaches maturity. The tables are, of necessity, calculated on a "point-in-time" basis.

Reprinted by permission of the Gaines Dog Research Center.

FEEDING FOR MAINTENANCE PURPOSES*

ON reaching maturity most dogs require only a good, nutritious maintenance ration. This is especially true if they are house pets and do not hunt or have other vigorous exercise. Following are some data on feeding during maintenance.

1. Did you know that during the maintenance period, medium-sized dogs (30-40 lbs.) require about ½ oz. (air-dry) of a good, dry dog food per pound of body weight? Larger dogs usually require slightly less—smaller dogs slightly more in order to stay in good body condition.

2. Inadequate or deficient diets fed to adult dogs can cause poor body condition, rough hair coat, and lower the body's resistance to disease.

3. Feeding once a day is adequate for adult dogs. It is desirable to feed about the same time each day—

---

*Feeding Research from the Purina Pet Center reprinted by permission.

usually in the evening since this tends to keep the dog quiet during the evening.

4. Dry self feeding is an easy and convenient way to feed mature dogs. This is done by many dogs' owners and most dogs will not overeat this way. Fresh water should be available at all times.

5. One of the frequent problems that occurs in feeding adult dogs is that they may overeat and consequently become overweight. Overweight dogs present a poor appearance and excess weight can shorten their life expectancy. Usually a dog that is fed all he will eat at each feeding without becoming excessively lean or fat is receiving an ample amount. This is probably the best way to gauge whether or not the dog owner is feeding enough, rather than by using a set pattern of feeding a certain amount. If a dog tends to become overweight, then he should be placed on limited intake to maintain normal weight. Many dog owners know that the adult weight depends on the size of the body framework. Unless a dog is being

A dog should be kept somewhat on the lean side. In this way he will be most active and will usually tend to lead a longer, healthier life.

used for show purposes, *we would recommend that he be kept slightly lean.* In this way he will be most active and will usually tend to lead a longer, healthier life.

6. Many people believe that their dog needs a variety of food, such as a regular change in the commercial dog food they buy or the addition of large amounts of table scraps. We have found that dogs do very well on one ration during their lifetime and do not need a change. This has been proven by many kennel and pet owners as well.

7. Occasionally dog owners will say their dog will not eat dry dog foods or is a finicky eater. Usually it is discovered that they are feeding table scraps or cooking meat and broth for their dog, which they naturally prefer, and therefore they refuse to eat the regular commercial dog foods. A dog fed in this way is not getting the balanced diet he would be receiving if a good commercial dog ration was being fed.

8. It is not unusual for dogs to often refuse to eat for a day or two or eat just a small amount sometimes. This condition is quite natural and unless it persists, there is nothing to become alarmed about since dogs vary widely in their food requirements, depending on age, size, activity, and the weather. Feeding according to body condition is a good sound method.

Feeding the Breeding Bitch

Feeding breeding bitches a well-balanced ration in the correct amount is important. Breeding stock in poor body condition and receiving an inadequate diet during gestation and lactation will have a low-milk supply and small pups.

Brood females can be kept on a maintenance ration between litters. At no time should she be overweight. An overweight female can have whelping problems and produce small litters. During the last two to three weeks of the gestation period, her feed consumption will tend to increase as much as 20 per cent as compared to the amount being consumed during maintenance. Usually if the female is fed on a maintenance level of ½ oz. of food per pound of body weight, her increased weight gain will boost food consumption adequately during gestation.

During lactation a bitch may consume 2½-3 times the normal maintenance level by the time the pups are three to four weeks of age. She should have all she wants to eat for the increased food intake necessary to meet the demands of heavy milk production. Since pups start eating solid food by the time they are three to four weeks of age, their feed consumption will increase while the dam's feed consumption will decrease. The ration the dam receives should also be available to her pups.

On the day of weaning the dam should not be fed but should have water available. The second day

feed ¼th the normal maintenance level; on the third day ½; on the fourth day ¾ths; and, on the fifth day the amount of food offered is brought up to the normal maintenance level. Cutting back on her food intake and then gradually increasing it helps decrease milk production and aids in the maintenance of a healthy mammary gland.

Stud dogs should be kept in good body condition without being overweight.

Feeding Orphan Puppies

Quite often the bitch will not nurse her puppies or perhaps has died from whelping complications. Here are some methods of handling the problem of orphan puppies.

Feeding—Good commercial bitch milk replacers, such as Borden's Esbilac, are available but if you find yourself in a bind with none available, the following formula can be used:

1 Cup Evaporated Milk
1 Tablespoon Corn Oil
+ Vitamin Drops for children
  (Deca-Vi-Sol mfg. by Mead Johnson)
1 Cup Water
1 Egg Yolk (no whites)
A Pinch of Salt

Warm the formula to body temperature and place in Pyrex baby nursing bottles like those used for feeding premature infants.

When feeding the puppies (every 8 hrs. is enough) hold the bottle so the puppy does not ingest air. Hold puppy's body parallel to the floor with the head slightly elevated. There is a tendency the first time to hold a pup's body vertically; this makes it easy for milk to enter the lungs. If milk flows into the lungs, pneumonia will result.

After each feeding take a piece of cotton dipped in warm oil or a clean, moistened wash cloth to massage the puppy and stimulate defecation and urination. Gentle massage of the back and sides before feeding is a form of passive exercise, stimulating circulation and awakening the puppy. Simple grooming is also best done at feeding time. Incubator conditions tend to dry the coat, so rubbing baby oil into the skin is often desirable. However, grooming can be overdone and the puppies should not be disturbed except at feeding time.

Weaning—Puppies can start eating (at 3 weeks of

Between-Meal-Snacks

Between-meal-snacks help to spoil the dog's appetite. They also tend to make beggars of dogs. The same thing happens when you feed snacks to the dog when you are eating. Your dog will become both a beggar and a nuisance.

age) on solid foods along with the mother's milk or milk replacer. By 6 weeks of age they can be fed entirely on solid foods. During the first several months of the puppy's life, keep food before him at all times.

Feeding Hard-Working Dogs

Working dogs use a lot of energy. To replace this energy a large amount of high quality, nutritious food is required. These dogs should be offered all of the dog food they want, but should not be allowed to become overweight.

Feeding once a day is ample, unless weight is a problem, and the dog is thin. Then twice a day feeding may be necessary. Usually the best time to feed is in the evening and dogs should not be fed just prior to being worked. Feed all of the dog food they will clean up—if fed moistened. If the dogs are self-fed dry, then a constant supply of dry food can be left in front of them at all times. If the dog is not maintaining good condition on dry feeding, then he should be switched to moistened dry dog food, since moistening the ration will increase acceptance and the dogs will eat more.

If a hard-working dog does not stay in good body

Bones

Dogs like to chew on bones. But don't give them chicken, turkey, or duck bones. These sometimes splinter and may get lodged in the throat or may puncture the stomach or intestine.

---

condition using a regular moistened dry dog food, then it is recommended that up to 20 per cent meat be added. The meat does not affect the nutritional balance of a good dry dog food but in most cases will increase the palatability and thus increase the food intake.

During the time a dog is not working, care should be taken to not overfeed, thus creating a weight problem. The average dog, not working, needs about 62 Calories (kcal.) per pound of body weight per day. This will vary according to age, weight, sex, breed, and previous nutrition.

PICA—Excessive Chewing and/or Eating of Undesirable Items

Dogs often chew on just about anything in sight, or have the bad habit of actually eating dirt, grass or even their own droppings. This problem is called coprophagy.

The problem of chewing is especially prevalent in young, teething puppies, and is usually outgrown by the time he reaches 8-10 months of age. Puppies will chew on wood, toys, articles of clothing, or anything else they can pick up or reach.

Several methods can be used to curb or prevent excessive chewing. If possible, items that the pups like to chew on should not be left in an area where they might be tempted. Discipline in the form of a swat with a rolled-up newspaper can also be used to put the point across in many instances. Since chewing is

Working dogs use a lot of energy and thus require a nutritious diet.

a natural tendency of the pup, and most pups are quite active, it may be advisable to give him a plaything or something that he can chew on for his own. This can be a rawhide bone or a toy made especially for dogs. Bones can be used, although if they are, they should be the large round beef bones or the ox tails and not pork chop or chicken bones. Certain plastic toys are not suitable for puppies and can cause impactions if swallowed.

The problem of dogs eating dirt, wood, sand, and their own droppings, or other items, is believed to be caused by several factors including confinement and boredom. This problem is not unusual, especially in confined dogs, and not only will dogs chew on these items but may actually eat them. As mentioned, the main causes of dogs eating undesirable items seems to be confinement and boredom. This occurs at all ages and in any breed although it seems to be more prevalent in the working and hunting breeds.

Currently we do not know how to inhibit this habit nutritionally and have no evidence to indicate that it is related to diet. It can occur on any commercial dog food as well as on home-made rations.

Here again, providing something to play with or chew on, such as hardwood sticks or toys made for dogs, may be helpful. It may also be beneficial to give the dogs more exercise or a larger area in which to run. As the dog owner has probably noticed, when he is playing or exercising his dog, the problem of eating undesirable items does not occur.

Quite often this problem begins in winter when the droppings are frozen. Dogs that are on a limited feed intake or those not receiving enough food may develop this habit. Once a dog starts chewing on items, and especially their droppings, it seems to become a habit. One dog seeing another doing this often acquires the habit.

There is no specific remedy that can be used to prevent dogs from eating undesirable items. Disciplining the dog, removal of the various items from the area, if possible, or giving the dog more exercise or something to play with may be helpful. As far as stopping dogs from eating their droppings, we know of no specific remedy. Some people have used a veterinary product called Ectoral, which is given to the dog at a low level for a few days to impart a bad taste to the droppings. (Ectoral is also used to control external parasites in dogs.) Ectoral can be obtained through your veterinarian.

The dog should also be checked for parasites and any disease problem that might be present. Some people feel that these factors contribute to coprophagy.

If the dogs are looking for something to chew on or eat, keep dry dog food in a self-feeder or pan where they can reach it at all times. This provides them with something to do and keeps them occupied.

Something Snappy

To keep your dog out of waste baskets, garbage pails, and off chairs, set un-baited small mousetraps under paper in those locations. The snapping trap won't hurt a pup over Chihuahua size, but the noise will scare him.

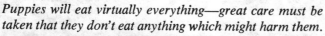

Puppies will eat virtually everything—great care must be taken that they don't eat anything which might harm them.

POPULARITY OF VARIOUS BREEDS

Dog breeds vary in popularity as the years go by. But the shift is gradual and changes among the more popular breeds occur only every five to ten years. Since the American Kennel Club is the largest of the registration agencies, their annual tables are fairly accurate for the entire dog fancy.

Breed	Rank
Poodles	1
German Shepherd Dogs	2
Dachshunds	3
Beagles	4
Miniature Schnauzers	5
Chihuahuas	6
Pekingese	7
Collies	8
Labrador Retrievers	9
Cocker Spaniels	10

Breed	Rank
St. Bernards	11
Basset Hounds	12
Irish Setters	13
Pomeranians	14
Shetland Sheepdogs	15
Doberman Pinschers	16
Boston Terriers	17
German Shorthaired Pointers	18
Fox Terriers	19
Brittany Spaniels	20

CHAPTER V
HEALTH

A healthy dog is a joy to behold, his coat and eyes shine and he is responsive. This healthy specimen is "D.J." an English Springer Spaniel owned by Dr. Milton E. Prickett, Lexington, Ky. "D.J." was the Best of Breed Winner of both the 1971 Westminster Dog Show and the 1971 International Dog Show. (Photo by William H. Oskay, SeeSharp Photography, Muncie, Indiana.)

HEALTH GUIDE

A S WITH people, good health is a key factor to a happy life for dogs. It is quite a simple matter to spot a healthy dog—his coat shines, his eyes shine, he runs and plays, his nose is cold and wet and he is responsive and has a good appetite. But, does the opposite mean that the dog is sick? If he displays a few symptoms, does this mean that he is ill or that you should wait until all the symptoms appear before contacting the vet? Of course, these questions are asked slightly in jest. But, it is surprising how many dog owners are really quite unaware of their dog's state of health. Some owners fuss over every little itch, scratch, discharge, or growl while others are so insensitive that they fail to see problems until it is too late.

The purpose of this Health Guide section is to assist the typical dog owner in determining whether the dog's problem is out of the ordinary and demands the services of the vet, or if the situation can be handled calmly at home. It isn't necessary or wise to run to the vet with every slight problem, yet knowing where to draw the line is often difficult. That is where having some guide lines is helpful.

A dog will assume a typical and individual behavior pattern which is, after a short period of time, quite predictable. Dogs like to live by a regular routine and they will happily follow it daily. They like to eat and sleep according to this schedule. As a dog owner, you will soon become aware of your dog's habits and general normal behavior. It will, therefore, be quite obvious to you when there is a change in behavior.

Digestive Problems

Loss of Appetite

When food, which is usually gobbled down in one minute flat, is left untouched for hours, you know something is disturbing this usually ravenous canine. However, lack of appetite by itself is no cause for alarm. All dogs will at some time or other refuse to eat a meal or two. They should be allowed to do this without being pestered to eat or coaxed with tempting tidbits. The cause for this disinterest in food may be purely adjusting to overeating on previous days or to indigestion. Very often a dog will also eat grass, and then he will vomit. This is nature's way of curing an upset stomach. As mentioned previously, this is

perfectly normal on occasion and should not be any reason for concern. However, should such poor eating habits or grass eating accompanied by vomiting occur more than once a week, then the dog's diet might be faulty and should be re-evaluated. If this persists after dietary changes, then an examination by the vet would be in order.

Vomiting

I. The habitual after meal vomiter

Some dogs who are healthy in every respect vomit quite regularly. This may be due to eating too rapidly and/or eating too much. These dogs will usually want to eat this regurgitated mass up again—there is nothing wrong with this, and they should be allowed to do so if they so desire. However, having such a mess regularly is not too pleasant especially when the dog lives in the house. It may be a relief to know that your dog isn't sick, but you will, in all probability, want to learn how to avoid this mess in the first place. Try these hints, and, if they don't help, consult your vet:

1—Let your dog rest about half an hour before feeding him.

2—Feed him in a quiet place away from the usual household commotion.

3—Feed him smaller portions—perhaps two small meals rather than one large one.

4—Let him rest after eating—avoid heavy exercise for at least half an hour.

II. Vomiting Yellow Stomach Juices.

Some dogs occasionally vomit stomach juices before their regular meal time. They will gag, ask to go out (if well trained) and then vomit a yellowy-foamy liquid. If this gets on carpeting, it makes quite a stain so wash it off immediately. As far as the dog is concerned, it is nothing to be overly concerned about. It's a build up of acid in the stomach when empty. This can sometimes be avoided by having a very regular meal time or by leaving a bowl with some dry kibble available at all times.

III. Continuous Vomiting.

An otherwise healthy appearing dog may start to vomit suddenly and continuously. If this vomiting continues and the dog can't keep anything down, then medical attention is required promptly. Excessive vomiting will cause dehydration, and, if this isn't treated, it can lead to death.

Puppies are particularly vulnerable to this type of situation. Like small children, they love to put things in their mouths and swallow them. Often, puppies will get something caught in their throat or lodged in their stomach, and this will cause the incessant vomiting. This misfortune can easily happen to a mature dog as well. That is why dog owners are cautioned not to give their dogs soft or small bones or rubber toys. These items, when chewed up, can create such a problem.

Constipation

This condition may be chronic or temporary. Insufficient exercise as well as the diet may be the cause. In chronic cases your vet may wish to examine the dog and prescribe a mode of treatment. When the problem is merely temporary, you might try giving your pet additional walks and exercise as well as some milk of magnesia or adding mineral oil to his food.

Diarrhea

Diarrhea is symptomatic of other problems. It may be caused by illness, intestinal parasites, or even emotional distress. The diarrhea can be treated, but the cause should be ascertained as well. Kaopectate can be administered. The quantity will depend on the size of the dog and the severity of the case. Check with your vet.

Some dogs have very "delicate" digestive systems and cannot tolerate rich food or certain types of table scraps. They must be maintained on specially prepared dog food in order to avoid any upset.

WHAT IS THE MORRIS ANIMAL FOUNDATION?

Morris Animal Foundation is an organization whose objective is to seek ways to prevent and cure diseases of companion animals (dogs, cats, horses) and zoo and wild animals and to learn how to provide better health for animals. It is a tax-exempt organization supported by gifts and legacies from individuals, clubs and organizations. Its studies into animal health problems are made through grants, usually to veterinary colleges, upon the recommendation of a scientific advisory committee. Persons seeking specific information about grants, animal diseases or the operation of the Foundation are urged to write the executive director.

Nervous, high strung animals will react to an exciting or stressful situation by having diarrhea. This is particularly annoying to pet owners when it is uncontrollable and occurs in the house. Veterinarians often prescribe tranquilizers as well as special diets to calm these types. Puppies suffering from this nervous digestive disturbance are particularly difficult to housebreak. Tremendous patience is required to cope with this dilemma.

Skin Problems

Allergic

Allergic skin problems are sometimes called "Summer itch," eczema, or dermatitis. Dogs are prone to many allergic conditions with one of the more common manifestations of the allergy being via the skin. Many dogs suffer from itchy skin due to an allergy to grass, fungus found on grass, carpet, food, lawn food, weed killer, or even to laundry soap used on their bed or towel. With so many possibilities, it is virtually impossible to determine the exact cause of the dog's problem. These allergic skin attacks often occur only seasonally—the beginning of Spring, Summer, Winter, or Fall. They will return each year at roughly the same time. Once the vet has diagnosed the skin problem as having an allergic basis, treatment can be initiated; the successful treatment can be repeated on each occasion that the symptoms reappear.

Skin problems should be treated promptly, as delay means needless discomfort for the dog as well as damage to the dog's coat. Only very rarely will a skin condition improve without any treatment. It seems as though once an area has been sufficiently irritated, even if the original source of the irritation is removed, the dog will continue to scratch or bite that area. This is due to the fact that the original allergic skin lesion has now become infected as a result of the dog's scratching and biting. Therefore, clearing up both the allergy and the infection must be done in order to restore the dog to proper health. Some breeds are more susceptible to skin ailments than others.

Infections

Only your vet can determine if your dog's skin condition is allergic, infectious or whether it is caused by external parasites such as fleas, ticks, or mites. Often, he can find the cause of the problem only by a microscopic examination of skin scrapings from the affected area. Once he makes the diagnosis, he can prescribe the specific therapy needed. Antibiotics are often used to combat these skin infections.

Until proven otherwise, any skin disturbance can be contagious to other dogs and possibly to humans. It is wise to be cautious and to take special precautions. Keep the dog's bed clean, wash your hands carefully after touching the affected area, avoid contact with other dogs so as not to expose them, and then be sure to continue treatment until all traces of the problem are removed.

External Parasites

Frequently the dog's skin disturbance is caused by an external parasite.

I. Demodectic Mange (Red Mange)

This skin disturbance is caused by mites. Symptoms usually appear first around the eyes and mouth, and then they spread to other parts of the dog's body. Loss of hair occurs in patches. If left untreated, super-infections usually complicate the situation. Your vet will probably prescribe a skin cream or powder, oral medication, and possibly dips or baths. Young dogs and particularly those with short hair seem to be especially prone to this condition.

II. Sarcoptic Mange (Scabies)

This is another skin condition caused by mites which results in severe itching, hair loss, and crusty lesions. Treatment is very similar to that for Demodectic Mange. *This type of mange is contagious to people as well as other dogs.*

Ringworm

This is a highly communicable disease of the skin which can be transmitted from animal to man. Its appearance is that of a round sore with crusts or scabs, and it is caused by a fungus. The size and number of the sores increases as the disease progresses. In order to make an accurate diagnosis, it is necessary to have a microscopic examination.

Your veterinarian will undoubtedly prescribe the following treatment:

1—Clean infected spots—remove hair and crusts.
2—Apply a fungicide regularly until healing has occurred.
3—Keep lesions washed to avoid secondary infection.
4—Careful hygiene is essential to avoid spread.

Ear Mites

These mites confine themselves to the dog's outer ear. They are quite irritating, and, as a result, the dog will scratch his ears and shake his head. If not treated promptly, the dog can damage himself with his intense scratching. Your vet should be consulted in order to care for this delicate problem. Since this is quite contagious to other dogs, if you have more than one dog, you'll probably have more than one victim.

Fleas, Ticks, and Lice

Fleas are amazing pests and can move from host to host—going from dog to cat to man very easily. Frequent scratching, bald spots, and inflammation of the skin can signal an invasion of fleas. Visiting the vet for definite diagnosis and treatment is recommended. Powders, sprays, dips, specially treated collars, or even oral medication may be prescribed. At the same time, it is of utmost importance that the dog's living quarters be completely cleaned and sprayed. Frequent cleaning and vacuuming of the pet's area also helps to remove eggs, larvae, and pupae. Destroying the fleas not only relieves your animal's discomfort, it also reduces his likelihood of getting tapeworms, as their eggs are carried by fleas.

Ticks are picked up in the great outdoors from shrubbery and undergrowth. They are quite visible to the naked eye and should be watched for during grooming. Dipping your dog in a medicated solution is the usual method of treatment. Spraying and regular cleaning of the dog's sleeping quarters can aid in controlling this pest. Serious skin infections or paralysis can occur if ticks are not removed promptly. They are also carriers of other diseases (Rocky Mountain Spotted Fever is carried by several types of ticks)—another good reason to eliminate their presence.

Lice are not only aesthetically unpleasant, and therefore, not "nice," they can become a source of danger for your pet—especially if he happens to be a puppy. Often dogs with just a few lice are very "itchy," while those harboring thousands of lice may not scratch themselves at all. So small they escape notice, some lice penetrate the pet's skin and suck the blood. The females will lay eggs which in just three weeks will hatch and develop into adult lice. The constant blood-sucking, if extensive, can cause severe anemia in puppies and greatly weaken mature dogs, particularly females with nursing puppies. The pest

---

Cold-Weather Coat

In winter, your dog undoubtedly spends much time indoors, and the dry air and indoor heat are not conducive to improving his coat. His skin will tend to dryness and his coat to dullness because of the heating conditions. Be sure that he has a balanced diet, and that his coat is brushed frequently to stimulate secretion of natural oils—brushing also will remove dead, dry hair, and help to improve the coat.

Flea Collars

Flea collars do a good job on fleas, but certain precautions need to be taken. After clipping or stripping, they may irritate the skin and should be removed for a few days. They have a bad effect in conjunction with anesthesia, so be certain to inform your veterinarian that your dog has been wearing one in case of surgery. Be certain never to use them in conjunction with any other insecticide or repellent.

can also be a source of irritation to cats and kittens.

Your veterinarian is your best source of help.

Dandruff

Some dogs display a dry, scaly skin which may become a perfect site for a more malicious skin eruption. Opinion differs as to the cause for this dandruff. Neglect in terms of brushing, combing, and bathing

Dogs can suffer from eye problems if their long hair irritates their eyes.

has been suggested. More likely is excessive bathing with a drying type soap and/or living in an overheated, overly-dry home. Additional brushing to stimulate the skin's natural oils is beneficial. Adding a special preparation to the diet and an oily dressing to the dog's coat can also be helpful.

Eye Problems

The eye is susceptible to a variety of problems. Foreign bodies can cause a slight irritation as well as serious damage. Symptoms of a problem in this area may be fluid running from the eye, as well as signs of distress, displayed by rubbing and pawing the irritated eye. Examine the eye and try to prevent the dog from doing additional injury to himself. Your vet can remove the foreign body and administer medication to combat infection. Any injury to the eye should be treated as rapidly as possible.

Infection

Symptoms of an eye infection are the same as those of a foreign body. Treatment usually involves administering an antibiotic eye ointment to the infected eye. Consult your vet.

Allergy

Allergic dogs usually have a variety of symptoms which may include not only the skin but also the eyes and nose. Itching, redness, discharge may all occur. Treatment with antihistamine (the same way doctors control hay fever) should help ease the animal's discomfort.

Cataracts and Blindness

Some breeds, because of excessive inbreeding, have developed a tendency to blindness and other visual problems. The best time to worry about this is *before* purchasing your puppy. Try to learn as much as possible about the breed which interests you, and if vision is a breed problem, try to be certain that there is no blindness in your pup's ancestors.

During old age, visual handicaps may develop in dogs of all breeds. Sometimes surgery can be of help. Usually blindness of old age comes on so gradually that the dog manages to compensate for his loss by using his other senses.

Blindness can be caused by specific illness, such as distemper, a serious eye infection, or an accident. Whether or not to destroy the dog with total blindness is a very personal decision.

Ear Problems

Infection

Symptoms of an ear infection may at first be rather generalized — little appetite, listlessness, whining.

When observed closely, they will give clues to their ear distress by rubbing the head on the ground and scratching and pawing at the throbbing ear as well as shaking the head. Your vet will be able to determine the necessary treatment.

Sometimes this condition is caused by a build up of natural wax plus grime. Ask your vet about cleaning your dog's ears. Some breeds require periodic ear cleaning.

Long-eared dogs seem to be particularly susceptible to ear infections because moisture doesn't have a good opportunity to dry, making it a fine spot for germs to proliferate. This is why extreme care should be taken when bathing a long-eared dog. Cotton should be inserted before the bath and the ears should be thoroughly dried after the bath. Another difficulty experienced by long-eared breeds is that the ears get soiled and become a fine culture media. Checking the ears frequently and keeping them clean is good hygiene.

Deafness

A small percentage of dogs are deaf from birth on. This is the reason for checking the hearing prior to purchase. Deafness in a puppy is probably a birth defect. Certain breeds have a predisposition toward deafness, thus, careful breeding practices should be followed. Deafness can also be caused by illness and by accidents. Prompt health care can prevent unnecessary difficulties.

Old age—the villain—may also cause deafness. But, if watched carefully and directed by hand signals rather than voice signals, the older dog with a hearing loss can still continue to function.

Tumors

Tumors, both malignant and benign, are to be found in dogs. If you become aware of any lumps or swellings consult the vet promptly. Early detection and modern surgery have made tumors less dreaded. Unspayed females are most vulnerable to tumors. A wise idea is to have your veterinarian give your pet a yearly complete check-up after the age of five.

Fits

Fits are muscular tremors which appear suddenly. They may be caused by illness, poisoning, or by emotional upset. It is best to allow the dog to calm down and to consult the vet.

Dog Psychiatry

Psychiatrists and psychologists are accepted in the area of human mental health care. Presently this is not the case in the dog world. Although there is an increased awareness of a "need" in this area there are still very few trained people to help the emotionally disturbed dog.

The study of doggy emotions is not new. Just as other animals, such as mice and rats, have been used in the psychology lab so the dog has also been studied. (Remember Pavlov's dog?) It has been found that dogs are prone to many of the disturbances seen in humans, such as neurosis, psychosis, and hysteria. Emotional problems may be exhibited by:

(1) **Severe nervousness**—a dog that is tense, anxious, can't relax, barks excessively, is always watching or prowling, won't allow himself to be touched or to play and relax is definitely abnormal. A pet displaying such a mode of behavior is difficult to live with and gives his owners little enjoyment.

(2) **The compulsive barker**—this dog barks continuously or frequently for no obvious reason. This is most annoying and disturbing to all those around him.

(3) **The fear-biter**—a most dangerous dog to keep because of the distinct possibility that he will injure someone. Dogs that have suffered some traumatic experience may respond to any fearful situation by attacking and biting.

(4) **Shyness and withdrawal**—this problem can be readily identified, a dog that hangs back or hides when greeted, or approaches people with his tail tucked between his legs and his head down is definitely suffering from this disturbance.

(5) **The sexual offender**—a male dog who masturbates excessively and who disturbs children and visitors with his behavior presents a definite problem.

(6) **The aggressive and hostile dog**—this type of animal is usually impossible to maintain in a regular home setting unless helped. A dog that attacks others or severely frightens them is not only suffering from a problem but is most certainly creating one for his owner.

These are a few examples of disturbed dogs that would need psychiatric help. Presently there are very few veterinarians available who can "treat" these problems. We know of a clinic in California that treats the disturbed dogs belonging to movie stars. However, there are more dogs with "problems" than there are professionals to treat them. The solution at the present time would seem to be to follow many of the suggestions for good mental health recommended for our own human population:

(1) Provide a happy, loving home.

(2) Keep stress and tension at a minimum.

(3) Prevent bad habits from forming—firmness not permissiveness.

(4) Have clear, well defined rules and limits and be consistent.

(5) Never allow cruelty to be inflicted.

(6) Don't breed a dog that shows personality deviations. (Unfortunately humans have not yet

attained this level of wisdom).

(7) Seek professional help when necessary.

Infectious Diseases

Canine Distemper

This is probably the most dreaded disease in the dog world. Statistics show that half of the dogs which contract distemper will die; the death rate among puppies sometimes reaches 80 per cent. Survivors of distemper are often left with damage to their nervous system or to their sense of smell, sight, or hearing. Partial or total paralysis is not unusual.

Canine distemper is an infectious disease. It is not necessary that a healthy dog come in contact with a diseased dog to become infected. The virus may be borne by air currents and inanimate objects. This, of course, increases the dangers of the disease since it

Sadness is a sick dog. (Photo by Maia Coven.)

virtually makes all susceptible dogs vulnerable to an attack. Canine distemper is found also in foxes, wolves and mink but not in cats. Canine hepatitis, another serious illness of dogs, often occurs simultaneously with canine distemper. Neither distemper nor canine hepatitis is transmissible to man.

The many signs of distemper are not always typical and for this reason treatment may be delayed or neglected. Usually the animal is listless and has a poor appetite. Congestion of the eyes may cause squinting or discharge. Cough, nasal discharge and diarrhea are

---

CANINE DISTEMPER

Canine distemper is the greatest single disease threat to the canine population. At least half of the dogs contracting distemper will die; the death rate sometimes reaches 80 percent among pups.

---

common. The virus may attack the nervous system, causing partial or complete paralysis, "fits," or a twitching in groups of muscles. Distemper is so prevalent and the symptoms so varied that any sick young dog should be taken immediately to your veterinarian for a definite diagnosis.

Practically speaking, it is nearly impossible to prevent exposure to canine distemper virus. Young dogs are more susceptible to the disease than older ones. However, some mature dogs leading comparatively isolated lives are very susceptible to the disease because they have not been recently exposed to the virus. This susceptibility may exist even though they were vaccinated when very young. No dog should be admitted into an area of possible exposure to distemper without immediate vaccination, unless it has been vaccinated within the last 12 months.

It is clear, therefore, that vaccination of your pet against canine distemper is not only highly recommended, but imperative.

Immunization against canine distemper provides the only effective means of control of the disease in the dog population. Since lasting protection, unfortunately, cannot be guaranteed as the result of a single series of inoculations, annual re-vaccination is strongly recommended.

Pups older than three to four months that have an unknown immune status should receive at least one dose of modified live virus vaccine. Younger pups should get at least two doses, the first one after weaning and the last at 12 to 16 weeks of age. Some authorities hold that vaccination should be commenced at six to eight weeks of age and then repeated every two weeks until the pup is three or four months of age. These regional variations in vaccination procedure are dictated by the infectivity of the distemper virus in a given area.

It is impossible for the average pet owner to determine the correct time for vaccination. This is a matter which requires the good professional judgment of your veterinarian, based on his experience and the general health of the dog.

The important thing to remember is that veterinarians are now able to provide most dogs with complete protection against canine distemper.

Rabies

Rabies remains a public health problem even though there have been few human fatalities recently. All warm-blooded animals can spread rabies—the majority of the animal rabies cases in the United States are found in wildlife such as skunk, foxes, and bats. Dogs and cats are the most commonly infected domestic pets. Thus, every pet owner has the responsibility of inoculating his animal in order to prevent rabies outbreaks.

Rabies is transmitted from animals to man by a bite from the infected animal. Everyone bitten by a domestic or wild animal need not undergo antirabies vaccinations. Following a bite, however, a physician should be consulted immediately. The animal should be confined by a veterinarian and observed for 14 days. If the animal remains well at the end of this period, then the rabies virus is not present. Confinement is necessary even for vaccinated dogs because the vaccine is only about 80 per cent effective. However, if rabies symptoms appear, then the administration of antirabies vaccine becomes necessary. The American Veterinary Medical Association makes the following suggestions to prevent rabies:

First of all, have your pet vaccinated if you haven't already done so. Veterinary medical scientists have developed safe and effective vaccines which give your pet maximum protection against rabies. To insure continued maximum protection, follow your veterinarian's advice and observe your local rabies control regulations.

Second, if bitten by an animal, thoroughly cleanse the wound with soap and irrigate with profuse quantities of running warm water. Contact your physician, Board of Health, or police department immediately. *Confine, do not kill the animal.*

Third, obey leash and licensing laws in your community.

Fourth, make sure your pet is identified by a license tag and a rabies inoculation tag.

Fifth, report stray dogs to the police or local pound department.

Finally, teach children not to play with strange pets and to avoid handling any wild animal, particularly when it appears to be tame. This is especially important when you are camping.

Leptospirosis

The organisms responsbile for leptospirosis are transmitted by the feces or urine of infected rats. In areas where rats are present, it is imperative that the dog's food be kept well-sealed so that it cannot be contaminated.

Symptoms of the disease are: vomiting, fever, diarrhea, jaundice, loss of appetite, and depression. Prompt veterinary attention is mandatory.

Prevention of the disease is now possible by vaccination. A yearly booster is recommended to maintain a good level of immunity.

Infectious Hepatitis

Infectious hepatitis is a viral disease which attacks the liver. Transmission is via the urine of infected dogs or viral carriers.

Symptoms are quite similar to distemper—fever, vomiting, diarrhea, pain, and anemia. This disease is often fatal.

A preventative vaccine is now available; and, there is a triple booster for distemper, hepatitis, and leptospirosis.

Coughs, Colds, Tonsillitis

Dogs kept in kennels are prone to a condition known as "kennel cough" which is a dry, gagging cough caused by an infection. Except for the cough, there usually aren't any other symptoms. Dog cough syrup may be used to relieve the soreness of the throat.

Coughing can also be caused by something caught in the throat. If you suspect this possibility, an X-ray may be necessary.

Many other conditions are characterized by coughs such as upper respiratory infections, distemper, sore throat, tonsillitis, pneumonia, heartworm, and asthma. Only your veterinarian can make a definitive diagnosis.

Manifestations of a cold may occur at any time. Symptoms are a watery discharge from the nose, possibly also from the eyes, listlessness and loss of appetite. Aspirin can help to reduce the discomfort.

Excessive licking of the lips is the most common sign of a sore throat and possible tonsillitis. Your vet can prescribe medication for this condition.

The Outdoor Dog

Keep the outdoor dog outside rather than expose him to cold, then heated quarters, and back outside again. Such a routine makes it difficult for the dog to maintain a steady body temperature and may bring on respiratory ailments, particularly in older dogs.

Two mature Shetland Sheepdogs—the dog on the right had rickets, caused by a dietary deficiency, as a puppy.

Dietary Deficiencies

Rickets

Rickets is a disease affecting the bones and teeth of puppies caused by a deficiency of vitamin D, calcium, and phosphorus. Proper diet, adequate sunshine, and vitamins can reverse this disease if treated in time. Symptoms of the disease are bowed legs, weak muscles, deformed joints, lack of vigor, arched neck, and a poor stance.

It is of utmost importance that bitches in pregnancy and lactation have sufficiently high amounts of vitamin D, calcium, and phosphorus. This is important both for maintaining their own health and for the proper formation of their puppies.

Black Tongue

Black tongue is a vitamin B complex deficiency disease which will not occur in dogs maintained on a good diet. It is not infectious or contagious. Treatment is only effective if the diet is corrected and nutritious foods high in the B vitamins are added, such as meat, milk, eggs, and liver.

Internal Parasites

Worming of Dogs

Dogs can be infested with different species of worms, including roundworms, hookworms, heartworms, tapeworms, and whipworms. Just as in poultry and livestock operations, worms can cause many dollars worth of damage in a kennel or breeding operation. Pups are most severely affected, with symptoms appearing as poor growth, rough hair coat, diarrhea, listlessness, and if the infection is severe death may occur.

In addition, roundworms and hookworms present a public health problem since the larvae from these species can infect humans.

All dogs should routinely have their droppings checked for the presence of worms by a veterinarian. Brood females should be wormed or checked prior to or within three weeks after breeding. Hookworm and roundworm larvae can pass from the dam via the bloodstream through the placenta to developing pups As a result, if the dam is infected, pups can be heavily infested with these species at birth.

Pups in good health can be wormed at four to five weeks of age if necessary. If dogs are heavily infested, worming should be repeated in three to four weeks. This is necessary since the life cycle of most worms is such that part of their life is spent in parts of the body other than the intestines. Even though worms are removed from he intestine the individual worms in the rest of the body soon mature and migrate to the intestines. This can be controlled by worming dogs periodically. Normally no problems occur if a reputable product is used and directions for treatment are followed. Never worm sick or weak dogs recently exposed to disease unless under veterinary supervision.

Hookworm eggs can be destroyed in dog runs by sprinkling a saturated salt solution over the area at a rate of one gallon per 100 square feet or sprinkling three pounds of dry sodium borate per gallon of water over the same amount of area. Both salt and borate destroy the eggs by dessication, or drawing the moisture out of the cell. Remember, salt is harmful to vegetation and care should be taken in its application. This treatment is effective against hookworm eggs only.

Roundworms

One of the most important parasites in dogs is the large intestinal roundworm (*Ascarids*). These white or yellowish colored worms, when mature, will measure two to eight inches in length.

The presence of roundworms in the intestines of a young dog is characterized by marked enlargement of the abdomen, unthriftiness, listlessness, and may be accompanied by digestive disturbances. If the infection is heavy or severe, worms may even be passed in the dog's droppings or in the vomit the dog produces when he coughs. The coughing is most prevalent when the larvae are passing through the lungs. When large numbers of larvae are present in the lungs, pneumonia may develop.

Many times it appears that adult dogs may develop an immunity against roundworms; therefore, it is a less serious problem in mature dogs than it is in young pups. However, roundworms can still be present in adult dogs and unless they are treated, the adult dogs will spread the worms to other dogs.

Just as the hookworm larva, the roundworm larva

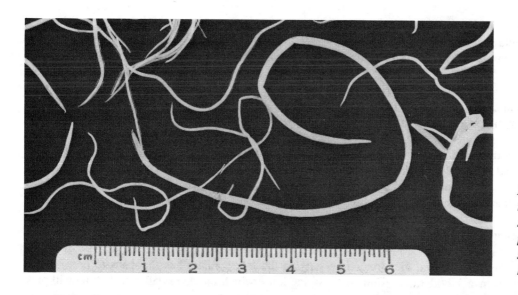

ROUNDWORMS —
the larvae of this para-
site can present a
public health problem
since it can invade the
human body.

can migrate through the blood system of the pregnant mother to her developing pups, and consequently, the pups may be heavily infected with worms at birth. This emphasizes the importance of worming the pregnant female early (at least the first three weeks) in her gestation period or even prior to breeding.

The larvae of the roundworm present a public health problem, since the Ascarid larvae can invade the body of humans and cause a condition known as visceral larva migrans. Generally, this disease develops in children less than three years of age, due to their habits of putting their fingers in their mouth, or eating dirt which may be contaminated.

There are many good roundworm treatments available, some of which contain piperazine. If this compound is used, the dog does not have to be fasted since the medication can be given right in his food.

Hookworm

The most injurious internal parasites in puppies are hookworms. These worms are common and can be found in dogs in most sections of the country. They are grayish-white in color, ½- to ¾-inch in length and as thick as a straight pin. These worms attach themselves with teeth or cutting blades to the lining of the mucosa of the dog's small intestine.

There are three kinds of hookworms; all have similar life cycles. The adult female worms attached to the small intestine deposit a large number of eggs which pass in the dog's droppings. If there is ample moisture available and a temperature of 72-86 deg. F, these eggs hatch in 12-24 hours. Extreme dryness as well as freezing temperatures kill the freshly hatched larvae. For this reason, the incidence and severity of hookworm infection is lowest during mid-Winter and highest in the Summer.

The larvae develop to a third or infective stage in a week, at which time they are picked up directly by the dog in contaminated feed, water, or when the dog licks any portions of his body that may have worm eggs clinging to it. The larvae go directly to the small intestine where they mature to adults. The infective

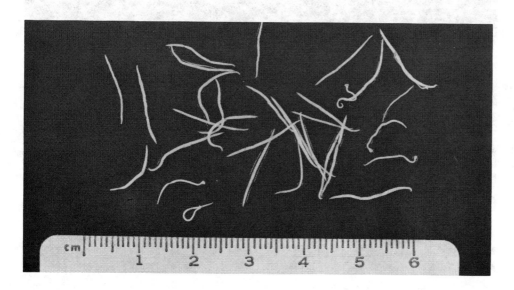

HOOKWORMS—the
most injurious parasite
in puppies. Heavy in-
festation can cause
anemia or even death
in young dogs.

115

larvae can also penetrate the dog's skin, going first into the blood stream and then into the lungs. In the lungs they are coughed up, swallowed and go to the small intestine.

Prenatal infection can occur in females during the gestation period. The migrating larvae go from the female via the blood stream to the placenta and pass into the developing young. Consequently, pups are sometimes heavily infected at birth. The main effects of hookworm on dogs, and the condition which makes them so serious, is the heavy blood loss they can cause. An infected dog may have continuous bloody diarrhea from persistent hemorrhaging caused by the hookworms in the intestine. In young dogs this can cause anemia or may even result in death. Many times young puppies that are heavily infected and treated properly may even be given a blood transfusion to help overcome the anemia. Failure to treat heavy hookworm infection will usually result in death of the pup. To illustrate the high blood loss, if there are 100 adult worms in the small intestine, it is estimated that these worms will take up as much as .25-.4 oz. of blood every 24 hours. It is easy to imagine what can happen if there would be several hundred worms present.

Symptoms of hookworm infection are poor stamina and general poor growth of the dog, along with the presence of blood in the droppings. If worms are present, the eggs or even some of the worms may be found in the droppings. The presence of hookworms can be determined by having your veterinarian check a droppings sample.

Diagnosis and treatment for hookworm should be done by your veterinarian. There are many wormers available which can be used in the treatment of hookworms, including pills or capsules and a wormer which is injected into the dog's subcutaneous tissue.

Tapeworms

There are at least 14 different species of tapeworms that can infect dogs in this country. Some of these species are limited to certain areas, but all depend upon suitable insects or other intermediate hosts to complete their life cycle.

Tapeworms vary in size from a fraction of an inch up to 30 feet depending upon the species and age of the worm. Intermediate hosts such as fleas, lice, rodents (rats, rabbits, mice), fish, and snakes are necessary in order for each specie of worm to complete its life cycle. Infection of the dog with a particular specie of tapeworm depends on the one present in the area and the intermediate host that the dog swallows or eats. If the intermediate host happens to be a flea or biting louse which the dog swallows, then he will pick up the larval stage of the particular species of the parasite this host is carrying. Other species can be picked up by the dog eating the intestines of rabbits, or the livers of rats or mice in which the immature stages of the worm are found.

Symptoms of tapeworm infestation in dogs are: digestive disturbances, abdominal pain, nervousness, and unthriftiness. Animals with mild cases probably suffer only abdominal discomfort and the inexperienced dog owner may not notice this. Heavy tapeworm infection may show up as persistent or alternating diarrhea and/or constipation. An important factor regarding tapeworms in dogs is that they may pass in the droppings and can, through the intermediate host, infest other livestock and man. The tapeworm segments passing in the droppings of infected dogs can contaminate furniture, dog bedding, and may even soil these items. The segments have a pinkish tinge when fresh, but are brown when dry and look like grains of rice.

TAPEWORM—transmitted through an intermediate host, the tapeworm can vary in size from a fraction of an inch to 30 feet depending on species and age.

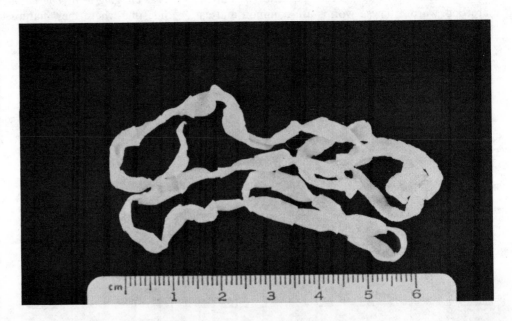

A dog infected with tapeworms may occasionally be seen sitting down and dragging his hind quarters over the floor or ground. This is partly attributable to the irritation that the segments cause when they pass through the intestines. The tapeworm can be detected by observing their segments in the dog's droppings. Also, if the veterinarian is given a sample of the dog's droppings, he can detect worm segments under a microscope, if they are present.

Treatment for tapeworm is by giving the dog a wormer designed for use against this parasite. Your veterinarian can give you information as to the most effective wormer for the particular species of worm which your dog may have.

Try to prevent your dog from coming in contact with the worm or intermediate host of a particular species of tapeworm. This can be done by controlling the rodent population around your area, and keeping your dog free of external parasites. As with most health problems, good management and prompt treatment upon diagnosis are necessary to help eliminate tapeworms in your dog.

Heartworm

One of the most difficult internal parasites to treat in dogs is the heartworm. This worm is most prevalent along the coastal areas of the United States although it is also found in the central and northern regions. The adult worm is slender, measuring ten to 12 inches in length with the female worm usually longer than the male. The adult worms most frequently live in the right ventricle of the heart.

The adult heartworm releases embryos or young worms, known as microfilariae, into the blood stream. These microfilariae circulate in the blood and do not develop further until they are ingested by a suitable intermediate host. This host is usually the mosquito although it has been found that fleas may also spread them. This is one reason for the high incidence of heartworms around the sea coast. When the mosquito takes in a small amount of blood containing the microfilariae the organism develops further in the insect's body. Complete embryonzation takes ten to 14 days at which time the microfilariae emerge as larvae. When the mosquito again feeds on another dog, this larvae can be transferred to the animal being fed upon. From this point there is little known about the remainder of the life cycle. It is thought that the larva migrates to certain connective tissue in the body and with the completion of the intermediate development, proceeds to the right ventricle by way of the veins. This completion of the life cycle may take three to four months from the time the young worm first enters the dog's body.

Signs of heartworm infection include a chronic cough and lack of stamina, especially after exercise. The presence of a large number of heartworms in the right ventricle can cause heart enlargement and subsequent heart damage. Continued infection can produce a strain on the heart which may eventually result in death of the dog.

Diagnosis of the presence or absence of microfilariae is made by observing a blood sample under the microscope. If microfilariae are present this indicates there are adult worms in the heart.

To date no single medication does a completely satisfactory job of treating both the larva and the adult heartworm. Surgery has been used to remove adult worms. Many of the wormers now available contain arsenicals which are effective in heartworm treatment. Treatment is difficult, not because the worms are hard to kill but from possible after effects. If all of the worms are killed at once there is a possibility that a clump of them may lodge in a major

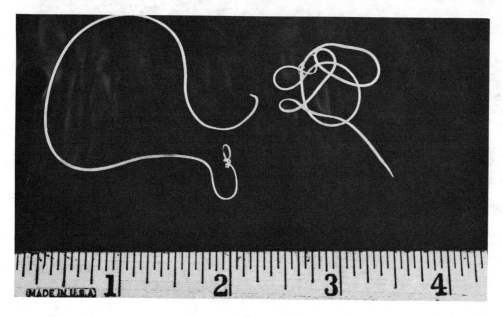

HEARTWORMS — one of the most difficult internal parasites in dogs to treat, the adult heartworm usually lives in the right ventricle of the host dog's heart.

blood vessel and cause death. Therefore, the worms should be killed a few at a time to prevent an accumulation. If an accumulation of dead worms occurs in the blood vessels of the lungs, pneumonia may result. Diagnosis for heartworms, and treatment if any are found, should be done by a veterinarian. The treatment period will usually be long and during this time the dog should have ample rest.

The best method for preventing recurrence of heartworms is to keep down the number of mosquitos in your area and prompt treatment of any infected dog. If heartworms prevail in your area, keep your home or kennel area screened so that the dog has minimum exposure to mosquitos. Drain all marsh lands and still water areas which are not in use as an aid in preventing mosquitos from hatching. Another manner for the prevention of infestation necessitates giving medicine daily during the mosquito season and for two months after a killing frost. The medicine is given only to dogs that have a negative blood test. This medicine destroys the microfilaria that may be introduced by mosquitos. Semi-annual blood tests for all dogs, preferably in March and November, are recommended.

Whipworms

Whipworms that are found in dogs have a white or gray colored whip-like body and are two to three inches long at maturity. They are usually found in the cecum (a blind pouch located between the large and small intestines) of the dog. The dog is infected by swallowing embryonated eggs picked up in contaminated water, feed, or by licking off eggs that may be clinging to his hair coat. The swallowed embryonated eggs hatch in the small intestine and in two to three months the young worms travel to the cecum.

Little is known about the damage whipworms cause to dogs. Symptoms of severe infection are chronic diarrhea, abdominal pain, prolonged nervousness, unthriftiness, and frequent periods of constipation and diarrhea. If diarrhea persists, blood may show up in the droppings. Animals affected with severe cases of whipworm may die if left untreated.

Identification of the worm can be made by a veterinarian upon microscopic examination of the droppings for whipworm eggs. Treatment is by a wormer designed for whipworm control. This wormer can be obtained from your veterinarian.

Routine checking of dropping samples for whipworms, prompt treatment if any are found, and good sanitation of the area in which the dog lives do much to prevent further spread and also aids in the elimination of these internal parasites.

Worming Precautions

The following precautions should be followed when worming your dog. Always follow the worming directions specifically. Dogs which are sick, weak or exposed to a disease, such as distemper, should not be wormed except under specific supervision of the veterinarian. Cleanliness of the dog and his kennel is a must for good worm control.

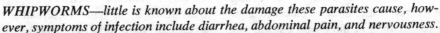

WHIPWORMS—little is known about the damage these parasites cause, however, symptoms of infection include diarrhea, abdominal pain, and nervousness.

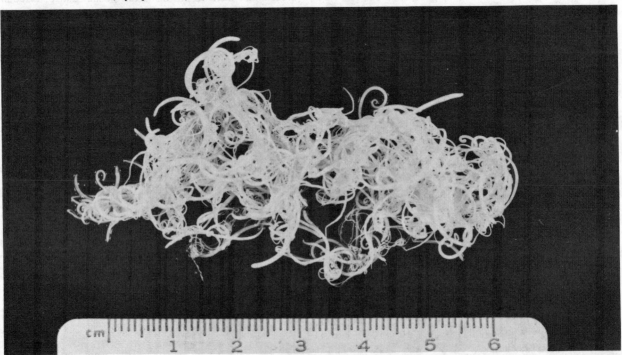

GENETIC DEFECTS

Hip Dysplasia

The symptoms of Hip Dysplasia are abnormal gait and eventual lameness in the severe cases, while the mild cases can only be diagnosed by X-ray. This defect occurs primarily in the large breed of dogs and appears to be most common in German Shepherds. The difficulty is caused by a hereditary flaw. The ideal way to avoid hip dysplasia is to breed only those animals which are proven to be free from the defect by X-ray examination.

Cleft Palate

Cleft palate is a hereditary defect, resulting in the failure of the tissues of the palate to close. Puppies with this condition are not able to suck properly. It is recommended that such puppies should not be allowed to survive as surgery is not successful.

Luxation of the Patella

Luxation of the Patella is actually a dislocation of the kneecap which makes walking painful and results in lameness. Although temporary relief can be given, a lasting solution has not been found. This problem occurs most frequently in miniature and toy breeds. Research indicates that this defect is genetic and, therefore, affected dogs should never be used for breeding.

Progressive Retinal Atrophy

Progressive Retinal Atrophy is a form of partial blindness to complete blindness. The onset of symptoms occurs between three to nine months of age. Research has found that it is a recessive defect; thus, breeders should avoid using affected animals or their litter mates for breeding purposes.

Blindness and Epilepsy

Although the research into these defects is not yet completed, it is strongly urged that affected dogs and their litter mates not be used for breeding.

Cryptorchidism

Cryptorchidism is a condition of the male which results in one or both testicles not descending into the scrotum. At birth, both testicles should be descended. If one has not descended normally (monochidism), it can often be brought down by administering doses of an anterior pituitary-like hormone. Surgery is required to correct this condition in the mature dog. Correction is recommended for several reasons; monochidism disqualifies the dog from the show ring; it may cause an unpleasant temperament, and it may become cancerous. A monochid dog may be fertile but should not be used for stud as this defect is believed to be hereditary.

Those dogs having two undescended testicles are always sterile.

Paralysis of the Hindquarters

This is a condition found in long-backed dogs, such as the Dachshund. Research is studying this defect presently but, as yet, the cause is uncertain. It may be due to a genetic cause or stress placed on the spinal column.

Entropion

Entropion is the term used when one or both eyelids are turned in. This results in the eyelashes brushing the eye, which causes pain and irritation. If untreated, this condition can result in blindness; fortunately, it can be corrected surgically. However, surgery of this nature will disqualify the dog from competition in American Kennel Club dog shows or obedience trials.

Overshot Jaw

It is believed that this defect is caused by a single recessive gene and results in the incisor teeth of the lower jaw to be outside of the upper jaw.

Semi Lethal Genes

Merle coloring is an example of a semi lethal gene. When two merle colored animals are mated, those puppies in the litter receiving a MM will be deaf, blind, sterile, and have completely white color markings. The recessive mm results in the absence of the merle color. Only the heterozygous Mm results in a merle colored dog.

OFA DYSPLASIA CONTROL REGISTRY PROCEDURE

It is important for the conscientious breeder to learn all he can possibly know about his breeding stock. The prevalence of hip dysplasia in pure bred dogs is a very real concern for all dedicated to the breeding of these fine animals. The Dysplasia Control Registry of the Orthopedic Foundation for Animals (OFA) offers breeders and practicing veterinarians expert unbiased evaluation of pelvic radiographs taken for interpretation of the status of the hip joints of mature and young adult animals.

When you have a dog X-rayed by your veterinarian, it is necessary for him to properly position the animal for good film evaluation. For most large dogs this requires a general anesthetic or heavy sedation to prevent motion and to allow for the proper extension of the hind limbs. It is advisable to make more than one film when the dog is anesthetized for future study and/or reference for comparative purposes. The manner in which additional films are produced depends upon the discretion of the vet making the film.

For submission of radiographs to the OFA, it is necessary to have the film permanently identified at the time the radiograph is taken with the following information: registered name, AKC registration number, birthdate, and owner's name. The veterinarian should identify the name of his hospital and date the film was taken on the radiograph. The age requirement for certification of a pelvic radiograph is one year or older since the dog's musculo-skeletal system is nearly mature at this time. For large, fast-growing breeds, an ideal time for taking pelvic films is the period between 18 and 30 months. It is necessary to submit with the radiograph a completed and signed application form, along with a service fee check for $10. Application forms are available from the Orthopedic Foundation for Animals, Inc., 817 Virginia Avenue, Columbia, Missouri 65201.

When your film is received at the Missouri Office, the film is screened as to diagnostic quality and proper positioning. An application number is assigned to each film of satisfactory quality which has a completed and signed application form. Groups of films are then air mailed to three different veterinary radiologists, all of whom are specialists in diagnostic pelvic radiography and who are qualified specialists in

radiology as certified by the American Board of Veterinary Radiology. When the first radiologist has completed his evaluation, the films are returned by air mail to the OFA with his interpretations for each film. The group of films is then sent to the second and third radiologists for their interpretations. None of the radiologists are aware of how the other radiologists evaluated the films until the final report has been sent to the owners to insure unbiased and objective evaluation. A consensus report is issued on the basis of the evaluations of the three radiological interpretations, and if the consensus is normal, a certificate of normalcy is issued to the owner of record and an OFA certificate number is issued for the dog, coded by breed. In the case of the dysplastic consensus, no certificate is issued and a confidential report is sent only to the owner and referring veterinarian. In the case of young dogs with marginal conformation of the hip joints, the radiologists may not be able to evaluate the true status of the hip joints and may request that another pelvic evaluation be made for comparative purposes. This may be an immediate request or an evaluation to be made when the dog has had additional time to mature. This re-evaluation is made without further charge.

A post card requesting permission to list the dog's name as being certified normal accompanies all normal certificates. If the owner desires to have his dog listed as normal by breed associations, he signs the card granting this permission and returns the signed card to the OFA. In all other cases, the results of the examination are held in strict confidence.

Films received for evaluation are retained by the OFA for research purposes and as a permanent record for future reference. This collection of radiographs, representing over 75 breeds, now comprises the largest single all breed collection in the world.

SOME ORTHOPEDIC PROBLEMS

Osteochondritis Dissecans
As A Cause of Shoulder Lameness in the Big Dog

Sudden forelimb lameness in the juvenile dog of the larger breeds may be a manifestation of osteochondritis dissecans, an increasingly diagnosed condition of the shoulder joint.

The disease has been reported as occurring most frequently in large and giant breeds between the ages of 5 and 12 months, a time at which the skeletal system is most susceptible to injury. A typical history of lameness after strenuous exercise of sudden stops in front of fences, and in connection with training or jumping is common.

The symptoms of lameness, refusal to use the affected limb, painful resistance to full extension of the forelimb and atrophy of the shoulder muscles are common findings. These symptoms are the result of an injury to the subchondral bone and cartilage of the shoulder joint. Pathologically, these lesions are seen as a bone necrosis of the central portion of the humeral articular surface with discoid plaques of cartilage at the site of injury.

A diagnosis of osteochondritis dissecans is most often made by the clinical symptoms of shoulder lameness after strenuous exercise. Radiographic diagnosis is helpful in severe or long standing cases, but in the acute stage lesions may not be apparent radiographically.

Fortunately, most dogs afflicted will make a functional recovery with rest and restricted exercise. Some veterinarians have used intra-articular injections of steriods to shorten the recovery period. More persistent cases of the disease may require surgical intervention to remove the bony lesion or pieces of detached cartilage within the joint capsule.

Although osteochondritis dissecans is more prevalent in some breeds and in some lines than others, breeders, trainers and large dog fanciers can help prevent this condition by exercising judgment in the amount of exercise a juvenile is allowed during this critical period of his development.

Canine Elbow Dysplasia

Elbow dysplasia is a descriptive term applied to a developmental abnormality of the elbow joint that is manifested by bony changes and foreleg lameness. Elbow dysplasia has been described in the German Shepherd Dog, St. Bernards, Irish Wolfhounds, Basset Hounds, Newfoundlands, Bloodhounds, Labrador Retrievers and Great Danes. This disease has been diagnosed in dogs ranging in age from three and a half months to three years, with six months the most frequently reported age of diagnosis. Elbow dysplasia has not been reported in the small breeds of dogs.

Clinical signs of the disease vary from slight lameness to refusal to bear weight on the affected limb. The lameness generally is gradual in appearance, inter-

---

CANINE PANOSTEITIS

Panosteitis is a disease of unknown origin which causes pain and lameness primarily in young growing dogs of the larger breeds. The disease has also been termed enostosis and eosinophilic panosteitis. Panosteitis has been reported in several breeds of dogs including the German Shepherd Dog, St. Bernard, Basset Hound, Great Dane, Doberman Pinscher, German Shorthaired Pointer, Irish Setter, Airedale Terrier, Samoyed and Miniature Schnauzer. Male dogs are more often affected and the condition is most frequently diagnosed between five and 13 months of age. Typical signs of the disease are a lameness which may affect one or more legs and shift from limb to limb intermittently over a period of several weeks. This lameness is usually not associated with injury. Diminished appetite and activity are common findings. Localized pain in the long bones of the legs can usually be demonstrated by firm pressure over the affected area. In the middle phase of the disease, diagnosis of panosteitis can be made radiographically. Characteristic radio-dense, patchy areas appear in the medullary canal of the long bones such as the humerus, femur, tibia, radius and ulna. Radiography is the most reliable means of differentiating lameness caused by panosteitis from other juvenile lameness such as hip dysplasia, elbow dysplasia or osteochondritis dissecans. The lameness caused by panosteitis is self-limiting and symptoms usually abate with time. Treatment with aspirin, corticosteroids have been helpful in the relief of pain associated with this condition.

mittent in nature and may become more pronounced after exercise. A frequent complaint is lack of drive in gaiting and loss of stamina. One leg or both forelegs may be affected. Severely affected dogs stand with bowed elbows and have swollen joints with increased joint fluid. These dogs resent forced movement of the elbow joint.

The diagnosis of elbow dysplasia is based on radiographic findings of an ununited anconeal process (which is a loose fragment of bone in the posterior portion of the elbow joint) and/or early osteoarthritis of the elbow with the arm flexed is a diagnostic clue for the observation of the anconeal process. Care must be taken in viewing radiographs of large dogs under 140 days of age since normal bony union is not complete until after this time.

Treatment of this condition is aimed at relief of pain by surgically removing the loose bone fragment within the elbow joint before osteoarthritic changes become aggravated. Experimental trial breeding of dogs with elbow dysplasia indicate the condition to be an inherited trait with a strong familial tendency. The mode of inheritance is thought to be that of three dominant genes controlling the appearance of the disease.

Since elbow dysplasia is an inherited abnormality, affected dogs should not be considered for breeding. Dogs with elbow dysplasia should be removed from breeding programs and preferably neutered for use as pet animals. Surgical removal of the ununited anconeal process has been useful in the relief of pain and lameness associated with the disease.

OTHER HEALTH HINTS

Taking a Dog's Temperature

There will be times when you may believe your dog is sick and has a fever. Possible clues that can signal the existence of a temperature are: (1) Heavy panting, (2) a hot, dry nose. The only way to know for certain whether the dog is sick is to take his temperature. The procedure is actually quite simple, but it must be done carefully to avoid accidentally injuring the dog:

- Use a rectal thermometer.
- Shake down the mercury.
- Apply some vaseline or other lubricant to the tip.
- Hold the dog in a standing position.
  Speak reassuringly to the dog while holding him.
- Insert thermometer gently and slowly into the rectum.
- Wait about three minutes and then remove gently.
- Normal temperature of dogs is 101 deg. to 101.5 deg. F.
- Any significant rise in temperature above this is a sign of illness. Consult your vet.

When to See the Vet

The American Veterinary Medical Association suggests you consult your veterinarian if your pet shows any of the following symptoms:

1—Abnormal behavior, sudden viciousness or lethargy.

2—Abnormal discharges from the nose, eyes, or other body openings.

3—Abnormal lumps, limping, or difficulty getting up or lying down.

4—Loss of appetite, marked weight losses or gains, or excessive water consumption. Difficult, abnormal, or uncontrolled waste elimination.

5—Excessive head shaking, scratching, and licking or biting any part of the body.

6—Dandruff, loss of hair, open sores, and a ragged or dull coat. Foul breath or excessive tartar deposits on teeth.

Choosing Your Veterinarian

If you are fortunate enough to live in an area served by more than one veterinarian, you will have the choice of selecting one. For many ardent pet owners this choice ranks in importance with the choice of the family doctor. Certainly you must consider proximity and availability as well as finding someone in whom you can have complete trust and confidence. Veterinarians are highly trained professional people who have devoted years of study in preparing for this field. All veterinarians are required to have a minimum of two years of pre-veterinary college study prior to four years of professional study in a college of veterinary medicine. Subsequent passing of a state board examination is required to be licensed to practice in any state or province. Thus, your pet should be in good hands and should receive the finest care available today.

Administering Medication

At some time or other your dog will have to take medicine. The easiest way is the best way! Attitude is most important, and your dog can sense it if you feel that you are going to do something unpleasant. Pretending that you have a great surprise will enlist his interest.

I. Giving Capsules and Pills

There are two ways to go about this—the professional way and the fun way.

The professional way involves holding the dog's upper jaw with one hand and pressing his cheeks inward to cover the teeth and pushing the capsule far back in the throat with the other hand. Then, closing his mouth with both hands and stroking his throat gently to make him swallow.

The fun and easy way is to wrap the pill or capsule in a small amount of liver sausage and watch the whole thing disappear in one bite. It's a pleasure to see the grateful look and to have him come running the next time it's pill time.

II. Giving Liquid Medicine

With a stubborn dog this is no easy trick. Most sources simply say to pull out the dog's lower lip to form a pocket and then to pour the liquid into this pocket with a spoon or dropper. Perhaps after doing this hundreds of times one becomes proficient. The typical pet owner, however, may find that giving liquid medicine is quite difficult. A quick shake of the dog's head and you are left standing there covered with medicine. We have found it necessary to be well covered before attempting this stunt. Our greatest success has come by mixing the liquid medicine into a taste tempting meal, i.e. liver and broth or chicken giblets au jus.

Care of the Recuperating Dog

When your pet is ill, he needs your love, care, and attention more than ever. That is why most animal authorities recommend nursing your dog back to health at home rather than in the animal hospital. By all means visit the veterinarian, have the dog examined and medication and treatment prescribed, but then take him home and let him recuperate in his own familiar surroundings with his own "family." You will have more patience in coaxing his reluctant appetite and more ability in cheering him up. That personal, warm touch will mean a faster and happier recovery.

Just remember to follow the veterinarian's directions and to give all the medication and treatment as prescribed. Call the vet if there are any changes in the dog's symptoms. If these steps are followed, the recovery should be rapid.

Heavy panting and a hot, dry nose are clues to the existence of a fever in a dog. The only way to be certain, however, is to take the dog's temperature.

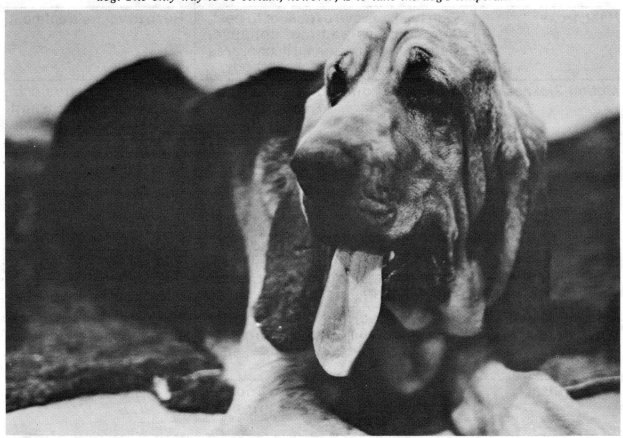

FIRST AID CHART

Condition	First Aid	Treatment
Burns	Use wet packs of cold water or ice cold water.	Consult your vet.
Choking	If possible remove foreign body from mouth or throat.	If not possible, consult your vet.
Diarrhea	When due to dietary changes, administer kaopectate according to dog's size.	If this continues, consult your vet.
Fits or Convulsions	Keep animal warm and quiet. If very wild try to prevent injury to self.	Consult vet.
Cuts	Minor cuts are licked clean by the dog. Wounds should be washed thoroughly and antiseptic and bandage should be applied if necessary.	Deep cuts should be stitched.
Dog Bites	Allow dog to lick them clean. If deep, wash them.	Deep bites should be stitched.
Fractures	Handle the dog carefully and muzzle him. Keep him warm and rush him to vet.	X-ray and setting of fracture are handled by vet.
Heatstroke	Due to excessive exposure to heat, dog displays panting, collapse, and fever. Place animal in cool area —administer wet packs to body.	Rush to vet for treatment.
Motion Sickness	Remove from moving vehicle. Allow stomach to settle before feeding.	Future trips should be pre-planned with anti-motion sickness medication.
Poisoning	Check container for correct antidote—administer immediately.	Rush to vet.
Porcupine Quills	Muzzle dog. Tie-clip ends of quills, then remove with pliers. Remove those near eyes and mouth first.	Vet may continue under anesthesia.
Shock	Caused by severe injury or illness. Keep animal warm and quiet. Cover with blankets.	Rush to vet.
Snake Bites	Cut X-shaped mark over fang print with sharp knife. Apply tourniquet between body and wound—suction out poison.	Rush to vet for anti-venom.
Stings (Insect)	Apply a paste of bicarbonate of soda or a weak solution of ammonia.	

Antidotes for Common Poisons

Cause vomiting—administer a mixture of half peroxide and water.

Poison	Source	Antidote
Acids	Batteries, etc.	Bicarbonate of soda
Alkali	Drain cleaners, etc.	Vinegar
Arsenic	Spray materials, etc.	Epsom salts
Food poisoning	Spoiled food, Garbage	Peroxide followed by epsom salts and a warm water enema
Lead	Paint	Epsom salts followed by milk
Mercury	Broken thermometer	Egg white and milk
Phosphorus	Rat poison	Peroxide
Sedatives	Medication	Strong coffee
Thallium	Insect poison	Table salt

First Aid—Restraint

Before you begin to administer first aid of any kind to an injured dog protect yourself by either muzzling the dog or by applying a self-made restraint. To make a restraint use anything readily available—a necktie or piece of rope—and loop it around the dog's mouth; tie above and then below and then bring up behind the ears and knot.

Safety Tips

Leashing

Many people still believe a dog is only happy when he is free to roam. They fail to realize that a dog is a remarkably adaptable creature and is far happier and safer when exercised in his own securely fenced yard or on a leash. To let your dog run loose, risking death or painful injury under the wheels of a fast-moving car, is downright cruelty.

Poison Prevention

Most dog poisoning isn't perpetrated by fiends. Careless dog owners are the culprits. Puppies especially will taste practically anything—paint, turpentine, insecticides, weedkillers, household bleaches and detergents. These common household supplies should be stored out of a curious pup's reach. After using insect sprays and fertilizers on your lawn, take care so that your dog doesn't get them on his feet and lick them off. When you suspect your dog has been poisoned, consult the veterinarian for emergency first aid treatment. Take him to the doctor as soon as possible.

Avoid Eye Injuries

When your dog rides with his head out the car window, he is in danger of incurring eye and ear injuries. Bits of grit blown with the force of a bullet into tender eye and ear tissues can start a painful infection.

Travel Notes

When traveling with your pet, always snap on his leash before you open the car door. An excited unleashed dog may dash headlong into traffic or scamper off to explore the countryside and get lost. In hot weather never leave your pet in a tightly closed car. Automobile interiors heat up rapidly, and dogs are very susceptible to heat prostration.

Dangerous Toys

Many dogs treasure a rubber bone or ball for years; others will chew them and swallow the pieces. If your dog attacks his toys like Jack the Ripper, avoid those made with metal rivets, staples or other materials he can tear apart and swallow. Many good, safe toys are available, so choose your dog's playthings carefully.

PROBLEMS OF OLD AGE

SYMPTOMS of old age begin at different times in different dogs. This "individual difference" may be due to the dog's breeding, diet, environment, life style, and general health. No one can tell how long a dog is going to stay fit or how long it's going to live. There are some general "rules of thumb" that can help the dog owner estimate the longevity of his dog. The larger breeds generally have a shorter life span than the smaller breeds. This seems to be due to their tend-

ency to "burn themselves out" more rapidly. It seems that a dog ages approximately seven "years" in one calendar year. Thus at five years of age a dog is roughly equivalent to a 35-year-old human. It shouldn't be surprising, therefore, to find six-year-old dogs with the typical problems of a middle aged man —cardio vascular disease, kidney disease, and digestive disturbances.

With the advent of modern medical therapy, the

Symptoms of heart disease in a dog include coughing, excessive tiring and fainting.

life span of your dog can also be extended. Problems which in past years were untreatable and could be solved only with euthanasia are today being medicated. Regular yearly check-ups can make early diagnosis and treatment possible, thus hopefully guaranteeing a longer and healthier life for your pet.

Kidney Disease

The most frequent affliction of the older dog is chronic kidney disease. Most deaths of older dogs are caused by this condition. The symptoms are increased thirst and urination, loss of appetite, and weakness. The diagnosis can be made by laboratory tests and prompt treatment may save the dog.

Heart Disease

Symptoms of this condition are coughing, excessive tiring, and fainting. If the disease is allowed to advance, it will lead to congestive heart failure signaled by fluid in the abdomen and swelling of the limbs. Your veterinarian can treat cardio-vascular disease with drugs, as well as recommending special diets and limited exercise.

Dental Problems

The older dog is often beset by loose or infected teeth; these should be extracted. This condition is due to natural aging as well as neglect. All dogs should have regular dental check-ups. Tartar should be removed before it is allowed to damage tooth enamel and gums. Periodic brushing of the teeth with salt and soda is recommended. Hard dog biscuits are also helpful in maintaining sound oral hygiene. If a dental problem is present, hard items should be avoided.

Diet

If your older dog is not displaying any digestive difficulties or gaining excess weight, then the regular maintenance diet can be continued. However, constipation and poor appetite often plague the older pet. Your veterinarian can prescribe a special diet to alleviate some of these problems.

Signs of Aging

At about six to seven years of age the dog's beard will probably begin to gray. Typically, then, the eyes begin to fail, followed by the hearing and finally the heart.

Whether to have your vet put the dog to sleep should only become a concern if the dog is suffering or if it becomes a real burden. Some dogs live to be 13 years or older, age gracefully, and then die peacefully and naturally. This will undoubtedly be a most painful loss, and in all probability the only grief that dog ownership will bring you.

The End

The question of disposing of the remains does arise. Some people have their veterinarian handle this task, other with strong emotional ties are desirous of a lasting memento. This need seems to have created a new commercial endeavor—the pet cemetery and pet coffins (see Chapter X). We know a family that is very active in the dog fancy—owns perhaps up to 40 dogs at one time, shows, breeds, grooms, etc.—and they have their favorite buried in the back yard under a special marker. Time will tell how you personally wish to handle this delicate matter.

What Next?

To ease the inevitable loss, consider getting another dog—perhaps a puppy—to keep your senior citizen company during his declining years. Frequently a young playmate instills new vim into an older pet and you may see frolicking and playing like never before. Avoid jealousy by still letting the older one have his own possessions, special spot and your love and attention. If you handle this successfully the results can be fantastic; your dog has a companion and when old age finally takes its toll you are not totally alone. The other solution is to adopt another dog after your pet departs. However, the difficulty is that finding the right one is often not so easy or so quick and with a saddened heart you may not be as discriminating and objective as you would wish. In any case, do get another dog! Don't believe that because of the grief just suffered that you won't do it again! Nonsense! If you've enjoyed dog ownership and all its rewarding experiences then by all means start anew. The next endeavor may be even more satisfying and enjoyable.

Dog Insurance

There is only one company that will write life insurance on a dog and that is Lloyd's of London. The rate is 13 per cent per hundred dollars of valuation. Thus, a dog valued at $200 would require an annual premium of $26.

Very few companies will insure your dog against theft and those that do will only do so if you transfer all your insurance to them. Proving theft is also extremely difficult.

Home owners insurance usually covers your dog for liability. If your dog bites someone or damages property, your insurance should cover the expenses.

At the present time there are no top line insurance companies which provide accident or health insurance for dogs.

BRUTUS–THE DOG WITH THE $230 LEG

This true story gives insight into the trials and tribulations of dog ownership.

IT WAS 6 P.M. on a rainy Friday in March when our 90-pound German Shepherd, fond friend of two bitches who live next door, crashed under the chain-link fence surrounding our back yard, to give chase to an imprudent Lothario half his size. It seems "the girls" were both in heat, and Brutus, self-appointed defender of virginity, had stood for all he was going to stand for.

Leaving dinner on the stove and two half-bathed children in the tub, I raced out the front door to see both dogs streaking full tilt toward the state highway at the end of our street. The squeal of brakes, the crash and the screaming of an injured animal came as no shock, for traffic was fast and heavy that night, and both dogs had obviously been heedless of anything but the chase.

Passing a helpful neighbor, I hollered something about getting the kids out of the tub and continued full speed to the head of the block. It was Brutus, all right. Thrown across four lanes of traffic by the impact, he was lying on the far side of the road. He seemed to be quiet then, lying on his right side, head up, and bleeding slightly from the mouth and the left hip.

"Dear God," I thought, "do I dare touch him?" I didn't relish being bitten by a panicky dog, but I had to see how badly he was hurt. The blood in his mouth seemed to be from a gash in his tongue, but the hip was obviously more serious.

"No ambulance available," called a neighbor who had rung up the vet. "You'll have to bring him in!" . . . And my husband not home yet.

Thank heaven for neighbors. One having rescued my children from imminent drowning, another had actually managed to find my purse and car keys (no mean feat in itself), and was maneuvering our station wagon into a driveway about ten yards from where Brutus lay. And believe it or not, I think he knew I couldn't carry him, because that dog managed to drag himself to the car and climb in on his own. Twenty minutes later, the X-ray revealed that his upper left rear leg was in nine pieces.

The following day, having consulted with several colleagues, our own vet called us in.

"There's no one here who wants to tackle that leg," he said. "The only man I know who may be able to save it is Dr. Wade Brinker at Michigan State."

My husband and I gaped blankly at him for a moment, and I finally managed to gulp, "You mean fly Dr. Brinker here?"

"No," he responded, "take the dog up there."

And so it was that the following Monday I set off on the 250-mile drive to East Lansing with our tranquilized dog and his leg in assorted pieces in the rear of our station wagon. He wasn't so tranquil, however, that he didn't raise the devil himself when we had a flat on the Indiana Tollway, and a Good Samaritan approached the car to lend a hand. My mother, who had volunteered to accompany me, and I hadn't even managed to get the spare out.

Late that afternoon, weary but relieved, we left the clinic, with the good doctor's assurances that he would call us immediately after the surgery.

Weeks of waiting followed, with our hopes rising each day, as Brutus continued to improve. They had inserted an eight-inch plate in his leg, and aside from the problem of the bones knitting, there was still a danger from post-operative infection, and a collapsed lung.

Finally it was home-coming! After two months in a cage, innumerable shots, tests and X-rays by strangers, would he be the same good-natured dog we had left with them nine weeks ago? That question, unspoken, lay between us all the way to East Lansing.

"He's weak," the doctor warned us. "And we've tranquilized him for the trip home." "Of course," I smiled, recalling the tranquilized, three-legged dog who had been ready to tear into a helpful stranger on the Indiana Tollway.

And out he staggered, scruffy, dirty, pitifully thin, and a bit foggy-looking. Then he saw us and such paroxysms of delight racked his body that he would collapse in a heap, only to struggle up again, fighting the drug, jumping and leaping in a fit of happiness.

Months have gone by, and each day that passes I watch our pet running, leaping, twisting with the artless grace some large dogs have, as he retrieves a toy thrown by the children. There is not a trace of a limp. And I marvel anew at the miracle of skill, patience and affection, on the part of Dr. Brinker and his staff, that gave us back our dog again, whole and normal and healthy in body, and —more important—in spirit as well. *Mary Becker*

DOGS IN ART

MAN has been drawing and painting animals since pre-historic times. Dogs being man's helpers and companions have figured prominently in artist's works. Actually, any art collection of consequence will contain paintings and sculptures depicting dogs.

The following paintings, all from the Prado Museum, Madrid, Spain, are representative of dogs portrayed in the world of art.

The Royal Family
by Diego Velázquez De Silva

Portrayal of an intimate setting in the royal palace including the faithful dog.

The Parasol by Francisco de Goya

A happy, sunny scene Goya painted with joy and naturally included an adorable lap dog.

Cardinal-Prince Don Fernando de Austria
by Diego Velázquez De Silva
Spanish royalty was often painted with a loyal hunting dog.

Shooting Party by Francisco de Goya
Sporting dogs have been teamed with hunters for hundreds of years. These dogs are undoubtedly ancesters of today's Spaniels.

Hunting Diana by Paul de Vos
Even mythological characters have their dogs.

Deer Pursued by a Pack of Hounds by Paul de Vos
These dogs appear to be more ferocious than today's hounds.

Dogs and Hunting Tools by Francisco de Goya
Dogs Goya portrays exemplifying the loyalty and devotion so highly prized in a sporting dog.

Hunting the Bull by Paul de Vos
The dogs de Vos shows in this scene actually do not resemble any of our pure breds today.

Spanish painters used children of nobility and small dogs as frequent subjects for their canvases. This small dog may be a Papillon or a Toy Spaniel.

Deer Hunting by Paul de Vos
Packs of dogs were used to hunt wild animals in Spain during the 17th Century. This was a popular sport indulged in by the monarchs.

CHAPTER VI
BREEDING/PREGNANCY/PUPPIES

SHOULD YOU BREED YOUR DOG?

FOR the professional breeder, this is primarily a question of genetics. For the non-professional, it is also a personal question of whether you want the additional work, excitement, and involvement that goes with breeding: 1) finding a suitable stud, 2) mating the dogs, 3) special care for the pregnant female, 4) staying at home around the time of birth, 5) helping care for the puppies, and 6) selling the puppies. The financial aspect must also be considered. Sometimes there are stud fees, vet fees, and then no living puppies.

Nevertheless, breeding can be a most enjoyable and rewarding experience. The difficulties encountered before the birth of the puppies are forgotten when the joys of watching cuddly pups frolic, eat, and sleep begin. Also, watching your female suddenly and naturally become a fine mother is a heartwarming experience. The children can become involved with the care of the puppies if you want to make this a family project.

An important factor to consider is the timing of the birth of the litter. There are many responsibilities involved in the birth and care of the litter—indicating that much time and energy is needed in order to provide proper care. Keep in mind that the gestation period is from 60 to 63 days. After the birth, the mother usually takes good care of her puppies, but supervision is needed to make sure all the pups are healthy, eating well and resting enough. Once the pups are weaned, they must be fed several times a day and soiled newspapers must be changed often.

If the litter is more than two puppies, small whelping quarters are soon outgrown. Large breeds grow very rapidly and if they aren't sold by eight weeks, they need a sizeable area. Some novice breeders have had to give away fine dogs because they didn't have enough room to keep them until they could be sold.

Before you even consider whether you have the time, money, space, and patience to start breeding, the genetic qualities of your bitch must be honestly evaluated. If she has serious faults, it would be best not to breed her, as these faults would be genetically carried on to her young. If she has no basic faults and is a healthy dog with a pleasant temperament, breeding can be considered.

There is work, planning, cost, and effort involved if the job is going to be done correctly. If the true love of dogs and wishing to further the improvement of the breed isn't your main goal, then you really shouldn't go into it. For the amateur, there is usually little, if any, profit to be made. Most amateur breeders consider this their hobby and operate at a loss. To become a professional requires extensive experience and a sizeable investment in order to have quality breeding stock and the adequate facilities of a true business venture.

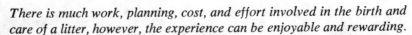

There is much work, planning, cost, and effort involved in the birth and care of a litter, however, the experience can be enjoyable and rewarding.

THE BREEDING PROCESS

Selecting the Male

UNLESS you are actively involved in the dog world, you may not know a good stud for your bitch. You can get help from your vet, from the breeder who sold you your dog, or from your local or national specialty breed organization. You should be able to get advice on whether to line breed, outcross, or possibly inbreed.

Inbreeding—This is the mating of very close relatives—father to daughter, brother to sister, mother to son. The novice or amateur breeder should not attempt this type of breeding. Inbreeding accentuates faults and is *not a good practice.*

Linebreeding—This is the mating of more distant relatives. Close linebreeding results in more predictable traits in the puppies.

Outcrossing—This is the mating of previously unrelated dogs of the same breed. Breeders usually use this method when they want to correct a fault or when they want to introduce another strain.

It is important to keep your breeding purposes in mind. Are you trying to get better hunting dogs, better show dogs, or dogs with fine temperament for children? Different purposes should result in a different selection of your stud.

This is just a very brief discussion of a complex subject. Those readers who wish to work on improving the breed should do a great deal of research in genetics and study what previous research findings have revealed. Breeding dogs can be most rewarding if done properly. Disappointments and needless expensive mistakes can be avoided by a careful approach.

The Stud

Locating a good stud dog for your bitch is of vital importance. Where you live can influence how difficult this may be. Sometimes if there isn't a quality stud available in your locale, the bitch must be transported to the stud, by rail or air.

Finding the stud can be accomplished by talking to people knowledgeable about dogs—such as breeders, handlers, your vet. All the investigating must be done prior to the time of your bitch's heat.

Once the stud has been selected, arrangements for the mating should be made. The best time to bring the bitch will be decided by her heat cycle. There is now a simple fertility test where Tes-tape is used to deter-

mine whether the bitch has ovulated. Many stud owners like to have the bitch arrive a day or so before the actual mating so that she can relax and be more at ease. Often they will keep a bitch for a few days so that the mating can be repeated. The details as to when to bring her to the stud, and how long to leave her, should be worked out in advance.

Stud Fee

The financial arrangement with the stud's owner should be discussed prior to the time of mating. Some stud owners prefer to be paid a set fee for this service, and they will usually give a repeat service if no living puppies result. Other stud owners ask for one or even two puppies, and they will usually specify that they want the "pick of the litter." Champion studs (those dogs that are already champions) usually get a higher fee than non-champions. Supply and demand also affect the fee. Some studs will only be bred to "approved bitches." That is, if the stud's owner doesn't feel the bitch is fine enough to breed, stud service won't be given.

Stud Service Certificate
(SIGNED GUARANTEE OF MATING)

This is to certify that: Certificate No._____

THE BITCH *MAR-ELS CREAM PUFF*
Breed *WEST HIGHLAND TERRIER* Registration No. *R-441969*
Owned by *Mrs. Susan K. Bernstein*
Address _____ *Glencoe, Ill.*
Was bred to my STUD DOG *Ch. Wig Mac Name Sak* Reg. No. *R-223895*
Date bred *DEC 9-10-11* 19*68* Due to whelp *FEB 9-10-11* 19*69*
Cash Fee $____Received Full Paym't $ *100* Rec'd PART paym't $_____
Additional Conditions:_____

_____

CONDITIONS OF SERVICE (and a part of this contract)

No fee refunded in whole or in part.
A guarantee of actual mating (and "tie") only is made and not of pregnancy or of puppies living or dead.
If bitch fails to be in whelp (pregnancy), the owner must give notice to me not later than fifty days after date of mating. A RETURN SERVICE will be given to the same stud without charge, at the next heat (and only this next best). If there is no pregnancy, owner of bitch to pay all express and shipping charges both ways. If such notice is given, the right to a return service is forfeited.
If my stud dies, is sold, or otherwise not available, I have the right to mate the bitch with one of my other studs, my choice, unless both parties agree mutually on another choice.
If bitch changes ownership, right of full return service is at my option.
In order to assure myself of the pregnancy condition of the bitch, the right to see and examine her is granted.
If puppy is to be received instead of cash fee, I will

make my choice of litter—at age of 8 weeks. One puppy constitutes a litter and if there is only one puppy, regardless of sex, this puppy shall constitute my choice of litter.
If all puppies are born dead, or none survive to age of 8 weeks, I have the postponed right to choice of puppy thru mating at next heat to my stud, but a repeat service is at my option. NO cash compensation is made. If same condition occurs at second whelping, obligations of both parties are terminated. These rights (choice of puppy) are not affected by change of ownership of bitch.
It is specifically agreed hereby that the owner of the stud is not obligated to sign application for registration of this litter until and unless the stud fee has been paid in full for, in case of puppy fee, the stud owner has gotten possession of puppy or puppies as agreed).
Important — Any ADDITIONAL or SPECIAL AGREEMENTS, conditions or provisions are noted on the other side of this certificate, over my written signature.

Signed *Mrs. E. N. Fischer*
                    Owner of stud dog
Signed *Mrs. Susan Bernstein*
                    Owner of bitch

This form is the property of and is sold by DOG WORLD MAGAZINE, 469 E. Ohio St., Chicago 11.
It must not be copied or imitated in any way.

The Female—In Heat

Scientifically, the reproductive period is called the "estrus cycle" or the "heat period" or "in season." A female puppy will "come into heat" after six months of age. Some breeds, usually large ones, may be older. After the first heat, the others will follow at fairly regular six-month intervals. Illness and change of climate can alter this regularity. The first indication of the beginning of the heat period is a swelling of the external genitalia. This is followed in a few days by a slightly pinkish, liquidy discharge which gradually becomes a darker red in color. Some dogs are very meticulous, and you will barely be able to observe any discharge. Others are not so neat, and great care must be taken so they do not soil carpets and furniture. This bloody discharge continues from about a week to ten days. There are "sanitary belts" for dogs on the market if you should find this necessary. When the discharge begins to diminish, the female is ready for mating. She may be receptive for approximately two to 14 days. If you do not plan to mate your dog, *extreme* care must be used to prevent any accidental encounters. The urine of a female in heat has an odor which is very attractive to all male dogs. Their appearance on your doorstep may well be your first indication that your female is in heat. Many people board their female in a kennel for the duration of this

During her "heat period" the female is usually happiest when able to remain at home. Great care must be taken to prevent accidental matings.

period. Others drive their female some distance from the house so she can urinate without attracting all the neighborhood males to the house. The female in heat must never be left out alone. Even a fenced yard is not safe.

There are some products available which claim to remove this "odor" from the female in season. However, none of them seem to be 100 per cent effective.

Actually, the female is happiest when able to be home with you during this time. So, if you can exercise care that no unplanned meetings occur, heat is really no problem. Often the puppy's first heat is quite distressing to her. She may have cramps and feel very uncomfortable. Affection and understanding will help her to be more at ease during this time. While in "heat," your female will ask to go out quite frequently. She will be somewhat anxious and may not be in the mood to play or frolic. Her appetite might increase. Such behavior is temporary and quite normal.

Mating the Female

Accidental

If an unplanned mating does occur, your vet can be of great assistance. Raising mongrel puppies is expensive and unnecessary! Your vet can give the female an injection which will end the pregnancy and will, in no way, prevent her from having future litters.

Planned

Should you intend to breed your female, planning must be done well in advance. Most dog authorities recommend not breeding at the first heat. Thus, the approximate date of ensuing heats should be calculated after the first.

The reproductive capacity of the female diminishes after age five, and, in many breeds, the reproductive cycle ends by age eight. However, there are great individual differences, and there have been numerous reports of bitches having litters well past this age.

Spaying

When puppies are not desired at any time, it is usually advisable to spay the female. This is an operation performed by the veterinarian which involves the removal of the ovaries. Today, when carried out in a modern animal hospital, this is a relatively safe operation. It is generally agreed that the best time for this procedure is after the dog has reached its full growth and not before. Spaying should, in no way, affect the dog's temperament or personality. It was once believed that dogs that had been spayed would become excessively fat. However, it has been found that this obesity is due to overfeeding and lack of exercise.

Bitches that have been spayed have a lower incidence of cancer of the reproductive system. Thus, this is a real advantage to the procedure. The "heat cycle" ceases, and the dog is safe from future pregnancies. Since this operation is irreversible, the female can never have puppies.

The cost of this operation will vary in different areas of the country. The cost should be weighed in terms of the advantages and other savings—no boarding while in heat—no accidental pregnancies!

The Male

As the owner of a male, you may wonder if you should use your dog as a stud. It seems like a relatively easy and appealing idea. For just a little work you can get a fee or a puppy. However, there is usually more to it than what meets the eye. First of all, some owners of male dogs find that the dog's personality changes when he is used for stud. Stud dogs can become very independent, not as affectionate as they previously were, and they may desire to roam. Most dog owners who have a single male, primarily as a pet, do not use them for stud as a general practice. However, there are occasions when a fine male is used, and it doesn't seem to do any real harm.

The basic question is whether the dog is of such quality to warrant his use as a stud. The purposes of the mating should be kept in mind. If the male is an outstanding hunting dog or a champion in conformation or obedience, it seems only natural to wish to perpetuate his remarkable qualities. A dog used for stud should himself be well-bred; he should have a good temperament and a constructionally sound build.

The care of the stud dog is most important. He should receive at least one good meal per day, and, if working hard, he should receive two. The meal should be well-balanced and high in protein. Ample exercise to keep him physically fit is vital.

Most breeders feel that ten months is the youngest age at which to begin using a male dog as a stud. The first mating must be handled carefully so that the novice stud can be taught everything that is necessary. It is best to use an experienced bitch the first few times. Mating no more frequently than once a month until the age of two years is recommended. After the age of two, a healthy stud can be used once a week. However, if he shows signs of tiring or disinterest, he should be rested for longer periods.

The fee for stud service is based on the average fee being charged for a specific breed. A stud who is a proven sire and a champion will command a higher fee than a non-champion.

It is the responsibility of the owner of the stud dog to care for the bitch while she is in his kennel or home for the mating. This means providing sleeping quarters, food, and exercise, as well as strict protection from unplanned matings.

If the use of the stud is to be a "genuine business enterprise," then he should probably be shown either for conformation, obedience, or field trials. Advertising in dog magazines would also be advisable.

All this work requires time, patience, and money. For the average dog owner, it is probably not the best idea. Even large kennels will often use other studs rather than maintaining their own.

The Mating

An experienced stud dog and an experienced brood bitch may need little assistance in mating, but, for the inexperienced, help is sometimes necessary.

The female will allow the male to mount her only when she is at the stage in her heat cycle when conception can occur. If she is watched carefully, this time is not too difficult to determine. She will become quite flirtatious and allow the male to make advances. It is considered advisable to repeat the mating twice. This repetition seems to give a better guarantee of conception. Although each female is different, noted dog authorities recommend breeding the 13th day and on alternate days until she again refuses.

The mating process itself should be handled slowly and carefully, allowing the bitch and stud to get acquainted in a controlled environment at first so that no fights can occur. Once they have familiarized themselves and seem interested, they can be allowed to come together. If the bitch is very nervous and aggressive, it is wise to use a muzzle so that she won't bite the male.

In the normal progression of mating, the male will mount the female and after the penis penetrates the bitch, the dogs will become "tied." This "tie" may last from just a few minutes up to an hour. Although a long-lasting tie is not necessary for conception, it is wise for the breeder to try to keep the dogs together for at least five minutes.

If there is a significant difference in size between the male and female, they may need special assistance. A male that is small may need a platform on which to stand and toy breeds are most easily mated on a table.

On occasion, the female will take a distinct dislike to a particular stud and not allow him to approach her. In such a case, it is wise, if possible, to use another stud.

Another problem is that sometimes the stud is not able at first to penetrate a willing female. It is best to separate them. Give the stud a rest of an hour or two and then, with much encouragement, let him try again. Never allow the stud to tire himself excessively in unsuccessful attempts.

After a mating, both dogs should be allowed to rest. Therefore, it is best not to rush the female home immediately after mating.

PREGNANCY

Care of the Expectant Mother

THE normal length of gestation (pregnancy) is 63 days. However, puppies can be healthy if born a few days earlier or later.

The care of the prospective mother is most important. She should be free of internal and external parasites. Worming should be done before the mating. She should be well fed but not overweight. During the first few weeks, she can have her regular diet, which can be supplemented with extra protein foods and vitamins. After the fifth week, she should be allowed additional food; however, she should not be allowed to get fat, as this will make her delivery very difficult. Cooked eggs, milk, and meat, in addition to a well-balanced commercial dog food, will give her the extra protein that she needs.

Plenty of exercise in the form of walking is best. Toward the end of her pregnancy, she should have several short walks rather than one overly long one. Undue stress and excitement should be avoided. Jumping and climbing stairs should not be allowed the last few days prior to whelping. She should be kept clean and well-groomed. The breast area should be clipped if necessary and any discharge from the vulva should be washed regularly.

False Pregnancy

False pregnancy can occur with or without a mating. The bitch develops all the signs of pregnancy—swollen nipples, enlarged abdomen, increased appetite—and yet she has not conceived.

Reabsorption

Sometimes a bitch will be pregnant and then, for some still unknown reason, will reabsorb the puppies.

Signs of Pregnancy

During the first few weeks, it is quite impossible to tell if the bitch is pregnant. After the fifth week, there is often an enlargement of the nipples. Then, after the sixth week, there may be a visible widening of the abdominal area. At this time, your vet can usually confirm the pregnancy.

WHELPING

FOR the novice breeder, this is a most exciting and somewhat frightening event, but, with proper planning and a clear understanding of what will and can occur, it need not be overwhelming.

It would probably be wise to take your dog to the vet to confirm the pregnancy. This confirmation is usually not possible until she is in the sixth week. Therefore, most authorities suggest that a high protein diet, vitamins, and exercise be administered from the breeding until delivery. When you visit the vet, he will check her to make sure she is in good health, and this is also a good time to ask for any suggestions that he may have for the whelping. If the bitch is very hairy, he may clip some of her hair around the nipples and the vulva area.

At least ten days before the due date, all the equipment for the whelping should be gathered. A *whelping box* of adequate size for the mother and pups should be placed in a warm and quiet place. Be certain it is large enough and that the sides are high enough to keep the puppies in, and that the mother can come and go comfortably. *Newspapers* should be saved, as they will be used in large amounts. Sterile *scissors, thread, rectal thermometer, hot water bottle, small towel-lined box* for the puppies, and clean *turkish towels* should all be readied.

To determine quite reliably when the puppies will arrive, check the bitch's temperature rectally at the same time at least once every day, beginning a week before she is due. Preferably, this can be done twice

WHELPING CALENDAR

Locate the date your bitch was bred in the left-hand column
and the expected whelping date is in the right-hand column.

Date bred	Date due to whelp	Date bred	Date due to whelp	Date bred	Date due to whelp	Date bred	Date due to whelp	Date bred	Date due to whelp	Date bred	Date due to whelp	Date bred	Date due to whelp	Date bred	Date due to whelp	Date bred	Date due to whelp	Date bred	Date due to whelp	Date bred	Date due to whelp	Date bred	Date due to whelp
January	March	February	April	March	May	April	June	May	July	June	August	July	September	August	October	September	November	October	December	November	January	December	February
1	5	1	5	1	3	1	3	1	3	1	3	1	2	1	3	1	3	1	3	1	3	1	2
2	6	2	6	2	4	2	4	2	4	2	4	2	3	2	4	2	4	2	4	2	4	2	3
3	7	3	7	3	5	3	5	3	5	3	5	3	4	3	5	3	5	3	5	3	5	3	4
4	8	4	8	4	6	4	6	4	6	4	6	4	5	4	6	4	6	4	6	4	6	4	5
5	9	5	9	5	7	5	7	5	7	5	7	5	6	5	7	5	7	5	7	5	7	5	6
6	10	6	10	6	8	6	8	6	8	6	8	6	7	6	8	6	8	6	8	6	8	6	7
7	11	7	11	7	9	7	9	7	9	7	9	7	8	7	9	7	9	7	9	7	9	7	8
8	12	8	12	8	10	8	10	8	10	8	10	8	9	8	10	8	10	8	10	8	10	8	9
9	13	9	13	9	11	9	11	9	11	9	11	9	10	9	11	9	11	9	11	9	11	9	10
10	14	10	14	10	12	10	12	10	12	10	12	10	11	10	12	10	12	10	12	10	12	10	11
11	15	11	15	11	13	11	13	11	13	11	13	11	12	11	13	11	13	11	13	11	13	11	12
12	16	12	16	12	14	12	14	12	14	12	14	12	13	12	14	12	14	12	14	12	14	12	13
13	17	13	17	13	15	13	15	13	15	13	15	13	14	13	15	13	15	13	15	13	15	13	14
14	18	14	18	14	16	14	16	14	16	14	16	14	15	14	16	14	16	14	16	14	16	14	15
15	19	15	19	15	17	15	17	15	17	15	17	15	16	15	17	15	17	15	17	15	17	15	16
16	20	16	20	16	18	16	18	16	18	16	18	16	17	16	18	16	18	16	18	16	18	16	17
17	21	17	21	17	19	17	19	17	19	17	19	17	18	17	19	17	19	17	19	17	19	17	18
18	22	18	22	18	20	18	20	18	20	18	20	18	19	18	20	18	20	18	20	18	20	18	19
19	23	19	23	19	21	19	21	19	21	19	21	19	20	19	21	19	21	19	21	19	21	19	20
20	24	20	24	20	22	20	22	20	22	20	22	20	21	20	22	20	22	20	22	20	22	20	21
21	25	21	25	21	23	21	23	21	23	21	23	21	22	21	23	21	23	21	23	21	23	21	22
22	26	22	26	22	24	22	24	22	24	22	24	22	23	22	24	22	24	22	24	22	24	22	23
23	27	23	27	23	25	23	25	23	25	23	25	23	24	23	25	23	25	23	25	23	25	23	24
24	28	24	28	24	26	24	26	24	26	24	26	24	25	24	26	24	26	24	26	24	26	24	25
25	29	25	29	25	27	25	27	25	27	25	27	25	26	25	27	25	27	25	27	25	27	25	26
26	30	26	30	26	28	26	28	26	28	26	28	26	27	26	28	26	28	26	28	26	28	26	27
27	31	27	30 (May)	27	29	27	29	27	29	27	29	27	28	27	29	27	29	27	29	27	29	27	28
28	1 (Apr.)	28	2 (May)	28	30	28	30	28	30	28	30	28	29	28	30	28	30	28	30	28	30	28	1 (Mar.)
29	2			29	31	29	1 (July)	29	31	29	31	29	30	29	31	29	1 (Dec.)	29	31	29	31	29	2
30	3			30	1 (June)	30	2	30	1 (Aug.)	30	1 (Sep.)	30	1 (Oct.)	30	1 (Nov.)	30	2	30	1 (Jan.)	30	1 (Feb.)	30	3
31	4			31	2			31	2			31	2	31	2			31	2			31	4

Courtesy Gaines Dog Research Center.

139

Everything is in readiness for the whelping—the whelping bed, newspaper, scissors, alcohol, towels, and you to give moral support.

a day, morning and evening. The temperature will drop about twelve hours before whelping. When her temperature drops, place her in the whelping box and stay with her. As the whelping time comes closer, the bitch will probably do a great deal of nesting. She will tear the paper in her whelping box or she may find another spot which she favors and start building a "nest." Encourage her to get accustomed to the box that you have provided and to sleep in it for several days before the big event.

When labor begins, stay with her constantly as she will need your encouragement. Since this is quite an emotional time for most dogs, it is best not to have any additional excitement; thus, limit the number of "visitors" into the delivery room. Try to keep as calm and quiet as possible. A puppy should be born about an hour after labor begins. Signs of labor differ between breeds and even between dogs in the same breed. Some bitches will whine and cry, and some will lie quietly, get up and scratch around and dig in their whelping box, and then suddenly push out a puppy without making a sound.

When a bitch strains hard for a long period of time without making any progress, there may be a problem. If nothing happens after one hour, call the vet and have him advise you. Don't wait too long—serious complications can result, such as the loss of pups and/or mother. The vet may want to see the bitch or he may tell you what to do. He may want to administer a shot to help things along or possibly a Caesarean section may be needed. This is a surgical procedure usually performed in a veterinary hospital. The bitch is given an anesthetic, and the pups are removed from the womb. This is necessary if the bitch is too small for normal delivery, if a pup is stuck in the

birth canal, or if the pup's head is too large. When such an operation is performed by a vet under proper conditions, it is not a dangerous operation. Usually the bitch can be taken right home afterwards and can nurse the puppies. Antibiotics to prevent infection are usually prescribed, which may be administered by injection or orally.

Some pups may arrive shortly after labor begins and others, with the vet's approval, may not be born for a day or two. The important factor is to have someone available to help her if necessary and to be certain that everything is going along correctly. Usually, a pup is born head first, but sometimes a pup may be breech—that is, come in another position rather than head first. Thus, the bitch may have difficulty, and you may have to assist her.

If part of the puppy is visible and yet keeps slipping back into the birth canal, then take hold of the puppy and pull gently in rhythm with each contraction. The membrane makes the pup wet and slippery so getting a firm hold may be quite difficult. Use a small piece of towel if you need a better grasp. Do not pull too hard or you may damage the pup.

As soon as the puppy is expelled, the membraneous sac in which it is enclosed should be torn open and removed and the umbilical cord cut. Then, the mother should lick the puppy clean and push it up to one of her teats to nurse. Again, you may have to assist here as some new mothers ignore their children. Quickly but gently dry and warm the puppy and place it by the mother to nurse.

After the whelping is finished, the mother is going to need a good cleaning. The breasts and bottom area should be washed with lukewarm water and mild soap, and then rinsed well. This will remove the discharges clinging to the mother from the delivery and will make for more sanitary conditions for her litter.

Reasons for a Caesarian Section

A puppy may be misplaced—sideways instead of head or feet first. It may be too large and thus be unable to move down the birth canal. On occasion, a puppy is dead, becomes stuck, and blocks the passage of the other puppies.

It is possible for a bitch to have more than one Caesarian operation. There are known cases of bitches having six such operations.

Assisting the Delivery

Surprisingly, instinct does not guide all bitches. Many are thoroughly confused as to what is happening to them and what they should be doing. It is not at all unusual for a bitch to expel a puppy and then to just sit there licking herself without doing her maternal job. The new mother *should* quickly tear open the sac which surrounds the puppy, bite off the um-

NEST BOX FOR WHELPING

A nest box has a lot to offer in good puppy management. Normally when the bitch approaches whelping time, she becomes restless and tries to find a secluded spot. A nest box seems to answer her needs and affords her a place to be alone and away from other dogs. It is normally placed in the pen five to seven days before whelping is expected. If the weather is cold, a heating pad is placed in the bottom of the nest box to help keep the pups from chilling.

In the illustration at right notice that all of the edges which the dogs can chew on are protected with metal strips. The top of the box is removable for easy cleaning and access to the pups. Construction is of one-half inch waterproof plywood. The dimensions of the box vary with the size of the dog.

The drawings below show the door opening with the metal shield. This shield is used in the lower part of the doorway as a barrier to keep the pups in the whelping box during the first three weeks; then it is removed. The whelping box is easy and inexpensive to build. It can be scrubbed and disinfected for good sanitation. With proper care, it will last for many years.

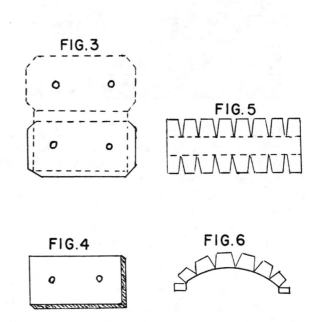

Size of Dogs	Box Dimensions				
	A	B	C	D	E
50 lbs. or less	24″	32″	21″	9″	14″
50 to 80 lbs.	28″	36″	23″	9″	15″
Tall dogs such as Greyhounds.....	28″	40″	30″	9″	19″

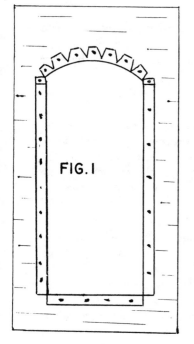

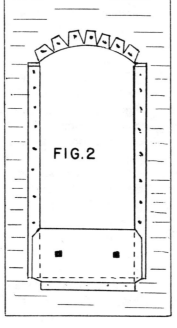

FIG.3

FIG.5

FIG.4

FIG.6

Fig. 1 shows the door opening with the metal strip covering all edges. Fig. 2 shows the shield in place. Notice how it is held in place by the metal overlap. Fig. 3 is the metal portion of the shield before it is folded over the wood. The one-half inch board, Fig. 4, is covered on both sides and the top with the metal (Fig. 3). Two small bolts hold them together. The metal being longer than the board forms a groove which enables the shield to be held in place in the opening. The metal corners are clipped off to prevent injury from the sharp points and to make it easier to put in and remove the shield from the opening. For smaller, short-legged dogs the shield should be 2½ inches high instead of 5 inches. In order for the metal to be curved on the top of the opening, it should be notched as shown in Fig. 5. Notch into the line where the metal is to be folded. The fold will be along the dotted line. The top line of the opening does not have to be curved, but can be straight. Fig. 6 shows the notched metal strip, cut, folded and ready to be nailed in place.

Courtesy Purina Pet Care Center, Ralston Purina Company

The new mother nursing her puppies—a healthy litter of four.

bilical cord and lick the puppy thoroughly to get it breathing and cleaned up. In your role as midwife be prepared to handle these matters if the mother neglects to do so. The most important thing is to quickly get the puppy out of the membrane sac in which it is enclosed at birth and to clear the lungs so that it can breathe. After removing the sac, cut the cord, rub the pup dry with a small turkish towel and hold it with its head downward and shake it gently. This should clear the lungs of fluid and help it to breathe. Too many puppy deaths have been attributed to respiratory failure which can be avoided. Fluid should be wiped off the puppy as it is expelled and the gentle downward shaking or swinging should be continued until no more fluid appears. Thoroughly drying the pup and keeping it warm is of utmost importance. The mother will probably eat the umbilical cord and the after birth which is perfectly natural and she should be allowed to do so as they seem to act as a laxative. If the litter is quite large it would be best to remove some of them so that she doesn't overdo a good thing. An afterbirth should be expelled after the delivery of each puppy. Any re-

maining within the uterus will cause infection and serious complications. Keep a paper and pencil near at hand to maintain an accurate record if the litter is large.

Frequently, there will be a little time between the births so that the new mother can rest and nurse her puppy. Once the straining of labor begins again, remove the puppies to the specially prepared puppy box close by. This is done in order to protect the pups from possible injury while the mother is giving birth. The box should be near enough, however, so that she can see and hear them for otherwise she may become needlessly concerned.

With the birth of each subsequent puppy the same procedure should be followed. If the mother is doing her part, don't interfere unless your services are needed. There may be times when a puppy is not breathing and the mother's licking and concern doesn't improve the situation. Take the puppy and rub it furiously with a towel to warm it and stimulate it. Shake it as described above. Continue working on it with rubbing and also proceed with mouth to mouth resuscitation. Open the pup's mouth and check for any obstruction.

Technique for Administering Mouth to Mouth Resuscitation

Put your mouth over the pup's nose and mouth and
(1) breathe into puppy's mouth

Yorkshire puppies and their mom on a most comfortable whelping bed. (Owned by Mrs. Dorothy Creeden.)

(2) inhale fresh air

(3) repeat.

Follow a regular breathing rhythm. Continue until breathing starts. Breathe gently as the puppies lungs are smaller.

When trouble arises it's so nice to have a veterinarian handy who can help you with: (1) oxygen—hold the oxygen mask over the pup's face for a few minutes (this is often quite successful), (2) an injection of adrenalin to stimulate respiration and the heart.

Difference of opinion exists as to how long it is wise to continue to attempt revival of a non-breathing pup. Some authors feel that it's never too late and to keep working vigorously until there is a response even if it takes hours. Most vets we queried felt that if the life processes didn't begin within a reasonable length of time after birth (approximately 15 minutes), even if the pup were revived, brain damage would have occurred. Since there is more to be gained from trying, it would be worthwhile to expend all the necessary time and energy to revive a "slow starting" puppy.

Most births are normal and follow a natural pattern. But one has to be prepared for any event. There are occasions when your bitch may expel an abnormal puppy. Remove it quickly so that the mother doesn't try to destroy it further or to eat it. When a bitch realizes that a pup is malformed or is going to die she may try to harm it. Sometimes bitches have been known to start this with one pup and then get hysterical and kill the entire litter. Such behavior is not usual but should be guarded against. If the bitch is highly agitated after the delivery and seems excessively rough with the pups—such as, biting them, ripping at their umbilical—then caution should be exercised. Separate her from the pups, if necessary, by putting them in their own heated, cozy box. Return them only for nursing every two hours until you see that the mother is acting normally. Consult your veterinarian—he may prescribe tranquilizers.

Usually during and after whelping, the bitch is quite tense, fearful, and overprotective of her new charges. Maintaining calm and quiet in her quarters at this time is highly recommended. Only family members should enter the nursery and they, too, should practice restraint. If the whelping box has been placed in a quiet and warm area, it is easy to maintain this necessary control. Veterinarians and breeders stress emphatically that for "preventative medicine" visitors should be kept from the "nursery" for several weeks. Infection spreads easily and avoiding unnecessary exposure is the wisest thing.

After you think the last pup has been born, consult with your veterinarian. He may wish to give the bitch an injection which would help to expel any matter still remaining in the uterus. Sometimes, there may even be another puppy.

Whelping is a strenuous experience for the bitch and she should get a tempting meal either between the delivery of pups or afterwards. She probably will not wish to leave her new charges so bring the food to her in the whelping box. Offer her some warm cereal with milk or cooked ground meat with broth —if she is reluctant to eat, coax her a little. Keeping her strength up at this point is most important for her and the nursing puppies. Allow her to go out to relieve herself. Probably it will be only for this purpose that she will leave her brood.

Compared to the human female the dog has a much quicker recuperation period. She is usually up and around all during whelping, running up and down stairs, immediately after and seemingly perfectly fit. Don't let this healthy appearance lull you into neglect. The postpartum period does have certain possible hazards. Beware of *eclampsia*—this is a type of convulsive paralysis which manifests itself by the dog shaking violently, its movement paralyzed, and high fever. Eclampsia is caused by a deficiency of blood calcium. Prompt administration of an injection of calcium gluconate should result in a remission of symptoms. Death can result if treatment is not initiated rapidly.

Peritonitis is an inflammation of the lining of the

abdomen that can result if the bitch does not completely expel everything from her uterus and birth canal. Signs of the existence of such a condition are: high fever and a greenish foul smelling vaginal discharge. Antibiotics may save the mother.

Mastitis is an infection of the breasts. It is another serious problem to be aware of. Should the breasts become red, swollen, hot and tender, immediate action is necessary. Puppies should not be allowed to nurse as they can become infected and die. Pups should be hand fed and the mother seen and treated by the veterinarian.

PUPPIES
Hand Feeding Puppies

There are occasions when the hand feeding of puppies becomes necessary. The possible reasons may be death or sickness of the mother, insufficient milk because of the litter size, or neglect by the mother. When hand feeding is indicated, your job of caring for the puppies can become quite an ordeal. Here is the best procedure to follow:

(1) Use a fully prepared formula created for this purpose such as Borden's Esbilac.
(2) Feed it warmed. Keep unused portion refrigerated.
(3) There are several methods of feeding—a dropper, a small nipple and bottle made for puppies, or a stomach tube.

Once the technique of using the feeding tube is mastered, it is the fastest, easiest, and probably the most reliable method. The vet can teach you how to insert

---

HOW TO TUBE FEED A PUPPY
Equipment
1. A 20 cc plastic disposable syringe.
2. One number eight infant feeding tube.
3. Prepared formula (Esbilac).

Have your veterinarian demonstrate the insertion of the tube the first time. At this time, mark the feeding tube to indicate the accurate depth of insertion necessary in order to place the formula into the stomach. Then, when feeding time arrives, attach the tube to the tip of the syringe and suck the warmed formula to fill the syringe with the required amount. Hold the puppy with one hand and gently insert the tube over the tongue and down into the stomach up to the mark on the tube. Very slowly, release the necessary amount of formula. Then, carefully withdraw the tube.

---

a feeding tube into the puppies' stomach and then to inject the required amount of formula into it with a syringe. In this manner, an entire litter can be fed in a short span of time and you can be certain of the amount ingested.

Using the dropper is a very slow process. The puppy must be held in an upright position and the milk is dripped onto the tongue and then swallowed. Great caution must be taken to prevent any liquid from getting into the lungs as this will result in pneumonia and death. There is also the fact that it is difficult to know how much milk the puppy has actually ingested as so much drips away. Using the scale before and after each feeding is the only way to know with certainty and this can become rather time consuming.

The nipple and bottle is also a slow feeding method which has the danger of allowing fluid to get into the lungs.

Since some controversy exists as to the frequency with which to feed puppies, your vet should be consulted. The amount to feed is determined by the size of the dog and he will advise you on this matter as well.

Be sure each puppy gets some colostrum from the mother. This is the watery looking substance which is the "first milk" that is so important in providing the pups with the vital immunities against infectious disease.

Post Whelping

After whelping, the bitch will have quite a copious blood-stained discharge for a week or two. This uterine discharge is normal and should stop after two weeks. The dam's temperature should return to normal at least forty-eight hours after whelping. If it is raised, an infection may exist and antibiotic treatment may be necessary.

Feeding the Bitch after Whelping

After delivery, the bitch will require a 50 to 100% increase in her normal food intake. For now, she must meet her own body needs as well as provide for her nursing puppies. Her diet should be rich in protein and provide ample liquid to help in the milk production. Eggs, meat, and milk can be added to enrich her diet. While she is nursing, she can be allowed to eat as much as she wants without fear of her becoming overweight.

Immediately after whelping, she may want her food brought to her in the whelping box—this should be done, because she is reluctant to leave her new litter. The first few days after whelping her diet can contain milk and milky preparations, such as cereal.

Often, bitches need to be coaxed to go out and relieve themselves during this time.

THE MATING, PREGNANCY AND BIRTH OF MISS PRISSY'S PUPPIES

Breeding your dog can be a real do-it-yourself project. This is a true story of how a novice breeder and inexperienced dogs successfully produced a beautiful litter.

MISS Prissy a black Labrador Retriever, came into our home when she was almost two years old. She is the sweetest, kindest and most gentle dog that I have ever seen. The most amazing aspect of her personality is her gentleness toward our children and other children.

After having had Miss Prissy for a year and a half and going through three periods of heat, we decided, or shall I say that I decided, that it was time for her to be mated and have a litter of puppies. It happened that in the neighborhood there was another black Labrador Retriever, whose owner was very interested

in having him used as a stud. The one condition for mating the two dogs was to make sure that they both had a good heritage. We exchanged papers (American Kennel Club papers) and, after examination, decided that Hogey would be a suitable father for Miss Prissy's pups.

On the appointed morning, Hogey arrived with a bow around his neck ready to do his job. Prissy was ready and quite excited. We proceeded to get them into the dog run and hoped that they would do what they were supposed to do, which we thought would happen immediately. (Neither had ever been mated.)

There was much playing around between the two dogs, many attempts by the male to climb on the back of the female, but unsuccessful tries for a connection or "tie." Finally we decided we had to enter into this union, so I held Prissy quietly and Hogey's owner lifted his front legs on Miss Prissy's back and held him up so that they could connect.

We finally succeeded in this process and the first "tie" was made. After about ten minutes, Hogey withdrew and he seemed exhausted whereas Miss Prissy was still quite playful. We made another date for the next morning; when we tried without success and made a date for later in the afternoon. The whole neighborhood turned out for the event. We had a successful "tie" at that time and then had another successful one the following morning. After each "tie," Hogey's owner and I were exhausted.

Now we had to wait for five weeks to determine whether all our work had been successful. The vet had advised us that this is the only way to determine whether it had worked. We watched and waited and finally took Prissy for a test. We were pretty sure that she was pregnant, because she seemed heavier in the stomach, as well as the fact that her nipples (there were ten) were growing larger. The vet confirmed the pregnancy and told us that she would have her puppies 63 days after the period of mating.

Approximately ten days before delivery, we took Prissy to the vet where she was X-rayed, given a bath and shaved so the puppies would have an easier time nursing from her nipples. The vet said he saw seven puppies but that there might be an eighth one hidden underneath the others.

To prepare for the event, we decided Prissy needed a whelping box. We took our specifications to a carpenter and had one made. The box had to be big enough to hold Prissy as well as her puppies. It also had to have a ledge built around the inner edges of the box so that the puppies would be able to lay near the wall and so that Prissy would not crush them. We began to give Prissy her food in the box so that she would become accustomed to it.

On the day before the birth, Prissy began to be fussy, nervous and scratched at everything. She ran around the house continuously and did not seem able to rest. This behavior continued through the evening and all night long. She went to the whelping box and tore papers up and made nests. At one point she took one of our children's stuffed dogs which has soft fur, placed it in her nest and licked it as if it was a real puppy. We watched her all night. I called the vet the

next morning, and he advised me it could happen anytime within the next 24 hours.

About 10:30 a.m., Prissy began to have contractions and we brought her to the whelping box. She had four or five very strong contractions and the first puppy appeared.

It was wrapped in a sac and had a long cord attached to it. Prissy cut the cord but did not open or cut the sac, and I felt that the puppy would suffocate so I cut the sac with scissors. After this Prissy took over by pulling the sac off and licking the puppy and eating the remains of the cord and sac. We then placed the puppy up to Prissy's nipples to nurse. When she began to have heavy contractions, we removed the puppy to another box, which was lined with turkish towels and a heating pad. Prissy proceeded to have four more puppies in the next hour and a half. She did all the work herself. In between the birth of each puppy, we put the others up to her to nurse and even though they could not see, they were able to find the nipples. After the first five were born, Prissy rested and then proceeded to have three more. At that point, we felt she had finished but we watched her for a while and when we were sure, we let her outside and then fed her a dish of ice cream and milk. She did not move away from the puppies for the next 24 hours except those few times when we let her outside. We felt that due to the number of puppies we would alternate nursing, four on and then the other four, which we tried to do at least once every hour. There were four girls and four boys, and all very black.

Prissy was very attentive to the puppies the first week, hardly leaving them except to go out for a few minutes. She cleaned up after them and there was never an odor in the room. The second week she continued to be attentive but the number of times the puppies nursed were fewer and Prissy left them for longer periods of time. The puppies were growing very fast at this time. The third week was her last week of being attentive. She seemed to lose her interest and the puppies seemed more hungry. We started feeding them baby formula and baby cereal but this presented problems for us because Prissy did not continue to clean up and lick the puppies clean. We had to move the whelping box to the garage, which was heated, as the odor was very strong.

At this point, we took Prissy to the vet and he gave her a shot to dry up her milk and the puppies were placed on puppy formula four times a day. This was a big job, but fortunately the weather was still fairly good and the feeding process could be done outside.

Six weeks after the puppies were born, we began to sell them and by the seventh week, seven were gone —we decided to keep one female.

Now that we have two dogs, we are content with having gone through this experience and we hope that others will have this opportunity. *Carol Gollob*

Pet Mania Miscellania

45.2 per cent of U.S. families own a cat, dog or both.
Average number of cats per family: 1.7
Average number of dogs per family: 1.3

THE PUPPIES

WHAT a surprise you'll have the first time you behold a newborn puppy. It's all wet, tiny, and really doesn't look anything like the breed standard. Don't panic. Their features will change and develop as they mature, even the color of their fur will change. For example, Dalmatian puppies are born without their spots. Sometimes puppies will have areas where fur is not present at first. Don't be overly concerned about these minor findings. If the puppy is healthy and well-formed, then wait for time to remove some of these youthful blemishes. However, if the pup is malformed

—and be sure this is so—then there is no sense in keeping it. At one time breeders would cut down the size of a litter by destroying those newborns who they felt were not "top" quality. Today, it is felt that a newly born puppy cannot be accurately evaluated. Sometimes the very one that you had intended to destroy may develop into a superior adult.

Weight

Weighing the pups at birth and then each day for the first week to ten days is good practice. By so doing, you can keep a close check on each pup and any that are not gaining sufficiently will come to your attention promptly. These should be allowed to nurse first so that the others don't push them aside. You may give them a supplemental bottle after each nursing period until they start to gain properly. Check with your vet as to the normal amount of weight gain desired for your breed.

> **REVIEW OF PUPPY CARE**
> 1. **Keep the babies warm and dry.**
> 2. **Watch their weight gain and, if necessary, give supplement feedings.**
> 3. **Keep the whelping box clean.**

"Crown Jewels Fiery Gold" very contented, looking over her new-born puppies just a few hours old. They are born white and at the age of three weeks, spots appear.

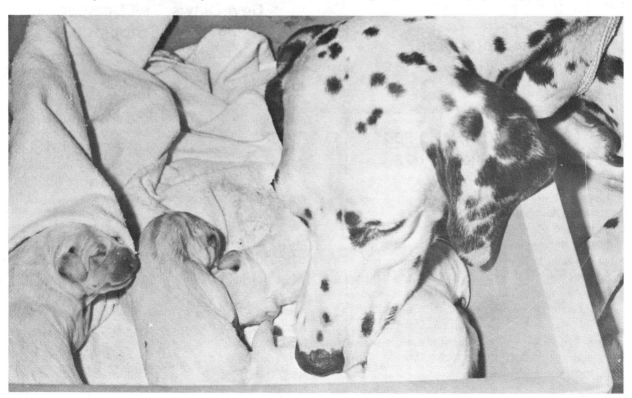

Temperature

Keeping the puppies warm is just as important as seeing that they are well-fed. The room should not only be warm, but also free from drafts. If the total room temperature cannot be maintained at 75 deg., then use well-protected heating pads. Take care that the cords are not exposed—dogs do have a tendency to chew on them. Another method of warming an area is to use a lamp. Place a room thermometer next to the whelping box so that you can be certain of the temperature in that spot.

Housekeeping

The whelping box itself should be kept dry and clean. After the births, remove all wet or soiled papers. The bottom of the box should be covered with several thick layers of newspaper. Some people like to stretch a towel across the bottom for extra warmth and softness. If you wish to do so, be sure to fasten it down well to prevent the pups from getting caught in or under it. The papers in the box should be changed as frequently as needed. For the first few weeks the mother usually is a terrific housekeeper. She will lick up any mess her children make. However, as they get older, this "clean-up patrol" will become your responsibility. If the nursery is not kept meticulously clean this becomes an invitation to infection and, needless to say, the odor can get rather overwhelming. Throw the soiled newspapers out of the house, otherwise your premises will rapidly develop a permeating reek.

Postnatal Care

After birth, most puppies are quite tired and may want to sleep. If it has been an easy delivery, the pup may wish to nurse immediately. The mother will usually lick the new puppy from head to toe to clean it up and to get its circulation going. The mother also must lick the puppy in order to help it to urinate and defecate.

A healthy, strong puppy should be able to suck well and satisfy his needs, sucking quietly, stroking the mother as it sucks. The rear nipples have the most milk and puppies having difficulties in getting enough to eat should be placed there. If a puppy is still not getting enough milk from the mother, supplemental feeding may be necessary. Puppies are both blind and deaf at birth; they do not open their eyes until about the tenth day.

Fading Puppies

This term is applied to puppies that are normal, healthy, and strong at birth, and then gradually sicken and die during the first week. The reason for this can be an infection in the puppies or in the mother which is being passed to the pups via the milk. That is why it is necessary to keep a close watch on the puppies and dam, to be certain that they are eating and growing—that they have fat, full tummies and are content. Sick puppies cry and crawl around aimlessly. Any signs of diarrhea should also be a warning. Contact your vet immediately if you see danger signals. Treatment immediately can often save you from needless loss.

Dew Claws, Tail Docking, and Ear Cropping

Your vet can remove your puppies dew claws. These are the "extra" nails slightly above the others, around ankle height. It is not necessary to remove them. However, they serve no useful purpose and just get in the way. This procedure is best done when the pup is four days old.

Many breeds require that their tails be docked for show purposes. This can be done at the same time as the removal of the dew claws. Again, since the docking should be done correctly, it should be handled by the vet.

A.K.C. Breeds Whose Tails Should Be Docked

Affenpinscher
Airedale
Australian Terrier
Bouvier des Flandres
Boxer
Brittany Spaniel
Brussels Griffon
Clumber Spaniel

CARING FOR HAND-FED OR ORPHANED PUPS

Normally the mother will lick her puppies in order to facilitate their urination and defecation. Should the puppies be orphaned—the mother ill or negligent—then this duty must be assumed. Gently wipe the anal area with a piece of moistened cotton until the puppy has a movement. With another clean piece of cotton, wipe the urinary area. This procedure should be followed before and after each feeding. It is essential to do this until the pups are mature enough to perform this bodily function independently.

Cocker Spaniel
Doberman Pinscher
Old English Sheepdog
English Toy Spaniel
Fox Terrier (smooth)
Fox Terrier (wire)
Toy Fox Terrier
German Shorthaired Pointer
German Wirehaired Pointer
Irish Terrier
Kerry Blue Terrier
Lakeland Terrier
Norwich Terrier
Pinscher (miniature)
Poodle (miniature)
Poodle (standard)
Poodle (toy)
Rottweiler
Schipperke
Schnauzer (giant)
Schnauzer (miniature)
Schnauzer (standard)
Sealyham Terrier
Silky Terrier
Springer Spaniel
Sussex Spaniel
Vizsla
Weimaraner
Welsch Corgi (pembroke)

Welsh Terrier
Wheaton Terrier

Some breeds should have their ears cropped. This operation should be conducted by a vet familiar with the breed standards. Cropping is usually done when the pups are eight weeks old. After surgery, the ears are taped and will heal by the time they are 12 weeks old.

A.K.C. Breeds Whose Ears Should be Cropped

Boston Terrier
Bouvier des Flandres
Boxer
Brussels Griffon
Doberman Pinscher
Great Dane
Manchester Terrier
Schnauzer (giant)
Schnauzer (miniature)
Schnauzer (standard)

Weaning

When the puppies are gradually taken off their mother's milk and given other food, this is called the weaning process. Depending on the breed and the size of the litter, weaning may take place between the age of three and six weeks.

Weaning can take place when the puppies are between three and six weeks old. Once the pups start eating solid food, the mother will not clean up after them.

WEANING

BY the time the babies are three weeks old they will begin to try and explore their environment. Life is no longer confined to eating and sleeping. They will enjoy being allowed to wander around outside their whelping box and may even become interested in relieving themselves on newspapers left directly outside their box. The mother will now leave them for longer periods of time and will hurry back merely to feed them. Sharp little teeth, as well as sharp little nails, which make their appearance at this time make nursing quite uncomfortable. Keep these trimmed and the bitch will be most grateful. Weaning is usually started at about four weeks of age and teaching the puppies to lap is the first lesson. Try using either infant formulae, Esbilac (substitute puppy milk), or mix up a combination of milk, cream, and a teaspoon of Karo Syrup. Offer the pups this in a shallow dish, but be prepared to encourage them by pushing their heads down a few times until they get the idea of how to eat from this new "dish." A week of milk nursing substitute beginning once a day and increased to four times a day is a good plan. Follow this the next few days with a milky mixture of pre-cooked baby cereal, enriched with a teaspoon of Karo Syrup and an egg yolk. At this point, your puppies should be eating heartily four times a day with the mother allowing them to nurse for only a few short times a day if at all. It is usually wise to give each pup his own pan of food in order to be certain that all are getting enough. Let them have as much as they want since this is the time of tremendous growth. Should you notice that one dog is monopolizing feeding time, then have him eat separately. Bitches will often regurgitate their own food to teach their pups to eat more solid food.

Usually by the fifth week, most pups are ready for a somewhat more substantial diet. If you have sufficient time to devote to the somewhat laborious task of preparing your own puppy food of cereal, eggs, and scraped meat or cooked hamburger, cottage cheese, enriched with vitamins, and you enjoy doing it then go ahead. On the other hand, if you can't afford the time or money required for this enterprise, then use a good quality puppy food starting at about six weeks. If fed moistened food, the pup should be fed three times a day until three to four months of age, then twice daily is adequate until he is eight to nine months of age. Feed all the moistened ration the pup will clean up at each feeding.

The period from weaning to approximately 20 weeks of age is the time when most pups grow fastest. During this period of rapid growth, medium-sized

Sharp teeth and nails make nursing quite uncomfortable as the pups grow older.

dogs, such as Pointer and Setters, require approximately three and one-half pounds of air-dry food to put on one pound of body weight gain. Larger breeds require slightly less, smaller breeds slightly more food per pound of gain. If canned dog foods are fed, three times as much canned food will normally be needed. Until the pups are about eight months old, they should have all the food they want.

When the pups are eight to ten weeks of age, they will consume the highest amount of feed in proportion to their body weight than at any other time in their lives except for lactating females. As the dog matures and gains weight, the amount of feed intake in proportion to body weight gradually decreases and levels off at maturity. If at any time during the growing period, the dog tends to become overweight, then his feed intake should be reduced.

Although most good quality commercial dog foods do contain vitamins and minerals in the suggested proportions, some veterinarians recommend adding vitamins and other additives. We would suggest you consult your own vet in this regard. A large and reputable dog food producer has the following to say about supplementing your dog's diet:

Many dog owners refuse to believe that good commercial dog foods contain all of the nutrients, except water, needed by normal dogs for all phases of their lives. Occasionally an individual dog may have a requirement for a particular nutrient that is higher than the average, but this is exceptional and is quite often the result of a metabolic abnormality.

Supplementation is costly, unnecessary and may cause nutritionally-induced physiological health problems. How can this happen?

Adding raw whole eggs to rations for puppies, or even mature dogs, is not uncommon. Raw egg white contains avidin, an enzyme, which ties up the vitamin, biotin, and if fed continually, a biotin deficiency can occur. Raw egg whites are used to produce biotin deficiencies experimentally. Symptoms include dermatitis, loss of hair, and poor growth. Although it is not necessary to add eggs to the diet, the addition of *cooked* eggs will not result in the destruction of biotin.

Adding supplemental minerals, such as calcium pills, to a regular diet can also be detrimental. It is known that both calcium and phosphorus must be present in the ration in ample amounts and in a proper ratio of 1.2:1 promotes maximum calcification. If additional calcium is added to make this ratio further apart, for example 5:1, there would be an inefficient assimilation of these two minerals even though the phosphorus was present in the correct amount. Rickets is one sign of a deficiency or imbalance of either of these two minerals in the diet of growing dogs.

Cod liver oil and wheat germ oil are sources of vitamins D and E. Adding excess cod liver oil can supply more vitamin D than is needed by the dog. Vitamin D must also be given in the proper proportion along with calcium and phosphorus for good bone and tooth formation.

If either of these two oils are in the process of becoming rancid, or if a rancid fat is added, this can destroy the vitamin E. In fact, low levels of rancid fish oil are often used to produce a vitamin E deficiency in experimental work. Vitamin E is needed for normal growth, reproduction, and lactation. All of the vitamins known to be required by normal dogs are added in sufficient quantities to most good commercial

Here's a litter of puppies enjoying a cafeteria style meal. Keeping them out of the food dish is quite a problem —one solution is to provide a small eating area.

151

dog foods. These vitamins are in stable forms and can withstand the heat and pressures that might occur during manufacturing and possible long periods of warehouse storage.

Many young puppies, especially prior to weaning, are fed a mixture of milk, baby cereal, vitamins, eggs, and meat. Besides being expensive, the preparation of a diet of this type is time-consuming and difficult. A good commercial dry dog food that has been moistened is highly palatable for pups and will supply them with the balanced nutrition that cannot be met by many home-mixes.

Occasionally charcoal is added to the diet. Unless fed in excessive amounts this ingredient is usually considered to be harmless, but there is no real advantage in using it. It is relatively indigestible and may take up some vitamins in the digestive tract and carry them out of the dog.

Hard-working dogs, such as racing Greyhounds, sled dogs and hunting dogs, require a high level of feed intake to meet their high-energy requirements. It is very important that they receive a highly palatable ration so they consume a high caloric intake. Many people add 20 to 25 per cent raw meat to the diet; this does not improve the nutritional balance of the ration but may increase acceptance. Meat fed at this level should not cause any problems. However, it is not advisable to feed extremely high levels of meat or only lean meat as the entire ration. Meat is deficient in certain minerals, including calcium, cobalt, iron and copper, as well as some vitamins. Young growing puppies fed only lean meat will develop severe rickets after being on this type diet for only three to four weeks. Meat is the only supplement we recommend adding to a dry dog food and this is only for normal dogs that have a high-energy requirement and need a food intake that is higher.

Supplementation is not necessary and may even prove to be detrimental at times. More and more dog owners are discovering that supplementation of a good commercial dog food offers no advantage for their dogs. This fact has been proven time and time again by the many thousands of dogs self-fed dry rations and water with excellent results.

Drinking water should be available at all times as puppies drink a lot and if only milk is offered it may be difficult later for them to adjust to water.

By the age of ten weeks regular milk can be used instead of the formula or enriched milk.

Try to feed your puppy on a schedule and be consistent in the hours. Here is a good schedule to follow:

Feeding Schedule

Age of Puppy	Morning	Noon	Evening
6 weeks to 6 months.....	X	X	X
6 months to a year......	X		X
Past one year			X

Selling Puppies

By the age of eight weeks puppies are customarily offered for sale. Occasional breeders make it a rule to keep their pups until they are 12 weeks of age in order to give them an extra "good start." For the breeder, keeping the puppies longer involves added expense and care. Food, innoculations, grooming and attention are required. When the litter is large, this can become quite a strain physically as well as financially. It is for this reason that it is usual to find dogs for sale as soon as they are weaned and independent from their mother. Thus, when considering your sales program, try to be mindful of these elements and plan accordingly.

Advertising in the local paper, city newspapers and special dog magazines is one of the best ways of reaching the public. Since most dog magazines appear only once a month, you will have to place your ad well in advance. Much time will be saved if you are explicit in your ad. State the breed, number, age, sex and lineage as well as price of your puppies and include your phone number or address. Vague ads result in numerous unnecessary and fruitless inquiries.

Inform your vet, stud owner, and local pet store about your saleable puppies. These people constantly get inquiries and may be able to steer customers in your direction. Once your puppies are offered for sale be prepared to spend a great deal of time on the phone answering a flood of questions and a great deal of time showing your babies to prospective buyers. People purchasing a dog do not usually rush into it and may want to spend hours observing them. It may be necessary for you to give specific appointments including a cut-off time. However, one can't be overly rigid as making sales is the purpose.

Setting a fair price can be difficult. It will be necessary for you to inquire as to the going rates for the particular breed that you have. Many factors come into price consideration, such as:

1—Breed
2—Blood lines—ancestry
3—Championships
4—Sex
5—Age
6—Innoculations received
7—Surgery performed (dew claws, ears cropped, tails docked).

Weigh these elements carefully to determine a fair price. Your price must be in line with other puppies on the market. If yours are significantly lower, perhaps you are undervaluing your goods, and you are hurting the market. Should your price be too high, you probably won't be able to make a sale. Don't be surprised if selling all the puppies takes quite a while and be prepared for this possibility. Finding the right home is not the easiest event in the world and there may be occasions when you will refuse to sell to a party. Most real dog lovers won't allow their puppies to go to families or homes that don't meet certain standards. If you have to make such a decision, don't feel badly—it's probably the wisest thing. Puppies that you have raised will undoubtedly become very dear to you and their welfare should be one of your prime concerns.

Most sources agree that it is never wise to give a puppy away or to sell it too cheaply since too many people equate worth with price. Thus, if you want your pup to be highly valued, you must ask a fair price for it.

The Sale

Be prepared for the sale of your puppies; if they are pure bred dogs, this event should have been anticipated and the litter registered with the A.K.C. All the necessary forms and pedigrees should be ready for the new owner. It's also a good idea to have a mimeographed diet sheet including instructions on care and training. This prepared information can save time and misunderstanding. Here's a handy list for you to check off:

Getting Puppy Ready for New Home . . .

☐ Fecal sample checked for worms. Worm if necessary according to internal parasites present:
    Roundworms
    Hookworms
    Tapeworms
    Whipworms
    Heartworms (in blood samples—vet cannot detect in puppies less than 12 weeks of age.)
☐ Clip toe nails and dew claws (remove dew claws during the first week after birth).
☐ Check teeth.
☐ Clean eyes if they contain foreign matter.
☐ Trim excess hair from around anal and urinary openings.
☐ Bathe and clip, trim or pluck if necessary (generally not before 6 weeks of age).
☐ Consult your veterinarian and follow immunization or protective health program.
☐ Acclimatize dogs by careful display and handling.
☐ Provide new owners with guarantees that their new pet will be found healthy by a veterinarian.
☐ Supply new puppy owner with an information sheet describing care, feeding, management, and sanitation for the new puppy.
☐ Have registration certificate ready.

Persons buying a puppy will often ask to see the parents of the pup. If you don't own the stud, it is helpful to have a good photograph to show.

LET'S HAVE PUPPIES

*A planned family with lots of professional help and advice
made this experience a happy and unforgettable one.*

"LET'S have puppies." "Sure, why not?" Why not? There were many reasons, but we ignored all of them. Here we were, a suburban family, with four teenagers, deciding to mate our two year old West Highland White Terrier bitch.

Puddy, listed on our American Kennel Club papers as Mar-El-Puddin, was our first pet. We had purchased her from a breeder when she was six weeks old. We had grown to love her dearly. After serious consideration we decided to give her the opportunity to fulfill her role of motherhood. So at the moment, as we observed Pud to be in season (her third), we ventured into the unknown of animal parenthood. We called Puddy's breeder, who had a champion stud. She would keep Pud for a week between the tenth and the 17th day of season. Bitches conceive on the 12th and 14th day. We were to pay her a fee, and if the mating didn't take, we could try again next time. Off Puddy went.

After Puddy returned we waited the weeks out to see if she was pregnant, and we began weighing the consequences of our decision.

My husband generously relinquished all responsibility to me. Peggy, my daughter, thought it was a great idea, and maybe when she returned from her summer in Europe, she could take a puppy to college. Nancy, our youngest, wanted me to be sure and call her at camp to inform her of the birth. This left Tom, Kathy, and me as the caring midwives. The group decision had already had some defectors.

We called the vet for support. He suggested vitamin pills, a blood test, and advised us not to depend on him other than office hours. It wasn't the kind of support an inexperienced family was looking for.

Pud was either pregnant or having a false pregnancy. Her nipples enlarged, her eating habits changed, and she was plumper. We decided to change vets. This was as traumatic as if I had changed obstetricians in the middle of my pregnancy. Our new vet was warm and kind over the telephone. He made house calls. When he stopped by to see Pud, he loved and hugged her. Upon examining her, he confirmed the pregnancy. He brought a new supply of vitamin pills and reassured us about the impending birth.

I was really unsure about the birth of Puddy's babies. At one time a dog handler had advised us against mating our dog. She had said our dog was very small, and this, along with the fact that Westies had a hard time delivering pups, made me concerned. I had also read a number of dog books, which made me nervous about my role as midwife. The vet said to read all of the books you like, and then put them away, and stop worrying. He also encouraged me to call him at any time. An understanding doctor is a great asset.

We built a whelping bed. The name sounds imposing, but it is really very simple. It is a box in which the dog can have her puppies, where the puppies can remain with the mother, and the mother can come and go as she likes. We bought two by fours at the lumber yard, and built a square box, with a removable opening that could be opened for Pud. The sides were low enough for her to climb over, but high enough to protect the babies. Our plan was that as soon as she started laboring to put her in the box and keep her there. This would avoid the danger and difficulty of having babies in a closet, or under the bed, or some other out-of-the-way place in the house.

Besides our vet, the breeder was also most encouraging. She urged me to call her with any questions; which I did. "Why did Pud eat so poorly?" "How would I know when she was ready to whelp?," and "How would I know when everything was going all right, and when we were in trouble?" Yes, Westies often eat badly during gestation. Take your dog's temperature daily during the last week. When there is a change babies can be expected within 24 hours. Call her as soon as labor starts. Also, have rubber gloves, clean towels, scissors, and thread ready.

Gestation is about 63 days. Ten days in advance we assembled the whelping bed in the breakfast room. This was a warm, quiet place with a telephone in close proximity. We put shredded newspaper in the bed.

Pud was due on Thursday. The previous week she had been dragging herself around. The babies caused her tummy to hang so close to the ground that we had to carry her up and down the stairs. She would crawl under the beds and furniture and furiously scratch. This, of course, was her natural instinct to get her whelping bed ready. We exposed her to the man-made bed regularly. The Sunday night before Pud was due, she was very restless. However, since there was no change in temperature, we assumed she was not ready. She continued being restless Monday morning.

When first Kathy and later Tom called me at the tennis courts about Pud's restlessness, I decided to come home. I knew the puppies were not due until Thursday, but maybe Kathy and Tom knew something I did not know! I arrived home at the moment the first pup was forcing its head out of the birth canal. Kathy, Tom, and Pud were all pretty tense and my noisy arrival only intensified the situation. Puddy didn't know what was happening to her. She resisted being in the whelping bed. Kathy was holding her in it. Tom was helping the baby in birth. He had to break the sack, as Pud didn't. Then, instinctively Pud began to lick the baby clean and eat the afterbirth. If Puddy could have spoken she would have said, "I sure don't know what's happening to me." At that moment Kathy and Tom were not so sure either.

It was 10:38 a.m. Monday, July 21, 1969. Man was walking on the surface of the moon for the first time and Puddy was giving birth to her first litter of puppies. The first pup was a female and all was well. Before we had time to recapitulate what had happened, Puddy strained again. Giving birth for Pud was like having a bowel movement. She would strain and turn in circles, and a puppy would push out.

This baby looked quite different from the first one. It wasn't breathing. We tried to start its breathing by massaging it, but to no avail. We put this strange baby down into the whelping bed and to our horror, Puddy began to eat it. This panicked us. We quickly got rid of what was left, and took the healthy pup out of the whelping bed.

A quick phone call to the vet helped. The second puppy was stillborn. To eat it is the mother's instinctive way of getting rid of anything improper. Just as she eats the afterbirth, so she eats anything not living. The vet gave us encouragement that all was well, and that we were lucky the stillborn was born, rather than blocking the birth canal and preventing subsequent births. We should call him if we had any more problems and he would be over to check on things in the early afternoon.

We had purposely put the whelping bed near the phone, anticipating the possible need of help. Throughout the day we spoke to the breeder and our dog-oriented friends. All the help novices can get, the better!

Pretty soon we had another puppy. Puddy did this with great ease. It was a healthy female. What more could we ask for.

By the time the vet arrived, we had had another male; three living puppies. Upon examining the mother, he felt there were more to come and gave Pud a shot to help things along. He examined the puppies and found them healthy but warned us that the next 36 hours were the most crucial.

Two more males had been born by five o'clock. Pud was tired but willing to go out for a minute and drink some water.

We spent a great deal of time trying to get the babies to nurse, but we didn't have much success. Our phone calls to our friends didn't give us the answers. Was it bad that the babies weren't eating? What should we do? How soon after birth should they eat? When we finally reached the vet, he reassured us that Westies are known to be hard to get started nursing, and we would have to help them. When Father arrived home for dinner, he saw three of us working with five fishlike babies attempting to attach them to their mother's nipples. We were a sight to behold. The whole day had passed; we had barely left the spot, and here we were with a tired mother and five stubborn babies.

Finally, by 10 p.m. all the babies had nursed and we were ready to settle down for the night. We turned off the light and were turning in when Tom decided to take one last look at Pud and the babies. He hollered for us to come quickly. There were no longer five babies, six babies were nursing. Puddy had had another baby without us! We now had two females and four males. Quite a litter for a dog that was too small to have babies.

Puddy may not have needed all the help we gave her but it was a fascinating experience for us.

The puppies grew strong and healthy. While Puddy was nursing them, she took complete charge. Each day was a change. They gradually began to use their legs, grow hair, open their eyes and move around. At three weeks we began to wean them and by five weeks we began to advertise that we had puppies for sale. By nine weeks we had sold all but the last female, which we decided to keep for ourselves. We named our baby Luna, in honor of the moonwalk on the day of her birth. We were no longer novices with one puppy. We had become experienced breeders and owners of two dogs.

As I see Puddy and Luna romp around the house today, it is hard for me to believe it happened to us. They play, they fight, they sleep in the same bed, they quarrel over their food, they mess up our house, they greet us when we come home. They bark when a stranger comes to the house. They climb on our laps when we're resting, they eat crumbs from the kitchen floor, and sleep on our beds at night. They give us an excuse for long Sunday walks on the beach. They keep each other company when we're away all day.

It has been a unique transition. From no pet, to a pet, to a pregnant pet, to puppies, to two pets all in two and one-half years. Who can tell what is in store for us next!

Margery Fridstein

155

HOW TO IDENTIFY THE ANCESTRY OF A MIXED BREED

If you have a mixed breed and you want to try to guess his ancestry, you can work on the problem from two ways. One is by studying his conformation. You can say: "He looks like . . ." And the second way is observing his actions. You can conclude that "he acts like . . ." You'll probably never know the truth, but you can have some fun, and you'll understand dogs better while doing it.

Scientists often catalog dogs by their jaw lengths. There are long-jawed breeds such as the Doberman Pinscher, German Shepherd, Greyhound, English and Irish Setters, and others. And there are short-muzzled dogs, such as the St. Bernard, Chow Chow, Chihuahua, Pomeranian, and others.

With some of these breeds, such as the Doberman Pinscher and the German Shepherd, there is a tendency, which is inherited, to be minus some of their premolars. Thus, the jaw length, plus the absence of teeth, might give you a clue. Do not confuse the short nose or short jaw with the pushed-in face of such breeds as Pekingese, Bulldogs, and Boston Terriers. These are difficult features to keep, even in purebreds. In mixed breeds the pushed-in face seldom is seen, though it may be slightly discernible in crossbreeds.

The ears also may be a clue. Spaniels and Poodles have longer than normal ears. So do Bassets and Bloodhounds. It is not known for certain, but it is believed that all prehistoric dogs had erect ears such as wolves, jackals, foxes, and hyenas have. So erect ears might indicate shepherd dog ancestry of some kind, or Arctic sled dog, or Chow blood. Drooping ears could indicate Spaniel, Poodle, or hound ancestry.

Some dogs, with very fine, short coats, become nearly hairless. This does not indicate Mexican or Chinese Hairless ancestry. More likely it is a little-understood disease called alopecia, or falling hair. But hair type can give you a clue.

Long, standoffish guard hair is a characteristic of the Chow Chow, and of many Arctic dogs. Long bristles that lie flat indicate some of the shepherd types. Hair which has a tendency not to fall out, but to get frizzy and curly, could indicate some terrier blood. Very short, fine hair is a characteristic of Dachshunds, Whippets, Miniature Pinschers, and similar dogs. The presence of a strong spotting pattern would indicate Dalmatian ancestry.

That ancient first ancestor of the dog, Miacis, had a long back. Dog people have been trying to breed out this tendency in most breeds for a very long time. German Shepherds are longer in body than they are tall. So are Dachshunds, Welsh Corgis, and a few others. A long-backed, short-legged, drop-eared dog would indicate Dachshund blood. If he had the first two characteristics, but erect ears, he might easily have some Corgi blood in him.

And now consider the possible ancestry of your dog just by studying his actions. Dogs that chase cars, bicycles, and running children inherit strong herding or cattle-driving instincts. The cattle-driving instinct is especially strong if the dog nips at the heels, without really trying to bite.

Some dogs grab and shake when trying to kill some creature or while fighting. This is a strong terrier instinct—the centuries-old methods of the great ratter. Dogs inheriting Greyhound instincts slash with their teeth, and duck in and out like great prize fighters. They also love to get out and run, whether or not they are chasing something.

In fighting, some dogs grab, then begin to chew while holding on, trying to get more of the enemy into their jaws. This is a habit developed in the Bulldogs and other pit-fighting dogs of the past. So if your dog shows such tendencies, he might have Bullterrier or Bulldog blood in him.

If, while out in the field, your dog tests wind scents instead of trailing foot scents (tracking), then he might have Setter, Pointer, or Spaniel blood in him. If he tracks, then he should have some hound ancestry. If he's crazy about jumping into cold water and just swimming about, he probably has Spaniel, Poodle or Retriever ancestry.

All these clues can make owning a mixed breed a lot of fun. You might even make a catalog of all the traits your dog shows. And in that case, you'd really find that your dog is ALL dog.

CHAPTER VII
SHOWING

Showing your dog can become a fascinating and rewarding hobby. Silky Terrier owned by Mr. and Mrs. Bob Brasaemle, Evans City, Pa. (Photo by William H. Oskay, SeeSharp Photography, Muncie, Ind.)

SHOWING

WHY show your dog? Without a doubt, most people show their dogs initially because they feel that their dog is a fine specimen of the breed and they wish others to see this as well. The competition of a show provides an excellent opportunity for dogs to be compared, contrasted, and evaluated. Win, lose, or draw —the show is always an educational experience for the owners as well as the spectators. Perhaps, the aftermath of a show will mean changes for your dog —better grooming, better training, or entry in other shows.

There is fun and excitement at a show and if your dog does make a good appearance you will be encouraged to pursue this endeavor. After several shows, who knows? You might even be ready to take this up as a hobby.

Showing Dogs—Quite a Hobby

Showing dogs can become a family hobby which is enjoyed by the members of all ages. Here is a hobby which has no special season—it goes on all year around. Dog fanciers can participate in this sport as much or as little as they desire. Many folks who show regularly state that their enthusiasm grows as they become more involved. First, they start with one dog, usually the family pet, and then if they are successful in their showing venture, they expand their enterprise. Attaining points for a champion is frequently the greatest incentive. Now, perhaps they will add an additional dog to the "family." If there are children, they will be indoctrinated by participating in the Junior Showmanship events. These junior shows give young people a chance to appear with their dog in front of an audience. They can develop poise and self-confidence through such participation.

Although there are costs and time involved, all the people we have queried feel that it's all worth it. They find that the closeness between the family is strengthened because of this joint enterprise. Any hobby involves expense and they find that showing requires no more than golf or bowling. A show is very exciting, challenging, and fun. Many also find it gives them an excuse to travel which they might otherwise not do. And, last but not least, this is an opportunity to meet and talk to many people and to exchange bits of interesting information and dog lore.

All in all, this is a hobby which many can enjoy and which you may find is just the thing for your family.

Showing—For a Serious Purpose

Should you desire to get involved with dogs somewhat seriously—let's say breeding or having a stud, or grooming—then the dog show exposure can give you valuable opportunities in (1) elevating your dog's status, (2) giving many people the opportunity to observe your dog, (3) giving you a chance to meet people interested in your services.

To learn where and when dog shows are held, write to the dog show superintendent and request that your name be placed on their mailing list; you will receive advance notice of the shows.

This dog show information which is sent is called the premium list. It will tell you the date of the show, the place, whether the show is benched or unbenched, and the amount of the entry fee. It will also give you the names of the judges, prizes, and when the last entries will be accepted. Should you decide to enter a show, send in the properly completed application with the required fee.

Showing can cost you a lot of money or it can be an inexpensive hobby. Hiring a professional handler to show your dog will be expensive, but he knows his trade and will present your dog at his best. Most dog owners handle their own dogs and, thus, can participate and enjoy all the excitement and if they win it is even more satisfying.

Preparing Your Dog for the Show
Training

The conformation class of a dog show is the opportunity for your dog to display his best physical qualities and his best performance. Thus, he must be groomed to make a fine appearance, and he must be trained in good conduct, for the judge will form his opinion based on what he sees—how the dog stands, walks, and runs.

Long before that exciting "first" show, you must train your dog to do the following:

1—Walk on the lead.

Holding the leash quite short, practice walking with the dog on your left side, training him to adjust to your speed and to stop when you stop. Conduct regular daily practice sessions which are fun, and yet instill pride and discipline.

159

2—Hold a pose.

Train your dog to allow you to pose him—to place him in the required stance position with the head up, alert expression, feet well-placed—thus displaying all his best features. Getting him used to this pose position from puppyhood to adulthood is good training.

3—Stand for examination.

In training your dog to allow the judge to examine him during a show, have friends examine him on a regular basis. This practice will help him to become accustomed to having his teeth checked and his body investigated.

ENTRY FORMS AND PREMIUM LISTS

Write to these superintendents for dog show information. By being on their mailing list, you will receive regular announcements of future shows.

Annually Licensed Superintendents

BEHRENDT, MRS. BERNICE, 470 38th Ave., San Francisco, Calif. 94121. Mrs. Helen M. Busby, Mrs. Norah F. Randolph.

BRADSHAW, JACK, III, 727 Venice Blvd., Los Angeles, Calif. 90015. Mrs. Jack Bradshaw, Barbara Bradshaw.

BROWN, NORMAN E., Route 2, Box 256, Spokane, Wash. 99207. Mrs. Anita W. Brown.

BURKET, MRS. HELEN ROSEMONT, 20 Sycamore, San Francisco, Calif. 94110. Bruce Burket, Mrs. Mary L. Hercsuth.

CROWE, THOMAS J., P.O. Box 20205, Greensboro, N.C. 27420. Ralph W. Cox, Miss Dorie Crowe, Mrs. Nina R. Crowe, Walter A. James, Mrs. Barbara Moss Mulvey, Stuart S. Sliney, Durwood H. Van Zandt.

JONES, ROY J., P.O. Box 307, Garrett, Ind. 46738. Mrs. Elizabeth F. Jones.

KELLER, LEWIS C., 2533 Garfield Avenue, West Lawn, Pa. 19609. Mrs. Lewis C. Keller.

MATHEWS, ACE H., 11423 S.E. Alder Street, Portland, Oregon 97216. Mrs. Nancy J. Mathews.

ONOFRIO, JACK, P.O. Box 25764, Oklahoma City, Ok. 73125. Raymond W. Loupee, Dorothy M. Onofrio.

SEDER, MISS HELEN, 9999 Broadstreet, Detroit, Michigan 48204. T. N. Bloomberg, Herbert H. Evans, Richard C. Heasley, Leon F. Krouch.

THOMSEN, JACK, Box 731, Littleton, Colorado 80120. Mrs. Ann Thomsen, Mrs. Nancy L. Walden, Herbert B. Wells.

WEBB, MARION O., 500 North Street, P. O. Box 546, Auburn, Indiana 46706. Mrs. Betty Dennis, Robert G. Foster, Mrs. Lillie Pion, Mrs. Dorothy Webb.

WINKS, ALAN P., 2009 Ranstead Street, Philadephia, Pa. 19103. Mario Fernandez, Thomas J. Gillen, John W. Houser, Robert P. Rio, Mrs. Joseph H. Spring.

Grooming

Trimming must be done weeks before a show. Hard coats grow more slowly than soft ones and thus must be started earlier. Until you are completely aware of the breed standards, your dog's assets and deficits, and are proficient in the proper grooming techniques, let a professional do the trimming. If you wish to eventually learn this aspect of dog care, then by all means analyze your dog's preparation and seek advice on how to do it. There are courses offered that can help you master this.

The night before the show is a good time for a bath if it is needed. Place the dog in a tub, wet his coat thoroughly with lukewarm water, apply dog shampoo, rub until thick and sudsy, massage starting at the neck and working back. Be sure to protect the eyes and ears. Use a spray to rinse until all soap is out. Dry well by using a dryer or thick towel. Brush out and pin a towel around the dog with large safety pins.

The day of the show, check the time your dog will be in the ring and gauge your grooming accordingly. You will want to allow ample time to brush, comb, and tidy up your dog but still not start too early so that he is wilted long before entering the ring.

Smooth, short-coated dogs need merely to be rubbed down with a grooming glove and if the coat needs a shine, rub on just a little hair cream.

Long, flat coats should be sponged to remove dust and then brushed well.

Terriers should not be bathed more than necessary as it softens their hard coat. White terriers can be chalked to clean and whiten the coat but this chalk must be brushed out thoroughly before the judging.

Light colored poodles can be powdered, but this must all be completely brushed out prior to entering the show ring.

Towels should be used to protect dogs that drool. Protect the long-eared dogs from soiling themselves while eating.

At your first few shows, observe the professional handlers. They are usually glad to share some of their knowledge with you.

How to Behave the Day of the Show

Don't tire or overexcite your dog. The trip, the new surroundings, the crowd, and the other dogs are all terribly exciting so try to instill a calm element by remaining as relaxed and as natural as possible. Nervousness is contagious and could hurt your dog's showing, so exercise self-control.

Let your dog rest as much as possible and do only the necessary grooming. Allow him to eat and relieve himself according to his normal schedule, if possible. Some authorities recommend feeding long before the judging so that the dog is more spirited and not sluggish after a heavy meal.

Left—A Yorkshire Terrier must go through elaborate preparations prior to a show. This is an example of how the Yorky looks after an oil spray and wrapping to preserve a good show coat. Below—Getting this dog's coat into show condition is going to be quite a chore.

The judging schedule will explain the time and ring in which your dog is to appear. Be on time as they will start without you if you are not there. Upon arrival at the ring, the attendant will give you an arm band bearing the entry number of your dog. This band is to be worn on the left arm.

When the group of dogs enters the ring, all the dogs are to be on their handlers' left side. Keep an eye on the judge and listen to his commands. Never block the judge's view of your dog. Try to keep your dog moving or posed while in the ring and have a special toy or treat in your hand to keep his attention.

Pose your dog carefully and be sure to allow yourself plenty of room. Place the forelegs so that they stand correctly; pull the head forward and up as you hold the tail in proper position.

When the judge makes his decision, accept it gracefully. Should you be a winner, that's fine. But, if your dog doesn't place in the winners' circle, please maintain a pleasant attitude. Judges try to make their selections fairly and carefully and their decisions should not be contested. If you wish to discuss your dog and get a candid opinion on how to improve his chances, most judges will be glad to talk to you briefly after the group is finished, when time permits. Dog shows are competitive and one must be prepared to lose as well as to win. As with any sport, it's how you play the game that counts. Enjoy the preliminary preparations and the show itself, and, then, winning needn't be so terribly important.

Professional Handlers

Many dogs are shown by professional handlers. About 1,000 handlers are licensed by the American Kennel Club. A professional handler is one who may board and train a dog to show, and, then, show it for the owner. For this, he charges a fee agreed upon for that show. Professional handlers may take many dogs to a single show. Professional handlers often arrange to take "strings" of dogs on "circuits" — a half-dozen or more shows held in towns and cities fairly close together so that the dogs and handlers move from one to another quite easily. For example, there are the Deep South Circuit, the Florida Circuit, the South Texas Circuit, etc.

Some professional handlers have full time jobs and go only to weekend dog shows. These handlers simply accept their clients' dogs at the shows. They bathe, trim and groom them, and then take them into the ring; whereas others own large kennels and board dogs for the general public as well.

Things to Remember

1—If the dog is having skin trouble or is out of coat, don't show him.

2—Be sure all innoculations against distemper, hepatitis, and leptospirosis are up to date.

3—Items to bring to the show for your dog are: collar and bench chain; show lead; dog food and water dish; comb, brush, sponge, towel, and all necessary grooming preparations.

4—Items to bring to the show for your own needs are: a folding chair; any refreshments you need and don't want to buy; paper and pencil to take notes; comfortable clothing with roomy pockets.

UNDERSTANDING A DOG SHOW

IN actuality a dog show is a canine beauty contest. Each breed has certain physical characteristics which distinguish it from other breeds. Within each breed there are the ideals for type and soundness. The dog show is designed to prove the quality, or lack of it, of each dog entered.

A dog show is also an elimination contest. The show may begin with thousands of dogs and gradually eliminate them until at the end one single dog is chosen as the best-in-show winner.

The primary purpose of a dog show is to enable dog owners to exhibit their dogs in competition with others of its kind. The ultimate objective is to improve the quality of all purebred dogs. This is achieved by an intelligent breeding program, using the dogs which have proven, through such competition to be the better representatives of their breeds.

A sanctioned or licensed dog show is only for purebred dogs which are registered or eligible for registration in the American Kennel Club. The entry form must show the dog's individual registration number or the litter registration number.

An eligible dog that is only litter registered may be shown no more than three times unless it has been given an indefinite listing privilege by the A.K.C.

Dog Show Registration and Rules

Excerpts from the official American Kennel Club Rules applying to Dog Shows are being included in order to impress the individual planning to enter his dog in a show with the thoroughness and fairness used in running an A.K.C. licensed show.

If you wish to study the complete pamphlet, write to the American Kennel Club, 51 Madison Avenue, New York, New York 10010 and request "Rules Applying to Registration and Dog Shows."

DOG SHOW CLASSIFICATIONS

SECTION 1. The following breeds and/or varieties of breeds, divided by groups, shall be all the breeds and/or varieties of breeds for which regular classes of The American Kennel Club may be provided at any show held under American Kennel Club rules. The Board of Directors may either add to, transfer from one group to another, or delete from said list of breeds and/or varieties of breeds, whenever in its opinion registrations of such breed and/or variety of breed in the Stud Book justify such action.

GROUP 1—SPORTING DOGS

GRIFFONS (WIREHAIRED POINTING)
POINTERS
POINTERS (GERMAN SHORTHAIRED)
POINTERS (GERMAN WIREHAIRED)
RETRIEVERS (CHESAPEAKE BAY)
RETRIEVERS (CURLY-COATED)
RETRIEVERS (FLAT-COATED)
RETRIEVERS (GOLDEN)
RETRIEVERS (LABRADOR)
SETTERS (ENGLISH)
SETTERS (GORDON)
SETTERS (IRISH)
SPANIELS (AMERICAN WATER)
SPANIELS (BRITTANY)
SPANIELS (CLUMBER)
SPANIELS (COCKER)
    Three varieties: Solid Color, Black.
                Solid Color Other Than Black including
                    Black and Tan.
                Parti-color.
SPANIELS (ENGLISH COCKER)
SPANIELS (ENGLISH SPRINGER)
SPANIELS (FIELD)
SPANIELS (IRISH WATER)
SPANIELS (SUSSEX)
SPANIELS (WELSH SPRINGER)
VIZSLAS
WEIMARANERS

GROUP 2—HOUNDS

AFGHAN HOUNDS
BASENJIS
BASSET HOUNDS
BEAGLES
    Two varieties: Not exceeding 13 inches in height.
    Over 13 inches but not exceeding 15 inches in height.
BLOODHOUNDS
BORZOIS
COONHOUNDS (BLACK AND TAN)
DACHSHUNDS
    Three varieties: Longhaired.
                Smooth.
                Wirehaired.
DEERHOUNDS (SCOTTISH)
FOXHOUNDS (AMERICAN)
FOXHOUNDS (ENGLISH)
GREYHOUNDS
HARRIERS
IRISH WOLFHOUNDS
NORWEGIAN ELKHOUNDS
OTTER HOUNDS
RHODESIAN RIDGEBACKS
SALUKIS
WHIPPETS

GROUP 3—WORKING DOGS

ALASKAN MALAMUTES
BELGIAN MALINOIS
BELGIAN SHEEPDOGS
BELGIAN TERVUREN
BERNESE MOUNTAIN DOGS
BOUVIERS DES FLANDRES
BOXERS
BRIARDS
BULLMASTIFFS
COLLIES
    Two varieties: Rough.
                  Smooth.
DOBERMAN PINSCHERS
GERMAN SHEPHERD DOGS
GIANT SCHNAUZERS
GREAT DANES
GREAT PYRENEES
KOMONDOROK
KUVASZOK
MASTIFFS
NEWFOUNDLANDS
OLD ENGLISH SHEEPDOGS
PULIK
ROTTWEILERS
SAMOYEDS
SCHNAUZERS (STANDARD)
SHETLAND SHEEPDOGS
SIBERIAN HUSKIES
ST. BERNARDS
WELSH CORGIS (CARDIGAN)
WELSH CORGIS (PEMBROKE)

GROUP 4—TERRIERS

AIREDALE TERRIERS
AUSTRALIAN TERRIERS
BEDLINGTON TERRIERS
BORDER TERRIERS
BULL TERRIERS
    Two varieties: White.
                  Colored.
CAIRN TERRIERS
DANDIE DINMONT TERRIERS
FOX TERRIERS
    Two varieties: Smooth.
                  Wire.
IRISH TERRIERS
KERRY BLUE TERRIERS
LAKELAND TERRIERS
MANCHESTER TERRIERS
    Two varieties: Standard, over 12 pounds and not exceed-
                ing 22 pounds
                Toy (in Toy Group)
NORWICH TERRIERS
SCHNAUZERS (MINIATURE)
SCOTTISH TERRIERS
SEALYHAM TERRIERS
SKYE TERRIERS
STAFFORDSHIRE TERRIERS
WELSH TERRIERS
WEST HIGHLAND WHITE TERRIERS

GROUP 5—TOYS

AFFENPINSCHERS
CHIHUAHUAS
    Two varieties: Smooth Coat.
                  Long Coat.

ENGLISH TOY SPANIELS
    Two varieties: King Charles and Ruby.
                Blenheim and Prince Charles.
GRIFFONS (BRUSSELS)
ITALIAN GREYHOUNDS
JAPANESE SPANIELS
MALTESE
MANCHESTER TERRIERS
    Two varieties: Toy, not exceeding 12 pounds
                Standard (in Terrier Group)
PAPILLONS
PEKINGESE
PINSCHERS (MINIATURE)
POMERANIANS
POODLES
    Three varieties: Toy, not exceeding 10 inches
                 Miniature (in Non-Sporting Group)
                 Standard (in Non-Sporting Group)
PUGS
SHIH TZU
SILKY TERRIERS
YORKSHIRE TERRIERS

GROUP 6—NON-SPORTING DOGS

BOSTON TERRIERS
BULLDOGS
CHOW CHOWS
DALMATIANS
FRENCH BULLDOGS
KEESHONDEN
LHASA APSOS
POODLES
    Three varieties: Miniature, over 10 inches and not
                 exceeding 15 inches
                 Standard, over 15 inches
                 Toy (in Toy Group)
SCHIPPERKES

SECTION 2. No class shall be provided for any dog under six months of age except at sanctioned matches when approved by The American Kennel Club.

SECTION 3. The regular classes of The American Kennel Club shall be as follows:
    Puppy
    Novice
    Bred-by-Exhibitor
    American-bred
    Open
    Winners

SECTION 4. The Puppy Class shall be for dogs that are six months of age and over, but under twelve months, that were whelped in the United States of America or Canada, and that are not champions. The age of the dog shall be calculated up to and inclusive of the first day of a show. For example, a dog whelped on January 1st is eligible to compete in a puppy class at a show the first day of which is July 1st of the same year and may continue to compete in puppy classes at shows up to and including a show the first day of which is the 31st day of December of the same year, but is not eligible to compete in a puppy class at a show the first day of which is January 1st of the following year.

SECTION 5. The Novice Class shall be for dogs six months of age and over, whelped in the United States of America or Canada, which have not, prior to the date of closing of entries, won three first prizes in the Novice Class, a first prize in Bred-by-Exhibitor, American-bred, or Open Classes, nor one or more points toward their championships.

SECTION 6. The Bred-by-Exhibitor Class shall be for

dogs whelped in the United States of America, or, if individually registered in The American Kennel Club Stud Book, for dogs whelped in Canada, that are six months of age and over, that are not champions, and that are owned wholly or in part by the person or by the spouse of the person who was the breeder or one of the breeders of record.

Dogs entered in this class must be handled in the class by an owner or by a member of the immediate family of an owner.

For purposes of this section, the members of an immediate family are: husband, wife, father, mother, son, daughter, brother, sister.

SECTION 7. The American-bred Class shall be for all dogs (except champions) six months of age and over, whelped in the United States of America, by reason of a mating which took place in the United States of America.

SECTION 8. The Open Class shall be for any dog six months of age or over except in a member specialty club show held only for American-bred dogs, in which case the Open Class shall be only for American-bred dogs.

SECTION 9. The Winners Class, at shows in which the American-bred and Open Classes are divided by sex, also shall be divided by sex and each division shall be open only to undefeated dogs of the same sex which have won first prizes in either the Puppy, Novice, Bred-by-Exhibitor, American-bred or Open Classes, excepting only in the event that where either the Puppy, Novice or Bred-by-Exhibitor Class shall not have been divided by sex, dogs of the same sex winning second or third prizes but not having been defeated by a dog of the same sex may compete in the Winners Class provided for their sex. At shows where the American-bred and Open Classes are not divided by sex there shall be but one Winners Class which shall be open only to undefeated dogs of either sex which have won first prizes in either the Puppy, Novice, Bred-by-Exhibitor, American-bred or Open

Classes. There shall be no entry fee for competition in the Winners Class.

After the Winners prize has been awarded in one of the sex divisions, where the Winners Class has been divided by sex, any second or third prize winning dog otherwise undefeated in its sex, which however, has been beaten in its class by the dog awarded Winners, shall compete with the other eligible dogs for Reserve Winners. After the Winners prize has been awarded, where the Winners Class is not divided by sex, any otherwise undefeated dog which has been placed second in any previous class to the dog awarded Winners shall compete with the remaining first prize-winners, for Reserve Winners. No eligible dog may be withheld from competition.

Winners' Classes shall be allowed only at shows where American-bred and Open Classes shall be given.

A member specialty club holding a show for American-bred dogs only may include Winners' Classes, provided the necessary regular classes are included in the classification.

A member club holding a show with restricted entries may include Winners' classes, provided the necessary regular classes are included in the classification.

SECTION 10. No Winners' Class, or any class resembling it, shall be given at sanctioned matches.

SECTION 11. Bench show committees may provide such other classes of recognized breeds or recognized varieties of breeds as they may choose, provided they do not conflict with the conditions of the above mentioned classes and are judged before Best of Breed competition.

Local classes, however, may not be divided by sex in shows at which local group classes are provided.

No class may be given in which more than one breed or recognized variety of breed may be entered, except as provided in these rules and regulations.

SECTION 12. A club that provides Winners classes shall also provide competition for Best of Breed or for Best of

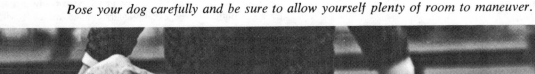

Pose your dog carefully and be sure to allow yourself plenty of room to maneuver.

Variety in those breeds for which varieties are provided in this chapter. The awards in this competition shall be Best of Breed or Best of Variety of Breed.

The following categories of dogs may be entered and shown in this competition:

Dogs that are Champions of Record.

In addition, the Winners Dog and Winners Bitch (or the dog awarded Winners, if only one winners prize has been awarded), together with any undefeated dogs that have competed at the show only in additional non-regular classes shall compete for Best of Breed or Best of Variety of Breed.

If the Winners Dog or Winners Bitch is awarded Best of Breed or Best of Variety of Breed, it shall be automatically awarded Best of Winners; otherwise, the Winners Dog and Winners Bitch shall be judged together for Best of Winners following the judging of Best of Breed or Best of Variety of Breed. The dog designated Best of Winners shall be entitled to the number of points based on the number of dogs or bitches competing in the regular classes, whichever is greater. In the event that Winners is awarded in only one sex, there shall be no Best of Winners award.

After Best of Breed or Best of Variety of Breed and Best of Winners have been awarded, the judge shall select Best of Opposite Sex to Best of Breed or Best of Variety of Breed. Eligible for this award are:

Dogs of the opposite sex to Best of Breed or Best of Variety of Breed that have been entered for Best of Breed competition.

The dog awarded Winners of the opposite sex to the Best of Breed or Best of Variety of Breed.

Any undefeated dogs of the opposite sex to Best of Breed or Best of Variety of Breed which have competed at the show only in additional non-regular classes.

SECTION 13. At specialty shows for breeds in which there are varieties as specified in Chapter 6, Section 1, and which are held apart from all-breed shows, Best of Breed shall be judged following the judging of Best of each variety and best of opposite sex to best of each variety. Best of Opposite Sex to Best of Breed shall also be judged. Dogs eligible for Best of Opposite Sex to Best of Breed competition will be found among the bests of variety or the bests of opposite sex to bests of variety, according to the sex of the dog placed Best of Breed.

At an all-breed show (even if a special club shall designate classes as its specialty show), the judge of a breed in which there are show varieties shall make no placings beyond Best of Variety and Best of Opposite Sex to Best of Variety.

SECTION 22. The Miscellaneous Class shall be for pure-bred dogs of such breeds as may be designated by the Board of Directors of The American Kennel Club. No dog shall be eligible for entry in the Miscellaneous Class unless the owner has been granted an Indefinite Listing Privilege, and unless the ILP number is given on the entry form. Application for an Indefinite Listing Privilege shall be made on a form provided by the AKC and when submitted must be accompanied by a fee set by the Board of Directors.

All Miscellaneous Breeds shall be shown together in a single class except that the class may be divided by sex if so specified in the premium list. There shall be no further competition for dogs entered in this class.

The ribbons for First, Second, Third and Fourth prizes in this class shall be Rose, Brown, Light Green, and Gray, respectively.

At present the Miscellaneous Class is open to the following breeds:

> *Akitas*
> *Australian Cattle Dogs*
> *Australian Kelpies*
> *Bichon Frise (eligible since Sept. 1, 1971)*
> *Border Collies*

Judges try to make their selections fairly and carefully and their decisions should not be contested.

165

Cavalier King Charles Spaniels
Ibizan Hounds
Miniature Bull Terriers
Soft-Coated Wheaten Terriers
Spinoni Italiani
Tibetan Terriers

CHAPTER 8
RIBBONS, PRIZES AND TROPHIES

SECTION 1. All clubs or associations holding dog shows under the rules of The American Kennel Club, except sanctioned matches, shall use the following colors for their prize ribbons or rosettes, in the regular classes of The American Kennel Club and the regular group classes.

First prize—Blue.
Second prize—Red.
Third prize—Yellow.
Fourth prize—White.
Winners—Purple.
Reserve Winners—Purple and White.
Best of Winners—Blue and White.
Special prize—Dark Green.
Best of Breed and Best of Variety of Breed—Purple and Gold.
Best of Opposite Sex to Best of Breed and Best of Opposite Sex to Best of Variety of Breed—Red and White.

and shall use the following colors for their prize ribbons in all additional classes:

First prize—Rose.
Second prize—Brown.
Third prize—Light Green.
Fourth prize—Gray.

SECTION 2. The prize ribbon for Best Local Dog in Show shall be Blue and Gold, and the prize ribbons in local classes and local groups shall be:

First prize—Rose.
Second prize—Brown.
Third prize—Light Green.
Fourth prize—Gray.

SECTION 3. Each ribbon or rosette, except those used as sanctioned matches, shall be at least 2 inches wide, and approximately 8 inches long; and bear on its face a facsimile of the seal of The American Kennel Club, the name of the prize, and the name of the show-giving club with numerals of year, date of show, and name of city or town where show is given.

SECTION 4. If ribbons are given at sanctioned matches, they shall be of the following colors, but may be of any design or size:

First prize—Rose.
Second prize—Brown.
Third prize—Light Green.
Fourth prize—Gray.
Special prize—Green with pink edges.
Best of Breed—Orange.
Best of Match—Pink and Green.
Best of Opposite Sex to Best in Match—Lavender.

SECTION 5. If money prizes are offered in a premium list of a show, a fixed amount for each prize must be stated. All other prizes offered in a premium list of a show must be accurately described or their monetary value must be stated. Alcoholic beverages will not be acceptable as prizes.

SECTION 6. A show-giving club shall not accept the donation of a prize for a competition not provided for at its show.

SECTION 7. All prizes offered in a premium list of a show must be offered to be awarded in the regular procedure of judging, with the exception of those prizes provided for in Sections 9 and 13 of this Chapter.

SECTION 8. Prizes may be offered for outright award at a show for the following placings:

First, Second, Third, Fourth in the Puppy, Novice, Bred-by-Exhibitor, American-bred or Open Classes, or in any division of these designated in the Classification.

First, Second, Third, Fourth in any additional class which the show-giving club may offer in accord with the provisions of Chapter 6, Section 11, and in the Miscellaneous Class (at all-breed shows only).

Winners, Reserve Winners, Best of Winners, Best of Breed or Variety, Best of Opposite Sex to Best of Breed or Variety. At all-breed shows only: First, Second, Third, Fourth in a Group Class and for Best in Show, Best Local in Show, Best Brace in Show and Best Team in Show.

SECTION 9. At specialty shows held apart from all-breed shows, prizes, for outright award, may also be offered for:

Best in Puppy Classes, Best in Novice Classes, Best in Bred-by-Exhibitor Classes, Best in American-bred Classes, Best in Open Classes, Best in any additional classes which the show-giving club may offer in accord with the provisions of Chapter 6, Section 11, in which the sexes are divided.

(In breeds in which there are varieties, a prize may be offered for Best in any of the above classes within the variety.)

SECTION 10. At all-breed shows, prizes may be offered on a three-time win basis for the following awards, provided permanent possession goes to an exhibitor winning the award three times not necessarily with the same dog, and further provided such prizes are offered by the show-giving club itself or through it for competition at its shows only:

Best in Show, Best Local in Show, Best in any one group class.

SECTION 11. At specialty shows, prizes may be offered on a three-time win basis for the following awards, provided permanent possession goes to an exhibitor winning the award three times not necessarily with the same dog and further provided such prizes are offered by the specialty club itself or through it for competition at its specialty shows only:

Best of Breed or Best of Opposite Sex to Best of Breed (Where a specialty club considers the classes at an all-breed show as its specialty show, there can be no award for Best of Breed in those breeds in which there are varieties.) Best of Variety of Breed or Best of Opposite Sex to Best of Variety, Best of Winners, Winners Dog and Winners Bitch.

SECTION 12. Perpetual prizes and such three-time win prizes as have been in competition prior to September 9, 1952 and which would not be allowed under the terms of the sections in this Chapter will continue to be permitted to be offered under the terms of their original provisions until won outright or otherwise retired. Should premium list copy submitted to the AKC for approval contain such non-allowable prizes, a certification by the Club Secretary stating that the prizes have been in competition prior to September 9, 1952 must be included.

SECTION 13. Annual Specials are prizes offered by member or non-member specialty clubs for outright award at the end of a twelve-month period, the award to be based on the most number of wins at shows, in a designated competition, throughout the period.

Only those clubs which have held specialty shows can offer annual specials.

CHAPTER 10
JUDGES

SECTION 1. Any reputable person who is in good standing with The American Kennel Club may apply for leave to judge any breed or breeds of pure-bred dogs which in his or her opinion he or she is qualified by training and experience to pass upon, with the exception of persons connected with any publication in the capacity of solicitor for kennel advertisements, persons connected with dog food, dog remedy or kennel supply companies in the capacity of solicitor or salesman, persons employed in and about kennels, persons who buy, sell and in any way trade or traffic in dogs as a means of livelihood in whole or in part, whether or not they be known as dealers (excepting in this instance recognized private and professional handlers to a limited extent as will later appear) and professional show superintendents.

No Judge shall be granted a license to be an annual superintendent.

SECTION 2. The application for license to judge must be made on a form which will be supplied by The American Kennel Club upon request and when received by said club will be placed before the Board of Directors of The American Kennel Club who shall determine in each instance whether a license shall be issued.

SECTION 3. The American Kennel Club will not approve as judge for any given show the superintendent, show secretary, or show veterinarians, or club officials of said show acting in any one of these three capacities, and such person cannot officiate or judge at such show under any circumstances.

SECTION 4. Only those persons whose names are on The American Kennel Club's list of eligible judges may, in the discretion of The American Kennel Club, be approved to judge at any member or licensed show, except that if it

becomes necessary to replace an advertised judge after the opening of the show and no person on the eligible judges list is available to take his place, the Bench Show Committee may select as a substitute for the advertised judge a person whose name is not on the eligible judges list provided such person is not currently suspended from the privileges of The American Kennel Club, is not currently suspended as a judge and is not ineligible to judge under the provisions of Section 1 and 3 of this Chapter.

SECTION 5. The American Kennel Club may in its discretion approve as a judge of any sanctioned match, futurity or sweepstakes a person who is not currently suspended from the privileges of The American Kennel Club or whose judging privileges are not currently suspended.

SECTION 6. Bench show committees or superintendents shall, in every instance, notify appointed judges of the breeds and such group classes upon which they are to pass, and such notifications shall be given before the publication of the premium lists.

SECTION 7. Bench show committees or superintendents shall not add to or subtract from the number of breeds or variety groups which a selected judge has agreed to pass upon without first notifying said judge of and obtaining his consent to the contemplated change in his assigned breeds or variety groups, and the judge when so notified may refuse to judge any breeds or variety groups added to his original assignment.

SECTION 8. A bench show committee which shall be informed at any time prior to A WEEK before the opening

Some of the trophies awarded at a recent International Dog Show in Chicago.

day of its show that an advertised judge will not fulfill his or her place, which substitute judge must be approved by The American Kennel Club, and shall give notice of the name of the substitute judge to all those who have entered dogs in the classes allotted to be judged by the advertised judge. All those who have entered dogs to be shown under the advertised judge shall be permitted to withdraw their entries at any time prior to the opening day of the show and the entry fees paid for entering such dogs shall be refunded.

Since an entry can be made only under a breed judge, changes in Group or Best in Show assignments do not entitle an exhibitor to a refund.

SECTION 9. Should a Bench Show Committee be informed at any time within a week before the opening of its show, or after its show has opened, that an advertised judge will not fulfill his or her engagement to judge, it shall substitute a qualified judge in his or her place, and shall obtain approval of the change from The American Kennel Club if time allows.

No notice need be sent to those exhibitors who have entered dogs under the advertised judge.

The Bench Show Committee will be responsible for having a notice posted in a prominent place within the show precincts as soon after the show opens as is practical informing exhibitors of the change in judges. An exhibitor who has entered a dog under an advertised judge who is being replaced may withdraw such entry and shall have the entry fee refunded, provided notice of such withdrawal is given to the Superintendent or Show Secretary prior to the start of the judging of the breed which is to be passed upon by a substitute judge.

SECTION 12. Any club or association that holds a dog show must prepare, after the entries have closed and not before, a judging program showing the time scheduled for the judging of each breed and each variety for which entries have been accepted. The judging program shall also state the time for the start of group judging, if any. The program shall be based on the judging of about 25 dogs per hour by each judge. Each judge's breed and variety assignments shall be divided into periods of about one hour, except in those cases where the entry in a breed or variety exceeds 30. A copy

of the program shall be mailed to the owner of each entered dog and shall be printed in the catalog.

No judging shall occur at any show prior to the time specified in the judging program.

SECTION 13. The maximum number of dogs assigned in the breed judging to any judge, in one day, shall never exceed 175.

If a futurity or sweepstakes is offered in connection with a specialty show, which is held as part of an all-breed show, the above figure of 175 shall be reduced to 150 for the specialty show.

SECTION 14. A judge shall not exhibit his dogs or take any dog belonging to another person into the ring at any show at which he is officiating, nor shall he pass judgment in his official capacity upon any dog which he or any member of his immediate household or immediate family (as defined in Chapter 6, Section 6) has handled in the ring more than twice during the preceding twelve months.

SECTION 15. A judge's decision shall be final in all cases affecting the merits of the dogs. Full discretionary power is given to the judge to withhold any, or all, prizes for want of merit. After a class has once been judged in accordance with these rules and regulations, it shall not be rejudged. A class is considered judged when the judge has marked his book which must be done before the following class is examined. If any errors have been made by the judge in marking the awards as made, he may correct the same but must initial any such corrections.

SECTION 16. A judge may order any person or dog from the ring. For the purpose of facilitating the judging, judges are required to exclude from the rings in which they are judging all persons except the steward or stewards and the show attendants assigned to the ring and those actually engaged in exhibiting.

SECTION 17. A judge shall be supplied with a book called the judge's book in which he shall mark all awards and all absent dogs. The original judges' books at shows shall be in the custody of the judge, steward, superintendent, or superintendent's assistant. None other shall be allowed access to them. At the conclusion of the judging, the book must

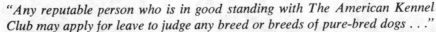

"Any reputable person who is in good standing with The American Kennel Club may apply for leave to judge any breed or breeds of pure-bred dogs . . ."

168

be signed by the judge and any changes which may have been made therein initialed by him.

SECTION 18. A judge's decision, as marked in the judge's book, cannot be changed by him after filing, but an error appearing in the judge's book may be corrected by The American Kennel Club after consultation with the judge.

SECTION 19. Only one judge shall officiate in each Group Class and only one judge shall select the Best in Show.

The Board of Directors suggests that whenever possible the Best in Show be determined by one who has not already judged any breed or group class of said show.

SECTION 20. If a judge disqualifies a dog at any show, he shall make a note in the judge's book giving his reasons for such disqualification. In computing the championship points for a breed, said dog shall not be considered as having been present at the show.

CHAPTER 11
HANDLERS

SECTION 1. And person handling dogs for pay or acting as agent for another for pay at any show held under the rules of The American Kennel Club must hold a license from The American Kennel Club.

Any reputable person who is in good standing with The American Kennel Club may apply to said Club for license to act as a handler or as an agent, which application must be made on a form which will be supplied by said Club upon request. When the application is received by The American Kennel Club the Board of Directors shall determine whether a license shall be issued to the applicant.

SECTION 2. The fee for being granted a license to be a handler or an agent, or an assistant to a handler or an agent, shall be determined by the Board of Directors of The American Kennel Club from time to time in its discretion. Any such license may be granted for any such period of time that the Board of Directors deems appropriate in its discretion. All granted licenses shall expire December 31 of the year in which they are granted.

Effective January 1, 1954, no fee is required with applications for Handlers or Assistant Handlers licenses.

No handler's license will be granted to a person residing in the same household with a licensed judge.

CHAPTER 16
DOG SHOW ENTRIES
CONDITIONS OF DOGS AFFECTING ELIGIBILITY

SECTON 1. No dog shall be eligible to be entered in a licensed or member dog show, except for dogs entered in the Miscellaneous Class, unless it is either individually registered in the AKC Stud Book or part of an AKC registered litter, or otherwise, if whelped outside the United States of America and owned by a resident of the U.S.A. or Canada, unless it has been registered in its country of birth with a foreign registry organization whose pedigrees are acceptable for AKC registration.

An unregistered dog that is part of an AKC registered litter or an unregistered dog with an acceptable foreign registration that was whelped outside the U.S.A. and that is owned by a resident of the U.S.A. or Canada may, without special AKC approval, be entered in licensed or member dog shows that are held not later than 30 days after the date of the first licensed or member dog show in which the dog was entered, but only provided that the AKC litter registration number or the individual foreign registration number and the name of the country of birth, are shown on the entry form, and provided further that the same name, which in the case of an imported or Canadian owned dog must be the name on the foreign registration, is used for the dog each itme.

SECTION 2. At every show held under the rules of The American Kennel Club, a recording fee not to exceed 25 cents may be required for every dog entered. This recording fee is to help defray expenses involved in keeping show records, and applies to all dogs entered. If a dog is entered in more than one class at a show, the recording fee applies only to first entry. The Board of Directors shall determine, from time to time, whether a recording fee shall be required, and the amount of it.

Effective June 1, 1954 recording fees are not required.

SECTION 3. Every dog must be entered in the name of the person who actually owned the dog at the time entries closed. The right to exhibit a dog cannot be transferred. A registered dog which has been acquired by some person other than the owner as recorded with The American Kennel Club must be entered in the name of its new owner at any show for which entries close after the date upon which the dog was acquired, and application for transfer of ownership must be sent to The American Kennel Club by the new owner within seven days after the last day of the show. The new owner should state on the entry form that transfer application has been mailed to The American Kennel Club or will be mailed shortly. If there is any unavoidable delay in obtaining the completed application required to record the transfer, The American Kennel Club may grant a reasonable extension of time, provided the new owner notifies the show records department of The American Kennel Club by mail within seven days after the show, of the reason for the delay. If an entry is made by a duly authorized agent of the owner, the name of the actual owner must be shown on the entry form. If a dog is owned by an association, the name of the association and a list of its officers must be shown on the entry form.

SECTION 4. To be acceptable, an entry must be submitted with required entry fee, on an official American Kennel Club entry form, signed by the owner or his duly authorized agent, and must include all of the following information: Name of the club holding the show; the date of the show; breed; variety, if any; sex; full description of the class or classes in which entered; full name of dog; individual registration number or AKC litter number or, for a dog entered in the Miscellaneous Class, ILP number; name and address of the actual owner or owners. For a dog whelped outside the U.S.A. that is not AKC registered, the entry form must show the individual foreign registration number and country of birth. In addition, an entry in the Puppy, Novice, Bred-by-Exhibitor, or American-bred class must include the place of birth; an entry in the Puppy Class must include the date of birth; and an entry in the Bred-by-Exhibitor class must include the name or names of the breeder or breeders.

No entry may be accepted unless it is received by the Superintendent or Show Secretary named in the premium list to receive entries prior to the closing date and hour as published in the premium list, and unless it meets all the requirements of the foregoing paragraph and all other specific requirements printed in the premium list.

SECTION 5. No entry shall be made and no entry shall be accepted by a Superintendent or Show Secretary which specifies any condition as to its acceptance.

SECTION 6. No change may be made in any otherwise acceptable entry form unless the change is received in writing or by telegraph, by the Superintendent or Show Secretary named in the premium list to receive entries, prior to the published closing date and hour of entries, except that a correction may be made in the sex of a dog at a show prior to the judging. No dog wrongly entered in a class may otherwise be transferred to another class. Owners are responsible for errors in entry forms, regardless of who may make such errors.

SECTION 7. No entry shall be received from any person

who is not in good standing with The American Kennel Club on the day of the closing of the entries. Before accepting entries, a list of persons not in good standing must be obtained by the Show Superintendent or Show Secretary from The American Kennel Club.

SECTION 8. No entry shall be made under a kennel name unless that name has been registered with The American Kennel Club. All entries made under a kennel name must be signed with the kennel name followed by the word "registered." An "exhibitor" or "entrant" is the individual or, if a partnership, all the members of the partnership exhibiting or entering in a dog show. In the case of such an entry by a partnership every member of the partnership shall be in good standing with The American Kennel Club before the entry will be accepted; and in case of any infraction of these rules, all the partners shall be held equally responsible.

SECTION 9. A dog which is blind, deaf, castrated, spayed, or which has been changed in appearance by artificial means except as specified in the standard for its breed, or a male which does not have two normal testicles normally located in the scrotum, may not compete at any show and will be disqualified. A dog will not be considered to have been changed by artificial means because of removal of dew claws or docking of tail if it is of a breed in which such removal or docking is a regularly approved practice which is not contrary to the standard.

When a judge finds evidence of any of these conditions in any dog he is judging he must, before proceeding with the judging, notify the Superintendent or Show Secretary and must call an official show veterinarian to examine the dog in the ring and to give the judge an advisory opinion in writing on the condition of the dog. Only after he has seen the veterinarian's opinion in writing shall the judge render his own decision and record it in the judge's book, marking the dog "disqualified" and stating the reason if he determines that disqualification is required under this rule. The judge's decision is final and need not necessarily agree with the veterinarian's opinion. The written opinion of the veterinarian shall in all cases be forwarded to The American Kennel Club by the Superintendent or Show Secretary.

When a dog has been disqualified under this rule or under the standard for its breed, either by a judge or by decision of a Bench Show Committee, any awards at that show shall be cancelled by The American Kennel Club and the dog may not again be shown unless and until, following application by the owner to The American Kennel Club, the owner has received official notification from The American Kennel Club that the dog's show eligibility has been reinstated. The American Kennel Club will not entertain any application for reinstatement of a male which has been disqualified as not having two normal testicles normally located in the scrotum until the dog is twelve (12) months old.

SECTION 9-A. A dog that is lame at any show may not compete and shall not receive any award at that show. It shall be the judge's responsibility to determine whether a dog is lame. He shall not obtain the opinion of the show veterinarian. If in the judge's opinion a dog in the ring is lame, he shall withhold all awards from such dog and shall excuse it from the ring. A dog so excused shall not be counted as having competed. When a judge excuses a dog from the ring for lameness, he shall mark his book "Excused —lame."

SECTION 9-B. No dog shall be eligible to compete at any show and no dog shall receive any award at any show in the event the natural color or shade of natural color or the natural markings of the dog have been altered or changed by the use of any substance whether such substance may have been used for cleaning purposes or for any other reason.

Such cleaning substances are to be removed before the dog enters the ring.

If in the judge's opinion any substance has been used to alter or change the natural color or shade of natural color or natural markings of a dog, then in such event the judge shall withhold any and all awards from such dog, and the judge shall make a note in the judge's book giving his reason for withholding such award. The handler or the owner, or both, of any dog or dogs from which any award has been withheld for violation of this section of the rules, or any judge who shall fail to perform his duties under this section shall be subject to disciplinary action.

SECTION 9-C. Any dog whose ears have been cropped or cut in any way shall be ineligible to compete at any show in any state where the laws prohibit the same except subject to the provisions of such laws.

SECTION 10. No dog shall be eligible to compete at any show, no dog shall be brought into the grounds or premises of any dog show, and any dog which may have been brought into the grounds or premises of a dog show immediately be removed, if it

(a) shows clinical symptoms of distemper, infectious hepatitis, leptospirosis or other communicable disease, or

(b) is known to have been in contact with distemper, infectious hepatitis, leptospirosis or other communicable disease within thirty days prior to the opening of the show, or

(c) has been kenneled within thirty days prior to the opening of the show on premises on which there existed distemper, infectious hepatitis, leptospirosis or other communicable disease.

SECTION 11. A club may engage dogs not entered in its show as a special attraction provided the written approval of The American Kennel Club is first obtained.

SECTION 12. No dog not regularly entered in a show, other than one engaged as a special attraction, shall be allowed within the show precincts, except when the club has stated in its premium list that space will be provided for dogs not entered in the show. The club must then provide an area, clearly identified by an appropriate sign. This area shall be exclusively for dogs which are either en route to or from other shows in which entered, or which are being delivered to new owners or custodians, or being returned to their owners. No dog may be placed in this area if it is entered in the show, nor unless it is registered or registrable and eligible to be shown under American Kennel Club rules and the standard for its breed.

An owner or agent who wishes to use this facility shall, upon entering the show, file with the Superintendent or Show Secretary a form giving the dog's registration data and the reason for its presence. The Superintendent or Show Secretary will then issue a tag identifying the dog. This tag is to be attached to the crate or container which the owner or agent must supply.

CHAPTER 17

THE CATALOG

SECTION 1. Every Bench Show Committee shall provide a printed catalog which shall contain all particulars required of exhibitors entering dogs as hereinafter provided. It shall also contain the exact location of the show, the date or dates on which it is to be held, the times of opening and closing of the show, a list of all officers and members of the Bench Show Committee names and complete addresses of all judges and of the Superintendent or Show Secretary, the names of the veterinarians or local veterinary association providing veterinary service at the show, and an alphabetical list of the names and addresses of all exhibitors.

CHAPTER 18
BENCHING OF DOGS

SECTION 1. At a Benched Show to which admission is charged, every dog twelve months old and over that is entered and present must be on its bench throughout the advertised hours of the show's duration, except for the necessary periods when it is actually being prepared for showing at its crate, or is being shown, or is in the exercise ring, or is being taken to or from these places. The advertised hours of the show's duration shall be hours from the scheduled start of judging to the time shown in the premium list for the closing of the show.

No such dog shall be in its crate during the advertised hours of the show's duration except by written permission of the Superintendent or Show Secretary, and except for a period of one hour before the time printed in the program for the judging of its breed or variety and, if it becomes eligible for its Group or for Best in Show, for a period of one hour before the time printed in the program for the judging of such competition.

SECTION 2. The provisions of Section 1 also apply to a dog under 12 months of age except that it need not be benched until after the judging of the breed classes for which it is entered or becomes eligible and it may be in its crate until the judging of those classes. At a two day show it is required to be present only on the day it is to be judged.

SECTION 3. Failure to comply with these rules may cause cancellation of the dog's winnings, and subject the owner, handler, and Superintendent or Show Secretary to a fine and suspension of license and privileges.

SECTION 4. No signs shall be displayed on a bench except the plaque or emblem of a show-giving specialty club to which the dog's owner belongs, and signs not over 11 x 14 inches offering dogs or puppies for sale, or giving the kennel name and address of the owner, or the dog's name and a list of awards won by it at that show, or the name of the show-giving specialty club of which the dog's owner is a member. No prizes or ribbons shall be displayed on the bench except those won by the dog at that show.

SECTION 5. At an Unbenched Show, a sign stating that the show is unbenched shall be prominently displayed wherever admission tickets are sold.

CHAPTER 19
MEASURING, WEIGHING AND COLOR DETERMINATIONS WHEN FACTORS OF DISQUALIFICATION IN BREED STANDARDS OR ELIGIBILITY UNDER THE CONDITIONS OF A CLASS OR DIVISON OF A CLASS.
CANCELLATION OF AWARDS

SECTION 1. Every dog entered and present at a show must compete in all competition in its breed or variety for which it is entered or becomes eligible, unless it has been excused, dismissed, disqualified or found to be ineligible, under the rules.

SECTION 2. Any club or association giving a dog show must provide arm cards and shall see that every person exhibiting a dog wears, when in the ring, an arm card containing thereon the catalog number of the dog being exhibited; but no badges, coats with kennel names thereon or ribbon prizes shall be worn or displayed, nor other visible means of identification used, by an individual when exhibiting a dog in the ring.

SECTION 3. The owner of a dog that is entered in a show, or the owner's agent, may request a determination of a dog's height or a dog's weight, if these factors are breed standard disqualifications, conditions of a class or conditions of a division of a class in which the dog is entered. Such requests may be made at any time after the opening of a show, but must be made before the scheduled time of the judging of the breed or variety. The determination, as made, shall be recorded on an American Kennel Club measuring and weighing form, and note of the height or weight of the dog, as the case may be, must promptly be made in the judge's book, by the superintendent or show secretary.

If the height or weight of the dog as determined under this Section is in accord with the breed standards or the conditions of the class or division thereof in which it is entered, the determination shall hold good for the duration of the show, and that show only and the dog cannot be in any way

Awaiting the judge's decision—a tense, anxious moment. (Photo by Maia Coven.)

challenged or protested as to height or weight at that show, except that a judge may request a reweighing of the dog when it comes under judgment, and a determination made at that time shall supersede the previous determination.

If the height or weight of the dog as determined under this Section is not in accord with the breed standard or the conditions of the class or division thereof in which it is entered, the dog shall immediately be declared ineligible to compete by the Superintendent or Show Secretary and shall be marked absent in the Judge's Book. Such a dog shall not be brought into the judging ring and may be excused from the show immediately. The eligibility of such a dog to compete at subsequent shows shall not be affected.

SECTION 4. In those breeds where certain heights or weights are specified in the standard as disqualifications, or in any class or division of a class the conditions for which include a height or weight specification, it shall be the judge's responsibility to initiate a determination as to whether a dog is to be disqualified or declared to be ineligible for the class.

If, in the judge's opinion, the height or weight of a dog under judgment appears not to be in accord with the breed standard or the conditions of a class or division thereof, the judge, before proceeding with the judging, must notify the superintendent or show secretary and request that the dog's height or weight be determined by persons appointed by the bench show committee for that purpose, unless the dog's height has previously been determined at the show, or unless the dog's weight has previously been determined at the show other than under the provisions of Chapter 19, Section 3. When a completed AKC measuring and weighing form has been submitted to the judge by such persons, giving the height or weight of the dog, the judge shall then disqualify the dog if its height or weight is such as to require disqualification under the standard of the breed, or shall declare the dog to be ineligible if its height or weight is such as to not conform with the conditions of the class or division in which it is competing, in either case making note of the fact in the judge's book.

If, in the opinion of any competing exhibitor or handler then in the ring, the height or weight of a dog under judgment (not previously determined at the show) appears not to be in accord with the breed standard or the conditions of a class or division thereof, such exhibitor or handler may, prior to the time the judge has marked his book, request the judge to proceed as above in obtaining a determination of the dog's height or weight. After the judge has obtained the completed AKC measuring and weighing form giving the height or weight of the dog, he shall then disqualify the dog if its height or weight is such as to require disqualification under the standard of the breed, or shall declare the dog to be ineligible if its height or weight is such as to not conform with the conditions of the class or division in which it is competing, in either case making note of the fact in the judge's book.

Any dog thus disqualified by the judge may not again be shown unless and until, following application by the owner to The American Kennel Club, the owner has received official notification from The American Kennel Club that the dog's show eligibility has been reinstated.

Any dog thus declared ineligible by the judge for a class or division thereof shall be considered to have been wrongly entered in the class and cannot be transferred to any other class or division at the show.

Any dog that has been found to be ineligible as to height under the conditions of a class may not again be shown in that class unless and until, following application by the owners to The American Kennel Club, the owner has received official notification from The American Kennel Club that the dog's show eligibility has been reinstated. However, without making such application to The American Kennel Club, the owner of such a dog may enter the dog in a different class,

provided the measurement made at the show is within the specified height limits of such class.

SECTION 5. Bench Show Committees shall be responsible for providing a suitable measuring stand and accurate scales at every show. Bench Show Committees must appoint three persons whose duty it will be, when called upon, to determine a dog's height or weight.

SECTION 6. In those breeds where certain colors or markings are specified in the standard as disqualifications, or in any class or division of a class where a certain color, or colors or combinations of colors are required by the conditions of the class or division thereof, it shall be the judge's responsibility to determine whether a dog is to be disqualified or declared to be ineligible for the class.

If, in the opinion of the judge, the dog's color or markings are such as to require disqualification, the judge shall disqualify the dog, making note of the fact in the judge's book.

If, in the opinion of the judge, the dog's color or markings do not meet the requirements of the class or division of a class in which the dog is competing, the judge shall declare the dog ineligible to compete in that class or division of class, making note of the fact in the judge's book.

If, in the opinion of any competing exhibitor or handler then in the ring, the color or markings or combination of colors of a dog under judgment are such as to disqualify under the standard or are such as not to meet the requirements of the class or division thereof, such exhibitor or handler may, prior to the time the judge has marked his book, request the judge to render an opinion of the dog's color(s) and markings. Before proceeding with the judging, the judge must write his opinion on an AKC form that will be supplied by the superintendent or show secretary for that purpose, and shall disqualify the dog if its color or markings are such as to require disqualification under the breed standard or shall declare the dog ineligible if the color or markings do not meet the requirements of the class or division thereof in which the dog is competing, in either case making note of the fact in the judge's book.

Any dog thus disqualified by the judge under the standard may not again be shown unless and until, following application by the owner to The American Kennel Club, the owner has received official notification from the American Kennel Club that the dog's show eligibility has been reinstated.

Any dog thus declared by the judge to be ineligible for a class or division thereof shall be considered to have been wrongly entered in the class and cannot be transferred to any other class or division at that show.

CHAPTER 20

PROTESTS AGAINST DOGS

SECTION 1. Every exhibitor and handler shall have the right to request through the superintendent or show secretary the examination, by one of a show's veterinarians, of any dog within a show's premises which is considered to endanger the health of other dogs in a show. The request is to be in writing and on a form obtainable from a superintendent or show secretary, whose duty it will be to see that the subject dog is promptly taken to the "Veterinarian Headquarters" by its owner or the owner's agent.

SECTION 2. A protest against a dog may be made by any exhibitor, entrant or any member of a member club of The American Kennel Club. It shall be in writing, and be lodged with the secretary of the show-giving club within seven (7) days of the last day of the show unless the same be made by The American Kennel Club, provided, however, that a protest calling for a decision as to the physical condition of a dog which can be determined only with the advice of a veterinarian or at the time of showing shall be made before the closing of the show.

No protest will be entertained unless accompanied by a deposit of five ($5.00) dollars, which will be returned if the protest is sustained. This does not apply to protests by The American Kennel Club, nor to a protest made in the ring previous to the rendering of his decision by the judge.

CHAPTER 21
CHAMPIONSHIPS

SECTION 1. Championship points will be recorded for Winners Dog and Winners Bitch, when Winners Classes are divided by sex, for each breed or variety listed in Chapter 6, Section 1, at licensed or member dog shows approved by The American Kennel Club, provided the certification of the Secretary as described in Chapter 9, Section 1, has been printed in the premium list for the show.

Championship points will be recorded according to the number of eligible dogs competing in the regular classes of each sex in each breed or variety, and according to the Schedule of Points established by the Board of Directors. In counting the number of eligible dogs in competition, a dog that is disqualified, or that is dismissed, excused or ordered from the ring by the Judge, or from which all awards are withheld, shall not be included.

If the Winners Class is not divided by sex, championship points will be recorded for the dog or bitch awarded Winners, based on the schedule of points for the sex of the breed or variety for which the greater number in competition is required.

SECTION 2. A dog which in its breed competition at a show shall have been placed Winners and which also shall have won its group class at the same show shall be awarded championship points figured at the highest point rating of any breed or recognized variety or height of any breed entered in the show have been designated Best in Show, shall be awarded championship points figured at the highest point rating of any breed or recognized variety or height of any breed entered and entitled to winners points in the show. The final points to be awarded under this section shall not be in addition to but inclusive of any points previously awarded the dog in its breed competition or under the provisions of this section.

SECTION 3. At shows in which the winners' classes of certain breeds are divided into recognized varieties of those breeds as specified in Section 1 of Chapter 6 of these Rules and Regulations, the procedure of computing championship points shall be the same as if each recognized variety were a separate breed.

SECTION 4. Any dog which shall have won fifteen points shall become a Champion of Record, if six or more of said points shall have been won at two shows with a rating of three or more championship points each and under two different judges, and some one or more of the balance of said points shall have been won under some other judge or judges than the two judges referred to above. A dog becomes a champion when it is so officially recorded by The American Kennel Club and when registered in the Stud Book shall be entitled to a championship certificate.

SECTION 5. Any dog which has been awarded the title of Champion of Record may be designated as a "Dual Champion" after it also has been awarded the title of Field Champion, but no certificate will be awarded for a Dual Championship.

CHAPTER 22
SUBMISSION OF A SHOW'S RECORDS TO AKC

SECTION 1. A show-giving club shall pay or distribute all prizes offered at its show within thirty (30) days after The American Kennel Club has checked the awards of said show.

SECTION 2. After each licensed or member club dog show a catalog marked with all awards and absent dogs, certified to by the superintendent or show secretary of the show, together with all judges' books, all original entry forms and a report of the show must be sent to The American Kennel Club so as to reach its office within seven (7) days after the close of the show. Penalty for noncompliance, one ($1.00) dollar for each day's delay and such other penalties as may be imposed by the Board of Directors of The American Kennel Club. All recording fees shall be paid to The American Kennel Club within seven (7) days after the close of the show.

Reprinted by permission of The American Kennel Club.

Aerial view of a typical dog show. Benching area is in foreground and competition rings in background.

JUDGING AT A DOG SHOW

THE judges are persons who have been licensed by the American Kennel Club to officiate at the shows. Some persons are licensed to judge only one breed; some are licensed to judge several or many breeds and a very few persons are licensed to judge every breed.

The judge is expected to judge each dog before him according to the standard as adopted by the particular breed club and approved by the American Kennel Club.

Physical conformation of the dog is of primary importance and other factors found in all standards are conditions of coat; ability to gait, or run, with an even movement; and general behavior in the ring.

Obviously all judges do not have the same opinion of each dog and a dog that wins at one show against the competing dogs may not win at the next show under a different judge and against other dogs. This is where the "sporting" factor enters for the exhibitor

and his dog and explains why each show is a new venture for both.

Dogs defeated at one stage or the other as the judging progresses are not necessarily inferior specimens of the breed in the judge's opinion—the judge has simply given his opinion that the winning dog is nearer the standard of perfection for the breed, considering the condition and appearance of all the entries on the day of the judging.

Five Classes

In each breed the exhibitor has the opportunity of entering his dog in one of five classes generally scheduled. In some of the breeds there are more than five classes as explained below. The same classes are provided for the male and female sexes and the classes for males are always judged first.

(1) **The Puppy Class** shall be for dogs six months and not exceeding twelve months of age. The age of a dog shall be calculated up to and inclusive of the day preceding the show.

(2) **The Novice Class** is for a dog that has never won a first prize in a regular class at any show, including Winners Class, wins in Puppy Classes, excepted. Only dogs whelped in United States and Canada are eligible.

(3) **Bred by Exhibitor Class** shall be for all dogs excepting Champions, six months of age and over which shall be presently owned and exhibited by the same person or kennel who were the recognized breeders on the records of the American Kennel Club.

(4) **The American-bred Class** is for all dogs (except champions) six months and over, born in the United States by reason of a mating which took place in the United States.

(5) **The Open Class** shall be for any dog six months of age or over except in a member specialty club show held only for American-bred dogs, in which case the Open Class shall be only for American-bred dogs.

"Winners" and "Reserve Winners"

After the winner of each of the classes has been selected, all of the class winners of the sex are brought together and the best among them is chosen and designated (6) "Winners Dog" (best male). The second best is designated (7) "Reserve Winners Dog."

The "Winner Dog" is awarded points toward his

MISCELLANEOUS ITEMS ABOUT JUDGING AT A SHOW

- In almost every breed, cowhocks are a fault.

- Noses should usually be black except in dogs where the nose color blends with the coat, such as brown or slate and the standards approve.

- There are about 2,400 people who are eligible as judges at American Kennel Club shows.

- Prize ribbons should always be presented by the judge to the winners.

- A dog show judge is not to see the show's catalog.

- A lame, monorchid, cryptochid, deaf, or blind dog is not to be shown.

Championship—the number of points depending on the number of males that were shown in the classes of the particular breed being judged. A dog must win points to become a Champion and no more than five points can be won at any show regardless of the number of dogs of the breed entered at the show.

The same classes for females are then judged and a (8) "Winners Bitch" (best female) and (9) "Reserve Winners Bitch" are selected. The "Winners Bitch" is likewise awarded a certain number of points toward her Championship, depending on the number of females that were shown in the classes for the breed.

The "Winners Dog" and "Winners Bitch" then compete against each other and the judge selects the better of the two and the award (10) "Best of Winners" is made to the one chosen.

"Specials Only"

Then the males and females entered in the class for (11) "Specials Only" (all of which must be champions of record) and any undefeated dogs which have competed at the show only in classes other than the regular classes are brought into the ring to compete against the male or female that has been chosen (10) "Best of Winners."

"Best of Breed"

From all these dogs the judge selects the best one in his opinion and awards the (12) "Best of Breed" or (12a) "Best of Variety of Breed" ribbon to the one selected. (Some breeds have two varieties, Beagles; some have three varieties, Cocker Spaniels.) That means the male or female selected has been judged to be the best dog of the (12) breed or (12a) variety entered in the show. In case no dogs are entered for (11) "Specials Only" the dog previously selected as (10) "Best of Winners" is automatically designated as (12) "Best of Breed" or (12a) "Best of Variety of Breed" without further judging.

Six Special Groups

After the best dog of each breed has been selected at the show the winning dogs meet in one of the six different groups—all Sporting dogs designated "Best of Breed" meeting in the (13) Sporting group, for example. This procedure is followed in the (14) Hound Group, the (15) Working Group, the (16) Terrier Group, the (17) Toy Group and the (18) Non-Sporting Group.

Ten Crown Jewel Dalmatian bitches on exhibit during the Chicago International Dog Show.

Final Judging Best in Show

The winner of each of these groups then is brought into the ring and one of the six dogs is judged to be (19) "Best Dog in Show."

Best American Bred Dog

This dog is selected from the six dogs which have been judged Best American Bred (20) in each of the Variety Groups. If the Best In Show is not an American Bred, the judge ascertains which dog in the group from which he selected his Best In Show, was judged the Best American Bred dog in that group and that dog should then come in the ring. If any of the five remaining dogs are not American Bred they leave the ring and the best American Bred in each of those five groups come in.

How Champions Are Made

To become a champion, a dog must win 15 championship points. Championship points are earned only by placing first in the Winners class. However, the dog chosen Best of Winners is entitled to the higher number of points won in the two sexes.

For example, if there were very few males competing and the Winners Dog won only one point, but beat the Winners Bitch, who had won five because of more competition, then he would also be entitled to five points.

Championship points are awarded on a scale drawn up by The American Kennel Club. The country is divided into four groups, then points for each breed are figured on the basis of national registrations and previous show entries for that area.

All show catalogs are required to carry the scale of points for all breeds in the section of the country where the show is held. This may vary for dogs and bitches of the same breed.

Five points is the largest number that can be won at one show. Rare breeds can combine the sexes for judging. This yields more championship points but only one winners class instead of the usual two.

The German Shepherd Dog is one of the most popular breeds and the most often shown dog. So it requires an average of between 50-60 males in actual class competition to yield five championship points; 55-65 bitches must compete to gain five points, depending on location of show.

There is one other way in which a dog can win championship points. If a dog comes up through the classes, wins Best of his Breed, then wins first of his group, he is entitled to the maximum number of points awarded to any other dog in the group.

A check system to prevent "cheap championships" is set by the rule that a dog must win two shows with three points or more under at least two different judges.

Who Runs the Show

The sponsor of a show is either a local all-breed dog club or a club whose members are fanciers of a particular breed. The latter often hold "specialty shows" restricted to the single breed. The active management of most shows is turned over to a show superintendent who supplies the necessary equipment and takes charge of all arrangements.

All dogs shows where championship points are awarded are held under the rules of the A.K.C., which has the responsibility of licensing judges and superintendents, registering pure-bred dogs, and keeping records of the awards and points given at every show.

Conduct In the Ring

Neatness in appearance is taken for granted. Simple unrestricting clothing is preferable. In Summer, the shows are out of doors, so a light weight cotton dress, trim and unadorned or a pair of culottes are perfect for the woman. The man may wear a fresh, neatly pressed slack and sport shirt. The Winter shows are inside, but many times the buildings are unheated. Dress accordingly. Pants suits for women are now permissable, and panty hose have proved a blessing as there is a great deal of stooping and bending in exhibiting a dog. Men usually wear suits and ties.

The judge is always well dressed. The woman wears a corsage and the man a buttonniere so that they are distinguished from the exhibitor.

Many times the exhibitor finds he is being crowded in the ring by the exhibitor next to him. This may be accidental or deliberate. Try to move to another place as quietly as possible, and without any disturbance. Never raise your voice or display anger, and above all do not chat with your neighbor. Any display of this kind may interfere with the judge's trend of thought and he may even find cause to dismiss you from the ring with a warning, or report you to the A.K.C. where a fine may be imposed. In the ring the judge is sovereign.

When judging has been concluded and the photographer has photographed the winning dog, with the handler and judge, you may enter the ring and address the steward if you have been nursing a grievance. Make your charge of misconduct to the steward, who will record the complaint, if he believes it is warranted. This report will go to the American Kennel Club for consideration. If the complaint is taken the offender may have his license revoked (if a professional handler) or a fine imposed and the dog may even be disqualified. All this must be done immediately, or within a couple of hours, or it will not be accepted.

Remember that you have spent a great deal of time training your dog to be well mannered in the ring, so you, too, must be beyond reproach.

OBEDIENCE TRAINING

OBEDIENCE training is training for proper behavior, and it gives the dog owner an education in dog management. It is a training course of regular and repeated work. To complete the Companion Dog course, the dog must successfully complete these six fundamental exercises:

1—Heeling on the Leash

On the signal "Heel!" the dog must voluntarily walk on the handler's left side with his right shoulder in line with the guide's left knee. The leash should hang loosely from the trainer's right hand. The dog must heel when the handler turns. The object of this exercise is to teach the dog to stay at your side. During training, a regular collar or a chain choke collar can be used.

When you stop, the dog must be taught to sit smartly at your side. To teach him to sit, push down on his back as you pull up slightly on the lead. Command "Sit" as you are doing this. Repeat this exercise until it becomes satisfactory. Praise the dog when he performs well.

2—Heeling Free

In this exercise, which is started after the dog has mastered heeling on the leash, the leash is removed and the dog should heel just as properly as if the leash were attached. To train him for this you will need to alternate having the leash on and off until the control is attained.

3—Stand for Examination

For this exercise, the dog is commanded to "Heel." Then, the handler orders "Stand-stay," and then he walks around and stands in front of the dog. The dog must remain standing while being examined by the judge. The dog stands until the handler returns to his side and the judge states "Exercise finished." The difficulty in this exercise is the dog must learn to stand here rather than to sit. Allowing a stranger to examine him may also be a true test for your dog. Train him for this by having friends examine him during this exercise.

4—The Recall

The dog is commanded to "Sit" and "Stay" as the handler walks away and then turns and faces the dog. At the signal, "Come," the dog should quickly return to the handler and sit down in front of him. At the next signal, the dog should walk around and sit down at the handler's left leg.

5—Long Sit

The dog is commanded to "Sit" and "Stay" while the handler moves away. Remaining in the sitting position for the duration of the exercise is the goal. During the "sitting three minutes" test, the handler remains out of sight and the dog must hold the "Sit-stay" until the exercise is finished.

NOTES OF INTEREST ON OBEDIENCE TRAINING

1—The purpose of training is to teach the dog how to please his master.

2—Obedience training is a relatively young idea. The first obedience club started in Chicago in 1933.

3—What is the best age to start training? Most professional trainers prefer to start a puppy no younger than ten to twelve months of age. Maturity is no barrier. An older dog *can* be taught new tricks!

4—What should you do if you don't have the time to train your own dog? There are training kennels which will do the job for you.

5—The American Kennel Club has set up four levels of obedience competition:

    Companion Dog—C.D.
    Companion Dog Excellent—C.D.X.
    Utility Dog—U.D.
    Utility Dog Tracker—U.D.T.

6—General training methods are:

    a—Demonstrate what you want the dog to do.

    b—Reward him with praise, a pat, or kind words.

    c—Repeat lesson until it is learned.

    d—Limit the length of time for beginning lessons to no more than five minutes at a time.

    e—Repeat exercise until it becomes second nature.

6—Long Down

On the command, "Down," the dog must lie down after which the handler walks away. He is to hold this down position for at least three minutes or till the handler returns and orders him to sit.

These exercises must be taught on a repetitive basis. Obedience training classes provide teaching and training for the handler in the proper procedures. In addition to class time, the dog must be worked with at home on a daily schedule if any progress is to be made. Patience and praise are extremely vital during this training period. If these exercises sound as though they would be useful for your dog to master, then give definite thought to enrolling in an obedience school. After successfully completing the course, you may wish to enter an official American Kennel Club Obedience Trial and compete for a degree. If you want, you can, with perseverance, train your dog at home without attending an obedience course.

If you go to obedience school:

1—Regular class attendance is essential.
2—Several short daily practice sessions are needed.
3—Constant praise and much patience are required.
4—Review, review, review is necessary.
5—When classes are over, practice should continue.
6—If your dog is successful in this first course, have some fun and enter an obedience trial.

The Professional Handler

The American and the Canadian Kennel Clubs license professional handlers who will exhibit dogs for others. The granting of a handler's license indicates that he or she is an experienced person skilled at grooming and showing dogs and that adequate kennels are maintained in which to keep dogs between shows.

Owners usually pay entry fees and board during the weeks between shows. Handlers get any prize money the dog might win. Trophies go to the owners of the winning dogs.

OBEDIENCE TRIAL REGULATIONS

The following excerpts from Obedience Regulations, *published by The American Kennel Club, have been selected because they should be of specific interest to the dog owner planning to compete in an obedience trial. The complete booklet can be ordered from The American Kennel Club.*

Purpose

Obedience trials are a sport and all participants should be guided by the principles of good sportsmanship both in and outside of the ring. The purpose of obedience trials is to demonstrate the usefulness of the pure-bred dog as a companion of man, not merely the dog's ability to follow specified routines in the obedience ring. While all contestants in a class are required to perform the same exercises in substantially the same way so that the relative quality of the various performances may be compared and scored, the basic objective of obedience trials is to produce dogs that have been trained and conditioned always to behave in the home, in public places, and in the presence of other dogs, in a manner that will reflect credit on the sport of obedience. The performances of dog and handler in the ring must be accurate and correct and must conform to the requirements of these regulations. However, it is also essential that the dog demonstrate willingness and enjoyment of its work, and smoothness and naturalness on the part of the handler are to be preferred to a performance based on military precision and peremptory commands.

General Regulations

Section 10. **Pure-Bred Dogs Only.** As used in these regulations the word "dog" refers to either sex but only to dogs that are pure-bred of a breed eligible for registration in the American Kennel Club stud book or for entry in the Miscellaneous Class at American Kennel Club dog shows, as only such dogs may compete in obedience trials, tracking tests, or sanctioned matches. A judge must report to The American Kennel Club after the trial or tracking test any dog shown under him which in his opinion appears not to be purebred.

Section 14. **Disqualification and Ineligibility.** A dog that is blind or deaf or that has been changed in appearance by artificial means (except for such changes as are customarily approved for its breed) may not compete in any obedience trial or tracking test and must be disqualified. Blind means having useful vision in neither eye. Deaf means without useful hearing.

If a judge has evidence of any of these conditions in any dog he is judging at an obedience trial he must, before proceeding with the judging, notify the Superintendent or Show or Trial Secretary and must call an official veterinarian to examine the dog in the ring and give to the judge an advisory opinion in writing on the condition of the dog. Only after he has seen the opinion of the veterinarian in writing shall the judge render his own decision and record it in the judge's book, marking the dog disqualified and stating the reason if he determines that disqualification is required under this section. The judge's decision is final and need not necessarily agree with the veterinarian's opinion. The written opinion of the veterinarian shall in all cases be forwarded to The

American Kennel Club by the Superintendent or Show or Trial Secretary.

The judge must disqualify any dog that attempts to attack any person in the ring. He may excuse a dog that attacks another dog or that appears dangerous to other dogs in the ring. He shall mark the dog disqualified or excused and state the reason in his judge's book, and shall give the Superintendent or Show or Trial Secretary a brief report of the dog's actions which shall be submitted to AKC with the report of the show or trial.

When a dog has been disqualified under this section as being blind or deaf or having been changed in appearance by artificial means or for having attempted to attack a person in the ring, all awards made to the dog at the trial shall be cancelled by The American Kennel Club and the dog may not again compete unless and until, following application by the owner to The American Kennel Club, the owner has received official notification from The American Kennel Club that the dog's eligibility has been reinstated.

Spayed bitches, castrated dogs, monorchid or cryptorchid males, and dogs that have faults which would disqualify them under the standards for their breeds, may compete in obedience trials if otherwise eligible under these regulations.

A dog that is lame in the ring at any obedience trial or at a tracking test may not compete and shall not receive any score at the trial. It shall be the judge's responsibility to determine whether a dog is lame. He shall not obtain the opinion of the show veterinarian. If in the judge's opinion a dog in the ring is lame, he shall not score such dog, and shall promptly excuse it from the ring and mark his book "Excused —lame".

No dog shall be eligible to compete if it appears to have been dyed or colored in any way or if the coat shows evidence of chalk or powder, or if the dog has anything attached to it whether for medical or corrective purposes, for protection, for adornment or for any other reason, except for Maltese, Poodles, Shih Tzu, and Yorkshire Terriers which may be shown with the hair over the eyes tied back as they are normally shown in the breed ring. The judge, at his sole discretion, may agree to judge such a dog at a later time if the offending condition has been corrected.

An obedience judge is not required to be familiar with the breed standards nor to scrutinize each dog as in dog show judging, but shall be alert for conditions which may require disqualification or exclusion under this section.

Section 15. **Disturbances.** Bitches in season are not permitted to compete. The judge of an obedience trial or tracking test must remove from competition any bitch in season, any dog which its handler cannot control, any handler who interferes willfully with another competitor or his dog, and any handler who abuses his dog in the ring, and may excuse from competition any dog which he considers unfit to compete, or any bitch which appears so attractive to males as to be a disturbing element. In case of doubt an official veterinarian shall be called to give his opinion. If a dog or handler is expelled or excused by a judge, the reason shall be stated in the judge's book or in a separate report.

Section 16. **Novice A Class.** The Novice A class shall be for dogs not less than six months of age that have not won the title C.D. No person who has previously handled a dog that has won a C.D. title in the obedience ring at a licensed or member trial, and no person who has regularly trained such a dog, may enter or handle a dog in this class. Each dog in the class must have a separate handler, who must be its owner or a member of the owner's immediate family. The same person must handle each dog in all exercises.

Section 17. **Novice B Class.** The Novice B class shall be for dogs not less than six months of age that have not won the title C.D. Dogs in this class may be handled by the owner or any other person. A person may handle more than one dog in this class, but each dog must have a separate handler for the Long Sit and Long Down exercises when judged in the same group. No dog may be entered in both Novice A and Novice B classes at any one trial.

Section 18. **Novice Exercises and Scores.** The exercises and maximum scores in the Novice classes are:

1. Heal on Leash .... 35 points
2. Stand for Examination .... 30 points
3. Heel Free .... 45 points
4. Recall .... 30 points
5. Long Sit .... 30 points
6. Long Down .... 30 points

Maximum Total Score .... 200 points

Section 19. **C.D. Title.** The American Kennel Club will issue a Companion Dog certificate for each registered dog, and will permit the use of the letters "C.D." after the name of each dog that has been certified by three different judges to have received scores of more than 50% of the available points in each of the six exercises and final scores of 170 or more points in Novice classes at three licensed or member obedience trials, provided the sum total of dogs that actually competed in the regular Novice classes at each trial is not less than six.

Section 20. **Open A Class.** The Open A class shall be for dogs that have won the C.D. title but have not won the title C.D.X. Obedience judges and licensed handlers may not enter or handle dogs in this class. Each dog must be handled by its owner or by a member of his immediate family. Owners may enter more than one dog in this class but the same person who handled each dog in the first five exercises must handle the same dog in the Long Sit and Long Down exercises, except that if a person has handled more than one dog in the first five exercises he must have an additional handler, who must be the owner or a member of his immediate family, for each additional dog, when more than one dog he has handled in the first five exercises is judged in the same group for the Long Sit and Long Down.

Section 21. **Open B Class.** The Open B class will be for dogs that have won the title C.D. or C.D.X. A dog may continue to compete in this class after it has won the title U.D. Dogs in this class may be handled by the owner or any other person. Owners may enter more than one dog in this class but the same person who handled each dog in the first five exercises must handle each dog in the Long Sit and Long Down exercises, except that if a person has handled more than one dog in the first five exercises he must have an additional handler for each additional dog, when more than one dog that he has handled in the first five exercises is judged in the same group for the Long Sit and Long Down. No dog may be entered in both Open A and Open B classes at any one trial.

Section 22. **Open Exercises and Scores.** The exercises and maximum scores in the Open classes are:

1. Heel Free .... 40 points
2. Drop on Recall .... 30 points
3. Retrieve on Flat .... 25 points
4. Retrieve over High Jump .... 35 points
5. Broad Jump .... 20 points
6. Long Sit .... 25 points
7. Long Down .... 25 points

Maximum Total Score .... 200 points

Section 23. **C.D.X. Title.** The American Kennel Club will issue a Companion Dog Excellent certificate for each registered dog, and will permit the use of the letter "C.D.X." after the name of each dog that has been certified by three different judges of obedience trials to have received scores of more than 50% of the available points in each of the seven exercises

---

A sanctioned or licensed dog show is for purebred dogs only and they must be registered or eligible for registration in the A.K.C. To be accepted the entry form must show the dog's individual registration number or the litter registration number.

---

and final scores of 170 or more points in Open classes at three licensed or member obedience trials, provided the sum total of dogs that actually competed in the regular Open classes at each trial is not less than six.

Section 24. **Utility Class.** The Utility class shall be for dogs that have won the title C.D.X. Dogs that have won the title U.D. may continue to compete in this class. Dogs in this class may be handled by the owner or any other person. Owners may enter more than one dog in this class, but each dog must have a separate handler for the Group Examination when judged in the same group.

Section 25. **Division of Utility Class.** A club may choose to divide the Utility class into Utility A and Utility B classes, provided such division is approved by The American Kennel Club and is announced in the premium list. When this is done the Utility A class shall be for dogs which have won the title C.D.X. and have not won the title U.D. Obedience judges and licensed handlers may not enter or handle dogs in this class. A dog may be handled in the Group Examination by a person other than the person who handled it in the individual exercises, but each dog must be handled in all exercises by the owner or a member of his immediate family.

All other dogs that are eligible for the Utility class but not eligible for the Utility A class may be entered only in the Utility B class to which the conditions listed in Section 24 shall apply. No dog may be entered in both Utility A and Utility B classes at any one trial.

Section 26. **Utility Exercises and Scores.** The exercises and maximum scores in the Utility classes are:

1. Scent Discrimination—Article No. 1. 30 points
2. Scent Discrimination—Article No. 2. 30 points
3. Directed Retrieve .... 30 points
4. Signal Exercise .... 35 points
5. Directed Jumping .... 40 points
6. Group Examination .... 35 points

Maximum Total Score .... 200 points

Section 27. **U.D. Title.** The American Kennel Club will issue a Utility Dog certificate for each registered dog, and will permit the use of the letters "U.D." after the name of each dog that has been certified by three different judges of obedience trials to have received scores of more than 50% of the available points in each of the six exercises and final scores of 170 or more points in Utility classes at three licensed or member obedience trials in each of which three or more dogs actually competed in the Utility class or classes.

Section 28. **Tracking Test.** This test shall be for dogs not less than six months of age, and must be judged by two judges. With each entry form for a licensed or member tracking test for a dog that has not passed an AKC tracking test there must be filed an original written statement, dated within six months of the date the entry is received, signed by a person who has been approved by The American Kennel Club to judge tracking tests, certifying that the dog is considered by him to be ready for such a test. The original statements cannot be used again and must be submitted to The American Kennel Club with the entry forms. Written permission to waive or modify this requirement may be granted by The American Kennel Club in unusual circumstances. Tracking tests are open to all dogs that are otherwise eligible under these Regulations.

This test cannot be given at a dog show or obedience trial. The duration of this test may be one day or more within a 15 day period after the original date in the event of an unusually large entry or other unforeseen emergency, provided that the change of date is satisfactory to the exhibitors effected.

Section 29. **T.D. Title.** The American Kennel Club will issue a Tracking Dog certificate to a registered dog, and will permit the use of the letters "T.D." after the name of each dog which has been certified by the two judges to have passed a licensed or member tracking test in which at least three dogs actually competed.

The owner of a dog holding both the U.D. and T.D. titles may use the letters "U.D.T." after the name of the dog, signifying "Utility Dog Tracker".

Section 30. **Obedience Ribbons.** At licensed or member obedience trials the following colors shall be used for prize ribbons or rosettes in all regular classes:

First Prize .... Blue
Second Prize .... Red
Third Prize .... Yellow
Fourth Prize .... White
Special Prize........................... Dark Green

and the following colors shall be used for non-regular classes:

First Prize .... Rose
Second Prize .... Brown
Third Prize .... Light Green
Fourth Prize .... Gray

Each ribbon or rosettes shall be at least two inches wide and approximately eight inches long, and shall bear on its face a facsimile of the seal of The American Kennel Club, the words "Obedience Trial", the name of the prize, the name of the trial-giving club, the date of the trial, and the name of the city or town where the trial is given.

Section 31. **Match Ribbons.** If ribbons are given at sanctioned obedience matches they shall be of the following colors and shall have the words "Obedience Match" printed on them, but may be of any design or size:

First Prize . . . . .Rose
Second Prize . . . . .Brown
Third Prize . . . . .Light Green
Fourth Prize . . . . .Gray
Special Prize . . . . .Green with pink edges

Regulations for Performance

Section 4. **Praise and Handling between Exercises.** Praise and patting are allowed between exercises, but points must be deducted from the total score for a dog that is not under reasonable control while being praised. A handler must not carry or offer food in the ring.

Imperfections in heeling between exercises will not be judged. In the Novice classes the dog may be guided gently by the collar between exercises and to get into proper position for the next exercise. There shall be a substantial penalty for any dog that is picked up or carried at any time in the obedience ring, and for a dog in the Open or Utility classes that is not readily controllable or that is physically controlled at any time, except for permitted patting between exercises, and posing, or if the judge requests the handler to hold his dog for measuring. Minor penalties shall be imposed for a dog that does not respond promptly to its handler's commands or signals between exercises in the Open and Utility classes.

Section 5. **Use of Leash.** All dogs shall be kept on leash except when in the obedience ring or exercise ring. Dogs should be brought into the ring and taken out of the ring on leash. Dogs may be kept on leash in the ring when brought in to receive awards, and when waiting in the ring before and after the group exercises. The leash shall be left on the judge's table between the individual exercises, and during all exercises except the Heel on Leash and group exercises. The leash may be of fabric or leather and, in the Novice classes, shall be of sufficient length to provide adequate slack in the Heel on Leash exercise.

Section 6. **Collars.** Dogs in the obedience ring must wear well-fitting plain buckle or slip collars of leather, fabric, or chain. Fancy collars, spiked collars or other special training collars, or collars that are either too tight or so large that they hang down unreasonably in front of the dogs, are not permitted, nor may there be anything hanging from the collars.

Section 7. **Misbehavior.** Any disciplining by the handler in the ring, any display of fear or nervousness by the dog, or any uncontrolled behavior of the dog such as snapping, barking, relieving itself in the ring, or running away from its handler, whether it occurs during an exercise, between exercises, or before or after judging, must be penalized according to the seriousness of the misbehavior, and the judge may expel or excuse the dog from further competition in the class. If such behavior occurs during an exercise, the penalty must first be applied to the score for that exercise. Should the penalty be greater than the value of the exercise during which it is incurred, the additional points shall be deducted from the total score under Misbehavior. If such behavior occurs before or after the judging or between exercises, the entire penalty shall be deducted from the total score.

A top brace—they won 18 Best in Show and 23 Group awards. (Champion Martin's Jingles Puff and Champion Martin's Bangles Puff, owned by Rena Martin, Highland Park. Ill.)

Section 8. **Commands and Signals.** Whenever a command or signal is mentioned in these regulations, a single command or signal only may be given by the handler, and any extra commands or signals must be penalized; except that whenever the regulations specify "command and/or signal" the handler may give either one or the other or both command and signal simultaneously. When a signal is permitted and given, it must be a single gesture with one arm and hand only, and the arm must immediately be returned to a natural position. Delay in following a judge's order to give a command or signal must be penalized, unless the delay is directed by the judge because of some distraction or interference.

The signal for downing a dog may be given either with the arm raised or with a down swing of the arm, but any pause in holding the arm upright followed by a down swing of the arm will be considered an additional signal.

Signaling correction to a dog is forbidden and must be penalized. Signals must be inaudible and the handler must not touch the dog. Any unusual noise or motion may be considered to be a signal. Movements of the body shall be considered additional signals except that a handler may bend as far as necessary to bring his hand on a level with the dog's eyes in giving a signal to a dog in the heel position, and that in the Directed Retrieve exercise the body and knees may be bent to the extent necessary to give the direction to the dog. Whistling or the use of a whistle is prohibited.

The dog's name may be used once immediately before any verbal command or before a verbal command and signal when these regulations permit command and/or signal. The name shall not be used with any signal not given simultaneously with a verbal command. The dog's name, when given immediately before a verbal command, shall not be considered as an additional command, but a dog that responds to its name without waiting for the verbal command shall be scored as having anticipated the command. The dog should never anticipate the handler's directions, but must wait for the appropriate commands and/or signals. Moving forward at heel without any command or signal other than the natural movement of the handler's left leg, shall not be considered at anticipation.

Loud commands by handlers to their dogs create a poor impression of obedience and should be avoided. Shouting is not necessary even in a noisy place if the dog is properly trained to respond to a normal tone of voice. Commands which in the judge's opinion are excessively loud will be penalized.

Section 9. **Heel Position.** The heel position as used in these regulations, whether the dog is sitting, standing, or moving at heel, means that the dog shall be straight in line with the direction in which the handler is facing, at the handler's left side, and as close as practicable to the handler's left leg without crowding, permitting the handler freedom of motion at all times. The area from the dog's head to shoulder shall be in line with the handler's left hip.

Section 10. **Heel on Leash.** The handler shall enter the ring with his dog on a loose leash and shall stand still with the dog sitting in the heel position until the judge asks if the handler is ready and then gives the order "Forward". The handler may give the command or signal to Heel, and shall start walking briskly and in a natural manner with the dog on loose leash. The dog shall walk close to the left side of the handler without crowding, permitting the handler freedom of motion at all times. At each order to "Halt", the handler will stop and his dog shall sit straight and smartly in the Heel position without command or signal and shall not move until the handler again moves forward on order from the judge. It is permissible after each Halt before moving again, for the handler to give the command or signal to Heel.

The leash may be held in either hand or in both hands, at the handler's option, provided the hands are in a natural position. However, the handler and dog will be penalized if, in the judge's opinion, the leash is used to signal or give assistance to the dog.

Any tightening or jerking of the leash, or any act, signal or command which in the opinion of the judge gives the dog assistance shall be penalized. The judge will give the orders "Forward", "Halt", "Right turn", "Left turn", "About turn", "Slow", "Normal", and "Fast", which order signifies that both the handler and dog must run, changing pace and moving forward at noticeably accelerated speed. These orders may be given in any sequence and may be repeated if necessary. In executing the About Turn, the handler will do a Right About Turn in all cases. The judge will say "Exercise finished" after the heeling and then "Are you ready?" before starting the Figure Eight.

The judge will order the handler to execute the "Figure Eight" which signifies that the handler may give the command or signal to Heel and, with his dog in the heel position, shall walk around and between the two stewards who shall stand about 8 feet apart, or if there is only one steward, shall walk around and between the judge and the steward. The Figure Eight in the Novice classes shall be done on leash only. The handler may choose to go in either direction. There shall be no About Turn in the Figure Eight, but the handler and dog shall go twice completely around the Figure Eight with at least one Halt during and another Halt at the end of the exercise.

Section 11. **Stand for Examination.** The judge will give the order for examination and the handler, without further order from the judge, will stand or pose his dog off leash, give the command and/or signal to Stay, walk forward about six feet in front of his dog, turn around, and stand facing his dog. The method by which the dog is made to stand or pose is optional with the handler who may take any reasonable time in posing the dog, as in the show ring, before deciding to give the command and/or signal to Stay. The judge will approach the dog from the front and will touch its head, body and hindquarters only, and will then give the order "Back to your dog", whereupon the handler will walk around behind his dog to the heel position. The dog must remain in a standing position until the judge says "Exercise finished". The dog must show no shyness nor resentment at any time during the exercise.

Section 12. **Heel Free.** This shall be executed in the same manner as Heel on Leash except that the dog is off the leash. Heeling in both Novice and Open classes is done in the same manner except that in the Open classes all work is done off leash, including the Figure Eight.

Section 13. **Recall and Drop on Recall.** To execute the Recall to handler, upon order or signal from the judge "Leave your dog", the dog is given the command and/or signal to stay in the sitting position while the handler walks forward about 35 feet towards the other end of the ring, turns around, and faces his dog. Upon order or signal from the judge "Call your dog", the handler calls or signals the dog, which in the Novice class must come straight in at a brisk pace and sit straight, centered immediately in front of the handler's feet and close enough so that the handler could readily touch its head without moving either foot or having to stretch forward. The dog shall not touch the handler nor sit between his feet. Upon order or signal from the judge to "Finish", the dog on command or signal must go smartly to the heel position and sit. The method by which the dog goes to the heel position shall be optional with the handler provided it is done smartly and the dog sits straight at heel.

In the Open class, at a point designated by the judge, the dog must drop completely to a down position immediately on command or signal from the handler, and must remain in the down position until, on order or signal from the judge, the handler calls or signals the dog which must rise and complete the exercise as in the Novice class.

Section 14. **Long Sit.** In the Long Sit in the Novice classes all the competing dogs in the class take the exercise together, except that if there are 12 or more dogs they shall, at the judge's option, be judged in groups of not less than 6 nor more than 15 dogs. Where the same judge does both classes the separate classes may be combined provided there are not more than 15 dogs competing in the two classes combined. The dogs that are in the ring shall be lined up in catalog order along one of the four sides of the ring. Handlers' armbands, weighted with leashes or other articles if necessary, shall be placed behind the dogs. On order from the judge the handlers shall sit their dogs, if they are not already sitting, and on further order from the judge to "Leave your dogs" the handlers shall give the command and/or signal to Stay and immediately leave their dogs, go to the opposite side of the ring, and line up facing their respective dogs. After one minute from the time he has ordered the handlers to leave their dogs, the judge will order the handlers "Back to your dogs" whereupon the handlers must return promptly to their dogs, each walking around and in back of his own dog to the heel position. The dogs must not move from the sitting position until after the judge says "Exercise finished".

Section 15. **Long Down.** The Long Down in the Novice classes is done in the same manner as the Long Sit except that instead of sitting the dogs the handlers, on order from the judge, will down their dogs without touching the dogs or their collars, and except further that the judge will order the handlers back after three minutes. The dogs must stay in the down position until after the judge says "Exercise finished".

Section 16. **Open Classes, Long Sit and Long Down.** These exercises in the Open classes are performed in the same manner as in the Novice classes except that after leaving their dogs the handlers must cross to the opposite side of the ring, and then leave the ring in single file as directed by the judge and go to a place designated by the judge, completely out

An example of a most attentive dog during an obedience exercise. The dog is receiving the "sit" and "stay" command. (Handler and trainer is Bob Scott.)

of sight of their dogs, where they must remain until called by the judge after the expiration of the time limit of three minutes in the Long Sit and five minutes in the Long Down, from the time the judge gave the order to "Leave your dogs". On order from the judge the handlers shall return to the ring in single file in reverse order, lining up facing their dogs at the opposite side of the ring, and returning to their dogs on order from the judge.

Section 17. **Retrieve on the Flat.** In retrieving the dumbbell on the flat, the handler stands with his dog sitting in the heel position in a place designated by the judge, and the judge gives the orders "Throw it", whereupon the handler may give the command and/or signal to Stay, which may not be given with the hand that is holding the dumbbell, and throws the dumbbell; "Send your dog", whereupon the handler gives the command or signal to his dog to retrieve; "Take it", whereupon the handler may give a command or signal and takes the dumbbell from the dog; "Finish", whereupon the handler gives the command or signal to heel as in the Recall. The dog shall not move forward to retrieve nor deliver to hand on return until given the command or signal by the handler following order by the judge. The retrieve shall be executed at a fast trot or gallop, without unnecessary mouthing or playing with the dumbbell. The dog shall sit straight, centered immediately in front of its handler's feet and close enough so that the handler can readily take the dumbbell without moving either foot or having to stretch forward. The dog shall not touch the handler nor sit between his feet.

The dumbbell, which must be approved by the judge, shall be made of one or more solid pieces of one of the heavy hardwoods, which shall not be hollowed out. It may be unfinished, or coated with a clear finish, or painted white. It shall have no decorations or attachments but may bear an inconspicuous mark for identification. The size of the dumbbell shall be proportionate to the size of the dog. The judge shall require the dumbbell to be thrown again before the dog is sent if, in his opinion, it is thrown too short a distance, or too far to one side, or against the ringside.

Section 18. **Retrieve over High Jump.** In retrieving the dumbbell over the High Jump, the exercise is executed in the same manner as the Retrieve on the Flat, except that the dog must jump the High Jump both going and coming. The High Jump shall be jumped clear and the jump shall be as nearly as possible one and one-half times the height of the dog at the withers, as determined by the judge, with a minimum height of 8 inches and a maximum height of 36 inches. This applies to all breeds with the following exceptions:

The jump shall be once the height of the dog at the withers or 36 inches, whichever is less, for the following breeds—

Bloodhounds
Bullmastiffs
Great Danes
Great Pyrenees
Mastiffs
Newfoundlands
St. Bernards

The jump shall be once the height of the dog at the withers or 8 inches, whichever is greater, for the following breeds—

Spaniels (Clumber)
Spaniels (Sussex)
Basset Hounds
Dachshunds
Welsh Corgis (Cardigan)
Welsh Corgis (Pembroke)
Australian Terriers
Cairn Terriers
Dandie Dinmont Terriers
Norwich Terriers
Scottish Terriers
Sealyham Terriers
Skye Terriers
West Highland White Terriers
Maltese
Pekingese
Bulldogs
French Bulldogs

The handler has the option of standing any reasonable distance from the High Jump, but must stay in the same spot throughout the exercise.

The side posts of the High Jump shall be 4 feet high and the jump shall be 5 feet wide and shall be so constructed as to provide adjustment for each 2 inches from 8 inches to 36 inches. It is suggested that the jump have a bottom board 8 inches wide including the space from the bottom of the board to the ground or floor, together with three other 8 inch boards, one 4 inch board, and one 2 inch board. A 6 inch board may also be provided. The jump shall be painted a flat white. The width in inches, and nothing else, shall be painted on each side of each board in black 2 inch figures, the figure on the bottom board representing the distance from the ground or floor to the top of the board.

Section 19. **Broad Jump.** In the Broad Jump the handler will stand with his dog sitting in the heel position in front of and anywhere within 10 feet of the jump. On order from the judge to "Leave your dog", the handler will give his dog the command and/or signal to stay, and go to a position facing the right side of the jump, with his toes about 2 feet from the jump, and anywhere between the first and last hurdles. On order from the judge the handler shall give the command or signal to jump and the dog shall clear the entire distance of the Broad Jump without touching and, without further command or signal, return to a sitting position immediately in front of the handler as in the Recall. The handler shall change his position by executing a right angle turn while the dog is in mid-air, but shall remain in the same spot. On order from the judge, the handler shall give the command or signal to Heel and the dog shall finish as in the Recall.

The Broad Jump shall consist of four hurdles, built to telescope for convenience, made of boards about 8 inches wide, the largest measuring about 5 feet in length and 6 inches high at the highest point, all painted a flat white. When set up they shall be arranged in order of size and shall be evenly spaced so as to cover a distance equal to twice the height of the High Jump as set for the particular dog, with the low side of each hurdle and the lowest hurdle nearest the dog. The four hurdles shall be used for a jump of 52" to 72", three for a jump of 32" to 48", and two for a jump of 16" to 28". The highest hurdles shall be removed first.

Section 20. **Scent Discrimination.** In each of these two exercises the dog must select by scent alone and retrieve an article which has been handled by its handler. The articles shall be provided by the handler and these shall consist of two sets, each comprised of five identical articles not more than six inches in length, which may be items of everyday use. One set shall be made entirely of rigid metal, and one of leather of such design that nothing but leather is visible except for the minimum amount of thread or metal necessary to hold the article together. The articles in each set must be legibly numbered each with a different number, and must be approved by the judge.

The handler shall present all 10 articles to the judge and the judge shall designate one article from each of the two sets, and shall make a written note of the numbers of the two articles he selects. These two handler's articles shall be placed on a table or chair in the ring until picked up by the handler who shall hold in his hand only one article at a time. The handler's scent may be imparted to the article only from his hands which must remain in plain sight. The handler has the option as to which article he picks up first. Before the start of the Scent Discrimination exercises the judge or the steward will handle each of the remaining 8 articles as he places them at random in the ring about 6 inches apart. The handler will stand about 15 feet from the articles with the dog sitting in the heel position. The handler and dog will face away from the articles that are on the ground or floor from the time the judge takes the handler's article until he orders "Send your dog". On order from the judge, the handler immediately will place his article on the judge's book or work sheet and the judge, without touching the article with his hands, will place it among the other articles.

On order from the judge to "Send your dog", the handler and dog will execute a Right About Turn to face the articles and the handler will simultaneously give the command or signal to retrieve. The dog shall not again sit after turning, but shall go directly to the articles. The handler may give his scent to the dog by gently touching the dog's nose with the palm of one open hand, but this may only be done while the dog is sitting at heel and the arm and hand must be returned to a natural position before handler and dog turn to face the articles. The dog shall go at a brisk pace to the articles. It may take any reasonable time to select the right article, but only provided it works continuously and does not pick up any article other than the one with its handler's scent. After picking up the right article the dog shall return at a brisk pace and complete the exercise as in the Retrieve on the Flat.

The same procedure is followed in each of the two Scent Discrimination exercises. Should a dog retrieve a wrong article in the first exercise, it shall be placed on the table

or chair, and the handler's article must also be taken up from the remaining articles. The second exercise shall then be completed with one less article in the ring.

Section 21. **Directed Retrieve.** In this exercise the handler will provide three regular full-size, predominantly white, work gloves, which must be open and must be approved by the judge. The handler will stand with his dog sitting in the heel position, midway between and in line with the two jumps. The judge or steward will drop the three gloves across the end of the ring in view of the handler and dog, one glove in each corner and one in the center, about 3 feet from the end of the ring and, for the corner gloves, about 3 feet from the side of the ring, where all three gloves will be clearly visible to the dog and handler. There shall be no table or chair at this end of the ring.

The judge will give the order "Left" or "Right" or "Center". If the judge orders "Left" or "Right", the handler must give the command to Heel and shall pivot in place with his dog in the direction ordered, to face the designated glove. The handler shall not touch the dog to get it in position. The handler will then give his dog the direction to the designated glove with a single motion of his left hand and arm along the right side of the dog, and will give the command to retrieve either simultaneously with or immediately following the giving of the direction. The dog shall then go directly to the glove at a brisk pace, and retrieve it without unnecessary mouthing or playing with it, completing the exercise as in Retrieve on the Flat.

The handler may bend his knees and body in giving the direction to the dog, after which the handler will stand erect with his arms in a natural position. The exercise shall consist of a single retrieve, but the judge shall designate different glove positions for successive dogs.

Section 22. **Signal Exercise.** In the Signal Exercise the heeling is done in the same manner as in the Heel Free exercise except that throughout the entire exercise the handler uses signals only and must not speak to his dog at any time. On order from the judge "Forward", the handler may signal his dog to walk at heel and then, on specific order from the judge in each case, the handler and the dog execute a "Left turn", "Right turn", "About turn", "Halt", "Slow" "Normal", "Fast." These orders may be given in any sequence and may be repeated if necessary. Then on order from the judge, and while the dog is walking at heel, the handler signals his dog to Stand in the heel position near the end of the ring, and on further order from the judge "Leave your dog", the handler signals his dog to Stay, goes to the far end of the ring, and turns to face his dog. Then on separate and specific signals from the judge in each case, the handler will give the signals to Drop, to Sit, to Come and to Finish as in the Recall. During the heeling part of this exercise the handler may not give any signal except where a command or signal is permitted in the Heeling exercises.

Section 23. **Directed Jumping.** In the Directed Jumping exercise the jumps shall be placed midway in the ring at right angles to the sides of the ring and 18 to 20 feet apart, the Bar Jump on one side, the High Jump on the other. The handler from a position on the center line of the ring and about 20 feet from the line of the jumps, stands with his dog sitting in the heel position. On order from the judge "Send your dog", he commands and/or signals his dog to go forward at a brisk pace toward the other end of the ring to an equal distance beyond the jumps and in the approximate center where the handler gives the command to Sit, whereupon the dog must stop and sit with its attention on the handler, but need not sit squarely. The judge will then designate which jump is to be taken first by the dog, whereupon the handler commands and/or signals his dog to return to him over the designated

Wirehaired Terriers in the show ring being "set up" for the judge.

jump, the dog sitting in front of the handler and finishing as in the Recall. While the dog is in mid-air the handler may turn so as to be facing the dog as it returns. The judge will say "Exercise finished" after the dog has returned to the heel position. When the dog is again sitting in the heel position for the second part of the exercise, the judge will ask "Are you ready?" before giving the order "Send your dog" for the second jump. The same procedure is to be followed for the dog taking the opposite jump. It is optional with the judge which jump is taken first but both jumps must be taken to complete the exercise and the judge must not designate the jump until the dog is at the far end of the ring.

The height of the jumps shall be the same as required in the Open classes. The High Jump shall be the same as that used in the Open classes, and the Bar Jump shall consist of a bar between 2 and 2½ inches square with the four edges rounded sufficiently to remove any sharpness. The bar shall be painted a flat black and white in alternate sections of about 3 inches each. The bar shall be supported by two unconnected 4 foot upright posts about 5 feet apart. The bar shall be adjustable for each 2 inches of height from 8 inches to 36 inches, and the jump shall be so constructed and positioned that the bar can be knocked off without disturbing the uprights. The dog shall clear the jumps without touching them.

Section 24. **Group Examination.** All the competing dogs take this exercise together, except that if there are 12 or more dogs, they shall be judged in groups of not less than 6 nor more than 15 dogs, at the judge's option. The handlers and dogs that are in the ring shall line up in catalog order, side by side down the center of the ring with the dogs in the heel position. Each handler shall place his armband, weighted with leash or other article, if necessary, behind his dog. On order from the judge to "Stand your dogs", all the handlers will stand or pose their dogs, and on order from the judge "Leave your dogs", all the handlers will give the command and/or signal to Stay, walk forward to the side of the ring, then about turn and face their dogs. The judge will approach each dog in turn from the front and examine it, going over the dog with his hands as in dog show judging. When all dogs have been examined, and after the handlers have been away from their dogs for at least three minutes, the judge will promptly order the handlers "Back to your dogs", and the handlers will walk

around behind their dogs to the heel position, after which the judge will say "Exercise finished". Each dog must remain standing at its position in the line from the time its handler leaves it until the end of the exercise, and must show no shyness nor resentment.

Section 25. **Tracking.** The tracking test must be performed with the dog on leash, the length of the track to be not less than 440 yards nor more than 500 yards, the scent to be not less than one half hour nor more than two hours old and that of a stranger who will leave an inconspicuous glove or wallet, dark in color, at the end of the track where it must be found by the dog and picked up by the dog or handler. The article must be approved in advance by the judges. The track-layer will follow the track which has been staked out with flags a day or more earlier, collecting all the flags on the way with the exception of one flag at the start of the track and one flag about 30 yards from the start of the track to indicate the direction of the track; then deposit the article at the end of the track and leave the course, proceeding straight ahead at least 50 feet. The tracklayer must wear his own shoes which, if not having leather soles, must have uppers of fabric or leather. The dog shall wear a harness to which is attached a leash between 20 and 40 feet in length. The handler shall follow the dog at a distance of not less than 20 feet, and the dog shall not be guided by the handler. The dog may be restrained by the handler, but any leading or guiding of the dog constitutes grounds for calling the handler off and marking the dog "Failed". A dog may, at the handler's option, be given one, and only one, second chance to take the scent between the two flags, provided it has not passed the second flag.

The Club or Tracking Test Secretary, after a licensed or member tracking test, shall forward the two copies of the judges' marked charts, the entry forms with certifications attached, and a marked and certified copy of the catalog pages or sheets listing the dogs entered in the tracking test, to The American Kennel Club so as to reach its office within seven days after the close of the test.

REGULATIONS FOR JUDGING

Section 8. **Announcement of Scores.** The judge shall not disclose any score or partial score to contestants or spectators until he has completed the judging of the entire class or, in case of a split class, until he has completed the judging of his division; nor shall he permit anyone else to do so. After all the scores are recorded for the class, or for the division in case of a split class, the judge shall call for all available dogs that have won qualifying scores to be brought into the ring. Before awarding the prizes, the judge shall inform the spectators as to the maximum number of points for a perfect score, and shall then announce the score of each prize winner, and announce to the handler the score of each dog that has won a qualifying score.

Section 9. **Explanations and Errors.** The judge is not required to explain his scoring, and should not enter into any discussion with any contestant who appears to be dissatisfied. Any interested person who thinks that there may have been an arithmetical error or an error in identifying a dog may report the facts to one of the stewards or to the Superintendent or Show or Trial Secretary so that the matter may be checked.

Section 10. **Rejudging.** If a dog has failed in a particular part of an exercise, it shall not ordinarily be rejudged nor given a second chance; but if in the judge's opinion the dog's performance was prejudiced by peculiar and unusual conditions, the judge may at his own discretion rejudge the dog on the entire exercise.

Section 11. **Ties.** In case of a tie for any prize in a class, the dogs shall be tested again by having them perform at the same time all or some part of one or more of the regular exercises in that class. In the Utility class the dogs shall perform at the same time all or some part of the Signal exercise. The original scores shall not be changed.

Section 18. **Orders and Minimum Penalties.** The orders for the exercises and the standards for judging are set forth in the following sections. The lists of faults are not intended to be complete but minimum penalties are specified for most of the more common and serious faults. There is no maximum limit on penalties. A dog which makes none of the errors listed may still fail to qualify or may be scored zero for other reasons.

Prizes are given to the winners in an obedience trial. This Alaskan Malamute handled by Bob Scott has just won first prize. Climate and weather allowing, obedience competitions are frequently conducted outdoors.

Section 19. **Heel on Leash.** The orders for this exercise are "Forward", "Halt", "Right turn", "Left turn", "About turn", "Slow", "Normal", "Fast", "Figure eight". These orders may be given in any order and may be repeated, if necessary, but the judge shall attempt to standardize the heeling pattern for all dogs in any class. The principal feature of this exercise is the ability of the dog to work as a team with its handler. A dog that is unmanageable must be scored zero. Where a handler continually tugs on the leash or adapts his pace to that of the dog, the judge must score such a dog less than 50% of the available points. Substantial deductions shall be made for additional commands or signals to Heel and for failure of dog or handler to change pace noticeably for Slow and Fast. Minor deductions shall be made for such things as poor sits, occasionally guiding the dog with the leash, heeling wide, and other imperfections in heeling. In judging this exercise the judge shall follow the handler at a discreet distance so that he may observe any signals or commands given by the handler to the dog, but without interfering with either dog or handler.

Section 20. **Stand for Examination.** The orders for this exercise are "Stand your dog and leave when ready", "Back to your dog". The principal features of this exercise are to stand in position before and during examination and to show no shyness nor resentment. A dog that sits before or during the examination or growls or snaps must be marked zero. A dog that moves away from the place where it was left before or during the examination, or a dog that shows any shyness or resentment, must receive less than 50% of the available points. Depending on the circumstances in each case, minor or substantial deductions must be made for any dog that moves its feet at any time, or that sits, or moves away after the examination is completed. The examination shall consist of touching only the dog's head, body and hindquarters with the fingers and palm of one hand. The scoring of this exercise will not start until the handler has given the command and/or signal to Stay, except for such things as rough treatment of the dog by its handler or active resistance by the dog to its handler's attempts to make it stand, which shall be penalized substantially.

Section 21. **Heel Free.** The orders and scoring for this exercise shall be the same as for Heel on Leash except that the Figure Eight is omitted in the Heel Free exercise in the Novice classes.

Section 22. **Recall.** The orders for this exercise are "Leave your dog", "Call your dog", "Finish". The principal features of this exercise are the prompt response to the handler's command or signal to Come, and the Stay from the time the handler leaves the dog until he call it. A dog that does not come on the first command or signal must be scored zero. A dog that does not stay without extra command or signal, or that moves from the place where it was left, from the time the handler leaves until it is called, or that does not come close enough so that the handler could readily touch its head without moving either foot or having to stretch forward, must receive less than 50% of the points. Substantial deductions shall be made for a slow response to the Come, depending on the specific circumstances in each case; for extra commands or signals to Stay if given before the handler leaves the dog; for a dog that stands or lies down; for extra commands or signals to Finish; and for failure to Sit or Finish. Minor deductions shall be made for poor or slow Sits or Finishes, and for a dog that touches the handler on coming in or sits between his feet.

Section 23. **Long Sit and Long Down.** The orders for these exercises are "Sit your dogs" or "Down your dogs", "Leave your dogs", "Back to your dogs". The principal features of these exercises are to stay, and to remain in the sitting or down position, whichever is required by the particular exercise. A dog that at any time during the exercise moves a substantial distance away from the place where it was left, or that goes over to any other dog, must be marked zero. A dog that stays on the spot where it was left but that fails to remain in the sitting or down position, whichever is required by the particular exercise, until the handler has returned to the heel position, and a dog that repeatedly barks or whines, must receive less than 50% of the available points. A substantial deduction shall be made for any dog that moves even a minor distance away from the place where it was left or that barks or whines only once or twice. Depending on the circumstances in each case, a substantial or minor deduction shall be made for touching the dog or for forcing it into the Down position. There shall be a minor deduction for sitting after the handler is in the heel position but before the judge has said "Exercise finished" in the Down exercises. The dogs shall not be required to sit at the end of the Down exercises.

If a dog gets up and starts to roam or follows its handler, the judge shall promptly instruct the handler or one of the stewards to take the dog out of the ring or to keep it away from the other dogs. The judge should not attempt to judge the dogs or handlers on the manner in which they are made to Sit. The scoring of the Long Sit exercise will not start until after the judge has given the order "Leave your dogs", except for such general things as rough treatment of a dog by its handler or active resistance by a dog to its handler's attempts to make it Sit.

During these exercises the judge shall stand in such a position that all of the dogs are in his line of vision, and where he can see all the handlers in the ring, or leaving and returning to the ring, without having to turn around.

Section 24. **Drop on Recall.** The orders for this exercise are the same as for the Recall, except that the dog is required to drop when coming in on command or signal from its handler when ordered by the judge, and except that an additional order or signal to "Call your dog" is given by the judge after the Drop. The dog's prompt response to the handler's command or signal to Drop is a principal feature of this exercise, in addition to the prompt responses and the Stays as described under Recall above. A dog that does not stop and drop completely on a single command or signal must be scored zero. Minor or substantial deductions shall be made for a slow drop, depending on whether the dog is just short of perfection in this respect, or very slow in dropping or somewhere between the two extremes. All other deductions as listed under Recall above shall also apply.

The judge may designate the point at which the handler is to give the command or signal to drop by some marker placed in advance which will be clear to the handler but not obvious to the dog, or he may give the handler a signal for the Drop, but such signal must be given in such a way as not to attract the dog's attention.

If a point is designated, the dog is still to be judged on its prompt response to the handler's command or signal rather than on its proximity to the designated point.

Section 25. **Retrieve on the Flat.** The orders for this exercise are "Throw it", "Send your dog", "Take it", "Finish". The principal feature of this exercise is to retrieve promptly. Any dog that fails to go out on the first command or a dog that fails to retrieve, shall be marked zero. A dog that goes to retrieve before the command or signal is given, or that does not return with the dumbbell sufficiently close so that the handler can readily take it without moving either foot or stretching forward, must receive less than 50% of the points. Depending on the specific circumstances in each case, minor or substantial deductions shall be made for slowness

in going out or returning or in picking up the dumbbell, mouthing or playing with the dumbbell, dropping the dumbbell, slowness in releasing the dumbbell to the handler, touching the handler on coming in, sitting between his feet, failure to sit in front or to Finish. Minor deductions shall be made for poor or slow Sits or Finishes.

Section 26. **Retrieve over High Jump.** The orders for this exercise are "Throw it", "Send your dog", "Take it", and "Finish". The principal features of this exercise are that the dog must go out over the jump, pick up the dumbbell and promptly return with it over the jump. The minimum penalties shall be the same as for the Retrieve on the Flat, and in addition a dog that fails both going and returning to go over the High Jump, must be marked zero. A dog that retrieves properly but goes over the High Jump in only one direction, must receive less than 50% of the available points. Substantial deductions must be made for a dog that climbs the jump or uses the top of the jump for aid in going over, in contrast to a dog that merely touches the jump. Minor deductions shall be made for touching the jump in going over.

The jumps may be preset by the stewards based on the handler's advice as to the dog's height. The judge must make certain that the jump is set at the required height for each dog. He shall verify in the ring with an ordinary folding rule or steel tape to the nearest one-half inch, the height at the withers of each dog that jumps less than 36 inches. He shall not base his decision as to the height of the jump on the handler's advice.

Section 27. **Broad Jump.** The orders for this exercise are "Leave your dog", "Send your dog", and "Finish". Any dog that refuses the jump on the first command or signal or walks over any part of the jump must be marked zero. A dog that fails to stay until the handler gives the command or signal to jump, or that fails to clear the full distance with its forelegs, shall receive less than 50% of the available points. All other penalties as listed under Recall shall also apply. It is the judge's responsibility to see that the distance jumped is that required by these Regulations for the particular dog.

Section 28. **Scent Discrimination.** The orders for each of these two exercises are "Send your dog", "Take it", and "Finish". The principal features of these exercises are the selection of the handler's article from among the other articles by scent alone, and the prompt carrying of the right article to the handler after its selection. The minimum penalties shall be the same as for the Retrieve on the Flat and in addition a dog that fails to go out to the group of articles, or that retrieves a wrong article, or that fails to bring the right article to the handler, must be marked zero for the particular exercise. Substantial deductions shall be made for a dog that picks up a wrong article, even though it puts it down again immediately, and for any roughness by the handler in imparting his scent to the dog. Minor or substantial deductions, depending on the circumstances in each case, shall be made for a dog that is slow or inattentive, or that does not work continuously. There shall be no penalty for a dog that takes a reasonably long time examining the articles, provided it is working smartly and continuously.

The judge shall select one article from each of the two sets and shall make written notes of the numbers of the two articles selected. The handler has the option as to which article he picks up first, but must give up each article immediately when ordered by the judge. The judge must see to it that the handler imparts his scent to the article only with his hands and that, between the time the handler picks up each article and the time he gives it to the judge, the article is held continuously in the handler's hands which must remain in plain sight. The judge or his steward must handle each of the eight other articles as he places them in the ring. The judge must make sure that they are properly separated before the dog is sent so that there may be no confusion of scent between articles.

Section 29. **Directed Retrieve.** The orders for this exercise are "Right", or "Center", or "Left", "Take it" and "Finish". The principal features of this exercise are that the dog stay until directed to retrieve, that it go directly to the designated glove, and that it retrieve promptly. A dog that fails to go out on command or that fails to go directly in a straight line to the glove designated, or that fails to retrieve the glove, shall be marked zero. A dog that goes to retrieve before the command is given or that does not return promptly with the glove sufficiently close so that the handler can readily take it without moving either foot or stretching forward, must receive less than 50% of the available points. Depending on the specific circumstances in each case, minor or substantial deductions shall be made for touching the dog or for excessive movements in getting it to pivot at heel facing the designated glove. All of the other penalties as listed under Retrieve on the Flat shall also apply.

Section 30. **Signal Exercise.** The orders for this exercise are "Forward", "Left turn", "Right turn", "About turn," "Halt", "Slow", "Normal", "Fast", "Stand", and "Leave your dog", and in addition the judge must give the handler signals to signal his dog to Drop, to Sit, to Come, to Finish. The orders for those parts of the eexrcise which are done with the dog at heel may be given in any order and may be repeated if necessary, except that the order to "Stand" shall be given when the dog and handler are walking at a normal pace. The signals given the handler after he has left his dog in the Stand position shall be given in the order specified above. The principal features of this exercise are the heeling of the dog and the Come on signal as described for the Heel and Recall exercises, and the prompt response to the signals to Drop, to Sit, and to Come. A dog that fails, on a single signal from the handler, to stand or remain standing where left, or to drop, or to sit and stay, or to come, or that receives a command or audible signal from the handler to do any of these parts of the exercise, shall receive less than 50% of the available points. All of the deductions listed under the Heel and Recall exercises shall also apply to this exercise.

Section 31. **Directed Jumping.** The judge's first order is "Send your dog", then, after the dog has stopped at the far end of the ring, the judge shall designate which jump is to be taken by the dog, whereupon the handler commands and/or signals his dog to return to him over the designated jump, the dog sitting in front of the handler and finishing as in the Recall. After the dog returns to the handler the order "Finish" is given followed by "Exercise Finished". The same sequence is then followed for the other jump. The principal features of this exercise are that the dog goes away from the handler in the direction indicated, stops when commanded, jumps as directed, and returns as in the Recall.

A dog that, in either half of the exercise, anticipates the handler's command and/or signal to go out, that does not leave its handler, that does not go out between the jumps and a substantial distance beyond, that does not stop on command, that anticipates the handler's command and/or signal to jump, that does not jump as directed, or a dog that knocks the bar off the uprights or climbs over the High Jump or uses the top of the High Jump for aid in going over, must receive less than 50% of the available points. Substantial deductions shall be made for a dog that does not stop in the approximate center of the ring, that turns, stops, or sits, before the command to Sit, or that fails to sit. Substantial or minor deductions shall be made for slowness in going out, and all of the minimum penalties as listed under Recall shall also apply.

The judge must make certain that the jumps are set at the required height for each dog by following the same procedure described for the Retrieve over High Jump.

Section 32. **Group Examination.** The orders for this exercise are "Stand your dogs", "Leave your dogs", and "Back to your dogs". The principal features of this exercise are that the dog must stand and stay, and must show no shyness nor resentment. A dog that moves a substantial distance away from the place where it was left, or that goes over to any other dog, or that sits or lies down before the handler returns to the heel position, or that growls or snaps at any time, must be marked zero. A dog that remains standing but that moves a minor distance away from the place where it was left, or a dog that shows any shyness or resentment or that repeatedly barks or whines, must receive less than 50% of the available points. Depending on the specific circumstances in each case, minor or substantial deductions must be made for any dog that moves its feet at any time during the exercise, or sits or lies down after the handler has returned to the heel position. The judge should not attempt to judge the dogs or handlers on the manner in which the dogs are made to stand. The scoring will not start until after the judge has given the order "Leave your dogs", except for such general things as rough treatment of a dog by its handler, or active resistance by a dog to its handler's attempts to make it stand. The dogs are not required to sit at the end of this exercise. The examination shall be conducted as in dog show judging, the judge going over each dog carefully with his hands. The judge must make a written record of any deductions immediately after examining each dog, subject to further deduction of points for subsequent faults. The judge must instruct one or more stewards to watch the other dogs while he conducts the individual examinations, and to call any faults to his attention.

Section 33. **Tracking Tests.** For obvious reasons these tests cannot be held at a dog show, and a person, though he may be qualified to judge Obedience Trials, is not necessarily capable of judging a tracking test. He must be familiar with the various conditions that may exist when a dog is required to work a scent trail. Scent conditions, weather, lay of the land, ground cover, and wind, must be taken into consideration, and a thorough knowledge of this work is necessary.

One or both of the judges must personally lay out or walk over each track after it has been laid out, a day or so before the test, so as to be completely familiar with the location of the track, landmarks and ground conditions. At least two of the right angle turns shall be well out in the open where there are no fences or other boundaries to guide the dog. No part of any track shall follow along any fence or boundary within 15 yards of such boundary. The track shall include at least two right angle turns and should include more than two such turns so that the dog may be observed working in different wind directions. Acute angle turns should be avoided whenever possible. No conflicting tracks shall be laid. No track shall cross any body of water. No part of any track shall be laid within 75 yards of any other track. In the case of two tracks going in opposite directions, however, the first flags of these tracks may be as close as 50 yards from each other. The judges shall make sure that the track is no less than 440 yards and that the tracklayer is a stranger to the dog in each case. It is the judges' responsibility to instruct the tracklayer to insure that each track is properly laid and that each tracklayer carries a copy of the chart with him in laying the track. The judges must approve the article to be left at the end of each track, must make sure that it is thoroughly impregnated with the tracklayer's scent, and must see that the tracklayer's shoes meet the requirements of these regulations.

There is no time limit provided the dog is working, but a dog that is off the track and is clearly not working should not be given any minimum time, but should be marked Failed. The handler may not be given any assistance by the judges or anyone else. If a dog is not trailing it shall not be marked or anyone else. If a dog is not trailing it shall not be marked Passed even though it may have found the article. In case of unforseen circumstances, the judges may in rare cases, at their own discretion, give a handler and his dog a second chance on a new track. A track for each dog entered shall be plotted on the ground not less than one day before the test, the track being marked by flags which the tracklayer can follow readily on the day of the test. A chart of each track shall be made up in duplicate, showing the approximate length in yards of each leg, and major landmarks and boundaries, if any. Both of these charts shall be marked at the time the dog is tracking, one by each of the judges, so as to show the approximate course followed by the dog. The judges shall sign their charts and show on each whether the dog "Passed" or "Failed", the time the tracklayer started, the time the dog started and finished tracking, a brief description of ground, wind and weather conditions, the wind direction, and a note of any steep hills or valleys.

Reprinted by permission of
The American Kennel Club.

REGULATIONS FOR JUNIOR SHOWMANSHIP

THESE *regulations have been adopted by the Board of Directors of AKC to implement the following dog show rule:*

A club or Association holding a show may offer Junior Showmanship if it so chooses. The classes and procedure shall conform to The American Kennel Club regulations governing Junior Showmanship as adopted by the Board of Directors.

The regulations are effective at shows where Junior Showmanship is offered, held on and after April 1, 1971.

Section 1. *Approval of Classes.* Any club that is approved to hold a licensed or member all-breed show or a specialty show held apart from an all-breed show, may also be approved to offer Junior Showmanship competition at its show.

Section 2. *Standard for Judging.* Junior Showmanship shall be judged solely on the ability and skill of the Juniors in handling their dogs as in the breed ring. The show qualities of the dogs shall not be considered. Junior handlers shall not be required to exchange dogs. The judge must excuse a handler and dog from the ring if, in his opinion, the handler cannot properly control the dog.

Section 3. *Approval of Judges.* Any person who is eligible to be approved to judge one or more breeds at AKC licensed or member shows, and any licensed handler, may be approved to judge Junior Showmanship, but no person approved to judge Junior Showmanship at a show shall exhibit or handle any dogs at that show. The name and assignment of each judge shall be included in the list of judges sent to AKC for approval. Junior Showmanship entries shall be included in computing judges' assignments under Chapter 10, Section 13 of the Dog Show Rules. A judge will not be disapproved for a Junior Showmanship assignment because of its proximity in time and distance to another Junior Showmanship assignment. Any change in judges shall be handled in accordance with the Dog Show Rules.

Section 4. *Classes and Divisions.* The regular Junior Showmanship classes shall be:

(A) *Novice.* This class shall be for boys and girls who are at least 10 years old and under 17 years old on the day of the show and who, at the time entries close, have not won a first place in a Novice class at a licensed or member show.

(B) *Open.* This class shall be for boys and girls who are at least 10 years old and under 17 years old on the day of the show, and who have won a first place in a Novice Junior Showmanship class at a licensed or member show. The winner of a Novice class shall automatically become eligible to enter and to compete in the Open class at the same show.

(C) *Junior and Senior Classes.* Either or both of these regular classes may be divided by age into Junior and Senior classes, provided the division is specified in the premium list. A Junior class shall be for boys and girls who are at least 10 years old and under 13 years old on the day of the show. A Senior class shall be for boys and girls who are at least 13 years old and under 17 years old on the day of the show.

(D) *Classes for Boys and Girls.* Any or all of these regular classes may also be divided by sex to provide a class or classes for Boys and a class or classes for Girls, provided the division is specified in the premium list.

(E) *Best Junior Handler.* A club offering Junior Showmanship may offer a prize for Best Junior Handler provided the prize is offered in the premium list. The Junior handler placed first in each of the regular Junior Showmanship classes, if undefeated in any other Junior Showmanship class at that show, shall automatically be eligible to compete for this prize.

Section 5. *Armbands.* Armbands with the catalog number of the dogs shall be worn by the Junior handlers.

Section 6. *Eligibility of Dog.* Each dog handled in a regular Junior Showmanship class must be entered and shown in one of the breed or obedience classes at the show, or must be entered for Junior Showmanship only. Each dog must be owned or co-owned by the Junior handler or by the Junior handler's father, mother, brother, sister, uncle, aunt, grandfather or grandmother. Every dog entered for Junior Showmanship must be eligible to compete in Dog Shows or in Obedience trials. At a Specialty show, each dog must be of the breed for which the show is held.

A dog that has been excused or disqualified by a breed judge or by a Bench Show Committee may still be handled in Junior Showmanship if eligible to compete in Obedience trials. A dog that has been rejected, dismissed or excused by the veterinarian for the protection of the other dogs at the show or for the protection of the dog excused, may not be handled in Junior Showmanship.

Section 7. *Premium List.* A club that has been approved to offer Junior Showmanship must list the classification in its premium list, with a description of the entry requirements for each class offered, and the name of the judge of each class. The number of entries in any or all classes may be limited, provided the limits are specified in the premium list.

Section 8. *Entry Forms.* To be acceptable each entry form must meet all of the requirements of Chapter 16, Section 4 of the Dog Show Rules, and in addition must be checked in the space provided to show that the dog is to be shown in Junior Showmanship, and must show in the spaces provided on the back of the form, the Junior Showmanship class in which the Junior handler is entered, the full name, address, and date of birth of the Junior handler and, if the dog is not owned or co-owned by the Junior handler, his relationship to the owner. The identification slip for the entry of the dog shall show the entry in Junior Showmanship and the class.

If a dog is to be handled in more than one Junior Showmanship class by different handlers of the same family, a separate entry form must be submitted for each Junior Showmanship class and each Junior handler.

Section 9. *Closing of Entries.* Entries for regular Junior Showmanship classes shall close at the same time that entries close for the show.

Section 10. *Judging Program.* The judging program shall list the Junior Showmanship classes, the ring(s) in which they are to be judged, the name(s) of the judge(s), the hour of judging and the number of entries in each class.

Section 11. *Catalog.* The information on any dog entered for Junior Showmanship only shall be listed at the end of the listing of its breed or variety. The dog's catalog number, the breed, and the name of the Junior handler shall be listed by classes under a separate section for Junior Showmanship.

Section 12. *Ribbons for Prizes.* The color of ribbons or rosettes for Junior Showmanship classes shall be:

First Prize — Rose
Second Prize — Brown
Third Prize — Light Green
Fourth Prize — Gray

They shall be at least 2 inches wide and approximately 8 inches long, and shall bear a facsimile of the AKC seal, the words Junior Showmanship, the name of the show-giving club, and the date.

All prizes and trophies must be described or value stated, and must be offered for outright award. No prize may be offered that is conditional upon the breed of the dog being handled.

Section 13. *Judges Book.* Each club holding Junior Showmanship shall provide for the judge a Judges Book which shall contain a separate sheet of the design prescribed by AKC for each Junior Showmanship class. The judge shall place the handlers First, Second, Third and Fourth and, after asking each placed handler to give his name, shall enter on the sheet the full names of the placed handlers, their armband numbers

"Don't worry—he's pedigreed!"

and the breeds of their dogs, and the total number of dogs competing in the class, and shall sign this book.

Section 14. *Limited Classes.* A club that is approved to hold a licensed or member all-breed show, may be approved to hold a Limited Junior Showmanship class or classes at its show, but no club will be approved to hold regular Junior Showmanship classes and limited Junior Showmanship classes at the same show.

Limited Junior Showmanship classes shall be open only to Junior handlers who have qualified by reason of certain wins in Junior Showmanship competition as specified in the premium list, within a specified period of about 12 months ending not more than 3 months prior to the date of the show; and may be further limited to Junior handlers who reside within a specified geographical area, or who have qualified at shows held within a specified geographical area.

Section 15. *Exceptions for Limited Classes.* All of these Regulations relating to regular Junior Showmanship classes shall also apply to Limited Junior Showmanship classes except that:

(A) The club may choose to prepare an announcement, separate from the premium list, which shall give all of the required information on the Limited Junior Showmanship and which shall be distributed, on request, to eligible Junior handlers. Special entry forms, identification slips, and arm-bands, may also be provided, if necessary.

(B) The premium list or separate announcement may specify a closing date for acceptance of entries in limited Junior Showmanship classes later than the date for closing of entries in the show.

(C) The dogs handled in Limited Junior Showmanship must be eligible for entry in Dog Shows or Obedience Trials. They may, but need not, be entered in breed or obedience at the particular show. Any limitation or restriction on entries in a show shall not apply to dogs that are brought into the show premises only to be handled in Limited Junior Showmanship.

(D) The information on dogs to be handled in Limited Junior Showmanship that are not entered in the show, and the names of the Junior handlers, may but need not be given in the catalog.

(E) The age limits specified in Section 4 shall apply to the age of each Junior handler at the time of the last win required to qualify for the Limited Junior Showmanship class, rather than to the age on the date of the Limited Junior Showmanship competition.

(F) If the entries in Limited Junior Showmanship warrant, the club may specify, in the first or in a later announcement, that preliminary classes will be held at the show, from which the judge(s) will select a specified number of Juniors to compete for Best Junior Handler, and no placements will be made in the preliminary classes.

Section 16. *Records.* The Superintendent or Show Secretary shall forward to The American Kennel Club, with the records of the show, the judges books for the Junior Showmanship classes.

Reprinted by permission of The American Kennel Club.

TOP BENCH SHOW WINNERS
The International Kennel Club of Chicago Best in Show Record

1938 Leonard Collins, Ch. Ideal Weather, Old English Sheepdog.
1939 Giralda Farms, Ferry v. Rauhfelsen of Giralda, Doberman Pinscher.
1940 Mr. and Mrs. A. Biddle Duke, Ch. Maro of Maridor, English Setter.
1941 Reg. P. Sparkes, Kamel White Knight, Bulldog.
1942 Mrs. James M. Austin, Ch. Che Le of Matsons Catawba, Pekingese.
1943 No Show (War Year).
1944 No Show (War Year).
1945 No Show (War Year).
1946 Claude J. Fitzgerald, Ch. Mighty Sweet Regardless, Boston Terrier.
1947 Fred Jackson, Ch. Frejax Royal Salute, English Springer Spaniel.
1948 Fred Jackson, Ch. Frejax Royal Salute, English Springer Spaniel.
1949 Mrs. Frank Cory, Ch. Charles River Color Sergeant, Irish Setter.
1950 Mrs. John G. Winant, Ch. Walsing Winning Trick of Edgerstoune, Scottish Terrier.
1951 Mrs. Harold M. Florsheim, Foxbank Entertainer of Harham, Wire Fox Terrier.
1952 Dr. and Mrs. W. Stewart Carter, Ch. Edgerstoune Troubadour, Scottish Terrier.
1953 Dr. and Mrs. George A. Richardson, Ch. Jodo von Liebestraum, German Shepherd Dog.
1954 William C. Sears, Ch. Ludar of Blue Bar, English Setter.
1955 Fred Jackson, Ch. Frejax Royalist, English Springer Spaniel.
1956 Mr. and Mrs. Jouett Shouse, Ch. Barrage of Quality Hill, Boxer.
1957 Mr. and Mrs. C. C. Venable, Ch. Chik T'Sun of Caversham, Pekingese.
1958 Hidden Lane Kennels, Ch. Ben-Dar's Winning Stride, English Setter.
1959 Mr. and Mrs. C. C. Venable, Ch. Chik T'Sun of Caversham, Pekingese.
1960 Blanche E. Reeg, Ch. Blanart Bewitching, Scottish Terrier.
1961 Frank and Katherine Wheatley, Ch. Conifer's Lance, Irish Setter.
1962 Mrs. Susan D. Phillips, Ch. Gladjac Royal Oslo, Norwegian Elkhound.
1963 Donald F. and Mary E. Smith, Ch. Treceder's Painted Lady, Boxer.
1964 Pennyworth Kennels, Ch. Courtenay Fleetfoot of Pennyworth, Whippet.
1965 Margaret Carveth, Ch. Ru-Mar's Tsushima, C.D., Doberman Pinscher.
1966 Serena and Hendrik Van Rensselaer, Ch. Fezziwig Raggedy Andy, Old English Sheepdog.
1967 Mrs. F. H. Gasow, Ch. Salilyn's Aristocrat, English Springer Spaniel.
1968 Mrs. James R. Getz and Mrs. Sally B. McCarthy, Ch. Shamrock Acres Light Brigade, Labrador Retriever.
1969 Dr. and Mrs. P. J. Pagano and Dr. Theodore S. Fickes, Ch. Arriba's Prima Donna, Boxer.
1970 Mr. and Mrs. James A. Farrell, Jr., Ch. Special Edition, Lakeland Terrier.
1971 Dr. Milton E. Prickett, Ch. Chinoe's Adamant James, English Springer Spaniel.

The Westminster K. C. Best in Show Record

1907 Winthrop Rutherfurd, Ch. Warren Remedy, Fox Terrier (Smooth)
1908 Winthrop Rutherfurd, Ch. Warren Remedy, Fox Terrier (Smooth)
1909 Winthrop Rutherfurd, Ch. Warren Remedy, Fox Terrier (Smooth)
1910 Sabine Kennels, Ch. Sabine Rarebit, Fox Terrier (Smooth)
1911 A. Albright, Jr., Ch. Tickle Em Jock, Scottish Terrier
1912 William P. Wolcott, Ch. Kenmare Sorceress, Airedale Terrier
1913 Alex H. Stewart, Ch. Strathtay Prince Albert, Bulldog
1914 Mrs. Tylor Morse, Ch. Slumber, Old English Sheepdog
1915 George W. Quintard, Ch. Matford Vic, Fox Terrier (Wire)
1916 George W. Quintard, Ch. Matford Vic, Fox Terrier (Wire)
1917 Mrs. Roy A. Rainey, Ch. Conejo Wycollar Boy, Fox Terrier (Wire)
1918 R. H. Elliott, Ch. Haymarket Fruitless, Bull Terrier
1919 G. L. L. Davis, Ch. Briergate Bright Beauty, Airedale Terrier
1920 Mrs. Roy A. Rainey, Ch. Conejo Wycollar Boy, Fox Terrier (Wire)
1921 William T. Payne, Ch. Midkiff Seductive, Cocker Spaniel
1922 Frederic C. Hood, Ch. Boxwood Barkentine, Airedale Terrier
1923 There was no BEST IN SHOW award this year.
1924 Bayard Warren, Ch. Barberryhill Bootlegger, Sealyham Terrier
1925 Robert F. Maloney, Ch. Governor Moscow, Pointer
1926 Halleston Kennels, Ch. Signal Circuit of Halleston, Fox Terrier (Wire)
1927 Frederic C. Brown, Ch. Pinegrade Perfection, Sealyham Terrier
1928 R. M. Lewis, Ch. Talavera Margaret, Fox Terrier (Wire)
1929 Mrs. Florence B. Ilch, Laund Loyalty of Bellhaven, Collie
1930 John G. Bates, Ch. Pendley Calling of Blarney, Fox Terrier (Wire)
1931 John G. Bates, Ch. Pendley Calling of Blarney, Fox Terrier (Wire)
1932 Giralda Farms, Ch. Nancolleth Markable, Pointer
1933 S. M. Stewart, Ch. Warland Protector of Shelterock, Airedale Terrier
1934 Halleston Kennels, Ch. Flornell Spicy Bit of Halleston, Fox Terrier (Wire)
1935 Blakeen Kennels, Ch. Nunsoe Duc de la Terrace of Blakeen, Standard Poodle
1936 Clairedale Kennels, Ch. St. Margaret Magnificent of Clairedale, Sealyham Terrier
1937 Halleston Kennels, Ch. Flornell Spicy Piece of Halleston, Fox Terrier (Wire)
1938 Maridor Kennels, Ch. Daro of Maridor, English Setter
1939 Giralda Farms, Ch. Ferry v. Rauhfelsen of Giralda, Doberman Pinscher
1940 H. E. Mellenthin, Ch. My Own Brucie, Cocker Spaniel
1941 H. E. Mellenthin, Ch. My Own Brucie, Cocker Spaniel
1942 Mrs. J. G. Winant, Ch. Wolvey Pattern of Edgerstoune, West Highland White Terrier
1943 Mrs. P. H. B. Frelinghuysen, Ch. Pitter Patter of Piperscroft, Miniature Poodle
1944 Mrs. Edward P. Alker, Ch. Flornell Rare-Bit of Twin Ponds, Welsh Terrier
1945 Mr. & Mrs. T. H. Snethen, Ch. Shieling's Signature, Scottish Terrier
1946 Mr. & Mrs. T. H. Carruthers, III, Ch. Hetherington Model Rhythm, Fox Terrier (Wire)
1947 Mr. & Mrs. Richard C. Kettles, Jr., Ch. Warlord of Mazelaine, Boxer
1948 Mr. & Mrs. William A. Rockefeller, Ch. Rock Ridge Night Rocket, Bedlington Terrier
1949 Mr. & Mrs. John Phelps Wagner, Ch. Marzelaine Zazarac Brandy, Boxer
1950 Mrs. J. G. Winant, Ch. Walsing Winning Trick of Edgerstoune, Scottish Terrier
1951 Dr. & Mrs. R. C. Harris, Ch. Bang Away of Sirrah Crest, Boxer
1952 Mr. & Mrs. Len Carey, Ch. Rancho Dobe's Storm, Doberman Pinscher
1953 Mr. & Mrs. Len Carey, Ch. Rancho Dobe's Storm, Doberman Pinscher
1954 Mrs. Carl E. Morgan, Ch. Carmor's Rise and Shine, Cocker Spaniel
1955 John A. Saylor, M.D., Ch. Kippax Fearnought, Bulldog
1956 Bertha Smith, Ch. Wilber White Swan, Toy Poodle
1957 Sunny Shay and Dorothy Chenade, Ch. Shirkhan of Grandeur, Afghan Hound
1958 Puttencove Kennels, Ch. Puttencove Promise, Standard Poodle
1959 Dunwalke Kennels, Ch. Fontclair Festoon, Miniature Poodle
1960 Mr. & Mrs. C. C. Venable, Ch. Chik T'Sun of Caversham, Pekingese
1961 Miss Florence Michelson, Ch. Cappoquin Little Sister, Toy Poodle
1962 Wishing Well Kennels, Ch. Elfinbrook Simon, West Highland White Terrier
1963 Mrs. W. J. S. Borie, Ch. Wakefield's Black Knight, English Springer Spaniel
1964 Pennyworth Kennels, Ch. Courtenay Fleetfoot of Pennyworth, Whippet
1965 Mr. & Mrs. Charles C. Stalter, Ch. Carmichaels Fanfare, Scottish Terrier
1966 Marion G. Bunker, Ch. Zeloy Mooremaide's Magic, Fox Terrier (Wire)
1967 E. H. Stuart, Ch. Bardene Bingo, Scottish Terrier
1968 Mr. & Mrs. James A. Farrell, Jr., Ch. Stingray of Derryabah, Lakeland Terrier
1969 Walter F. Goodman and Mrs. Adele F. Goodman, Ch. Glamoor Good News, Skye Terrier
1970 Dr. and Mrs. P. J. Pagano and Dr. Theodore S. Fickes, Ch. Arriba's Prima Donna, Boxer
1971 Dr. Milton E. Prickett, Ch. Chinoe's Adamant James, English Springer Spaniel

CHAPTER VIII
THE OUTDOOR DOG

BIRD DOGS AND THEIR JOBS

WHAT DO THEY DO?

Retrievers

The retrievers remain quietly at the hunter's side; their job begins when the shot is fired. Remembering where the bird fell and, upon command, fetching the downed bird promptly is their bailiwick. They must find their bird on land or in water and track down the cripple.

Spaniels

Spaniels have a full time job. They work in front, seeking out and flushing upland birds, and then they retrieve the birds after they have been downed.

Pointing Dogs

The pointing dog's purpose is to point at the game and to hold his point (staunch) until the handler flushes the birds. There are pointers who are trained to "point dead," signaling the hunter as to the downed bird's location. Pointing dogs are not natural retrievers, but they can be trained.

Suiting the Dog to the Game

When selecting your sporting dog, consider the type of hunting you will be doing and then choose accordingly.

Waterfowl

The retrievers—Labrador, Golden Chesapeake, and Irish Water Spaniel—are best for the hunter who is after waterfowl and shore birds.

Pheasant

For those hunting pheasant in open country, the English Setters and Pointers are good choices. In restricted covers, the German Shorthair, German Wirehair, and Brittany will work better. Some authorities insist that the spaniels are the most perfectly suited for hunting pheasant in restricted cover.

Ruffed Grouse

The flush-type dogs are probably best for grouse hunters; spaniels or retrievers work equally well.

Woodcock

Woodcock and Ruffed Grouse are frequently found in the same terrain. Thus, a dog suitable to hunt Ruffed Grouse is again used here.

Bobwhite Quail, Chicken, Hungarian Partridge

Pointing dogs are tops for hunting quail, chicken, and partridge. Choose the Pointer or the English Setter. For areas that are in dense cover, the German Pointers, Brittany, Irish or Gordon Setters can be used.

Field Trial Clubs

For those interested in an outdoor sport, in the breeding of better dogs, and in improved game conditions, membership in a Field Trial Club is the answer. These clubs offer a fine opportunity to observe or participate in an exciting and exhilarating sport. The club provides opportunities for sharing and exchanging ideas on dog care, training, handling, breeding, health, and hunting.

THE ABC's OF TRAINING A BIRD DOG

MANY think that obtaining a bird dog for the first time and getting him trained to a degree where you can shoot birds over him is an all but impossible task. The thought is completely false. It *does* take *much* knowledge, patience, and hours of work to arrive at "finished" bird dog performance, but teaching your pointing dog, retriever, or spaniel the basics, so that he is prepared to go afield to hunt with you, can be done with relative ease.

Many new bird dog owners come home with a pup of eight to 16 weeks. This age is ideal! But, regardless of age, you can begin basic training a few weeks after you bring your new pup home.

A most important consideration before you go to pick up your pup is a kennel—that is, unless you plan to make a house dweller out of your future hunting companion, and there's certainly nothing wrong with doing that. A clean, dry, warm, "escape-proof" kennel should be constructed before you bring your pup home if you are going to make an outside dog of him. I say escape-proof because once a youngster learns to get out of confinement a few times, there's no keeping him in after that. They become veritable "Houdinis."

Introduce your dog to a collar as soon as you get him home. Make it tight enough that he can't work it over his head with his paws. He won't like it at first, and he'll try to get rid of it. But he'll soon get used to the collar. In a few days try snapping on a lead or leash, and walk him around your yard or driveway. Many canines fight the lead the first time you snap one on, but it is a most important training tool, one they *must* become accustomed to.

The first week or so at home, away from its mother, should not involve any intensive training. Your concern for this initial period is to transfer the confidence and friendship the pup had for his mother and other members of the litter, to you. Spend all the time you can with the dog. Avoid scolding or harsh tones of your voice. Wear old clothes so you can really love him up. Permit him to jump on your clothes. Better manners can be learned in time.

Now there comes a split in recommendations. If you have a retrieving dog or a spaniel, the first command to teach is "Sit!" If you've brought home a pointing dog, I recommend "Heel" first. But let's name the breeds in each classification, so there's no misunderstanding.

The retriever breeds are as follows: Labradors, Chesapeakes, Goldens, and Curly Coated and Flat Coated Retrievers. The Spaniel breeds are numerous, but only a few are used regularly as hunting dogs. They are: Springers, American Water Spaniels, Irish Water Spaniels, and Cockers.

The major pointing breeds are: Pointers (usually called English Pointers, but this is a misnomer), English Setters, Irish Setters, Gordon Setters, Brittany Spaniels, Vizslas, German Shorthaired Pointers, German Wirehaired Pointers, Griffons, and Weimaraners.

Training Spaniels and Retrievers

Let's take up training of spaniels and retrievers first. "Sit" is the first command for him to learn. It's easy. Grasp the dog by the collar with one hand, and push down on his rump with the other. Just prior to shoving down, give the command, "Sit." (Spaniel owners may want to say "hup" instead.) Never say another word but this one during this exercise. Keep your lessons on a fun basis, especially initially. Your tone of voice and general attitude must be appealing to the dog if you are going to achieve results quickly. Let's face it, some people will be better at it than others, but even if you don't have a talent for training dogs, you can get the basics across with perseverance.

Lessons should be frequent, but short. Four or five times is plenty for the first try at "Sit." But you should return often to redo the exercise. Four, five times a day, even more if you can swing it, is the key. Once the dog is sitting, it's time to teach the next command, "Stay."

With palm outstretched, start backing away from the sitting dog, giving the single word command, "Stay." The tendency for the dog will be to get up and follow you. Return to him, pull him back to the original spot where he sat, and "resit" him. Back away again, palm outstretched toward the dog, the sole word commanded, "Stay."

Again, short lessons, repeated numerous times, are the key. If you'll follow the recommendations, your new pup will soon come around. Once the pup is sitting and staying on command to your satisfaction, he's in a perfect state of mind to learn the important command, "Here" or "Come." Merely call the word, clap your hands, and start in the opposite direction—away from the sitting pup. No problems here. He'll rush in to get to you.

So with relative ease you have your new youngster sitting, staying, and coming to command. If you are

Retrieving is important for all bird dogs. I tell this Shorthair "Whoa," and toss out a boat fender dummy. Retrieving should be happy and most dogs love it.

persistent, make your lessons short and happy, and conduct them often, you'll have accomplished this phase of training in about two weeks. You may get results quicker, but continue them so they are well ingrained in the dog's head.

Retrieving is the most important thing a retriever must learn and it's high on the list of things a spaniel must do. Bouncing a rubber ball or tennis ball on a hard surface where your dog can see it is a good initial tool to use to gain and nurture his retrieving interest.

Bounce the ball until he is in a frenzy, wanting to catch it himself. Have a check cord of about 15 feet in length snapped on the pup's collar. Toss the ball out only a short distance. He'll pounce on it immediately. Give the command, "Fetch," and drag him back to you before he has a chance to run off with the dummy. Some precocious pups will charge back with the ball readily, but others will want to run off— being possessive with this new toy. Don't let that thought get developed too far.

Retrieving, too, should be play time for a young pup. Don't get harsh with the dog. Make sure your attitude remains calm and on an even keel. As the dog progresses with his training, you can move to a different type of training dummy. Corn cobs are light, and the right size for a three- to six-month-old pup. As the dog gets older you should move up to a training dummy made from a boat fender. You may also want to increase the dog's interest in retrieving by

adding commercial bird scent to the dummy. Another way to do this is affix a wing of a duck or pheasant to the dummy.

Once the dog is fetching the dummy with vigor, it is time to teach him to stay with you until commanded to fetch. Again, the check cord is your tool. Tell the dog "Sit." When he does, tell him to "Stay," and tramp on the length of check cord. Next give the command, "Mark," and toss the dummy high into the air.

The dog will lunge after the bird, but with your feet firmly on the check cord, he'll be stopped short. Return him to the sit. Release him to go retrieve the dummy with "Fetch" or the dog's name. Keep the check cord on the dog until you are certain he will not break without it. Again make the lessons short, but repeat them often. If you are going to have a dog with great interest in retrieving, you shouldn't overdo it with too much dummy tossing at one session. Toss it a few times each session, but make the sessions often. Sometimes intense Summer heat can take the desire out of a retrieving dog quickly.

Next step is to start throwing the dummy in taller weeds where he'll have to search for it with his nose. Training scent or a freshly tied-on bird wing is imperative here because the dog will have to use his scenting powers to find the dummy.

It is best to introduce your dog to water by taking him to the pond or lake with another dog that loves to swim. If you don't have one of these swimmers

Start a dog in water by tossing the bird in shallow water—where he'll only have to wade in. Gradually extend your tosses as the dog gains more confidence in his swimming ability and grows to love the water.

yourself, perhaps you know someone that does. If not, the best answer is to don swimming trunks yourself and wade in. Do that and your pup will be more anxious to wade in after you.

Start with shallow water where your pup can walk around, then proceed to deeper water where he can swim. There will be much splashing initially, and it is necessary for a dog to venture into deeper water to learn to swim adeptly. He should learn to swim with powerful strokes, forelegs remaining in the water rather than needlessly splashing the surface.

Once your dog is in the shallow water you can urge him to the deeper areas by tossing the retrieving dummy. If he's an eager retriever on land, he'll be just as eager in water, perhaps even more so. Start by tossing the dummy only a short distance, so that the dog can fetch it by wading. Extend your tosses until he is eventually swimming a short distance to get to it. Once you've progressed this far, it's only a matter of another trip or two to the pond until you can heave the dummy out as far as you can. The dog will soon be jumping into the water from a high bank with gusto!

Now your spaniel or retriever is almost ready for a session in the hunting field or duck blind. Introduce him to gunfire by shooting a training pistol over him at feeding time. Start by shooting it at a distance, then, each day move closer. Next graduate to a centerfire pistol with blanks; then a shotgun, fired in the field while the dog is some distance from you, interested

in something else. This same procedure should be used for pointing dogs, too.

Once introduced to gunfire, your retriever or spaniel is ready for gunning. One more refinement is recommended, though. Purchase a few pigeons to shoot over your dog. Place the bird in a cage and set it in a field. Now bring in the dog at heel. About 15 feet from the cage, command the dog to sit. Walk ahead of him, flush the bird out of the cover, and shoot it.

If you can have a friend hold the dog on a check cord, it will keep him from breaking until you give the command to fetch. Several pigeons shot over a youngster just prior to the season will give him all the experience he needs to give you a satisfying day his very first time out with you. Now pointing dogs!

Training the Pointing Dog

The first command for a pointing dog is "Heel," but unless the pup is particularly bold, I don't like to teach it until he has several months of age under his belt and has all the confidence in the world in me. I *never* teach a pointing dog to sit unless he is to double in a duck blind. If that's the case, I wait a year or so before teaching sit. While waiting for your pup to become old enough to teach heel, you can have fun with retrieving. Merely follow the procedures outlined previously for retrievers and spaniels.

You can even introduce pointing dogs to water,

Above—This handler works his dog into a planted pigeon. Note the checkcord. Right—one man tosses up the pigeon, while the other fires a blank pistol over the dog. The man on the left is also tramping on the check cord. Thus if the dog decides to break shot, he won't go far!

again using the same recommendations previously given for retrievers and spaniels. Many pointing dog breeds double as water dogs when the occasion arises. Griffons, Wirehaired Pointers, Brittanies, and German Shorthairs are noted for being excellent water dogs. But even the other pointing breeds will not suffer by learning how to swim. When hot weather precludes running the fields and forests to keep in good physical condition, you can swim your pointing dog and give him all the exercise he needs.

You can teach heel in your driveway or yard. Again the check cord is used. Command "Heel," and pull the dog with you as you move forward. If he charges ahead, give the command again, and jerk him back. It is most important to be in a good frame of mind and not lose patience. Otherwise it is likely you will affect the dog's disposition, making him less bold.

As with the previous training recommendations, the key is short lessons repeated often. Once a day is hardly enough at the beginning, though it's plenty once the dog knows the commands and it's only necessary to keep him brushed up. If you are training a retriever or spaniel and he has the other "basics" under his belt, why not teach him to heel next?

When the pointing dog is heeling well, it's time to try the next command, an important one, "Whoa." Do it by heeling the dog, suddenly stopping yourself, at the same time commanding "Whoa" in an authoritative voice. Jerk back on the check cord if the dog doesn't stop. As the dog gets the hang of this exercise, command the word "Whoa" and keep moving forward yourself.

The tendency for the dog will be to keep walking with you. If he does, return him to the point you gave the command and make him stop. Remember repetition, repetition! Soon the dog will be stopping each time you sing out the word, "Whoa."

Now, when he is loose in the yard or field, but still with the check cord on, give the command "Whoa" when he is, say, 15 yards from you. If the dog doesn't stop in his tracks, get to him, and return him to the spot he was at when you gave the command originally. Then make his stay there for a while.

As time passes you will be able to stop your dog with this one word under all circumstances. It gives you a wonderful degree of control over him in the field, something most casual hunters can never get out of their canines!

You can start the command, "Here" by letting your dog trail a long 35-foot check cord in the field. If he won't come in when you call him, sing out "Whoa," then go get him! If you've ingrained him well with "Whoa," you'll have little trouble with "here," unless the dog is overly ambitious and bold.

So now you've progressed through retrieving, water, heel, whoa, and come or here, plus some pretty good handling response. But you have a pointing dog. How about pointing? At a tender age you can use the bird wing on a fish pole technique to give your pup the idea. But don't overdo this one because pointing must ultimately become a response to scent, not sight. But to get started, swing the bird wing, hung from a length of line and fishing pole. The dog will go wild to catch it, but don't let him do that.

Eventually he'll tire and start stalking the bird wing like a cat! Now is the time to let the wing lie still. If the dog lunges in, jerk it away. If he points, encourage him with soothing "Whoas," and try to get your hands

on him to stroke him softly, conveying to him how pleased you are with his point. Remember, don't overdo the sight pointing lessons!

You can use caged birds or pen raised birds to bring your pup along the training trail, but there is nothing better than wild birds and natural conditions. It is my opinion they benefit a dog most. Travel to your hunting grounds at every opportunity prior to the open season. (The same goes for spaniels, too.) The tendency for a young dog is to perhaps flash point his game, then charge in, flushing the birds and giving merry chase. This is fine for increasing the dog's desire to hunt, but too much chasing, without some pointing, is certainly not good.

Your "Whoa" command is of benefit here. If the dog is chasing too much, you have to begin stopping him. Make him drag the check cord at all times. If he won't stop on command, the check cord makes it easier to get to him. It is more work to get a pointing dog ready than it is a retriever or spaniel, no question about it, but many hunters are not happy unless a steady point is a part of their hunt, and I'm one of them, though I train and hunt over spaniels and retrieving dogs, too.

You have to hope that the dog eventually starts pointing, then you encourage him to hold. Professional help should be sought if you have trouble here, for each individual dog varies, and different recommendations may be in order for each. Once your dog is on point, you should not continually say, "Whoa," unless you are positive he has a bird in front. One "Whoa" is enough. Then walk in and try to flush the bird. If the dog breaks, chasing the bird, bring him back, scolding him to a degree to match his age and

disposition. But if you start saying "Whoa" continually, and there is no bird there, you will be encouraging your pup to false point, a very bad fault, and a very hard, if not impossible one, to break.

Many pups love to chase song birds, meadowlarks, sparrows, and what not. Though you don't want to scold a youngster for doing this, you don't want to encourage it either. If you do, you may have a five-year-old that points more robins than he does pheasants. Use your common sense and a degree of discretion.

A release pen for quail is used by many to augment the native bird supply, but most first-time dog men will seldom make the purchase. Regardless, it's a good investment. The pen and birds can run from $30-$40. The idea is that you release half the birds in the pen to work your dogs on, those remaining call the released ones back after the training session (through a funnel-type opening that allows birds to crawl in, but not out). Using a quail recall pen also means you need some acreage close to home in order to release the birds and work your dogs. If you make use of this method, don't forget the check cord!

Pigeons are a cheaper investment, and should be used along with some type of cage to hold the birds while you are working the pointing dog. The use of pigeons lacks a little in that training conditions cannot be as natural as with released quail. Plant the pigeons in good cover, in a cage. Work your dog with the check cord until he makes a point. In many cases points will not be stylish with these birds. Nevertheless, it gives young dogs an initial contact with flying birds, and there are no closed seasons on pigeons. Shoot the ones your dog points. A few birds shot, shortly before the season opens, would be my recommendation. Don't overdo it!

With these basics you can have a young pointing dog, retriever, or spaniel ready for the hunting season in a relatively short period of time. It is my opinion that spaniels and retrieving dogs can be taught the basic techniques necessary for scoring on game a little quicker than the pointing dogs. But for many, the extra effort involved to gain a steady point is worth it.

Don't neglect taking up the exciting sport of bird hunting with a dog because you think it's too complicated a procedure and involves too much training time. You can accomplish much in a matter of weeks or months taking a few minutes at a time at frequent intervals. Training a young pup is enjoyment if you go at it with the right attitude. The result is a young dog that aids you tremendously in filling the game bag. And, more importantly, you have gained a hunting companion, one that says nothing when you miss a rooster or mallard, one that is never late in the morning, and one that gives his all to assist you in having an enjoyable day on the gunning grounds! What more could a hunter ask?   *Nick Sisley*

199

WHAT IS A WELL-TRAINED FIELD SPRINGER?

ON THE way to the field, whether on or off the leash, the dog walks gently at heel without playing, tugging or forging ahead. It will sit (hup) instantly on the handler's command to await further orders. When cast off with the command "Hi-On," it springs instantly into action, hunting with great speed, keenness and desire in the direction indicated by the handler's arm signal. Its enthusiasm and eagerness are such that it glances at the handler only when a whistle or voice command is given.

It will quarter back and forth in front of the handler, always keeping within gun range and turning on whistle signals.

When the dog scents game, it becomes very animated with tail and stern action ("making game"). It will drive in hard on the hiding bird and flush it boldly into the air or catch it. If the bird has run, the dog will track it until able to catch up and flush it. As the bird becomes fully air-borne, the dog will drop to flush ("Hup") and will stay down ("steady to shot") while the bird is dropped. If the handler doesn't give a command, the dog should "hup" automatically.

The dog is constantly alert, watching the flying bird ("marking") and its fall to the ground, but stays hupped ("steady") until commanded to retrieve. At the command to fetch (usually the dog's name), it will race to the vicinity of the fall and search eagerly until the bird is located. If the bird is only wounded and running, the dog will track it, seldom allowing a cripple to escape. When the bird is found, the dog will seize it firmly but gently in its mouth and return rapidly to the handler. It will deliver the bird directly and without a struggle, after which it will sit obedi-

("Grant" owned by Mr. Edward Porges.)

ently until cast off again or heeled from the field.

The dog is silent throughout his performance, neither whining nor barking.

THE WORKING TERRIER

A working terrier can be of any terrier breed. The test he must pass is functional, for he is judged solely by performance. If he will work and is dead game he is accepted into the fraternity of the working terrier class.

The word terrier comes from the Latin, *terra,* which means earth. In absolute definition a "working terrier" is one which hunts below ground. The very nature of a terrier is to pursue all those animals which burrow. The fox, badger, skunk, hare, rabbit, woodchuck, weasel, etc., are the terrier's natural quarry. His attitude toward all vermin is implacable.

200

From the earliest days of working terriers the fox has stood as one of its most significant adversaries. When going to ground to fox the terrier is often successful in causing the fox to bolt, that is, run out a back entrance from the earth. However, if the terrier cannot make the fox bolt (there may be no escape-hatch), he then grabs hold and either kills or draws the fox from the earth. Sometimes it is not possible to get a hold, then the terrier will corner the fox and start baying, informing the diggers of their whereabouts.

Terrier owners not fortunate enough to be living in the country need to become acquainted with farmers and other country dwellers. Let these people know you have terriers which need work. They will gladly watch for any fox or woodchuck activity. This will save a great deal of scouting time. Make it clear that all earths will be filled in and no damage to property will occur.

When you arrive at an occupied fox den, tether all except one terrier, providing you have more than one. When the terrier goes to ground station yourself near the escape hole so you can shoot the fox when he attempts to bolt. Turn any other terriers loose so they can join in the worry. In a manner of speaking the worry (shaking the dead fox) is the terrier's reward. Strict discipline is mandatory for all dogs and persons while a terrier is working in an earth. Only if all is quiet will the fox bolt.

There is always the possibility that the fox cannot bolt, or that the terrier cannot get a hold to draw it. Wait until the terrier barks from the same spot for several minutes telling that he has the fox cornered. Then begin to dig. Follow the hole and keep the trench wide. What seems wide enough when you start can become far too narrow as you dig down into the earth. Keep the hole open; you do not want to shut off the terrier. Stop and listen often. They may be up a side hole. As soon as you reach the fox, kill it quickly.

STARTING PUPPIES

Woodchucking is a good way to start puppies. We like to start our Lakelands with some above-ground work. It is first necessary to know the location of an active den and the best time to find the chuck out feeding. Note wind direction, being careful to keep it in your face as you work cautiously across the field. Take your time. Have a couple of puppies and one adult terrier on leashes under strict control. Much of the way you will be on your hands and knees. Get as close as you can and when you are certain the adult terrier sees the chuck release him. He will be there in a flash, maneuvering himself so as to block the chuck from the den entrance. Now let the puppies go. With encouragement and a protective guard furnished by the adult terrier the youngsters soon learn to handle themselves with audacity. We like the pup-

pies to have several encounters with the chucks above ground before we let them enter. Also, we like to work them on woodchucks before they work foxes.

The terrier is rarely able to get a hold on a chuck in an earth due to the smallness of the hole. For the chuck to try to escape by running is futile. The chuck's short-legged, waddling gait prohibits his making a run for it. Not being able to make the chuck bolt, the terrier will corner him and begin to bay. Always wait until the barking comes from one place for several minutes before starting to dig.

These are two ways which terriers are worked. There are many others. However, it must not be thought that working a terrier is a wanton sport for destroying wildlife. Farmers and conservationists are fully aware of the destruction brought about by fox, woodchuck, rat, skunk, etc. Working terriers contribute toward the necessary balance of natural resources in a safe, humane manner.

It must be emphasized that no terrier should be allowed to go off hunting by himself. Early training can enforce the boundaries, beyond which he does not venture alone. The risk of losing a trapped terrier is omnipresent. Generally a rescue can be effected if the terrier's whereabouts is known. Woe to the terrier which goes off hunting alone and becomes trapped in the ground. He is a lucky dog indeed if he is rescued. And never, never allow a terrier to go to ground wearing his collar.

Good shovels, at least two pairs of strong arms, a small tube of penicillin ointment, clean rags, and water are necessary things to have along whenever the terriers are out working. After being in the earth for a time a terrier should be given a drink, his eyes washed out, and any bites or scratches attended to.

It is my opinion that a working terrier should weigh between 12 and 15 pounds, with 14 the ideal weight. The coat must be thick to protect against the cold and wet. Color is of no importance, nor is length of leg. Some believe that a long-legged terrier cannot get down in a small hole. Not true. No terrier walks into an earth. He lies on his side and scratches his way in. The terrier to reject immediately is the one with thick shoulders or turned out elbows, or a wide chest. A terrier with any of these could not get into an earth, or if he did he would most likely become stuck. The true working terrier temperament possesses both pluck and discretion. If the terrier is foolhardy he will spend most of his days in the hospital. There are good workers to be found in many of the terrier breeds.

Those of us who work our terriers enjoy nothing as much as a day's outing with the dogs. We prize the working qualities, and cherish a good terrier as the Dutch scholar, Erasmus, who wrote, "And upon the last day, oh little one, thou shalt wag a tiny tail of gold."

Patricia A. Lent

201

THE WHYS AND WHEREFORES OF COON DOGS

THE DISTANT baying was increasing in tempo now, for the hounds were narrowing the gap between them and their prey, that ringtailed, bandit-faced, fur-bearer that continues to gain new aspirants for his hide each year—the wily raccoon. And what a challenging, brainy critter he is, matching wits with both man and hound.

As we sat on the ridge above the valley, drinking in the thrilling sounds of the chase, the dogs pushed their victim until only a short distance separated them. The coon scurried up a small cherry tree, his only resort now. The hounds went mad, talking "treed" with an increased chatter in their voices.

Our group continued to sit in silence for some brief moments, listening to that great hound music. None of us wanted to have such an enjoyable moment end too quickly. There wasn't one of us who didn't have a tingle of satisfaction and excitement go up and down his spine.

Coon hunting is a growing, All-American sport. It's done at night with the aid of carbide, wet or dry cell battery lamps, or any type of light that will help light up the dark night woods and aid you in shining

Bluetick coonhounds, jumping at a tree that harbors a coon, and telling their master about that fact in no uncertain terms.

a tree for telltale coon eyes. It's growing because the figures say so: the sale of coon dog pups, the number of dogs being registered, and the increased number of new names on the registry certificates. This fact is undeniable.

And coon hunting is truly an All-American sport, not one we inherited from our old world forefathers. Bird hunting with pointing or flushing dogs, fox hunts, and rabbit chases are dog oriented sports that originated on the Continent or the British Isles prior to the settlement of the New World. The old world hunter certainly would have enjoyed hunting the raccoon, but the raccoon is native to North America. We Americans are the only ones privileged to chase this masked bandit with our long-eared, loud-mouthed, scent-crazy hounds.

The growth of sport hunting in America enjoys a popularity that can be matched nowhere else on earth. In other countries, hunting is almost always a pastime for the rich and their guests. Game populations are managed with great expenditures of money and full-time employees to serve the fancies of a few.

In the United States 17,000,000 hunters take to the gunning fields each season. They are in pursuit of many different kinds of game, over a wide expanse of varying terrain. The average guy can hunt in America with relatively little expense. But when it comes to coon hunting, state that fact double — in spades! This is a sport that most down-to-earth Americans can enjoy to the utmost.

Why? I think it's the aura that surrounds a coon hunt that brings hunters to the fold and keeps them there. There's something about going out at night, hunting in the darkness that gives a sense of self-satisfaction. In reality, it's a whole new view of nature. Senses are more aroused than in daytime. You use varying terrain. The average guy can hunt in America don't use on rabbit and bird hunts. Your ears are carefully tuned to every distant murmur of the hounds' voices, consequently you hear the mournful tones of the hoot owl, scurrying animals in the distance, even leaves falling and touching the ground. These are but a few of the tangible results of your new perceptiveness! Because it's dark and you have only the glow of light from your lantern to light the way, your eyes are always searching, actually seeing things that you might miss in daylight.

And every night out is different, even if you go back to some places many times during the course of the year. The overhead clouds present eerie patterns that are always changing. In stark black and white tones, lit by the moon, their ghostly appearance is usually sobering. Once the hounds are turned loose, there's the anticipation. Will the dogs strike a trail tonight? Will it be a coon or trash game? Will they run the coon to tree him and stick to the tree until you get there like they should? A thousand and one other questions enter your mind—then you hear Old Blue open! Your heart jumps! What a deep, mellow tone he has! How that voice carries!

It starts raining, a storm cloud has gathered quickly, and you didn't notice it in the excitement. You're wet, but you're running after the hounds, for they have the prey treed, at least it sounds like it. There's a hidden limb. You see it too late. It catches you in the shin, and down you go. Lights out, both figuratively and literally! Bruised and sore, you're soon back up again, cursing a little under your breath, but soon forgetting the fall; you're concentrating on getting to the dogs more than ever now.

You don't even notice that stretch of briars or the next patch of thorn apples just before you get to the dogs, even though you leave a patch of your shirt and a few thousand red corpuscles on one of the latter.

At last you're at the tree. Hope to devil they don't have a 'possum up. You search with the light. No eyes. You keep flashing the light over the tree, urging the dogs all the while to keep up their chiming voices. Is that him? No! Yes, by gosh, it is. The hounds have done it again. Talk about satisfaction.

You talk to your companion, say a few good words about his dog, for it took both hounds' cunning and knowledge to bring this coon to the tree. You know how much work went into getting both dogs this far along. The satisfaction suddenly doubles.

This is part of the aura that surrounds coon hunting, some of the treasures that make it so loved by an ever-increasing number of dog lovers. But there are numerous prospective coon hunters that don't know too much about the sport. How can they get started?

With rabbit dogs and bird dogs it's usually a matter of buying a young puppy, one or more good books on the subject of training, and going to work. This is the way *not* to start coon hunting. The way to start is to accompany a person you know who is an experienced coon hunter. Take a look at how his dogs work, and if you can talk him into it, take your new pup along some night in the future. This oldtimer will, in effect, show your youngster how it is done. For the most part coon hounds, though there must be plenty of it bred

An unregistered hound of the black and tan variety.
One can readily see this hound loves to tree coon.

203

into them, learn by seeing it done right by others. And if they see it done wrong, they learn that, too, unfortunately!

If you don't know an experienced coon hunter, better get to know one. There are plenty of them around. If all else fails, you can purchase a completely trained and broke coon hound, but he'll cost you up to a month's pay. Another possibility is to buy a "pup trainer," an old coon dog past his prime, and a young pup. Hopefully the old dog will have enough time left in him to get your puppy well started.

Coon dogs are large, flap-eared, mouthy rascals that have a nose to smell old tracks and the yen to open their yaps and tell the world when they get a whiff. Some years ago the United Kennel Club was formed, and they currently recognize six separate breeds of coon hounds. By buying a dog that is registered, you can trace his family, hopefully finding out that he came from some darn good working hounds. If so, breeding should tell. Your chances of getting a good dog are usually better with a registered dog.

However, with coon hounds there are plenty of the unregistered variety. The U.K.C. registers by color, but some coon hunters will mix the color, breeding one to another, and parents that compliment each other should make good coon dogs—regardless of color.

The six breeds that the U.K.C. registers are Treeing Walkers, Black and Tans, Plotts, Blueticks, English, and Redbones. The Treeing Walkers descended from the Walker Fox Hounds, and color can run the gamut —any color is acceptable here. Redbones, naturally have the reddish color, Blueticks have a distinctive ticking that makes their coat appear blue, Black and Tans are mostly black with tan ears and several other spots, Plotts are brindle colored, and English can have coats of varying color.

The aspiring coon hunter will usually have one of these colors to choose from, even if you don't buy a registered dog. You'll find that most hounds, even the crossbreeds, will look like one of the registered hound's colors.

Once you have a pup in your possession, don't expect miracles. On the average, it takes many months, usually several years, of intensive exposure to get a hound to the point where he can run a track and tree a coon without help from another, more experienced coon dog. There are exceptional pups, of course, that are treeing their own coon or "almost" when less than a year old. Most will not be so precocious.

Perhaps an unrecognized reason that coon hunting has become so popular is both the abundance of this animal and his spread to new areas. Twenty-five years ago the raccoon wasn't so plentiful in the Midwest; he didn't even inhabit much of it. The same goes for Western states, where he seems to increase in numbers every year.

The dog looks bigger than the boy! Another unregistered type of hound, but he knows there's a coon up that tree.

Even in the country that lies East of the Mississippi, the coon was a scarce item until recent decades. In the depression he was hunted relentlessly for his valuable fur. When fur prices went down, hunters quit chasing them. Another factor is our country's increasing annual corn crop. Raccoon have taken to corn like bees take to clover. On a recent trip to New Brunswick, Canada, where corn has only recently become an important crop, I was amazed at the number of raccoon. As soon as the dogs entered a corn field and barked a few times, coon came out everywhere. It was mass confusion, the dogs had too much scent and too many tracks to run!

But if there is an abundance of coon, there is also an abundance of trash or off game to tempt the hounds from running what we want them to—coon. A coon hound is worthless to you if he takes a fox track, deer track, etc., at night. In the first place, since we can't smell, we have to depend on the dog to chase the right animal. But, the young, inexperienced hounds run scent, and many times don't know what animal lies at the end of that scent trail. They just want to chase down what is leaving that smell, and tell the world about it while they are doing the job!

Your coon hound *must* be trash proof. How do you get him that way? Many times it's a difficult job, and it becomes tougher in relation to how long your hound has been getting away with chasing unwanted critters. Scent pads can sometimes work wonders. Let's say your hound runs deer consistently. You buy a collar with a specially designed pad holder and soak the

Below—Two registered Redbone hounds at the tree. Right—Sometimes the hunter can't see coon eyes by shining. Maybe there's too much foliage, the dogs have treed in an evergreen, or who knows what. To verify the coon's presence and satisfy their own curiosity, climbing a tree has to be an expected part of the hunt.

pad completely with commercial deer scent. Now your dog smells deer all the time. When he puts his nose in a deer track, he shouldn't be able to tell the deer scent trail from the heavy deer odor on his neck collar. But, he can still pick out the smell of other animal trails, and let's hope it's a coon trail that he shoves his nose into next—so he'll get back on the right track.

Electric shock sticks are also available. Again, you use the commercial deer scent, fox scent, whatever trash your hound is running. You put a saturated pad on the end of the shock stick. Your dog smells it eagerly, but receives an unpleasant shock on the nose in the process. If he persists, he continues to get shocked each time. Several such lessons have been known to straighten out many a trash running coon hound.

Electric shock collars are probably most effective, but also most expensive. In this case you take your hound right to the deer, perhaps spotting them in a field. Take your hound in. When he takes off barking, you give him a jolt with the electric collar (from the magic button on the radio-control transmitter receiver you hold in your hand). One session may do the trick, but many dogs will require several.

Once you have a coon hound, and he's started, make certain you stay *with* him. Don't let a young hound get on a tree so far away that you can't tell where he is. With a young hound it's good to give him many long minutes treeing before you walk in. This tends to make him stick to the tree well. But if you

can't hear the dog when he trees the coon, it may be hours until you eventually get to him. He will leave the tree after a time if you don't come in, making it doubly difficult to make a tree dog of him in the future.

Getting a top tree dog is perhaps the most difficult coon hunting trick to turn. Most any dog will run a track—the scent is there and he will just do it. Sure, there are some old coon that know one track after another to throw the dog off the trail, and a young hound will lose plenty during the learning process. But, getting a hound to bark at the tree and stay there while telling you to "come on," is, in a way, asking the dog to do a rather unnatural thing. In the wild state if a wild dog or wolf ran game up a tree, he'd simply leave it, aiming for another animal in some new hunting territory. A true tree hound? He should be treasured above all others!

But in conclusion, let's return to the hunt taking place at the start of this article.

When we came down off that mountain to get our treeing hounds, we spotted the coon, only eight feet above his wildly jumping pursuers. The hounds were in a frenzy, but, to make the perfect ending to the story, we leashed the hounds, and started walking for home, smiles on our faces, happiness in our hearts. The coon would like to run another day. We gave him back to the wilds, like returning a trout unharmed, back to the stream from which we just caught him. Now how many hunting sports allow a fellow to do that??? Coon hunting's one of 'em!   *Nick Sisley*

FIELD TRIALS

IN THE United States, Field Trials are competitions by sporting dogs of the same type under conditions which are similar to those found in the natural hunting environment.

The first Field Trial was held in the United States on October 8, 1874, near Memphis, Tennessee. The contest was to find the best pointer or setter, but only nine participants were involved. Slowly, the sport flourished and expanded. Today, there are nearly 250,000 dogs competing in various field trials each year. Field trials are considered to be the fastest growing recreational activity in the United States.

In the final analysis, field trials serve several basic purposes: they are an enjoyable sport; they can result in better breeding; they make sportsmen conservation minded.

The good field trial dog is usually not the best for ordinary hunting purposes, and the best training for field trial work differs markedly from regular shooting dog training.

Field trials are held under the sanction of either the American Kennel Club or the Amateur Field Trial Clubs of America. Trials are conducted for Beagles, hounds, spaniels, pointers, and retrievers. Those trials for the pointing breeds (pointers and setters) are the most numerous. Field Trials are classified as amateur or open, depending on the standing of the dog's handler. They are also classified by the age of the dogs (Puppy Stakes, Derby Stakes, All Age Stakes).

Bird Dog Trials

In *bird dog trials,* dogs are run in pairs, and the time run is called a "heat." Heats in the same stake are of equal duration. The club announces the time duration of each heat. The dogs are judged on speed, range, hunting intelligence, response to handling, game finding, style, intensity, and game and gun manners.

Spaniel Field Trials

In *field trials for spaniels,* there is no time limit. These dogs are judged on pace, range, response to handling, style, game finding, marking of fallen game, retrieving—tender or hardmouthed—carry of game, and steadiness to flush and shot.

Hound Field Trials

Beagle trials are the most numerous of the hound field trials. They are run in pairs (braces), and there is no time limit for the heat. Judges select the winner on the basis of hunting ability, keen nose, ability to carry a trail, and work out checks or losses without undue delay.

In *Foxhound Trials,* all of the dogs are turned loose and judged by mounted judges on hunting, trailing, speed, driving, and endurance.

The ideal field trial dog should possess the following qualities:

Ambition and Courage
Stamina
Speed
Intelligence
Style
Dash
Olfactory powers of high order
Good blood lines and conformation

Purchasing a Hunting Dog

The best ways to select a hunting dog are to see the dog perform and to see records of his field-trial performance. There are field trials held all over the United States during most of the year so there should be ample opportunities to see dogs in action. Although these performers are usually not for sale, their offspring usually are.

Getting a puppy is preferable since there is a very small selection of older dogs available, and the good dogs will command a high price. Hunting dogs are most devoted to their masters, and, thus, if you own and hunt with them from puppyhood, they will truly be yours.

If you want to buy a mature dog, remember you are taking a chance of getting a dog with some real faults. If this is necessary, then try out the dog. Have the owner show you how the dog works. Should you be unable to observe the dog personally, ask a professional handler in the area to give you an opinion.

Don't wait until the hunting season to buy your dog. Remember, you will need time to train your dog and to learn to function as a team.

A good hunting dog must have the daring and energy to find the game; he must also have a good temperament in order to live in the house. He should have the proper physical conformation, and he must be trainable.

They're off! The 1971 National Shooting Dog Championship, Union Springs, Alabama. (Photo courtesy of American Field.*)*

THE VARIOUS FIELD TRIALS

William F. Brown, editor of *The American Field,* classifies Field Trials as follows:

(a) POINTING DOG TRIALS, for Pointers, English Setters, Irish Setters and Gordon Setters, Brittany Spaniels and German Shorthairs, Griffons and Weimaraners, to name the principal breeds that point their game.

(b) BEAGLE TRIALS, for the merry little silvery-voiced Hounds, with thirteen-inch and fifteen-inch classes, and exciting competitions on rabbits.

(c) RETRIEVER TRIALS, for the recognized Retriever breeds, notable Labrador Retrievers, Golden Retrievers, Chesapeake Bay Retrievers, Irish Water Spaniels, Flat-Coated and Curly-Coated Retrievers. The function of the regular Retriever is to mark the fall of the game, upon order go briskly to the fall, find the game and return rapidly to deliver right up to hand. Land and water tests are given.

(d) SPANIEL TRIALS, for the accepted Spaniel breeds, chiefly for Springer Spaniels and Cocker Spaniels, the dog required to cover the ground within ordinary shooting range, find game and upon flushing, stop immediately, assuming a sitting position, then exhibit steadiness to wing and shot; expected to retrieve only on command. The Spaniel, effective for land work, takes readily to water, and those bred from hunting strains are natural retrievers.

(e) HOUND TRIALS, of different kinds for the various Hound classifications. Foxhound meets have been esteemed over a goodly span; Coonhound trials are gaining rapidly in popularity, and there are trials for Bassets.

There were approximately 7,142 Field Trials conducted in the United States last year. The American Kennel Club approved 3,192 of these events which were conducted under their rules and regulations. This number includes 887 Member and Licensed Field Trials and 2,305 Sanctioned Field Trials. These American Kennel Club Field Trials were conducted for Basset Hounds, Beagles, Pointers, Retrievers and Spaniels and there were 104,911 starters.

Coon Dog clubs conducted over 3,000 Field Trials the past year under the rules and regulations of the United Kennel Club. This includes Day Trials and Night Trials, with over 100,000 starters. Current Coon Dog magazines are carrying advertisements of an annual Coon Dog Field Trial at Kenton, Ohio. $50,000 in cash is offered as prizes and 10,000 dogs are expected on the grounds, including those entered in the Field Trial and those brought along "for sale or trade." It is not unusual for these champions to sell from $3,000 to $10,000 each.

The American Field recognized 750 Field Trials last year conducted under their rules and regulations, with over 36,000 starts. These were mostly Bird Dog Field Trials for Pointers and Setters.

Foxhound enthusiasts conduct over 200 Field Trials annually under the rules and regulations of the National Foxhunters Association and are exclusively for American Foxhounds. There are approximately 20,000 starters at these Trials.

Therefore, in practically every state in the union and during every week of the year, a Field Trial is in progress somewhere in the United States, bringing together more than a quarter million dogs in these 7,142 Field Trials.

A. K. C. FIELD TRIAL RULES AND PROCEDURES FOR POINTING BREEDS, DACHSHUNDS, RETRIEVERS, SPANIELS

THE following excerpts from the American Kennel Club's publication, "Registration and Field Trial Rules and Standard Procedures for Pointing Breeds, Dachshunds, Retrievers, Spaniels," (Amended to January 1, 1971) list some of the rules and standards to be observed in an A.K.C. sanctioned field trial.

CHAPTER 17
RULES FOR POINTING BREED TRIALS

Held By Specialty Clubs For the Following Breeds:

BRITTANY SPANIELS
POINTERS
GERMAN SHORTHAIRED POINTERS
GERMAN WIREHAIRED POINTERS
ENGLISH SETTERS
GORDON SETTERS
IRISH SETTERS
VIZSLAS
WEIMARANERS
WIREHAIRED POINTING GRIFFONS

(Chapters 1 through 16 also apply)

SECTION 2. Any of the following regular stakes may be offered at such trials:

Open Puppy Stake for dogs six months of age and under fifteen months of age on the first advertised day of the trial.

Open Derby Stake for dogs six months of age and under two years of age on the first advertised day of the trial.

Gun Dog Stake (Open or Amateur) for dogs six months of age and over on the first advertised day of the trial.

All-Age Stake (Open or Amateur) for dogs six months of age and over on the first advertised day of the trial.

Limited Gun Dog Stake (Open or Amateur) for dogs six months of age and over on the first advertised day of the trial which have won first place in an Open Derby Stake or which have placed first, second, third or fourth in a Gun Dog Stake. A field trial-giving club may give an Amateur Limited Gun Dog Stake in which places that qualify a dog have been acquired in Amateur Stakes only.

Limited All-Age Stake (Open or Amateur) for dogs six months of age and over on the first advertised day of the trial which have won first place in an Open Derby Stake or which have placed first, second, third or fourth in any All-Age Stake. A field trial-giving club may give an Amateur Limited All-Age Stake in which places that qualify a dog have been acquired in Amateur Stakes only.

In an Amateur Stake at a licensed or member field trial all dogs must be owned or handled by persons who, in the judgment of the Field Trial Committee, are qualified as Amateurs.

SECTION 4. Bitches that are in season or which, in the opinion of the Field Trial Committee, appear to be in season, are ineligible to compete in licensed or member field trials, and should be removed from the field trial grounds. The Field Trial Committee may remove any dog from the field trial grounds if it considers that such removal is necessary for the smooth running of the field trial.

SECTION 5. A dog is not eligible to be entered or to compete in any field trial in any stake in which championship points are given, if a judge of that stake or any member of his family has owned, sold, held under lease, boarded, trained, or handled the dog, within one year prior to the date of the field trial.

FIELD CHAMPIONSHIP

At present a dog of one of the Pointing Breeds will be recorded a Field Champion after having won 10 points under the point rating schedule below in regular stakes in at least three licensed or member field trials, provided that 3 points have been won in one 3 point or better Open All-Age, Open Gun Dog, Open Limited All-Age, or Open Limited Gun Dog Stake, that no more than 2 points each have been won in Open Puppy and Open Derby Stakes, and that no more than 4 of the 10 points have been won by placing first in Amateur stakes;

EXCEPT THAT a Brittany Spaniel shall not be recorded a Field Champion unless it has won a 3 point or better Open Gun Dog, Open All-Age, Open Limited Gun Dog, or Open Limited All-Age Stake that was open only to Brittany Spaniels;

EXCEPT THAT a German Shorthaired Pointer, German Wirehaired Pointer, Vizsla, or Weimaraner, shall not be recorded a Field Champion unless it has won at least 4 points in Shoot-to-Kill Stakes at field trials held by Specialty Clubs for one of these four breeds;

AND EXCEPT THAT a German Shorthaired Pointer, German Wirehaired Pointer, or Weimaraner, shall not be recorded a Field Champion unless it has also been certified by two of the approved judges to have passed a Water Test at a licensed or member field trial held by a Specialty Club for one of these three breeds. In the case of a Weimaraner, if it has been certified by the Weimaraner Club of America to have passed an All-Age Water Certification Test, or to have been given a rating of Retrieving Dog or Retrieving Dog Excellent, it shall be considered to have met the Water Test requirement.

Championship points shall be credited only to dogs placed first in regular stakes. The number of points shall be based on the actual number of eligible starters in each stake according to the following schedule:

4 to 7 starters	1 point
8 to 12 starters	2 points
13 to 17 starters	3 points
18 to 24 starters	4 points
25 or more starters	5 points

AMATEUR FIELD CHAMPIONSHIP

At present a dog of one of the Pointing Breeds, except for Brittany Spaniels, will be recorded an Amateur Field Championship after having won 10 points under the point rating schedule below in regular Amateur stakes in at least three licensed or member field trials, provided that 3 points have been won by placing first in one of 3 point or better Amateur All-Age, Amateur Gun Dog, Amateur Limited All-Age, or Amateur Limited Gun Dog Stake;

EXCEPT THAT a German Shorthaired Pointer, German Wirehaired Pointer, Vizsla, or Weimaraner, shall not be recorded an Amateur Field Champion unless it has won at least 4 points in Amateur Shoot-to-Kill Stakes at trials held by Specialty Clubs for one of these four breeds;

AND EXCEPT THAT a German Shorthaired Pointer, German Wirehaired Pointer, or Weimaraner, shall not be recorded an Amateur Field Champion unless it has also been certified by two of the approved judges to have passed, with an amateur handler, a Water Test at a licensed or member field trial held by a Specialty Club for one of these three breeds. In the case of a Weimaraner, if it has been certified by the Weimaraner Club of America to have passed an All-Age Water Certification Test, or to have been given the rating of Retrieving Dog or Retrieving Dog Excellent, with an amateur handler, it shall be considered to have met the Water Test Requirement.

Amateur Championship points shall be credited to dogs placed first, second, or third, in regular Amateur stakes in accordance with the following schedule, based on the actual number of eligible starters in each stake:

| | Placement | | |
	1st	2nd	3rd
4 to 7 starters	1 point		
8 to 12 starters	2 points		
13 to 17 starters	3 points	1 point	
18 to 24 starters	4 points	2 points	
25 or more starters	5 points	3 points	1 point

Championship points from first placements in Amateur stakes that are credited towards a Field Championship, will also be credited towards an Amateur Field Championship.

WATER TEST

If a German Shorthaired Pointer, German Wirehaired Pointer, or Weimaraner club wishes to hold a Water Test in conjunction with its licensed or member field trial, request for approval of the Water Test should be included on the date application for the trial. If approved, the Water Test must be specified on the questionnaire form and announced in the premium list.

The Water Test shall be judged by two of the judges of the field trial. The dog shall retrieve a live or dead game bird from water after a swim of about 20 yards to the bird. The handler shall stand 6 feet from the water, and the dog must demonstrate its willingness to enter the water, to swim, and to retrieve, at the direction of its handler without being touched or intimidated. Style shall not be considered. The dogs shall not be placed, but shall either pass or fail. The judges shall certify on the judging sheets provided, the particulars of each dog that passed the test.

STANDARD PROCEDURE FOR POINTING BREED FIELD TRIALS

Held By Specialty Clubs For the Following Breeds:

> BRITTANY SPANIELS
> POINTERS
> GERMAN SHORTHAIRED POINTERS
> GERMAN WIREHAIRED POINTERS
> ENGLISH SETTERS
> GORDON SETTERS
> IRISH SETTERS
> VIZSLAS
> WEIMARANERS
> WIREHAIRED POINTING GRIFFONS

PROCEDURE 1. STANDARD OF PERFORMANCE

1-A PUPPY STAKES. Puppies must show desire to hunt, boldness, and initiative in covering ground and in searching likely cover. They should indicate the presence of game if the opportunity is presented. Puppies should show reasonable obedience to their handlers' commands, but should not be given additional credit for pointing staunchly. Each dog shall be judged on its actual performance as indicating its future as a high class Derby dog. Every premium list for a licensed or member trial shall state whether or not blanks are to be fired in a Puppy Stake. If the premium list states that blanks

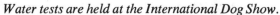

Water tests are held at the International Dog Show.

A Weimaraner on point. (Photo courtesy of American Field)

will be fired, every dog that makes game contact shall be fired over if the handler is within reasonable gun range. At least 15 minutes and not more than 30 minutes shall be allowed for each heat.

1-B DERBY STAKES. Derbies must show a keen desire to hunt, be bold and independent, have a fast, yet attractive, style of running, and demonstrate not only intelligence in seeking objectives but also the ability to find game. Derbies must point but no additional credit shall be given for steadiness to wing and shot. Should birds be flushed after a point by handler or dog within reasonable gun range from the handler, a shot must be fired. A lack of opportunity for firing over a Derby dog on point shall not constitute reason for non-placement when it has had game contact in acceptable Derby manner. Derbies must show reasonable obedience to their handlers' commands. Each dog is to be judged on its actual performance as indicating its future promise. At least 20 minutes and not more than 30 minutes shall be allowed for each heat.

1-C GUN DOG AND LIMITED GUN DOG STAKES. A Gun Dog must give a finished performance and must be under its handler's control at all times. It must handle kindly, with a minimum of noise and hacking by the handler. A Gun Dog must show a keen desire to hunt, must have a bold and attractive style of running, and must demonstrate not only intelligence in quartering and in seeking objectives but also the ability to find game. The dog must hunt for its handler at all times at a range suitable for a handler on foot, and should show or check in front of its handler frequently. It must cover adequate ground but never range out of sight for a length of time that would detract from its usefulness as a practical hunting dog. The dog must locate game, must point staunchly, and must be steady to wing and shot. Intelligent use of the wind and terrain in locating game, accurate nose, and style and intensity on point, are essential. At least 30 minutes shall be allowed for each heat.

1-D ALL-AGE AND LIMITED ALL-AGE STAKES. An All-Age Dog must give a finished performance and must be under reasonable control of its handler. It must show a keen desire to hunt, must have a bold and attractive style of running, and must show independence in hunting. It must range well out in a forward moving pattern, seeking the most promising objectives, so as to locate any game on the course.

Excessive line-casting and avoiding cover must be penalized. The dog must respond to handling but must demonstrate its independent judgment in hunting the course, and should not look to its handler for directions as to where to go. The dog must find game, must point staunchly, and must be steady to wing and shot. Intelligent use of the wind and terrain in locating game, accurate nose, and style and intensity on point, are essential. At least 30 minutes shall be allowed for each heat.

1-E BACKING IN GUN DOG, ALL-AGE, LIMITED GUN DOG, AND LIMITED ALL-AGE STAKES. If a dog encounters its brace mate on point it should back on sight, preferably without caution from its handler. Failure of a dog to back when it sees its brace mate on point must be penalized, and a dog that steals its brace mate's point shall not be placed. A backing dog shall not be sent on by its handler until after it has demonstrated complete steadiness to wing and shot, unless directed by a judge in case of an unproductive find; nor until after the retrieve has been completed, if game is killed. A backing dog shall receive no less credit if its brace mate's point was unproductive.

1-F In a Gun Dog, All-Age, Limited Gun Dog, or Limited All-Age Stake held by a German Shorthaired Pointer, German Wirehaired Pointer, Vizsla, or Weimaraner Club, any dog placed 1st or 2nd must have demonstrated backing in addition to the basic requirements for hunting and pointing as described above. If a dog that is being considered for either 1st or 2nd placement has not had an opportunity to back, the judges must set up a brace or braces for this purpose after all braces in the stake have been run. The judges will then select a dog from among those that have run in the stake, and shall have it placed on point in an open location on a live planted bird. The dog to be tested for backing shall be cast off not less than 100 yards from the dog on point, and shall be permitted to hunt freely until it has established a back. It must back until it has demonstrated complete steadiness to wing and shot. In a Shoot-to-Kill stake the dog must back until the retrieve has been completed. A dog that backs when a back is set up in this manner shall receive the same credit as a dog that has demonstrated equal quality in backing during the normal course of running.

PROCEDURE 2. JUDGES

2-A Each stake must be judged by two Judges.

2-B The judges may place the dogs 1st, 2nd, 3rd, and 4th in each stake. They should withhold placement from any dog if its performance does not merit the crediting of any championship points.

PROCEDURE 4. DRAWING AND BRACING

4-A The dogs shall generally be run in braces, and each dog in a brace must have a separate handler.

4-B If every dog entered in a stake at a licensed or member field trial has a different handler, the bracing of the dogs in that stake shall be established by a straight drawing and the braces shall then be run in the order drawn.

PROCEDURE 5. COURSES AND BIRDS

5-A Stakes at licensed or member field trials may be run on any of the following types of courses, all of which must include sufficient acreage, adequate cover for birds, and suitable objectives:

(1) *Single Course With Bird Field* consisting of a back course and a bird field which has sufficient cover to hold birds and which is of adequate size to permit a dog to hunt naturally without excessive backing. A bird field must not be less than 5 acres, and 10 acres is recommended. At a licensed or member trial no less than two birds must be released in the bird field for each brace in first series in all stakes except the Puppy Stake. Additional birds may be released either in the bird field or on the back course.

(2) *Single Course Without Bird Field* consisting entirely of a course without any specific bird field, on which birds are released in suitable places around the course. At a licensed or member trial no less than two birds must be released for each brace at a suitable place on the course in all stakes except the Puppy Stake.

(3) *Continuous Courses* consisting of a series of courses on which each brace starts where the last brace was picked up. On such a course it is assumed that there is adequate natural or released game.

(4) A stake may be run on Continuous Courses for first series, with a second series consisting of nothing but bird field work for the dogs selected by the judges, provided this is specified in the premium list.

5-E Birds should, if possible, be released in natural cover rather than in artificially created cover. They should not be placed in holes nor in such cover as will impede their ability to fly or run. Hobbles are highly undesirable, and must never be used if there is adequate cover. If hobbles are used they must be of soft yarn which the birds themselves can remove, and must allow a minimum of three inches space between the birds' feet. Other artificial restraints may never be used. Birds may be rocked or dizzied but not to such an extent as to affect their ability to fly. Game stewards should wear gloves and should not hold birds against their bodies. Successive birds should not be released in or near the same spot.

CHAPTER 18
RULES FOR DACHSHUND TRIALS
(Chapters 1 through 16 also apply)

SECTION 4. A Derby Stake at a Dachshund field trial shall be for dogs whelped on or after the first day of January of the year preceding that year in which the field trial is run.

SECTION 5. A Non-Winners Stake at a Dachshund field trial shall be for dogs which never have won first place in any field trial stake at a licensed or member Dachshund field trial.

Note: In all Stakes the principal qualifications to be considered by the Judges are good noses, courage in facing punishing coverts, keenness, perseverance, obedience and willingness to go to earth. Should a rabbit lodge in any earth, or run through any drain large enough for the Dachshunds to enter, the dogs should, of course, be expected to enter without hesitation; and failure to do so should automatically render them ineligible for first award, even though their performance was in all other respects outstanding.*

SECTION 15. Championship points for Dachshunds shall be awarded only to the first and second place winners of Open All-Age Stakes. A Dachshund winning first place in an Open All-Age Stake will be awarded a number of championship points equal to the number of actual starters in the stake in which it competed. A Dachshund winning second place in an Open All-Age Stake will be awarded one-third as many points as the first place winner of the stake, provided there are nine or more actual starters in the stake.

CHAPTER 19
RULES FOR RETRIEVER TRIALS
(Chapters 1 through 16 also apply)

SECTION 1. Wherever used in this chapter and in the Standard Procedure for Non-Slip Retriever Trials, the word Retriever shall be deemed to include the several breeds of Retrievers and/or Irish Water Spaniels.

SECTION 5. Only stakes which are run on game birds and on both land and water shall be permitted to carry championship points. Premium lists should specify the kind of game to be used in each stake, and, unless otherwise specified in the premium list, only pheasants and ducks may be used in stakes carrying championship points, and pheasants or pigeons and ducks in other stakes.

SECTION 10. A Derby Stake at a Retriever Trial shall be for dogs which have not reached their second birthday on the first day of the trial at which they are being run. For example, a dog whelped May 1, 1965, would not be eligible for Derby Stakes at a trial starting May 1, 1967, but would be eligible at a trial the first day of which was April 30, 1967.

A Qualifying Stake at a Retriever Trial shall be for dogs which have never won first, second, third, or fourth place or a Judges' Award of Merit in an Open All-Age or Limited All-Age or won first, second, third or fourth place in an Amateur All-Age Stake, or won two first places in Qualifying Stakes at licensed or member club trials. In determining whether a dog is eligible for the Qualifying Stake, no award received on or after the date of closing of entries shall be counted.

An Open All-Age Stake at a Retriever Trial shall be for all dogs.

A Limited All-Age Stake at a Retriever Trial shall be for dogs that have previously been placed or awarded a Judges' Award of Merit in an Open All-Age Stake, or that have been placed first or second in a Qualifying or placed or awarded a Judges' Award of Merit in an Amateur All-Age Stake carrying championship points.

An Amateur All-Age Stake at a Retriever Trial shall be for any dogs, if handled in that stake by persons who are Amateurs (as determined by the Field Trial Committee of the trial-giving club).

At present, to acquire an Amateur Field Championship, a Retriever must win: (1) a National Championship Stake, handled by an Amateur, or a National Amateur Championship Stake or (2) a total of 10 points in Open All-Age or Limited All-Age Stakes or a total of 15 points in Open All-Age, Limited All-Age or Amateur All-Age Stakes, which may be acquired as follows: In each Open All-Age, Limited All-Age or Amateur All-Age Stake, there must be at least 12 starters, each of which is eligible for entry in a Limited All-Age Stake, and the handler must be an Amateur (as determined by the Field Trial Committee of the trial-giving club), and the winner of first place shall be credited with 5 points, second place 3 points, third place 1 point, and fourth place ½ point, but before acquiring a championship, a dog must win a first place and acquire 5 points in at least one Open All-Age, Limited All-Age or Amateur All-Age Stake open to all breeds of Retriever, and not more than 5 points shall be acquired in trials not open to all breeds of Retriever.

At present, to acquire a Field Championship, a Retriever must win:

(1) a National Championship Stake or (2) a total of 10 points, which may be acquired as follows:—In each Open All-Age or Limited All-Age Stake there must be at least 12 starters, each of which is eligible for entry in a Limited All-Age Stake, and the winner of first place shall be credited with 5 points, second place 3 points, third place 1 point, and fourth place ½ point, but, before acquiring a championship, a dog must win first place and acquire 5 points in at least one Open All-Age or Limited All-Age Stake open to all breeds of Retriever, and not more than 5 points of the required 10 shall be acquired in trials not open to all breeds of Retriever.

STANDARD PROCEDURE FOR NON-SLIP RETRIEVER TRIALS

BASIC PRINCIPLES

1. The purpose of a Non-Slip Retriever trial is to determine the relative merits of retrievers in the field. Retriever field trials should, therefore, simulate as nearly as possible the conditions met in an ordinary day's shoot.

Dogs are expected to retrieve any type of game bird under all conditions, and the Judges and the Field Trial Committee have complete control over the mechanics and requirements of each trial. This latitude is permitted in order to allow for the difference in conditions which may arise in trials given in widely separated parts of the United States, which difference well may necessitate different methods of conducting tests.

2. The function of a Non-Slip Retriever is to seek and retrieve "fallen" game when ordered to do so. He should sit quietly on line or in the blind, walk at heel, or assume any station designated by his handler until sent to retrieve. When ordered, a dog should retrieve quickly and briskly without unduly disturbing too much ground, and should deliver tenderly to hand. He should then await further orders.

Accurate marking is of primary importance. A dog which marks the fall of a bird, uses the wind, follows a strong cripple, and will take direction from his handler is of great value.

23. The Judges must judge the dogs for (a) their natural abilities including their memory, intelligence, attention, nose, courage, perseverance and style, and (b) their abilities acquired through training, including steadiness, control, response to direction, and delivery. Decisions to eliminate a dog from a stake as a result of faulty performance must be the consensus of the Judges.

LINE MANNERS

25. When called to be tested, a dog should come tractably at heel and sit promptly at the point designated by his handler and remain quietly where placed until given further orders. Retrievers which bark or whine on line, in a blind or while retrieving should be penalized. Loud and prolonged barking or whining is sufficient cause to justify elimination from the stake.

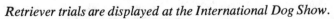

Retriever trials are displayed at the International Dog Show.

THE RETRIEVE

29. When ordered to retrieve, a dog should proceed quickly and eagerly on land or into the water to marked falls or on the line given him by his handler on falls he has not seen. He should not disturb too much ground or area and should respond quickly and obediently to any further directions his handler might give him. Failure to enter either rough cover, water, ice, mud or any other situation involving unpleasant or difficult going for the dog, after having been ordered to do so several times, is sufficient cause to justify elimination from the stake.

A dog who pays no attention to many whistles and directions by his handler can be said to be "out-of-control", and unless in the opinion of the Judges there exist valid mitigating circumstances, should be eliminated from the stake.

38. A dog should be eliminated for hard mouth or badly damaging game, but, before doing so, all Judges should inspect the bird and be satisfied that the dog alone was responsible for the damage.

CHAPTER 21
RULES FOR SPANIEL TRIALS
(EXCEPT BRITTANY SPANIELS AND IRISH WATER SPANIELS)
(Chapters 1 through 16 also apply)

At present to acquire a Field Championship an English Springer Spaniel must win (1) a National Championship Stake or (2) two Open All-Age Stakes or two Qualified Open All-Age Stakes or one Open All-Age Stake and one Qualified Open All-Age Stake at different trials with at least ten starters in either stake.

At present to acquire a Field Championship a Cocker Spaniel or English Cocker Spaniel must win (1) a National Championship Stake or (2) two Open All-Age Stakes or two Qualified Open All-Age Stakes or one Open All-Aged Stake and one Qualified Open All-Age Stake at different trials with at least six starters in either stake.

At present to acquire an Amateur Field Championship an English Springer Spaniel must win (1) a National Amateur Championship Stake or (2) two Amateur All-Age Stakes at different trials with at least ten starters in each stake.

STANDARD PROCEDURE FOR SPANIEL FIELD TRIALS

1. The purpose of a Spaniel field trial is to demonstrate the performance of a properly trained Spaniel in the field. The performance should not differ from that in any ordinary day's shooting, except that in the trials a dog should do his work in a more nearly perfect way.

2. The function of a hunting Spaniel is to seek, find and flush game in an eager, brisk, quiet manner and when game is shot, to mark the fall or direction thereof and retrieve to hand. The dog should walk at heel or on a leash until ordered to seek game and should then thoroughly hunt the designated cover, within gun shot, in line of quest, without unnecessarily covering the ground twice, and should flush game boldly and without urging. When game is flushed, a dog should be steady to flush or command, and, if game is shot should retrieve at command only, but not until the Judge has instructed the handler. Dogs should retrieve quickly and briskly when ordered to do so and deliver tenderly to hand. They should then sit or "hup" until given further orders. Spaniels which bark and give tongue while questing are objectionable and should be severely penalized.

3. If a dog, following the line of a bird, is getting too far out he should be called off the line and later he should again be cast back on it. A dog which causes his handler and gun to run after him while line running, is out of control. Handlers may control their dogs by hand, voice or whistle, but only in the quiet manner that would be used in the field. Any loud shouting or whistling is evidence that the dog is hard to handle, and, in addition, is disturbing to the game.

4. A dog should work to his handler and gun at all times. A dog which marks the fall of a bird, uses the wind, follows a strong runner which has been wounded, and will take direction from his handler is of great value.

5. When the Judge gives a line to a handler and dog to follow, this must be followed and the dog not allowed to interfere with the other contestant running parallel to him.

6. The Judges must judge their dogs for game-finding ability, steadiness, and retrieving. In game finding the dog should cover all his ground on the beat, leaving no game in his territory and showing courage in facing cover. Dogs must be steady to wing and shot and obey all commands. When ordered to retrieve they should do this tenderly and with speed. No trials for Spaniels can possibly be run without retrieving, as that is one of the main purposes for which a Spaniel is used.

7. In judging a Spaniel's work Judges should give attention to the following points, taking them as a whole throughout the entire performance rather than giving too much credit to a flashy bit of work.

Control at all times, and under all conditions.

Scenting ability and use of wind.

Manner of covering ground and briskness of questing.

Perseverance and courage in facing cover.

Steadiness to flush, shot and command.

Aptitude in marking fall of game and ability to find it.

Ability and willingness to take hand signals.

Promptness and style of retrieve and delivery.

Proof of tender mouth.

Where facilities exist and Water Tests are held in conjunction with a stake the manner and quality of the performance therein shall be given consideration by the Judges in making their awards. Such tests should not exceed in their requirements the conditions met in an ordinary day's rough shoot adjoining water. Land work is the primary function of a Spaniel but where a Water Test is given, any dog that does not complete the Water Test shall not be entitled to any award.

Reprinted by permission of The American Kennel Club.

"Excellent retriever, but he can't swim."

AMATEUR FIELD TRIAL CLUBS OF AMERICA FIELD TRIAL RULES AND REGULATIONS FOR ALL POINTING BREEDS

THE following are excerpts from the Amateur Field Trial Clubs of America Running Rules (1969) as adopted by Amateur Field Trial Clubs of America, Inc., The American Field Publishing Company and The Field Dog Stud Book.

MINIMUM REQUIREMENTS FOR FIELD TRIALS FOR ALL POINTING BREEDS

Section 2. RECOGNIZED STAKES ARE:

(a). **Puppy Stakes.** From January 1 to July 1 in each year for dogs whelped on or after January 1 of the year preceding. From July 1 to December 31 of each year for dogs whelped on or after June 1 of the year preceding.

(b). **Derby Stakes.** From July 1 to December 31 in each year for dogs whelped on or after January 1 of the year preceding, and from January 1 to July 1 in each year for dogs whelped on or after January 1 of two years preceding.

(c). **All Age Stakes.** For dogs of any age. An "open stake" is one in which there are no limitations with respect to either dogs or handlers. An "amateur" stake is one in which all handlers are amateurs as defined by Article VIII, Section 1, herein.

Winners in Members and Gun Dog or Shooting Dog stakes shall be recorded, and win certificates issued, but winners of children's, ladies', brace, and other stakes not conforming to the definitions contained under this article will not be recognized.

Section 3. The minimum length of heats for all stakes other than Puppy Stakes shall be thirty minutes, on the basis of the time that an average brace takes to negotiate the course. In the case of one-course trials, no more than eight minutes of the thirty shall be spent in the bird field. Minimum length of heats for Puppy Stakes shall be fifteen minutes.

RULES AND REGULATIONS FOR FIELD TRIALS

ARTICLE II

Championship Stakes

Section 1. Amateur Field Trial Clubs of America, Inc. shall hold each year,

A

A National Amateur Quail Championship

B

A National Amateur Pheasant Championship

C

A National Amateur Shooting Dog Championship

D

A National Amateur Pheasant Shooting Dog Championship

E

A National Amateur Chicken Championship

F

Such other championships as the Board of Trustees may determine for dogs of all pointing breeds, registered or eligible for registration, regardless of previous wins, that have qualified as follows:

Section 2. For qualification in the National Amateur Quail Championship a dog shall have previously won a place, under an amateur handler, in a one hour multiple course all age stake, or a first place win in a one course or thirty minute all age stake duly held by an active member of this corporation in accordance with its regulations, or winner or runner-up in a Regulation Championship sanctioned by this corporation.

Section 3. For qualification in a National Amateur Pheasant Championship or a National Amateur Chicken Championship, a dog shall have previously won a place, under an amateur handler, in a derby, all age, or Regional Championship Stake duly held by an active member of this corporation in accordance with its regulations.

Section 4. For qualifications in a National Amateur Shooting Dog Championship and in a National Amateur Pheasant Shooting Dog Championship, a dog shall have won a place, under an amateur handler, in a shooting dog stake held by an active member of this corporation, in accordance with its regulations. Gun Dog Stakes and Shooting Dog Stakes shall be considered one and the same.

Section 5. Within the meaning of this article and "All Age Stake" shall include Open Championships recognized by the American Field Publishing Company and Derby Stakes shall include all recognized Futurities.

Section 6. **Championships.** The National Amateur Quail Championship. The National Amateur Pheasant Championship, The National Amateur Shooting Dog Championship, The National Amateur Pheasant Shooting Dog Championship, and the National Amateur Chicken Championship shall be held annually at a place and date to be determined by the action of the President of this corporation. The winner of the first place in the National Amateur Quail Championship shall be declared the National Amateur Quail Champion of America for that year. The winner of first place in the National Amateur Pheasant Championship shall be declared the National Amateur Pheasant Champion of America for that year. The winner of first place in the National Amateur Shooting Dog Championship shall be declared the National Amateur Shooting Dog Champion of America for that year. The winner of first place in the National Amateur Pheasant Shooting Dog Championship shall be declared the National Amateur Pheasant Shooting Dog Champion of America for that year. The winner of first place in the National Amateur Chicken Championship shall be declared the National Amateur Chicken Champion of America for that year.

Section 7. A champion must be declared in all championships. The naming of a runner-up in all the championship events is optional with the judges.

Trophies

Section 8. A Championship trophy, to be won three times by the same owner, but not necessarily by the same dog, will be presented to the owner of the Champion in each stake, each year, to remain in his possession until the time of the running of the next such championship stake, when it must be returned in good condition to the Secretary of this corporation. The corporation will cause the name of the dog, the name of the owner, and the year of the win to be engraved on each championship trophy each year. In addition to the regular championship trophies, the outright award to a suitable trophy of value shall go to the owner of the respective champions each year. If the judges declare a runner-up, his owner shall also be awarded a suitable trophy to commemorate the win. The Hawfield Trophy and the Championship Trophy in the National Amateur Quail Championship; and the Mary M. Phillips Trophy in the National Amateur Shooting Dog Championship, and the W. H. McNaughton Trophy for runner-up in the National Amateur Shooting Dog Championship; the W. Lee White Trophy in the National Amateur Pheasant Shooting Dog Championship; and the Gunsmoke Trophy in the National Amateur Pheasant Championship; being presently in competition shall each, upon being won three times by the same owner, become the property of said owner.

All trophies other than the Brooke Week's Memorial Trophy and the Chimes Mississippi Jack Trophy, which are perpetual trophies, that are now, or may be in the future, offered for competition shall, upon being won three times by the same owner, become the property of said owner.

ARTICLE III
The National Shooting Dog Championship

The National Shooting Dog Championship is an Amateur Free-for-All Championship run by the National Shooting Dog Championship Association at Union Springs, Alabama. Dogs are qualified for the championship finals in a preliminary qualifying series.

Section 7. **Handlers.** A dog must be handled by his amateur owner, or a member of his family who is an amateur, or he may be handled by any other amateur handler, but that person must be a member in good standing of an active member of this corporation. An individual handler must be designated at the time of the drawing and such handler, if present and physically able to handle or scout, must handle the dog as drawn. If two dogs handled by the same handler should be drawn in the same brace, the second dog so drawn shall change place with the next dog to be handled by another handler.

Section 8. **Length of Heats.**

1. In the National Amateur Quail Championship the first series heats shall be one and one-half hours in length.

2. In the National Amateur Pheasant Championship, the National Amateur Chicken Championship, the National Amateur Shooting Dog Championship, and the National Amateur Pheasant Shooting Dog Championship the first series heats shall be one hour in length.

In each stake the judges may run as many additional series as they deem necessary and the time of running therein shall be determined solely by the judges.

Section 9. **Shooting.** No dog shall be placed in a Championship Stake until shot over when birds are flushed to his point. The shot shall be fired by the handler of the pointing dog only, with a gun not less than .32 calibre.

Section 10. **Conduct of Handlers.** All handlers must conform to any and all regulations and rules and directions of the judges which do not conflict with the regulations and running rules of this corporation, and should any such regulation be disregarded, the judges shall have authority to disqualify such handler and/or his dogs, or they may leave the matter to the Stake Manager for his action.

The judges are expected to prescribe and rigidly enforce a strict rule upon the interference of handlers with the opponents' dog.

Handlers shall be at liberty to inquire of the judges at any time as to any regulations within their province or of the Stake Manager concerning any rule beyond the jurisdiction of the judges.

Section 11. **Scouting.** No scouting other than by an amateur shall be permitted. It shall be illegal for anyone to scout for a handler unless permission of the judges has first been obtained. Lagging behind the field trial party for the purpose of locating dogs shall constitute scouting to the same extent as leaving the field trial party to go in any other direction.

(a). **Scouting in Shooting Dog Championships.** No scouting is permitted in a Shooting Dog Stake except that a person, with the permission of a judge, may be designated to go and see if a dog is on point at a specific location.

Section 12. **Handling Dogs.** During the running of a heat no dog in competition therein shall be removed from the ground for an appreciable length of time, placed on a leash or worked otherwise than in the accepted manner of handling by voice, whistle or signal.

(a). The use of any electronic device for the handling of a dog in competition in a field trial is forbidden.

Section 13. **Backing.** In an all-age or shooting dog stake, it is mandatory that a judge order a dog up if that dog in the opinion of the judge, demonstrates conclusively that he refuses to back his bracemate.

Section 18. **Blank Ammunition.** The use of live ammunition is banned in all trials held by member clubs of the Amateur Field Trial Clubs of America, Inc. and in all Amateur Championships sanctioned by the Amateur Field Trial Clubs of America, Inc.

ARTICLE VI

Section 1. **Definition of Professional and Amateur.** Any person who receives or has received, either directly or indirectly, compensation for training or handling dogs, or who has accepted a cash prize or prizes, or other valuable consideration for handling dogs other than his own in field trial competition, or any person who works for or has worked for a professional handler in the training of dogs, or any member of the family of a professional handler who assists him in the training of dogs is classified within the meaning of these regulations as a professional handler. All handlers not so classed as professional shall have amateur standing.

"He can't stand the sight of blood."

NATIONAL AMATEUR QUAIL CHAMPIONSHIP

Year	Location	Winner	Owner
1961	Albany, Georgia	Pineland Johnny pointer dog	Murray Fleming Albany, Georgia
1962	Rossville, Tennessee	Mack's Chief Warhoop pointer	Mrs. E. M. Berol and Mr. and Mrs. J. G. Franks Ridgeland, South Carolina
1963	Quitman, Georgia	Kilsyth Sparky pointer dog	Mrs. G. M. Livingston Quitman, Georgia
1964	Albany, Georgia	Vendetta pointer dog	Harold Sharp Atlanta, Georgia
1965	Paducah, Kentucky	Primo's Rowdy pointer dog	Frank Stout Madison, Mississippi
1966	Hoffman, North Carolina	La Strega pointer dog	Lloyd Reeves Woodstock, Vermont
1967	Waynesboro, Georgia	Haberdasher's Southerner pointer	Dr. W. H. McCall Asheville, North Carolina
1968	Stillwater, Oklahoma	Rinski's Little Sam pointer	Jack McClain Nevada, Missouri
1969	Paducah, Kentucky	A Rambling Rebel pointer	W. S. Richardson Richmond, Virginia
1970	Albany, Georgia	Gunsmoke's Admiration pointer bitch	H. N. Holmes Springfield, Illinois

NATIONAL AMATEUR PHEASANT CHAMPIONSHIP

Year	Location	Winner	Owner
1961	Beale Air Force Base, Cal.	Orinda's Debutante pointer bitch	J. Marion Thomas San Francisco, California
1962	Killdeer, Ohio	Warhoop Jake II pointer dog	John O'Neall, Jr. Hatchechubbee, Alabama
1963	Baldwinsville, New York	Chaney Farm's Dan pointer dog	W. C. Chaney Sumter, South Carolina
1964	Killdeer, Ohio	Tybabe's Willing Doctor pointer dog	Ernest Mimms Belleville, Michigan
1965	Killdeer, Ohio	Cannonade pointer dog	H. N. Holmes Springfield, Illinois
1966	Killdeer, Ohio	Cannonade	H. N. Holmes
1967	Killdeer, Ohio	Smokepole pointer dog	H. N. Holmes
1968	Killdeer, Ohio	Gunsmoke's Admiration pointer bitch	H. N. Holmes
1969	Killdeer, Ohio	Haberdasher's Royal Ace pointer dog	Dr. W. H. McCall Asheville, North Carolina
1970	Killdeer, Ohio	Mr. Thor setter dog	John O'Neall, Jr. Hatchechubbee, Alabama

NATIONAL AMATEUR SHOOTING DOG CHAMPIONSHIP

Year	Location	Winner	Owner
1961	Orange, Virginia	Warhoop Jake II pointer dog	John O'Neall, Jr. Hatchechubbee, Alabama
1962	Paducah, Kentucky	Jack's Delivery Joe pointer dog	J. P. Kennedy Madisonville, Tennessee

NATIONAL AMATEUR SHOOTING DOG CHAMPIONSHIP (Continued)

Year	Location	Winner	Owner
1963	Holly Springs, Mississippi	Warhoop Paladin pointer dog	W. R. Johnson Rossville, Tennessee
1964	Hoffman, North Carolina	Snipes Delivery Jim pointer dog	W. S. Richardson Richmond, Virginia
1965	Crab Orchard, Illinois	Smokepole pointer dog	H. N. Holmes Springfield, Illinois
1966	Neosho, Missouri	Rinski's Little Sam pointer dog	Jack McClain Nevada, Missouri
1967	Orange, Virginia	My Sallee pointer bitch	Parke Brinkley McLean, Virginia
1968	Waynesboro, Georgia	Cannonade pointer dog	H. N. Holmes Springfield, Illinois
1969	Ardmore, Oklahoma	Wahoo's Trouble Dot pointer bitch	Raymond Rucker Oklahoma City, Oklahoma
1970	Neosho, Missouri	Neosho Jake pointer dog	Dr. G. C. Olive Neosho, Missouri

NATIONAL AMATEUR PHEASANT SHOOTING DOG CHAMPIONSHIP

Year	Location	Winner	Owner
1961	Baldwinsville, New York	Potato Patch Sue pointer bitch	Dr. A. H. Nitchman Cranbury, New Jersey
1962	Baldwinsville, New York	Potato Patch Sue	Dr. A. H. Nitchman
1963	No Trial	——	——
1964	Oroville, California	Tigar's Jocko Brittany Spaniel	John Munson San Lorenzo, California
1965	Oroville, California	Title Withheld	——
1966	Allenwood, Pennsylvania	Trachaven Nellie pointer bitch	Eugene Strausbaugh York, Pennsylvania
1967	Allenwood, Pennsylvania	Trachaven Nellie	Eugene Strausbaugh
1968	Allenwood, Pennsylvania	Grouse Ridge Will setter dog	Dr. T. M. Flanagan Norwich, New York
1969	Allenwood, Pennsylvania	Grouse Ridge Will	Dr. T. M. Flanagan
1970	Ohio, Illinois	Amos' Duke pointer dog	M. J. Williams Fairfield, Illinois

NATIONAL AMATEUR CHICKEN CHAMPIONSHIP

Year*	Location	Winner	Owner
1967	Gleichen, Alberta	Happy's War Bonnet pointer dog	R. F. Hester and Doug Gonyea Portland, Oregon
1968	Gleichen, Alberta	Gunsmoke's Admiration pointer bitch	H. N. Holmes Springfield, Illinois
1969	Solon Springs, Wisconsin	Happy's War Bonnet pointer dog	L. E. Tippett Portland, Oregon
1970	Gleichen, Alberta	Paladella's Delivery pointer dog	A. H. Bohren Beaverton, Oregon

*This trial was started in 1967

BEAGLE FIELD TRIALS

FOR rabbit hunting, the Beagle is the ideal dog. With a minimum amount of training, with few special skills required, and for little cost, the sport of Beagle Field Trials can be enjoyed. As with all field trials, the purpose is two-fold—the sport and the improvement of the breed.

The American Kennel Club sanctions most of the Beagle trials. The stakes are divided by height into two divisions. There are stakes for Beagles up to 13 inches in height, another for those over 13 inches, but not over 15 inches in height.

The following excerpts are from The American Kennel Club's booklet, "Beagle Field Trials Rules and Standard Procedures," (amended to January 1, 1971).

BEAGLE FIELD TRIAL AND REGISTRATION RULES

CHAPTER 5
FIELD TRIALS DEFINED

SECTION 1. A MEMBER FIELD TRIAL is a field trial at which championship points may be awarded, held by a club which is a member of The American Kennel Club.

SECTION 2. A LICENSED FIELD TRIAL is a field trial at which championship points may be awarded, held by a club which is not a member of The American Kennel Club but which has been licensed by The American Kennel Club to hold the specific field trial designated in the license.

SECTION 3. A SANCTIONED FIELD TRIAL is a field trial at which dogs may compete but not for championship points, held by a club, whether or not a member of The American Kennel Club, or by a Beagle Association, by obtaining the sanction of The American Kennel Club.

SECTION 4. A BEAGLE FIELD TRIAL SEASON is a period of twelve months starting July 1.

CHAPTER 7
RIBBONS, MONEY PRIZES, AND SPECIAL PRIZES

SECTION 1. A club holding a licensed or member field trial shall offer prize ribbons or rosettes of the following colors in the four regular classes:

> First prize—Blue.
> Second prize—Red.
> Third prize—Yellow.
> Fourth prize—White.
> N.B.Q.—Dark Green.

For additional non-regular classes, a club holding a licensed or member trial shall offer ribbons or rosettes of the following colors:

> First prize—Rose.
> Second prize—Brown.
> Third prize—Light Green.
> Fourth prize—Gray.
> N.B.Q.—Orange.

SECTION 2. Each ribbon or rosette at a licensed or member field trial shall be at least 2 inches wide and approximately 8 inches long and shall bear on its face a facsimile of the seal of The American Kennel Club, the words Field Trial, the name of the prize, the name of the field trial-giving club, and the date of the trial.

SECTION 3. If ribbons or rosettes are given at sanctioned field trials they shall be of the following colors, and shall bear the words Field Trial, but may be of any design or size:

> First prize—Rose.
> Second prize—Brown.
> Third prize—Light Green.
> Fourth prize—Gray.
> N.B.Q.—Orange.

SECTION 4. If money prizes are offered, a fixed amount or percentage of the entry fee for each prize shall be stated.

SECTION 5. All special prizes not money which may be offered shall be accurately described or the value stated. Stud services shall not be accepted as special prizes.

DESCRIPTION OF CLASSES AND CHAMPIONSHIP REQUIREMENTS

SECTION 1. All licensed and member Beagle field trials shall be run under one of the three following procedures:

> A. Braces on Rabbit or Hare.
> B. Small Packs on Rabbit or Hare.
> C. Large Packs on Hare.

At a licensed or member Beagle field trial the regular classes shall be:

Open Dogs not exceeding 13 inches in height.

Open Bitches not exceeding 13 inches in height.

Open Dogs over 13 inches but not exceeding 15 inches in height.

Open Bitches over 13 inches but not exceeding 15 inches in height.

However, if when the entries are closed, it is found that there are less than six hounds of a sex eligible to compete in any class, that class shall be combined and run with both sexes in a single class is possible, but no classes shall be combined under any other circumstances.

No hound shall be eligible to run in more than one of these classes at any field trial.

A club may be approved to hold additional non-regular classes, provided a description of the eligibility requirements appears in the premium list.

SECTION 2. Splitting of prizes or places is prohibited.

SECTION 3. Field Championship points for Beagles shall be awarded only to hounds placing in licensed or member trials in Open Classes in which there were six or more starters. The championship points shall be awarded on the following basis:

> 1 point to the winner of first place for each starter;
> 1/2 point to the winner of second place for each starter;
> 1/3 point to the winner of third place for each starter;
> 1/4 point to the winner of fourth place for each starter.

A starter is an entered eligible hound that has not been disqualified and that is not measured out for second series or for the winners pack, and that has been cast or laid on a line with its brace mate at the start of its first series heat at a brace trial; or that has been cast at the start of its first series pack at a pack trial; or that has been cast at the start with the rest of the pack at a large pack trial.

SECTION 4. The total number of wins and championship points necessary for a Beagle to be recorded a Field Champion by The American Kennel Club shall be established by the Board of Directors of The American Kennel Club. The wins and points may be acquired in both the 13 inch and 15 inch divisions.

To be recorded a Field Champion, a hound of either sex must have won three first places and 120 points in classes with not less than six starters at licensed or member field trials.

SECTION 5. A Beagle that has won the required number of classes and championship points will, when registered in the Stud Book, be recorded a Field Champion, and a championship certificate will be issued to the owner. A hound becomes a Field Champion when it is so officially recorded by The American Kennel Club.

SECTION 6. A Field Champion may be designated as "Dual Champion" if it has also been awarded the title of Champion. No certificate will be awarded for a Dual Champion.

STANDARD PROCEDURES

GENERAL PROCEDURES GOVERNING BEAGLE FIELD TRIALS RUN IN BRACES, SMALL PACKS OR LARGE PACKS

All of these procedures apply to sanctioned field trials as well as to licensed or member field trials except for those procedures that state specifically that they apply to licensed or member trials.

PROCEDURE 1. MANAGEMENT

1-A The Field Trial Committee shall have full charge of the organization and management of the trial, and shall have the power subject to the by-laws, rules and procedures of The American Kennel Club, to interpret any special rules published by the club holding the field trial, and to decide any matter, whether arising from an unforeseen emergency or not, which is not specifically provided for in these rules and procedures. Whenever such matters arise, the Field Trial Committee shall exercise the specific powers and carry out the duties described in these rules and procedures and submit a complete report of the incident to The American Kennel Club.

1-B Each club holding a licensed or member field trial must have at least three members of the Field Trial Committee present on the grounds at all times during the running of the trial. If a split class or two classes are run at the same time on different running grounds there must be at least three members of the Field Trial Committee on each grounds throughout the running, unless the separate running grounds are immediately adjacent to each other. A club which fails to comply with this requirement will not be approved for a licensed or member field trial during the next field trial season.

1-C The Field Trial Committee shall appoint a Marshal or Marshals to carry out the orders of the Judges. Marshals may advise Judges but must carry out the instructions of the Judges whose decision is final. At a trial run in Large Packs no person shall act as Marshal for a class in which he has a hound entered; and at a trial run in Small Packs no person shall act as Roving Marshal for a class in which he has a hound entered. Marshals shall be identified by badges or arm bands carrying the designation "Marshal."

1-D At a field trial run in Small Packs there shall be two Marshals. One Marshal shall guide and supervise the gallery. The other Marshal, known as the Roving Marshal, shall assist the Judges and supervise the handlers.

1-E At a trial run in Large Packs there shall be three or more Marshals. One of the Marshals shall assist Judges in becoming acquainted with the running grounds and act as guide and liaison man between the Judges, the other Marshals, the Field Trial Committee and the gallery. The other Marshals shall keep owners, handlers and spectators out of the running grounds, and report to the Judges immediately in writing any hound that has pulled out of the running pack, together with the number, time, and length of time out of the pack. After the class is completed, one Marshal shall account for all hounds and guide the handlers from the running grounds.

1-F At a field trial run in Braces or Small Packs each class or division of a class shall be judged by two Judges. At a field trial run in Large Packs there shall be two Judges for each class or division of a class up to 30 hounds, three Judges for 31 to 40 hounds, four Judges for 41 to 50 hounds, and so forth. If substitute Judges are required, or if additional Judges are required for a split class or for a Large Pack class of more than 30 hounds, they may be appointed by the Field Trial Committee at the trial provided they are persons in good standing with The American Kennel Club. When such Judges are used they should, if possible, act in conjunction with one or more of the advertised Judges provided this does not prevent any advertised Judge from completing the judging of a class which he has already started. If two such Judges have to judge together without one of the advertised Judges, at least one should be an experienced Judge of American Kennel Club licensed Beagle field trials. The American Kennel Club shall be promptly notified of additional or substitute Judges officiating.

1-I One person only may handle or hunt each hound, whether it be the owner, his agent or the agent's deputy. All others must remain in the gallery at a licensed or member trial. At a sanctioned trial no persons except the handlers of the hounds shall follow the hounds, unless specific permission is obtained from the Judges and handlers.

When game is raised or the hounds are away on the trail, the gallery shall stand fast or change position only as instructed by the Judges or the Marshal.

At trials run in Large Packs everyone except Judges and Marshals must go to an advantageous point designated by the Judges or Marshal, and may change positions only at the discretion of the Judges or Marshal.

1-J If unforeseen circumstances make it impossible to complete the judging of a licensed or member field trial on the last date applied for and approved by The American Kennel Club, the Field Trial Committee may continue the judging on one or two days immediately following the last date approved. The Field Trial Secretary's report to The American Kennel Club shall include a report of the circumstances requiring the extension and a list of the classes or series judged on each additional day.

1-K At a licensed or member trial run in braces or small packs, no hounds shall be put down after 30 minutes following official sunset. The Field Trial Committee and the Judges shall be responsible for enforcement of this Procedure.

2-B Castrated dogs and spayed bitches are ineligible for entry and shall not be permitted to compete in Beagle field trials.

2-C In a class for combined sexes, any bitch which in the opinion of the Field Trial Committee is in season, shall be ineligible to compete and shall be excluded from the running grounds and regular kennels. A separate kennel shall be provided for such bitches.

2-D All entered hounds must be present on the field trial grounds at the time entries close at a licensed or member trial when entries close on the day the class is to be run.

2-E No hound which is entered and present may be withheld from competition at any trial and no hound may be withdrawn during the running of a class, unless it is disqualified by the Judges, or is found to be ineligible, or is excused by the Field Trial Committee after consultation with the Judges. No hound will be excused by a Field Trial Committee except in the most unusual and deserving circumstances, and never to meet the convenience or caprice of its owner or his agent. If any hound should be withheld or withdrawn with or without the consent of the Field Trial Committee, that committee shall make a full report of the incident in writing and the report shall be forwarded to The American Kennel Club by the Field Trial Secretary. At a licensed or member trial the committee shall also use its authority under Chapter 14, Section 2, if the evidence justifies such action.

PROCEDURE 3. MEASURING

3-A At all Beagle Field Trials hounds shall be measured in accordance with the following procedures; except that measurement shall not be required for any hound with whose entry form the owner or agent has submitted an official American Kennel Club measurement card; and except further that such measurement will not be required at certain sanctioned trials the announcements for which specify that all hounds shall be measured in advance or that a hound may be entered without measurement in the class into which it was measured on some specified earlier occasion.

(1) *Brace and Small Pack Trials.* At field trials run in Braces or Small Packs, only the hounds called back by the Judges for second series or for the winners pack shall be required to be measured; except that if there are eight or less entries in a class, all hounds in that class shall be measured before the drawing. The actual measuring shall be done by the Judges, who may select a third person to assist them, and shall be done in the presence of the owners or handlers of all hounds called back, before starting second series or the winners pack. Such measuring at a Brace trial shall be done immediately following the conclusion of judging of first series and prior to announcement of second series bracings.

The owner or handler of any hound whose eligibility for the height requirements of the class may be considered doubtful may notify the Field Trial Secretary when he presents the completed entry form entering the hound in a specific class, that he wants the hound measured before closing of entries.

All hounds on which such advance measurement has been requested shall be measured at the place where the drawing will be held within one-half hour prior to the closing time for entries for the class in which the hounds are entered, and the start of such advance measuring shall be publicly announced by the Field Trial Secretary. The actual measuring shall be done by the Judges of the class who may select a third person to assist them. As each hound is measured the owner or handler shall give its name to the Judges and the name and measurement shall be announced to the spectators by the Field Trial Secretary or Field Trial Committee Chairman.

A hound measured in advance on request shall not be subject to further measurement at that trial. The owner or handler or a hound that, prior to the drawing, measured out of the class in which it has been entered, shall have the option of having his entry fee returned or of transferring the entry to a class at that trial for which the hound is eligible as measured, if entries for such other class have not yet closed, and the hound shall not be counted as an entry in the class from which it was measured out. Hounds measured out after being called for second series or winners pack shall not be eligible to run in another class at that trial.

(2) *Large Pack Trials.* At a Large Pack trial all hounds entered in each class shall, before they are numbered, be measured by the Field Trial Committee or by one or more measuring committees, each consisting of at least three persons appointed by the Field Trial Committee. The measuring shall be done only during the hours specified in the premium list and in any advertising the club may decide to use, except that measuring immediately before the numbering may continue after the published time if it is impossible to measure all hounds within the time advertised.

3-B The actual and recorded owner of a Beagle 18 months of age or older registered with The American Kennel Club, which has not completed its Field Championship, may apply to The American Kennel Club for an official determination of his hound's height. . . .

PROCEDURE 4. JUDGING

4-A All Judges prior to assuming their duties shall familiarize themselves with these rules and procedures and make their findings in accordance therewith. If any Judge shall fail to judge in accordance with these procedures, the Field Trial Committee shall report the irregularity in detail to The American Kennel Club.

4-B In all classes the judges shall award places as follows: 1st, 2nd, 3rd, and 4th. After these places have been awarded the Judges shall designate the next best qualified hound as "N.B.Q." N.B.Q. is not a place and in case of disqualification of a placed hound at a licensed or member trial, the N.B.Q. hound shall not be moved up.

4-C No person shall make any remarks nor give any information which might affect the actions of the persons handling the hounds or the running of the hounds. Any person so offending may be expelled from the running grounds on orders from the Judges, and points of merit shall not be allowed any hound whose handler acts upon such information. The Judges must be informed of any such misconduct before the close of the race in which it occurs, and their decision shall be final.

PROCEDURE 5. STANDARD FOR JUDGING

5-A Foreword

(1) The Beagle is a trailing hound whose purpose is to find game, to pursue it in an energetic and decisive manner, and to show a determination to account for it.

(2) All phases of its work should be approached eagerly, with a display of determination that indicates willingness to stay with any problem encountered until successful. Actions should appear deliberate and efficient, rather than haphazard or impulsive.

(3) To perform as desired, the Beagle must be endowed with a keen nose, a sound body, and an intelligent mind, and must have an intense enthusiasm for hunting.

(4) Beagle Field Trials are designed and conducted for the purpose of selecting those hounds that display sound quality and ability to the best advantage.

5-B Definitions—Desirable Qualities

Searching ability is evidenced by an aptitude to recognize promising cover and eagerness to explore it, regardless of hazards or discomfort. Hounds should search independently of each other, in an industrious manner, with sufficient range. In trials run in Braces or Small Packs, hounds should remain within control distance of the handler, and should be obedient to his commands.

Pursuing ability is shown by a proficiency for keeping control of the trial while making the best possible progress. Game should be pursued rather than merely followed, and actions should indicate a determined effort to make forward progress in the surest most sensible manner by adjusting speed to correspond to conditions and circumstances. Actions should be positive and controlled, portraying sound judgment and skill. Progress should be proclaimed by tonguing. No hound can be too fast provided the trail is clearly and accurately followed. At a check, hounds should work industriously, first close to where the loss occurred, then gradually and thoroughly extending the search further afield to regain the line.

Accuracy in trailing is the ability to keep consistent control of the trail while making the best possible progress. An accurate trailing hound will show a marked tendency to follow the trail with a minimum of weaving on and off, and will display an aptness to turn with the trail and to determine direction of game travel in a positive manner.

Proper use of voice is proclaiming all finds and denoting all forward progress by giving tongue, yet keeping silent when not in contact with scent that can be progressed. True tongue is honest claiming that running mates can depend on.

Endurance is the ability to compete throughout the duration of the hunt and to go on as long as may be necessary.

Adaptability means being able to adjust quickly to changes in scenting conditions and being able to work harmoniously with a variety of running mates. An adaptable hound will pursue its quarry as fast as conditions permit or as slowly as conditions demand. At a loss, it will first work close, and then, if necessary, move out gradually to recover the line.

Patience is a willingness to stay with any problem encountered as long as there is a possibility of achieving success in a workmanlike manner, rather than taking a chance of making the recovery more quickly through guesswork or gambling. Patience keeps a hound from bounding off and leaving work undone, and causes it to apply itself to the surest and safest methods in difficult situations.

Determination is that quality which causes a hound to succeed against severe odds. A determined hound has a purpose in mind and will overcome, through sheer perseverance, many obstacles that often frustrate less determined running mates. Determination and patience are closely related qualities and are generally found in the same hound. Determination keeps a hound at its work as long as there is a possibility of achievement and quite often long after its body has passed the peak of its endurance. Determination is desire in its most intense form.

Independence is the ability to be self-reliant and to refrain from becoming upset or influenced by the actions of faulty hounds. The proper degree of independence is displayed by the hound that concentrates on running its game with no undue concern for its running mates except to hark to them when they proclaim a find or indicate progress by tonguing. Tailing, or watching other hounds, is indication of lack of sufficient independence. Ignoring other hounds completely and refusing to hark to or move up with running mates is indication of too much independence.

Cooperation is the ability to work harmoniously with other hounds by doing as much of the work as possible in an honest, efficient manner, yet being aware of and honoring the accomplishments of running mates without jealousy or disruption of the chase.

Competitive spirit is the desire to outdo running mates. It is a borderline quality that is an asset only to the hound that is able to keep it under control and to concentrate on running the game rather than on beating other hounds. The overly competitive hound lacks such qualities as adaptability, patience, independence, and cooperation, and in its desire to excel is seldom accurate.

Intelligence is that quality which influences a hound to apply its talents efficiently, in the manner of a skilled craftsman. The intelligent hound learns from experience and seldom wastes time repeating mistakes. Intelligence is indicated by ability to adapt to changes in scenting conditions, to adapt and to control its work with various types of running mates, and to apply sound working principles toward accomplishing the most under a variety of circumstances.

The hound that displays the aforementioned qualities would be considered the Ideal Beagle for all purposes afield, capable of serving as a field trial hound, a gun dog, or a member of a pack, on either rabbit or hare.

5-C Definitions—Faulty Actions

Quitting is a serious fault deserving severe penalty and, in its extreme form, elimination. Quitting indicates lack of desire to hunt and succeed. It ranges from refusing to run, to such

There are times when I have the feeling that that dog of yours means more to you than I do . . . !"

221

lesser forms as lack of perseverance, occasional let up of eagerness, and loafing or watching other hounds in difficult situations. Quitting is sometimes due to fatigue. Judges may temper their distaste when a hound becomes fatigued and eases off, if such a hound has been required to perform substantially longer than those with which it is running. During the running of a class a hound may have to face several fresh competitors in succession. In such instances a short rest period would be in order. Otherwise, Judges should expect hounds to be in condition to compete as long as necessary to prove their worthiness, and no hound that becomes unable to go on should place over any immediate running mate that is still able and willing to run.

Backtracking is the fault of following the trail in the wrong direction. If persisted in for any substantial time or distance it deserves elimination. However, hounds in competition sometimes take a backline momentarily, or are led into it by faulty running mates. Under these circumstances Judges should show leniency toward the hound that becomes aware of its mistake and makes a creditable correction. Judges should be very certain before penalizing a hound for backtracking and, if there is any doubt, take sufficient time to prove it to be either right or wrong. Backtracking indicates lack of ability to determine direction of game travel.

Ghost trailing is pretending to have contact with a trail and making progress where no trail exists, by going through all the actions that indicate true trailing. Some hounds are able to do this in a very convincing manner and Judges, if suspicious, should make the hound prove its claim.

Pottering is lack of effort or desire to make forward progress on the trail. Hesitating, listlessness, dawdling, or lack of intent to make progress, are marks of the potterer.

Babbling is excessive or unnecessary tonguing. The babbler often tongues the same trail over and over, or tongues from excitement when casting in attempting to regain the trail at losses.

Swinging is casting out too far and too soon from the last point of contact, without first making an attempt to regain scent near the loss. It is a gambling action, quite often indicating over-competitiveness or an attempt to gain unearned advantage over running mates.

Skirting is purposely leaving the trail in an attempt to gain a lead or avoid hazardous cover or hard work. It is cutting out and around true trailing mates in an attempt to intercept the trail ahead.

Leaving checks is failure to stay in the vicinity of a loss and attempt to work it out, bounding off in hopes of encountering the trail or new game. Leaving checks denotes lack of patience and perseverance.

Running mute is failure to give tongue when making progress on the line.

Tightness of mouth is a failure to give sufficient tongue when making progress. This will often be evidenced by the hound tightening up when pressed or when going away from a check.

Racing is attempting to outfoot running mates without regard for the trail. Racing hounds overshoot the turns and generally spend more time off the trail than on it.

Running hit or miss is attempting to make progress without maintaining continuous contact with the trail, or gambling to hit the trail ahead.

Lack of independence is a common fault that is shown by watching other hounds and allowing them to determine the course of action. Any action which indicates undue concern for other hounds, except when harking in, is cause for demerit.

Bounding off is rushing ahead when contact with scent is made, without properly determining direction of game travel.

ADDITIONAL STANDARD PROCEDURES FOR BEAGLE FIELD TRIALS RUN IN LARGE PACKS ON HARE

PROCEDURE 9. MARKING AND DRAWING

9-A The hounds shall be numbered as entered and measured, starting with the number "1". Each hound shall have its number painted on both its sides with a durable paint, the figures to be at least 3½ inches high and clearly visible. The Field Trial Secretary and his assistant, if any, shall be the only persons to record each number against the name of the corresponding hound. These numbers shall be used in any drawing and in the running of the packs and the names of the hounds must not be used.

9-B All entries in a class shall run as a pack; except that when there are more than 25 starters the pack may, at the option of the Field Trial Committee, be split and the two Divisions run simultaneously for not less than two hours, with at least one advertised Judge with each pack if possible. If the Field Trial Committee decides to split the pack, the hounds shall be drawn so that their handlers will not have a choice of Judges or running grounds. . . .

PROCEDURE 10. INSTRUCTIONS TO JUDGES

10-A In Open Classes the pack shall run for not less than 3 hours, and Derbies shall run for not less than 1½ hours.

10-B Before each class the Judges shall agree upon a uniform point system of crediting and demeriting hounds and shall inform the Chairman of the Field Trial Committee of the system they are going to use, and he in turn shall inform the handlers of this system.

10-H Judges are to consider that the Beagle is primarily a hunting hound and that its object is first to find game and second to drive it in an energetic and decisive manner and show an animated desire to overtake it.

10-I Trailing game other than announced shall not be considered a demerit, nor shall any hound be demerited for failing to pack if the pack shall be proven to be on game other than announced. . . .

10-J The number of times a hound finds game shall not necessarily give it the preference, but the quality of the performance shall be given first consideration. Ability and desire to hunt are or first importance. These points are evidenced by intelligence, the method of working ground, and the ambition and industry displayed whether game is found or not.

10-K When a hound gives signs of being on game, the Judges shall allow it opportunity to prove whether or not it is on true trail. Judges shall not penalize or fault a hound without ample proof. If reasonable doubt exists, the hound shall be given the benefit of the doubt.

10-L The Judges shall give credit to the hound that is a better searcher and sticks to its work. A hound will be expected to maintain an efficient range throughout a race and to show hunting sense in its work. Hunting sense is shown by the desire to hunt for game, the selection of likely places to hunt in, the method of hunting the places, the industry in staying out at work, and the skill in handling and trailing the game after it is found.

10-M At a check all hounds should work industriously, close to where the loss occurred, before going further afield to look for the line.

10-N Undue credit shall not be given a hound with an outstanding voice, when not seen by the Judges, nor for speed nor flashy drive if the trail is not clearly followed. Accuracy in trailing, proper use of mouth, endurance, good pack qualities, should be the principal points of merit.

Reprinted by permission of The American Kennel Club.

A CONVERSATION WITH A FIELD TRIAL JUDGE

FOR the past 20 years, Mr. Edward Porges has been a trainer, handler, and judge of English Springer Spaniels that are used in pheasant hunting competitions called field trials. Here, he answers questions about the Springer Spaniel and Field Trials.

Is the English Springer Spaniel hunting dog similar in appearance to any of our popular breeds?

The Springer Spaniel looks very similar to our American Cocker Spaniel except that he is about twice as large and weighs twice as much.

Where did the English Springer Spaniel come from?

Old English writings tell us that this breed came from Spain to England several hundred years ago. The Spanish words *Espania* and *Espaniol* are very close to the word Spaniel.

Has the English Springer always been a hunting breed?

Yes. It was used by the English long before guns were used for hunting. Old writings and prints show that these dogs were used by hunters who carried trained hawks on their wrists. When the dogs would find game such as pheasants or rabbits, the dogs would spring on the game, that is, put it into the air or cause it to run, and the hawks, when released, would pounce on the game and bring it back to the hunter. Springing the game was the reason for the name Springer.

At what age does training start?

Simple retrieving of a stick with feathers attached starts at about eight weeks. Serious training starts at about six months and continues until the dog is about two years old, when he is ready for competition.

A Springer Spaniel retrieving. (Photo courtesy of American Field.)

About how many hours of training are required?

About 600 hours. You will understand why this many hours when I tell you later what these dogs are required to do in field trial hunting competitions.

What is a field trial and where did these trials originate?

A field trial is a competition for dogs under actual hunting conditions. In England on the large estates, wild pheasants have always been raised as a crop to to be marketed, just as we raise a crop of corn or oats. When the birds were ready to be harvested, Springer Spaniels were used to find and flush or spring the birds for the shooters. Because the estates took great pride in the abilities of their dogs, competitions developed between the dogs of the various estates. This was the beginning of Springer Spaniel field trials.

What procedure is used in the United States field trials to test the abilities of the Springers?

In England many large estates, covering thousands of acres, provide a test for the dogs in fields holding hundreds of pheasants. However, in the United States we have no such estates, and our field trials must be run more artificially—although one should not underestimate our ability to quickly detect the weaknesses in any dog. In the average United States trial, two or three large fields are used, approximately a mile in length. A row of stakes is placed in line down the center of each field. On the right side of this row of stakes is one dog's course to be hunted and on the left side of stakes is a second dog's course to be hunted. When the trial is ready to start, men called game planters are ordered to release pheasants on the courses to be hunted. These planters release pheasants purchased from the game farms about every 70 yards down the entire length of the two courses. Next, two dogs are called up with their handlers. One dog is placed on each course with his handler. They are both ordered to hunt, and they move down the courses with judges closely behind. It does not take long for one of these fast hunting dogs to find a pheasant. The dog flushes or springs the bird into the air, sits down and never moves, but watches the flight. The bird is

---

THE AMERICAN FIELD

The American Field conducts the Field Dog Stud Book, which is an authentic registry of all breeds, but specializes in hunting dogs and, principally, the pointing breeds.

In addition, the American Field publishes a weekly magazine devoted to bird dog events. There are about 800 yearly pointing dog trials recognized by the American Field, and information about them is carried in this weekly magazine.

shot, and the dog watches the point of fall. He will not dare to move until the judge orders the handler to send his dog. The dog must then run exactly to the place where the shot bird fell, find the bird quickly, and deliver it to the handler. In the meantime, as soon as the second dog, that has been hunting the other course, hears the shot, he must immediately sit down and never move until the first dog has delivered the shot bird to his handler. The dogs are ordered to hunt again until a judge has seen enough of a dog's work. Then another dog is called up. A trial usually starts with about 30 dogs. After all the dogs have been hunted, the judges confer and eliminate certain dogs who may have committed errors. After about a day and a half of hunting, the dogs which have not been eliminated are each given a water test. Each dog is brought to the edge of a lake, a pheasant is shot over the water, and the dog must enter the water, even though it may be near freezing, swim out and bring back the pheasant. The judges now confer, the first, second, and third place trophies are awarded, and the trial is over.

Are most of the dogs' owners usually pleased with the decisions of the judges?

The owners of first, second, and third place dogs are usually very happy. The others usually go home mad at the judges.

Are top flight field trial dogs often sold?

In the United States, rich men or poor men would rather sell their homes, their autos, or even their good wives, before they will sell a top flight dog.

In England where the raising of pheasants and dogs is more commercialized, top flight dogs may often be bought.

How much do you have to pay for one of these English dogs?

I'd rather not answer that question, because in past years I bought two good dogs in England and if I told you what I paid, my wife would kill me.

What is done with the pheasants that are shot in the field trials and also in training?

There is a strict code among Spaniel field trial men. All pheasants shot in training reach someone's table. The birds are never wasted. The pheasants shot in field trial competition are either sold or are donated to institutions for table use.

Do the conservation commissions encourage field trials and the training of hunting dogs?

The conservation commissions strongly encourage field trials and the training of hunting dogs—because trained gundogs save wild game. With a capable hunting dog, game that is shot seldom hides or crawls away to die and be wasted. This may happen too often to hunters not using trained dogs.

CHAPTER IX
THE WORKING DOG

DOGS SERVING THE MILITARY

THROUGHOUT man's history, dogs have served in wartime. Dogs were used by invading armies to haul supplies and herd the "food on the hoof." They were even known to fight when necessary, to act as messengers and sentries, and to guard soldiers.

At the beginning of World War I, dogs were being used to haul loads, work on guard and sentry duty, and to locate injured soldiers. When the United States

Nemo, a heroic sentry dog, lives in honored retirement in a special kennel at Lackland AFB. The German Shepherd was wounded by Viet Cong guerrillas and has undergone special treatment by veterinarians at Lackland. (U.S. Air Force photos)

became involved in the conflict, it was decided to use dogs for similar purposes; however, there was no supply of trained dogs prepared for this type of work and the war ended before any significant use of the dogs was made.

When the United States entered World War II, again there were no dogs trained for war duty. Nazi Germany, on the other hand, had trained hundreds of thousands of dogs for war work. Quick work on the part of enthusiastic people resulted in the formation of an organization called Dogs for Defense. The dogs serving in the United States Armed Forces formed the K-9 Corps. Initially, Dogs for Defense carried on exclusively in procuring, training, and shipping dogs to where they were needed. Once these trained animals proved their worth, the Army took over training of the large number of dogs required, while Dogs for Defense continued to procure the dogs.

The training program prepared dogs for sentry duty, scout work, messengers, sledge and pack dogs, and for mine detection. Although, at first, many breeds were tried, only five proved acceptable. They were:

German Shepherds
Belgian Sheepdogs
Doberman Pinschers
Collies (farm type)
Grant Schnauzers and—
Crosses of these breeds

For sledge work, Malamutes, Eskimos, and Siberian Huskies were used, and St. Bernards and Newfoundlands were favored for pack work.

Throughout their war service, the K-9 Corps served admirably. There are numerous stories of the heroic feats performed by these four-footed soldiers.

When World War II ended, the dogs were "demilitarized", and Dogs for Defense helped in retraining them for civilian life.

The Korean War again called on dogs, and they served faithfully as scouts and as patrols on the front. Today, dogs are an indispensable part of our Viet Nam forces.

Currently, military dogs are trained to fulfill one of five different functions—Sentry Dog, Patrol Dog, Scout Dog, Tracker Dog or Marijuana Dog. A brief description of each function follows:

Sentry Dog

The sentry dog team is used to increase security of

such areas as distant perimeter posts, ammunition dumps, warehouse areas and isolated radar sites. When on post, a sentry dog's primary function is that of a detection and warning device. This function has been performed when the sentry dog detects and alerts his handler to the presence of an intruder. A secondary function of the sentry dog is to pursue, attack and hold any intruder who attempts to evade or escape apprehension.

Patrol Dog

The patrol dog is a composed, discriminating, controllable and observant animal, capable of detecting and detaining unauthorized personnel in both combat and criminal situations. The patrol dog is trained to work with a combat unit or among base personnel and their dependents, on or off leash and with complete safety. In addition to performing sentry duties the dogs are trained to locate hidden persons in large buildings or open areas by airborne scent. They can be used to track criminals from crime scenes, or find lost children by following scent tracks which may be 24 hours old or more. They are capable of locating lost, abandoned, or hidden articles, no matter how small. They will attack only on command, without savaging, and can be called off an attack if necessary. Finally, they can be used with complete safety to control crowds or disperse large, unruly mobs.

Scout Dog

The scout dog, used primarily by the U.S. Army is trained to provide a warning capability for forces engaged in offensive operations against the enemy. Normally used at the squad or platoon level of operations, the scout dog team provides point detection for the partol force and insures protection from ambushes, booby traps, etc.

Tracker Dog

The tracker dog, a Labrador Retriever, is trained to pursue ground scents in support of Army Combat Tracker teams. A most difficult training procedure, the dogs selected for this program must meet strict temperament criteria and must display an active interest in tracking.

Marijuana Dog

Being trained on an experimental basis by Army and Air Force training units, German Shepherd dogs are being trained to detect the presence of marijuana in support of law enforcement and border clearance

activities. It is anticipated that the successful use of these dogs will greatly enforce the control of marijuana within the Armed forces.

Military Dog Training

Responsibility for military dog training for the U.S. Armed Forces was transferred to the Air Force from the Army in 1958, and the function was assigned to the Dog Training Branch at Lackland AFB, Texas. Dogs also are trained at Kadena AB, Okinawa, and Wiesbaden AB, Germany. The Air Force is the sole Department of Defense user of patrol dogs. Sentry dogs are used by the Army, Navy, and Marine Corps.

Patrol dog handlers receive 12 weeks of training while the sentry dog handlers attend an eight-week training course. In addition to actual training with a dog, they also receive instruction in psychology of dogs, prevention of canine diseases, first aid and care of dogs, and principles of dog training.

Breed of Dogs Used

The German Shepherd was selected as the breed best suited to needs of the Armed Forces. This determination was based on the breed's demonstrated traits of keen sense of smell, endurance, reliability, speed,

Handler carries training equipment and canteen on his hip. The German Shepherd's choke chain will be replaced by the heavy working collar when the dog and trainer combine on a training problem.

power, tracking ability, courage, and adaptability to almost any climatic condition.

The German Shepherd is a workdog; strong, agile, well-muscled, alert, and full of life. It has a distinct, direct, fearless, but not hostile expression; a self-confident personality; and a certain aloofness that does not lend itself to indiscriminate friendship. His long effortless trot covers maximum ground with a minimum number of steps. The dog is capable of learning about 100 commands.

Behavior and Instincts

The dog's world differs from the human's in specific ways. His vision is inferior to the human's although he can detect movement, however slight. He depends less on visual impressions than on his superior senses of hearing and smell. A dog's hearing ability is about 20 times better than man's; he can detect sounds above and below the frequencies a human is capable of hearing. If a dog wishes to examine an object, he moves downwind to take advantage of his keenest sense—smell—and then moves in close.

Training

Once the handler-dog relationship has been established, motivation which finds its roots in the sentimental attachment of canine and man is brought into play. The entire training of dogs is based upon a proper use and development of the natural instincts of the animal. They are:

- Instinctive companionship for man is turned into comradeship with his handler;
- Instinctive response to human attitudes is used as the basis of training; the dog is praised and encouraged when he does well and is corrected and reprimanded when he does badly; and,
- Instinctive urge for prey is heightened by agitation, and allowing him to pursue the agitator.

Vocal commands are given firmly and clearly. The tone and sound of voice, not the volume, are the qualities that will influence the dog. Patience, coupled with firmness, is one of the prime requisites of a good dog handler. The trainer must never lose patience or become irritated. If he does, the dog will become hard to handle.

From the very beginning of training, the dog is never permitted to ignore a command or fail to carry it out completely. He is never allowed to suspect that there is anything for him to do but obey. Laxity may result in an attitude or mood of disobedience that means difficulty and delay in training.

A dog does not understand right and wrong according to human standards. Rewards and punishment are the means of teaching him the subject areas desired. Real punishment is inflicted as a last resort and only for deliberate disobedience, stubbornness,

Security police dog handler instructor at Lackland AFB demonstrates to a student the proper technique to search an apprehended person while the trained patrol dog, unleashed, remains on alert. (U.S. Air Force photos)

or defiance. The word "no" is used to indicate to the dog that he is doing wrong. "No" is the only word used as a negative command. A dog is never slapped with the hand or struck with the leash. The hand is an instrument of praise and pleasure to the dog and he must never be allowed to fear it. Beating with the leash will make him shy of it and lessen the effect of its proper use.

Patrol Dogs

To the uninformed, little distinction can be drawn between the patrol dog and a sentry dog. In both cases, the German Shepherd is chosen; the difference rests with the training.

The Air Force first became interested in the use of patrol dogs during tests at Andrews AFB, Md., in 1968 in conjunction with the Washington, D.C., Police Department. Later, 30 security policemen from Vandenberg and Castle Air Force Bases in California, and Davis-Monthan AFB, Ariz., completed a 14-week training course with patrol dogs at Lackland. Subsequent evaluation at the three bases proved the dogs far superior to the sentry dogs in meeting Air Force security needs.

Initial classes for dogs and handlers began at Lackland in August 1969. After assignment to a Security Police unit, continuing obedience training is provided the dog. Training objectives for the new patrol dog seek a composed, discriminating, controllable animal

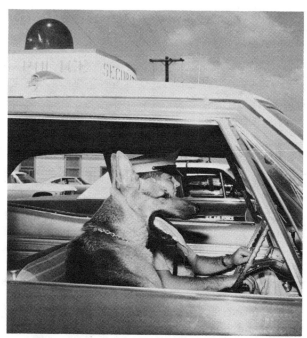

Security policemen and patrol dog on a tour of duty. The dog is trained to remain in the vehicle when the security policeman dismounts to question a suspect, however, the dog will attack without command at any sign of resistance to the policeman.

for detection of unauthorized intruders, and for subsequent attack at the command of the handler.

The patrol dog is not disturbed by the approach of another person and discriminates between a definite threat and acceptance of the person by the handler. He remains alert, but is not excited by strangers moving about him. He willingly enters vehicles with other persons and dogs without becoming hostile.

The patrol dog has the same degree of obedience when off-leash as on. He may be sent by his handler into an empty building to search for hidden persons or to cover an area to find a lost or concealed object. He will press an attack of another person at the command of his handler with the same aggressiveness as the sentry dog, but unlike the sentry dog, may be called off the attack at any point.

Training methodology for the patrol dogs differs from the sentry dog procedures.

- Basic obedience drills are continued daily;
- Training aspects are introduced earlier; and,
- Several training procedures may be practiced in a sequence.

Agitation and attack drills to build the dog's confidence and increase the biting power of his jaws (400-700 pounds per square inch) are important objectives.

Sentry Dogs

A "sentry dog team" consists of a handler and dog.

Normally, the handler is drawn from security and law enforcement personnel of the service he represents. As a sentry or patrol dog handler, he does not lose his identity as a policeman, but rather, he receives additional training which qualifies him to employ an item of special equipment—his dog.

Designed as a defense against the possible saboteur or espionage agent, the sentry dogs are trained to be hostile and aggressive toward all persons except their regular handlers. The dogs can be retrained, however, to accept a new handler when the original handler leaves the unit.

Procurement of Military Dogs

At present, the Air Force procures only German Shepherd dogs in support of the Military Working Dog Program in the continental United States and overseas. It is neither economical nor practical for the Armed Forces to raise their own dogs. The Air Force prefers to obtain its dogs from private owners, since dogs are more easily trained if they have been raised in a home environment. The Air Force accepts donations or pays up to $150 for acceptable dogs. An owner agrees in writing that once he sells or donates his pet, it becomes the property of the U. S. Government. An unacceptable dog, however, will be returned to the owner at Government expense, unless the owner prefers that his rejected dog be disposed of by the Air Force. When a dog can no longer work due to age or disease, it will be disposed of in a humane manner in accordance with military regulations.

Military working dogs receive excellent care and treatment from their handlers and are provided the best medical care possible from military dog veterinarians wherever they are assigned.

Every month the Air Force receives in excess of 1,000 mail and telephone inquiries or offers from private dog owners. The so-called "good" offers outnumber the unacceptable ones by about two to one. A good offer is one in which a private German Shepherd dog's owner indicates that his dog meets the current specifications of height (23 inches high at the shoulder), age (1-3 years) and weight (at least 60 pounds). Female dogs must be spayed at least 60 days before acceptance. All-white dogs are not acceptable.

The San Antonio Air Materiel Area (SAAMA) working dog procurement Center (Detachment 37) at Lackland AFB mails the owners the necessary procurement forms and requests they have their dog examined by a licensed veterinarian. Military veterinarians are authorized to examine dogs at no expense to the owner. The owner returns the completed forms to Detachment 37 giving a description of the dog's general characteristics and condition (including a snapshot) and indicates whether he desires to donate or sell his dog to the Government.

CANINE PATROL

Police departments all over the United States are adding canines to their ranks. The Chicago Police Department's program is a typical example of the services of the Canine Patrol.

The Chicago Police Department has approximately 50 man-and-dog teams. Two man-and-dog teams generally work together and use a kennel-type vehicle for travel to and from assigned beats or specific locations. (Chicago Police Department photos)

A GOOD police dog possesses several important qualities. He has a lively intelligence. He has the persistence to concentrate on his task. He has the mobility to pursue a suspect where a man on foot would have little success. Because of his keen sense of smell a dog is also able to proceed where darkness would baffle an officer traveling alone. He is also able to hear sounds that are fainter and higher-pitched than his master is capable of hearing.

Man-and-Dog Teams

Guided by their masters, Chicago Police dogs are used in the patrol of areas where the incidence of street crimes is particularly high. Studies of selected high-crime areas have shown that the use of man-and-dog teams has been especially effective in the reduction of the major crimes of assault, burglary and auto theft.

Man-and-dog teams also patrol secluded areas of parks, beaches and boat harbors and at hospitals and auto pounds. They are often called upon to search buildings for suspects, to track suspects who have abandoned vehicles and to search areas for discarded crime evidence such as clothes, guns and tools. Several of the dogs are trained to recognize the presence of marijuana.

The Canine Section

The Chicago Police Department has approximately 50 man-and-dog teams. These units work in three eight-hour shifts and are available 24 hours a day. Two man-and-dog teams generally work together and use a kennel-type vehicle for travel to and from assigned beats or specific locations.

The teams are members of the Canine Section, one of several units in the Task Force. In accordance with Task Force requirements, assignments of the teams are made at Canine Section headquarters, 1179 South State Street. Vehicles of the Canine Section are radio-equipped for two-way contact with the Communications Center.

Training

Dogs of the Department's Canine Section are all of the German Shepherd breed and weigh from 90 to 120 pounds. To qualify for training they must be male, nine months to two years of age, and weigh at least 75 pounds. They must be of even temperament —neither shy nor vicious—and be intelligent-looking and alert.

Each dog must also pass a complete physical examination by the Canine Section's veterinarian and a variety of tests for intelligence, mobility, persistence and interest in training.

The dogs are given training at the Department's Canine Training Center, located northwest of O'Hare Airport. They also receive specific training in the city in vacant buildings and at park and waterfront locations.

Obedience

The initial training course takes 14 weeks. The dog and his handler are trained together. The dog is taught to obey only one man, and a relationship of close affection, trust and understanding is built up between the team-mates.

During his obedience training the dog is highly praised for each successful accomplishment. The dog learns to respond to commands to heel, sit, stay, lie down and come to his master. He also learns to overcome obstacles that include boxes and steps and a scaling wall that can be adjusted for heights from four to nine feet.

Pursuit

Fully trained for obedience, the dog now learns to respond to every command his handler may issue in the course of apprehending a suspect.

Upon command, the dog will instantly leap into pursuit and persist in following his quarry regardless of twists and turns in the suspect's flight or any distraction the dog may encounter en route. If the officer sees that the suspect is safely cornered and cannot run any farther, he commands the dog to halt and simply stand guard until his master can take charge.

Tracking and Seeking

A dog trained to track must learn to discriminate among various scents. During the dog's training he and his handler work together with one or more other teams. Each handler first conceals an object bearing his scent, then teaches his dog to seek and retrieve only the object belonging to him.

A police dog can follow the scent of the human body whether deposited by bare feet or by the wearer's footwear. He can quickly search a large building or a wide area. He is encouraged to bark when he finds the source of the scent—suspect or victim—and direct the handler to the spot.

Refresher Training

To insure a high standard of efficiency every handler and his dog are given refresher training under

A police dog can follow the scent of the human body whether deposited by bare feet or by the wearer's footwear. He can quickly search a large area and is trained to bark when he finds the source of the scent.

Departmental supervision. One day per month they go to the Canine Training Center for refresher training, and one night per month they receive in-service training on the street. However, the basic responsibility for maintaining a dog's efficiency rests with the handler, who must continually develop learnings the dog acquired during the initial training course.

The Dog at Home

Officers who wish to serve as handlers are carefully selected. An applicant must have a deep affection for dogs and be wholeheartedly interested in this type of work. He must be under 40 years of age and possess adequate police experience, with at least two years "on the street."

Each dog lives at his handler's home. To further qualify for service as handler the officer must therefore receive his wife's permission, own his own home or rent from a relative, receive the consent of neighbors on both sides and to the rear of his home and, finally, agree to have no other dogs on his premises.

In his home, the dog becomes a loving, devoted pet and enjoys playing with the handler and members of his family. The Department pays for the dog's food and it provides a kennel for the officer's backyard.

A handler devotes one hour of duty time each day to the exercise and grooming of his dog and to the maintenance of its equipment. Veterinary care to guard the dog's health is provided by the Department Veterinarian.

Since man-and-dog teams generally work in pairs and share the same kennel car, one of the handlers parks the vehicle at his home during off-duty hours.

DOGS AND THE U.S. CUSTOMS

THE introduction of detector dogs on a broad scale, as a major tool in the stepped-up drive on narcotic smuggling along the borders and at the country's major gateways, was announced by U. S. Commissioner of Customs, Myles J. Ambrose.

The program is part of the crackdown mounted by the Bureau of Customs, an arm of the Treasury Department, on drug smuggling. The drive is directed principally against hard drugs such as heroin and cocaine, but is also aimed at interdicting the large-scale smuggling of marijuana and hashish, the use of which has reached epidemic proportions.

Detector dogs have been tested by the Customs Service for several years. They have proved their effectiveness in locating marijuana and hashish (its concentrated derivative), particularly in mail parcels and cargo sent to the United States from abroad, and in vehicles at border stations.

The dogs are being trained and assigned to their stations at Mexican border ports and mailrooms where there are large volumes of packages. So far the dogs have proved their worth:

On his first test assignment in Laredo, a Customs detector dog indicated that marijuana was concealed behind the door panel of a previously searched car. The marijuana was so professionally hidden that Customs officers found no indications that the door panel had been tampered with. When the panel was removed, five pounds of marijuana were found and two smugglers were arrested.

In Miami, when a Customs dog pawed the surface of a wooden table he indicated the presence of hashish. Customs officers polished out the scratch marks and sent the table, under surveillance, to the addressee. When the table was disassembled 20 pounds of hashish were seized and the violator was arrested.

In a cooperative arrangement with the Bureau of Customs, the Department of Defense is providing dogs and the facilities in which to train them in detecting marijuana and hashish. The U.S. Army and the U.S. Air Force are also helping to unite discharged Vietnam veteran dog handlers with new jobs as handlers for Customs.

The San Antonio Air Materiel Area Military Working Dog Program at Lackland A.F.B., Texas, procures the dogs and provides kennel facilities and training areas.

The Air Force and the Physical Security Branch of the Provost Marshall General of the Army also provide Customs with names of veteran dog handlers who have been or are about to be discharged and who might be interested in the Customs law enforcement program. In some cases, Customs has been successful in hiring servicemen even before the end of their tours of duty under the "early out" for law enforcement purposes.

Former senior military noncommissioned officers, skilled in dog and dog handler instruction, handle the training.

When the dogs arrive for training, they undergo a physical examination and "personality tests." Only dogs with a naturally "gentle disposition" are selected for Customs training. (Although normally the dogs are not in direct contact with the public, Customs takes this additional precaution to assure that the dogs are good-natured.)

Training for each dog and handler takes approximately two months.

Initially, Customs officers instruct the handler in Customs laws, procedures, and search techniques. Then a training program matching each dog handler with two dogs is set up. During this phase, the dogs learn to find and point out concealed marijuana and the handler learns to respond to each dog's method of alerting him.

Prior to graduation, the dogs must successfully complete intensive tests, including finding marijuana concealed among parcels of foodstuffs and disguised by odor-masking chemicals. In one of the tests, marijuana is buried in a fruit jar under a gravel road. The dog must walk along the road, locate the jar, and dig it up.

Once training is completed, narcotic detector dog teams are assigned to Customs international mail facilities, cargo docks and terminals, and border ports, where they screen mail, cargo, unaccompanied baggage, ships, and vehicles suspected of carrying illicit drugs. So far, dogs have been successfully used at Boston, Miami, Seattle, San Francisco, Los Angeles, Chicago, and San Antonio, Dallas, Laredo, and Roma, Texas.

During one 2-week trial period, the dogs made 18 seizures of illicit drugs.

After teams have been assigned and during subsequent training phases, the Bureau of Customs will continue to explore additional opportunities for using dogs in detecting marijuana and hard narcotics.

THE INCREDIBLE TRACKING DOG

Lost hunters, game-law violators, even armed robbers—all turned up when Reo went to work

JIM BURMAN started out by himself from his home in Kamloops, where I was stationed then as a British Columbia game warden, on the morning of September 19, 1943. He intended to hunt in rough country above Savona, at the west end of Kamloops Lake. It was an area he was not familiar with, but he told his wife not to worry, that he'd stay close to the road.

Mrs. Burman phoned me late the next afternoon, a very anxious woman. Her husband had planned to be home by dark the first day. He was now 20 hours overdue, and she was sure he'd had an accident or was lost. I had to agree.

Would I lend a hand? That was part of my job.

I loaded Reo, the tracking Doberman Pinscher that I owned and had trained, into my car and drove to the Burman place. Mrs. Burman told me what she could. I'd be looking for a man in his early 40's, with some experience as a hunter, who worked for the Kamloops Public Works Department. He had left home carrying a big lunch and a bottle of pop in a packsack.

Mrs. Burman gave me a sock that her husband had worn. That was all Reo would need to pick up the track.

I found Burman's car parked at the end of the lake, two miles west of Savona. There was no snow on the ground. The job would be entirely up to the dog. I gave him a good smell of the sock and the car, and attached his harness and leash. I never buckled that harness onto Reo unless he was supposed to track someone down, and he knew its meaning as well as I did. We were ready to go.

Reo lined out without a second's delay, going straight north, in the direction Burman had said he intended to hunt. But it was plain from the start that the man had not followed his plan of keeping near the road. He hadn't even stayed near a trail.

The country was open sagebrush hills for about two miles. Then we came to timber. By that time I realized that the missing man had started for the Cooper Creek road but failed to reach it. And Reo and I were not far into the timber when I discovered the reason. Jim Burman had become confused and started to travel in a big circle about four miles across. At that point he was really lost, and his tracks showed that he was running.

Just before dark I could see that he was dragging something on the ground.

Reo found and picked up three empty cartridges as we followed the track. The brass cases were some distance apart, which meant that they had not been fired as a signal. Two of them were in places where no deer would have been sighted, and I had no idea what the man was shooting at. But I was sure of one thing. I was dealing with a panic-stricken lost hunter. He had been out for two days and a night, with a second night coming on. It was a safe bet that Reo and I would find him in bad condition.

The dog and I stayed on the track all night. Just as day was breaking I heard a shot not far ahead. Reo was tugging hard on his rope now. We were closing in. Then, on the slope of a hill, I saw what we were looking for.

He was stumbling along, holding his rifle by the barrel and dragging the butt on the ground, obviously exhausted. I called his name.

He wheeled and gave me a wild stare. "Jim," I called, "it's Ellis, the game warden."

He started to run away, stumbled and fell, got up and staggered a few steps, and went down again. He was plainly a man demented, and I didn't want to rush him. Insead I turned up a draw, got out of his sight, and ran to head him off. When I looked over the top of the hill he was sitting on a log, watching back where he had last seen me, and he had the rifle across his knees, ready for use. The search for a lost man was turning into a hunt for one berserk instead.

If I called his name again he'd be likely to take off, and if I tried to run him down I stood a good chance of getting shot. I tied Reo to a tree and started a sneak, stalking Burman as I'd stalk a deer.

When I was only a few feet away I spoke his name in a low voice. He bounded to his feet to run but was so tired that he went down in a heap, and before he could get up I had the rifle and was talking to him very quietly.

The first thing he asked for was a drink. He needed it desperately. I gave it to him—opening the bottle of pop that was still in his packsack. He had touched neither it nor his lunch.

We sat and talked for a long time before he began to come back to reality. He told me that wolves had

233

come for him while he was trailing a wounded deer, and had followed him all night. He had shot all but one of his shells at them but couldn't drive them off, he said. He was not even in wolf country.

I finally walked him slowly back to his car, but when we got there he didn't recognize it.

One more day and night in the woods would probably have been too much for Jim Burman. Reo had added another name to the list of lost people—men, women, and children—who owed their lives to his incredible ability to track. I had Reo for 11 years, and the list grew long.

I worked as a game warden for the British Columbia Fish and Wildlife Branch from 1938 to 1965, when I retired. I was stationed first at Kamloops and then at Kelowna, where I live now. Of the many people with whom I had dealings in those 27 years, I am sure that not more than a handful ever knew that I owed the job in the first place to a keen-nosed fantastically intelligent dog, the most remarkable animal I have ever known.

The chain of adventures started in 1936, while I was working for the city of Kelowna as a truck driver. That fall a little four-year-old girl wandered away from her home on the Bear Lake road 12 miles out of Kelowna.

She was lost in country with no deep canyons and no water that a child could drown in. But although 400 men combed the area for days and cougar hounds were brought in (in case she had been carried off by a cougar or bear), no trace of her was ever found.

A few days after that tragedy I was talking about it with a friend, George Sutherland, and I remarked that it was too bad the local game warden, the provincial police, or someone else didn't have a tracking dog for use in such cases.

The suggestion took hold with Sutherland. That was in the hungry 30's, and we had no money for buying a trained dog, even if we could have located one. But George did have a few bucks in the bank, and he took me up on the idea.

"You've trained dogs for hunting," he said. "You know how to go about it. If you can find a young dog that you think would make a good tracker, I'll put up the money. You train it, and if it turns out O.K. we'll give it to Mac Maxson, the game warden."

That was how I came to own Reo. I got the name and address of a man in Vancouver who was raising a very good strain of Dobermans, and George and I arranged to buy a six-month-old male for $50.

The name on the dog's papers was Reo van Papen, but before he died 11 years later he was known all over British Columbia as Don Ellis's Reo.

I started the dog's training the morning after he arrived, taking him in my truck and getting acquainted with him. I realized from the outset that I was dealing with an exceptionally intelligent dog, one that seemed to understand every word that was said to him.

Before long Reo developed his tracking instincts to such a point that I'd come home from work and offer my kids a quarter if they could hide where Reo couldn't find them. In those lean days a kid would do most anything for a quarter, but very rarely did I have to pay off.

I fitted the dog with a harness and a light leash of rope, using them only when he was on tracking job. He learned very quickly what that harness meant, and he loved the work.

I had to discipline him only once. That time, he left a man track for a fresh coyote track. I paddled him, and he never forgot the lesson. From then on he hated the very smell of coyote. In fact he reached the point of refusing to take any track but a human's.

Reo got his first workout by accident. When I'd had him about two months I took him to George Sutherland's home to show him off. George had two daughters, Ella and Mabel, who were eight or nine (they're grown and married now), and as I left that night one of them said, "If we go and hide next Sunday, will you come with Reo and find us?"

I said sure, thinking they'd forget all about it. Then I proceeded to do the forgetting myself. The next I heard of it was the following Sunday evening. I arrived home about 9 o'clock and was no sooner in the house than the phone rang. It was Mrs. Sutherland, and she was worried and mad.

Ella and Mabel had been as good as their word. They had taken a lunch and gone up Knox Mountain, counting on me to keep my end of the bargain. It was now dark as a black cat, the girls had not come home, and their mother had been trying for hours to reach me. It was my turn to be worried—and good!

Knox Mountain is rough and rocky and covered with cactus, a hard place to search for lost children. I hotfooted it for the Sutherland place, got a slipper belonging to one of the girls, and let Reo have a smell. He went at the job as if he had been doing it for years, straining on his rope and half-dragging me up the mountain.

Near the top he slowed down and started to whine. I found out later that all four of his feet were stuck so full of cactus spines that I had to carry him down. But he didn't quit.

He led me to a cave just big enough for a man to crawl into, and when I shone my flashlight inside I saw the two little girls huddled together at the far end, crying quietly. I felt like doing a little crying myself, for the whole thing was my fault.

Reo went up to them and licked their faces, and we started for home. What Mrs. Sutherland said to me when we got there sounded a lot like, "You and your big mouth!" And I didn't blame her. But at least I knew I had a tracking dog.

Before that summer was over, Reo, young as he was, turned in another performance that gave me a lot of satisfaction and did much to establish his reputation.

Another child turned up missing, again a four-year-old girl from Kelowna. A family named Ryder had just suffered the loss of a two-year-old boy, and the parents were not sleeping well. One hot moonlit evening they and their little daughter drove out to Hydraulic Creek for a picnic, and after eating they decided to take a nap in the car. They put the tot on the front seat. When the parents awoke at midnight they found that she had opened the car door and wandered away.

They made a quick, frantic search, and then the father raced to town to get me, leaving the mother at the scene.

Reo smelled a coat that the child had left behind and picked up the track at once, heading up the creek. A mile from the picnic ground he led me to a hole in the bank, where a big tree had blown down. The girl was curled up there, sobbing.

When I'd had Reo for a year, there came the day that I had been dreading.

"Don't you think it's about time you turned him over to the game warden?" George Sutherland asked me one day. I had to agree. The only roadblock I could think of was that Reo seemed to be strictly a one-man dog and I didn't know whether Maxson could handle him.

The next day I took him around to the warden's house, ready for the parting. Mac Maxson was in the yard skinning a coyote, which Reo hated. The warden came over to the truck and put his hand through the door to pat the dog. Reo smelled coyote and sank his teeth into the hand. Naturally, Maxson wanted no part of him after that. I couldn't have had better news.

That fall I trained a bird dog for Gordon Wismer, British Columbia's Attorney General. He had heard of Reo's exploits, and when he came to pick up his dog he said, "We could use you and that dog of yours. How would you like a job with the game department?"

I started work the first of May 1938, and that was the beginning of more than a quarter-century on the most interesting and challenging job I could have found—thanks to Reo.

At first I was assigned to drive a truck for a fish hatchery, but I didn't get much chance to do that. We had no phone at the hatchery, but time and again the inspector would drive in to say that they needed my dog and me for a tracking job.

Reo brought off one of his most amazing feats that summer. A woman picnicking at Penantan Lake, two miles from the hatchery, lost a valuable diamond ring in six-inch-high grass and came to us for help.

I didn't have much hope for success, but I took Reo to the lake, let him smell another of the woman's rings, covered his eyes (as I did when I threw something for him to search for), removed the blindfold, and told him to find.

I had given up and was having a cup of coffee in the lodge when the dog came trotting up to me with the ring in his mouth. The search had taken him two hours.

One of Reo's lost-man exploits that I remember best was the tracking of two young hunters. They had gone hunting in rough country west of Kamloops—an area of willow, timber, creeks, and swamps—and had become confused and, as so often happens, had started to walk in a circle. I got the call for help from the mother of one of the hunters, and Constable Hall of the British Columbia Provincial Police came with me.

We found their car in midmorning, and Reo had no trouble with the track. We followed it for the rest of that day, stopping at noon and again just before dark to boil tea in a billy-can and to eat.

It took a good man to stay with Reo on a long search like that. But most of the time he pulled me along on his leash, especially going uphill, and maybe because of the excitement of what we were doing I never seemed to feel tired until the job was finished.

Hall and I went on in the darkness, using our flash-

"Forgive me if I don't join you tonight."

235

lights to get over logs. We were about ready to give up and camp under a tree until morning when the dog made a sharp turn to the right and lunged ahead in his harness. The lost hunters were curled up under a big fallen tree, trying to keep each other warm.

It was after midnight when the constable and I made the find. We had been on the track since 8 a.m. The hunters had been out for two days, a night, and half of the second night when we caught up with them.

Before the four of us got back to the highway both boys were assuring us that they had not been lost. They had just run out of time and couldn't make it out to the road, they explained.

I can recall only two occasions when the person Reo tracked down did not come out alive. One was a woman, known to be in a very depressed frame of mind, who left her husband's car and disappeared while he was in the house talking with the owner of a neighboring ranch.

I got the call at midnight of an ink-black night, during a hard rainstorm.

The unfortunate woman had left her hat on the car's seat, and that was enough for Reo. He tracked her across the ranch, through two fences, and to the shore of a nearby lake. She had left her handbag and coat there, and her body was floating face-down 150 yards out. A cowboy from the ranch rode his horse into the lake and brought her ashore.

The second person we didn't find in time was also a suicide, a young woman who drowned herself in the Thompson River. Reo tracked her to a big eddy where the water boiled under a logjam. Then he sat down, staring at the swirling current.

"Where is she, boy?" I asked, and he dived in headlong, and if it hadn't been for his leash, that would have been the end of him.

It took men with pike poles to get the girl's body out. How Reo knew she was there under the logjam, I'll never understand. An extra sense that dogs have, I guess.

All his life Reo excelled at three things: finding lost people, sniffing out game-law violations, and tracking down men wanted by the police. He was as good at one as at another, combining an incredibly keen nose with an almost-human understanding of what was required.

Some of his encounters with violators were so amusing that even the men who paid the fines got a kick out of his performance.

Checking duck hunters one morning, I stopped a car with Vancouver license plates and asked the four men in it for a look at their hunting licenses and kill. They acted nervous, explaining that they were hurrying home to be on time for work.

"I won't hold you up long," I promised.

They had six ducks. Their licenses and everything else seemed to be in order. But when they were ready to drive off I missed Reo.

"Hold it a minute till I see where my dog is," I said.

He was under the car, chewing on a leather shoestring with which the men had tied an illegal blue grouse to the frame. He brought the grouse out, went back, and retrieved three more, one at a time. The hunters didn't get back to work in Vancouver that day, but they took their punishment with complete good nature.

Another time, I was checking anglers on Jackpine Lake, and while sitting in my car eating lunch I heard shooting. Grouse season was not open, so I investigated. I found six fishermen eating around a campfire and saw one coming across the lake in a boat. When the boatman saw me he turned around, beached the boat, jumped out, and ran. He came back to the boat in a few minutes and rowed across and joined his party at the campfire.

I took him and Reo back to where he had beached the boat, and put Reo on his track. The dog was back in nothing flat with a grouse. He brought me two more, and the best excuse the embarrassed violator could think of was, "Well, I only shot three."

Of the 50-odd searches on which I used Reo during his 11 years, the longest was a three-day and three-night manhunt for an armed prison escapee in 1941.

We didn't have much to go on, just faint scent from a blanket the man had used. And heavy rain fell much of the time. But right after dawn on the fourth morning the dog led the posse to where the convict had holed up in a shallow depression in the ground.

The man started shooting, and Reo went for him, something the dog never did to a lost person. When that happened and the posse started to return the fire, the wanted man changed his mind and stood up with his hands in the air.

Reo's attitude toward the people he tracked down was, under ordinary circumstances, very unusual. Though he was never friendly to strangers, I have seen him jump up on someone he had found, wagging all over with friendliness, as if he wanted to be thanked.

I've had three tracking dogs since Reo, and one of them was very good at it. But if you didn't watch him he'd attack the person he had found, and I believe he would have killed if he had got the chance.

One of Reo's most spectacular performances involving crime was finding an empty cartridge alleged to have been used in a murder. He was blindfolded and allowed to smell another cartridge that had been handled by the suspected murderer. It took him four hours to make the find in a pile of wood chips near the cabin in which the killing had taken place.

Perhaps Reo's most unbelievable achievement happened in connection with the robbery of a store at Chase.

One of the bandits dropped his hat in the store, and the dog had no trouble picking up the track. But the robbers had made their getaway in a car, and the trail soon ended.

Two weeks later, as Reo and I were walking the street in Kamloops, we met a stranger, and as he passed, the dog got his scent, turned on him, and growled. A policeman nearby took the man into custody. It's hard to believe, but the stranger turned out to be the owner of the dropped hat.

Once more, Reo had found his man.

I lost Reo in 1947. He was restless that night, refusing to lie down on the rug at the foot of my bed where he slept, coming back time after time for a customary pat on the head. The end came quietly. Sometime after midnight I felt him dragging my blanket off. By the time I turned the light on he was dead.

As a newspaperman friend of mine put it, in the tribute he wrote to Reo, a gallant dog had gone west. I have never known another like him.   *Don D. Ellis*

Reprinted from *Outdoor Life:* Copyright © 1969 Popular Science Publishing Company, Inc.

THE DOGS THAT HELP THE BLIND

UNDOUBTEDLY, one of the most noble and outstanding contributions to mankind made by dogs is to serve as eyes for those who have lost their vision.

In the United States, there are several organizations that train dogs for this most worthwhile purpose. They are:

- Eye Dog Foundation,
  Los Angeles, California

- Leader Dogs for the Blind,
  Rochester, Michigan

- Master Eye Foundation,
  Minneapolis, Minnesota

- The Seeing Eye,
  Morristown, New Jersey

- Guide Dogs for the Blind,
  San Rafael, California

- Guiding Eyes for the Blind, Inc.,
  New York, New York

- Pilot Dogs,
  Columbus, Ohio

- Second Sight Guide Dog Foundation,
  Forest Hills, New York

EYE DOG FOUNDATION

THE PARENT corporation was founded in 1939 and devoted itself to the broad spectrum of aiding the blind. In 1952 Eye Dog Foundation was founded as a subsidiary for the purpose of devoting itself to the exclusive function of giving guide dogs to the blind. In 1954 Eye Dog Foundation became an independent entity, still retaining its exclusive function. Since April, 1956, it has operated a school for the blind students and Guide Dogs at Beaumont, California.

Supported entirely by public contributions, the Foundation receives its major financial aid from the endowments and bequests contained in wills as well as annual donations from public-spirited individuals.

The policy of Eye Dog Foundation is to supply (free of charge) eyes for the blind in the form of a guide dog along with harness and leash. Not only do they receive a guide dog free of charge, but while in attendance for the one month's training the students live on Eye Dog Foundation premises in a dormitory provided by the Foundation where they are housed and fed free of charge.

Prior to the commencement of the class wherein the blind person is trained with the dog, the dog is put through an intensive six months training period by a trainer, licensed by the State of California.

The Foundation has found that the German Shepherd is the most suitable for guide dog work and insist that they be purebred with papers. In addition, since the female is more gentle in temperament, only she is used. The dog must be between ten and 30 months of age. The reason for this is that maturity is an essential element in the potential guide dog. With maturity comes the responsibility required to guide the blind person through all the obstacles encountered by the sighted person; this then becomes a matter of life and death to the blind individual. However, another factor to be considered is the life span of the dog and therefore the length of service to the blind; thus the rule that the Foundation limits the beginning training to dogs not over 30 months of age. Aside from the fact that the German Shepherd is one of the most intelligent breeds, the short hair reduces the chore of the blind person in keeping her clean.

Your Dog and the Law

As the owner of a dog, you are legally responsible or liable if your dog should bite someone. The law is quite explicit about this; thus, it is highly advisable that anyone owning a "guard" dog be very experienced in training and handling them.

The first step in the training of the dog is that she learn to obey basic obedience commands such as: Come, Sit, Down, Fetch, Forward, Right and Left. Once that hurdle is attained, the dog must be trained under traffic conditions to:

• Stop at the curb at the end of each block as well as to stop at intersections where there are no curbs.

• To go forward on command only if it is safe to do so.

• To cross the street straight to the opposite curb and stop so the blind person will not stumble.

• The dog is taught to work at the left side of the blind person, but in addition is taught to clear her master safely of all obstacles on the right side as well as of any overhanging obstacles, low objects and manholes.

• To wait while approaching automobiles pass and not to guide the blind person too closely to any automobile.

• To pass other animals (such as dogs, cats, birds, etc.) without being distracted from her work.

• Not to be distracted by noise or traffic.

• To guide her master to a bus, elevator, airplane, car or other vehicular transportation and ride with him.

• To find doors in and out of buildings.

• To stop at the top and bottom of stairways so that her master will not fall.

• To lie quietly under a table in a restaurant.

To insure complete safety to the blind recipient, at various stages during the training the trainer works with a blindfold. This determines whether the dog is completely dependable in her work. The dog must learn to meet every situation expected to be encountered in her life's work.

Once this training is completed, the class is scheduled and the students are brought in to the Foundation. Since Shepherds range in size from very large to small, it becomes a matter of matchmaking for the trainer to match the proper sized dog with the individual student. Further, it is necessary that the temperament and character of the dog be compatible with that of the student. These are only minor phases of the ultimate goal though they prove extremely important as the pair begin to exist together.

For additional information contact:
Eye Dog Foundation
257 South Spring St.
Los Angeles, California
Phone: (213) 626-3370

LEADER DOGS FOR THE BLIND

LEADER Dogs For The Blind is a school for blind people who want desperately to remain active in the community. Well over 200 blind men and women visit the school each year to get Leader Dogs. Great effort is made to guarantee every eligible person will be trained with a Leader Dog if he makes application. The school in Rochester, Michigan, is dependent entirely upon voluntary contributions.

Historically, the problem of blindness has been dealt with on an emotional basis. Predominate attitudes of the public still vacillate between stifling sympathy and avoidance. Even the more sophisticated of our fellow citizens frequently assume that blindness is synonomous with dependence.

The blind man wants to produce and enjoy the fruits of his labor the same as those who can see. He doesn't want sympathy. He wants to become a customer for the goods which all the world wants to sell. Leader Dogs for the Blind provides the means of mobility so the blind man can resume his responsibility, so he can seek the same opportunities as any other citizen. The School hopes to put the man back on his feet with a Leader Dog.

For additional information contact:
Leader Dogs For The Blind
1039 S. Rochester Rd.
Rochester, Michigan
Phone: (313) 651-9011

Left—New animals are identified and given thorough physical examinations. Leader Dogs must be friendly, companionable and willing to accept a great deal of responsibility.

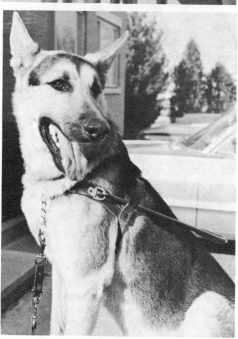

Above—It takes four weeks of intensive training to achieve the ability to move briskly with a Leader Dog. The dog is already trained when it is assigned to a student, and will serve the master for approximately eight years. The instructor is always very close by for the first weeks of training. Later the student is told to "get lost"; he is on his own with his Leader Dog. Left—A Leader Dog with its "leading" equipment.

239

THE MASTER EYE FOUNDATION OF AMERICA

THE Master Eye Foundation of America, which operates in Minneapolis, Minnesota, is another non-profit organization which supplies trained dogs entirely without charge to qualified blind persons of all creeds, color, and origins in all fifty states, Canada, and Mexico. They have trained guide dogs for the blind since 1926. Once accepted into their program, they will pay transportation from any place in the United States, and they will pay room and board for the three to four weeks required to pair dog with master and to train them to work smoothly together as a team.

Ray Kempf, a graduate of the Master Eye Foundation, describes the eight indispensable traits of any guide dog and relates them to his dog Sonny.

TEMPERAMENT

"He has that calm, Nordic-like temperament seen so much and loved so much in our part of the world. He will lie still, keeping his cool in the midst of a gathering of people which, to an ordinary dog, would be highly distracting.

COORDINATED SENSES

"Sight, smell, hearing, touch, all working smoothly together like a finely oiled machine. Sonny must be constantly sensitive to what I am doing, even what I may *intend* to do under given circumstances . . . responding with trained reflexes conditioned to all external dangers such as moving traffic, bodies of water, projecting objects, holes in the road or sidewalk, steep curbs and the like.

"If you could see Sonny now, you would find him totally relaxed, eyes closed, apparently asleep. But don't you believe it! You will see his forepaw resting lightly on my instep from time to time, feeling my motions. Should I move radically from my present position, giving Sonny the word we're moving on, he'd be on his feet instantly, ready, able and willing to guide me safely wherever I command.

MEMORY

"Sonny must remember all the places I've been and, when I leave, bring me back there on command when the occasion arises. Sounds impossible, doesn't it? When we travel by bus, train, plane or ship, it is Sonny's job to return me to my seat or stateroom when I leave it for whatever purpose. When we stop at a motel and go for a walk or on business in a strange city, he must not only return me to my motel, but to my door!

"And here's an even tougher one. Several years ago, when Sonny and I first paired up, I had occasion to visit my dentist, high in the Medical Arts Building in Minneapolis. With aid of a bystander or two, we eventually found our way to the right office. Every six months since then, when I return for my semi-annual examination, Sonny guides me unerringly to the proper door at the command, 'Dentist!'

VOCABULARY

"Sonny has, by actual count, a vocabulary of 30 words! He responds to them faithfully . . . *up, down, come, go, sit, stay, right, left,* etc. This is not too unusual. Every Master Eye Guide Dog, bred, trained and certified for release by LaSalle Kennels, can duplicate this feat. It seems to be bred deep in their bones!

LOYALTY

"Of course, this is a two-way street. Sonny gives *me* the same degree of loyalty as I give *him!* That's why the Master Eye Foundation is so persnickety about who gets their carefully trained guide dogs. They make certain from the start that a two-way working relationship exists between dog and master. Otherwise, no soap!

"Naturally, I care for that dog as a sighted person would care for two precious eyes . . . which he *is!* I don't pamper him as a play-time companion or hobby. When his harness is on, he's my loyal business partner . . . he's *all* business, *his* and *mine*—no pause to greet fellow dogs, to chase cats or bow and scrape to be petted by passersby. It's Sonny's job to look out for me and me alone, when I'm in motion.

RESPONSIBILITY

"I have touched lightly upon this in considering some of the previous traits but this one is of such import as to require treatment in depth. I'm quite sure Sonny has an alarm clock ticking in his head! Every morning, precisely at six, he's up and nudging me awake with his cold nose! So I hop out of bed, open the door to let him outside until my breakfast is completed. Then, harness in hand, when I stand in the door and call him just once, he's quickly there, nosing my left hand, telling me he's ready to receive the harness and be off with me at a brisk pace.

"What a reassuring feeling to have such dependable responsiveness ready to serve as my eyes and protector anytime of the day or night, without grumble, with no demand for overtime, no pay raises, no days off, no week-end passes, no coffee breaks, just constant great-hearted devotion to my welfare. Dog's life? If that's what it is, it's a *good* one for *him* and for *me!*

"The mention of 'coffee breaks' leads me to Sonny's interesting eating habits. When I attend business breakfasts, luncheons or dinners, Sonny lies quietly at my feet, totally oblivious to all the luscious food smells. I'm often asked, 'When does *he* eat?' The answer is simple. He eats only when I'm asleep and he knows he won't be needed to guide me. If this is not an example of the kind of *responsibility* that would do credit to any man or beast, then I don't know the meaning of the word!

WORKLIKE HABITS

"Sonny and I have developed what I like to call 'Harness Talk.' I can tell instantly by the feel of the harness when Sonny veers left or right, begins holding back or surging forward. When danger threatens, I can feel the warning pressure of his body against my left leg. When danger comes too close for his liking, he'll block my path entirely. Obviously, this says, 'Stop' as emphatically as the spoken word. When we approach a hole or obstruction, he gives me the signal in advance. As he steps off the curb when the coast is clear, I can tell by the tilt of the harness how steep the curb is. Back pressure on the harness says, 'Slow.'

Forward pull on the harness says, 'Speed up, chief!'

"Let Sonny see a known friend of mine approaching from as far away as a city block, his delighted body movements telegraph through the harness accompanied by tail-thumps against my legs, that I'm to get set to greet a friend. It never fails!

GENTLEMANLINESS

"In this context, you might enjoy a true dog story told me by the Executive Vice President of the Master Eye Foundation. During a recent three years in England, he made his home at Canwick Hall, a rambling stone house built in 1700. It had an acre or so of front garden, in the northwest corner of which, tucked away beneath some ancient trees, was a small, moss-encrusted tombstone marking the grave of the original estate owner's favorite hunting dog. The simple inscription, carved deep into the aging stone, read, 'Laddie . . . He Was A Gentleman.' "

For additional information contact:
Master Eye Foundation
Produce Bank Building
Minneapolis, Minnesota
Phone: (612) 336-1833

THE SEEING EYE

HELPING blind people to free themselves from this restriction by making use of the capabilities of the dog is the work of The Seeing Eye. To date, more than 6,000 Seeing Eye dogs have given service to blind people all over the country. They have helped these determined men and women to win livelihoods and to further their careers in over a hundred different fields.

The Seeing Eye came into existence officially on January 29, 1929, when it was incorporated at Nashville, Tennessee. Its roots, however, go back several years before then—to one woman's vision, to a magazine article she wrote, and to a blind young man who could see its implications and who did something about them.

To old friends of The Seeing Eye the story is familiar. The woman was Dorothy Harrison Eustis of Philadelphia, then living in Switzerland. She was initially interested in the scientific selection and breeding of German shepherd dogs. Mrs. Eustis and her staff realized, however, that only through the dogs' performance could the effectiveness of the breeding program be measured. The breeding activities were therefore augmented by a training program whose "graduates" soon demonstrated their ability to render outstanding service to the Swiss Army and to several

"The dog is a liberating factor in life to some blind . . ., not a luxury . . ."—Dorothy Harrison Eustis, founder of The Seeing Eye.

metropolitan police units in Europe. Thus, Mrs. Eustis had a good idea of what these dogs could do. But even she was unaware of their full potential until she visited a German school where she saw shepherd dogs being trained as guides for blinded war veterans. Deeply impressed and deeply moved, she wrote an article for the November 5, 1927 issue of the *Saturday Evening Post*. Its title, as it turned out, was prophetic: "The Seeing Eye."

A few weeks later, the article came to the attention of a twenty-year-old Tennessean, Morris Frank, who immediately wrote to Mrs. Eustis: ". . . Thousands of blind like me abhor being dependent on others. Help me and I will help them. Train me and I will bring back my dog and show people here how a blind man can be absolutely on his own . . ." Morris Frank was invited to come to Switzerland. A dog was selected and trained for him, and then he himself was trained.

Back in the United States again, he crossed and recrossed the country, putting himself and his dog Buddy to the test under every conceivable traffic situation.

Mrs. Eustis, too, returned to America, to found The Seeing Eye and to dedicate herself to the task of opening this new path to freedom for blind Americans.

The first Seeing Eye class was held in Nashville during February 1929, with two members in attendance. By the end of that year, 17 blind men and women had found freedom through their Seeing Eye dogs. Freedom, of course, was from the very beginning the goal of The Seeing Eye and of those who came for training. But freedom for what? Mrs. Eustis put it this way: *"The dog is a liberating factor in life to some blind . . ., not a luxury. . . . It is not our idea to advocate the placing of dog guides with all the blind— far from it. The dog guide is suitable for the man who can use him in his daily life, who wants an aid in making himself a free economic unit . . ., who wants a wider freer life. . . ."*

For additional information contact:
The Seeing Eye
Morristown, New Jersey 07960

GUIDE DOGS FOR THE BLIND, INCORPORATED

CALIFORNIA is the only state having laws governing the operation of a Guide Dog School. The school and the instructors must be licensed by the State Dog Board. The non-profit school is not connected with any other training center and does not receive State or Federal aid. Guide Dogs For The Blind, Inc. operates under License No. 1 from the California State Guide Dog Board.

As of June 19, 1971, Guide Dogs For The Blind, Inc. had enrolled 2,192 sightless persons. Although its costs approximately $3,000 to produce each man-dog team, no charge is made either for the valuable animal or room and board during the four-week training period. Since more and more early trainees are returning to the school for dogs to replace those who have died or grown too old to work, even more applications are expected in the near future. In addition to replacement and first-time guide dog users, the sad situation exists once again of blinded servicemen returning home from yet another conflict. For more information write: Guide Dogs for the Blind, Inc., Box 1200, San Rafael, Cal.

One of the most important commands a Guide Dog must learn is to "fetch" immediately, as oftentimes a blind person may drop a coin or important paper and a properly trained dog will immediately retrieve the article and bring it to his master.

GUIDING EYES FOR THE BLIND, INCORPORATED

GUIDING EYES for the Blind is a national service incorporated in the State of New York with its principal area of service being the United States and its territorial possessions.

The primary purpose of the agency is to provide independent mobility via guide dogs to those visually handicapped individuals who are physically, mentally and emotionally prepared to benefit from it.

The agency is a voluntary, non-profit organization supported through the contributions of the public.

In its comparatively brief 15 year history, Guiding Eyes for the Blind has graduated approximately 1200 units — dog and master — and currently has units operating in over 40 states and Puerto Rico.

Services of the agency stem from two basic departments, the Breeding Division and the Training School.

Breeding Division

The work of this department is an essential element in providing the best unit possible through the breeding and development of the most suitable dogs for guide dog work.

Guiding Eyes for the Blind breeds Labrador Retrievers, Golden Retrievers, and German Shepherds. However, other breeds are also used, such as Smooth Haired Collies, Bouvier des Flandres, and Boxers. It is the dog rather than the breed that is important. The animal must meet GEB standards in order to qualify for guide dog work.

A program of observation and initial development of the puppy is conducted in cooperation with 4-H Clubs in New York State to determine whether puppy has the basic characteristics necessary for guide dog work — intelligence, temperament and trainability.

The 4-H'er is assigned a puppy from eight weeks of age through one year, which is minimum maturity for guide dog training.

His objective, recognized and rewarded as a formal 4-H Club program, is to raise a happy, healthy puppy, ready to start his "education" as a guide dog at the age of about one year.

Training School

A staff of professionally trained instructors conducts a prescribed 26 day course designed to teach capable visually handicapped persons the techniques and procedures necessary to properly utilize the services of a well-trained guide dog.

Twelve classes are offered in any one year of instruction. A maximum of twelve students can be accommodated in any one session. No more than six students will be assigned to any one instructor, assuring both instructor and student sufficient opportunity to deal with the subject matter covered in the course.

Training of dogs and students takes place in three separate communities varying in size and complexity, as well as in a number of rural areas. Each location has been selected because of its particular set of mobility problems. This system of coverage will prepare dog and master to cope with every conceivable mobility situation from a simple street crossing to the New York subway, regardless of where their future will take them.

Each dog is put through an intensive three-and-a-half to four months course of instruction before being placed in class with a blind student. In learning responsibilities required in guiding blind persons safely, the dog is being taught two basic principles — obedience and disobedience. Ability to reject the master's command in the view of impending danger is often the difference between safety and accident. Capacity to make decisions is a major difference between a trained dog and a Guiding Eyes for the Blind guide dog.

For additional information contact:
Guiding Eyes For The Blind
106 East 41st St.
New York, New York
Phone: (212) 683-5165

Guiding Eyes For The Blind, Inc. breeds Labrador Retrievers, Golden Retrievers and German Shepherds, however, other breeds such as Smooth Haired Collies, Bouvier des Flandres and Boxers are also used.

OLD DRUM
A TRIBUTE TO THE DOG

A Tribute to the Dog
SENATOR VEST'S SPEECH TO THE JURY, SEPTEMBER 23, 1870

Gentlemen of the Jury: The best friend a man has in this world may turn against him and become his enemy. His son or daughter that he has reared with loving care may prove ungrateful. Those who are nearest and dearest to us, those whom we trust with our happiness and our good name, may become traitors to their faith. The money that a man has, he may lose. It flies away from him, perhaps when he needs it the most. A man's reputation may be sacrificed in a moment of ill-considered action. The people who are prone to fall on their knees to do us honor when success is with us may be the first to throw the stone of malice when failure settles its cloud upon our heads. The one absolutely unselfish friend that a man can have in this selfish world, the one that never deserts him and the one that never proves ungrateful or treacherous is his dog.

"Gentlemen of the Jury, a man's dog stands by him in prosperity and in poverty, in health and in sickness. He will sleep on the cold ground, where the wintry winds blow and the snow drives fiercely, if only he may be near his master's side. He will kiss the hand that has no food to offer, he will lick the wounds and sores that come in encounters with the roughness of the world. He guards the sleep of his pauper master as if he were a prince. When all other friends desert he remains. When riches take wing and reputation falls to pieces, he is as constant in his love as the sun in its journey through the heavens. If fortune drives the master forth an outcast in the world, friendless and homeless, the faithful dog asks no higher privilege than that of accompanying him to guard against danger, to fight against his enemies, and when the last scene of all comes, and death takes the master in its embrace and his body is laid away in the cold ground, no matter if all other friends pursue their way, there by his graveside will the noble dog be found, his head between his paws, his eyes sad but open in alert watchfulness, faithful and true even to death."

Burden vs Hornsby 1869-70

When Senator George Graham Vest paid his famous tribute to the dog in the old Court House in Warrensburg, Mo., in 1870, he appealed to the hearts of dog lovers everywhere when he said: "The one absolutely unselfish friend that a man can have in this selfish world, the one that never deserts him, the one that never proves ungrateful or treacherous, is his dog."

That Eulogy of Senator Vest won the case for Charles Burden whose favorite hound, Drum, was shot by a neighbor, Leonidas Hornsby, who had sworn to kill the first dog that came on his place after he had lost a number of sheep. Though Hornsby had hunted with Drum, and acknowledged him to be one of the best hunting dogs he had ever seen, he stubbornly insisted on carrying out his threat when one dark night a dog was found prowling in his yard. That dog was Old Drum.

Immediately Burden sued Hornsby for damages and the trial became one of the strangest in the history of this section of the country. Each man was determined to win his case, and several appeals were made till Hornsby finally took it to the Supreme Court of Missouri. Burden, however, was awarded $50 damages for the loss of his favorite hunting dog, Drum. Vest's Eulogy to the dog, which he made in his final appeal to the jury, won the case and became a classic speech.

Through the direction of the Warrensburg Chamber of Commerce, and coordinated efforts of many dog lovers over the country, Old Drum was immortalized in a statue on the Johnson County Courthouse lawn, in Warrensburg, Missouri, September 23, 1958. Dog lovers all over the country responded quickly to the national announcement of the placing of this statue to Old Drum, who has become a kind of symbol of all dogs that people have loved.

When Senator Vest said: "Gentlemen of the jury, a man's dog stands by him in prosperity and poverty, in health and sickness," he touched a common bond of relationship in all dog lovers.

Vest's Memorial Ass'n., St. Louis, has already placed a plaque on the old Court House, scene of Vest's famous Eulogy, recognizing it as an historic spot in the state. Since then, restoration of the Old Courthouse where the famous trial took place, has been underway and at present is open for visitations on summer weekends.

—Courtesy of The Warrensburg Chamber of Commerce

STAMPS AND DOGS

Dog pictures are popular on stamps and have been used by most of the nations of the world. Here are samples of just a few of these.

CHAPTER X

CAREERS WITH DOGS

THE phenomenal increase in the pet population in this country certainly would suggest that careers involving dogs should prove to be successful. Presently, a great number of people earn their living through some involvement either directly or indirectly from dogs. For those who want to expand their love of dogs from a sport or hobby into a career, here are some possibilities. However, to be successful at any of these vocations, they must be approached as a serious business and not as a hobby. Frequently, people are drawn into these fields initially through their hobbies, but, once it becomes a career, a more purposeful and serious attitude must prevail.

SOME STATISTICS

Pet Spending

$1,000,000,000 for pet supplies and accessories, including equipment for tropical fish
$1,400,000,000 for cat and dog foods
$30,000,000 for bird food
$5,000,000 for fish food
$300,000,000 for health care
$100,000,000 to buy pets
$150,000,000 for grooming

VETERINARIAN

SINCE 1854, when the first veterinary college in the United States was established, veterinary medicine has grown to the stature of a highly diversified profession with nearly 30,000 doctors of veterinary medicine in North America.

Veterinary medicine is an autonomous profession having its own system of education, licensure, and organization, and adhering to a strict code of ethics.

As the profession has advanced scientifically and its members have become more numerous, the affairs of veterinary medicine have become increasingly complex. The profession today has many facets. Not only are veterinarians actively engaged in diagnosis, treatment, and control of a broad spectrum of diseases among many species of animals, but they are also key members in the nation's medical, public health, research, and military teams.

Demands for veterinary medical services continue to rise. A recent report estimates that North America will need 44,000 veterinarians or almost twice today's number, by 1980.

Veterinarians in the
 United States ....27,500 (estm.)
Veterinarians in Canada ..... 2,500 (estm.)
Membership in the AVMA ...20,110
Veterinary Colleges in the U.S.   18
Veterinary Colleges in Canada   3
Figures according to the 1970 records of the American Veterinary Medical Association.

VETERINARY MEDICAL EDUCATION

There are 18 colleges of veterinary medicine in the United States, and three in Canada. Most are associated with a public university. Collectively, they graduate approximately 1,150 veterinarians each year.

The number of faculty members — engaged in teaching and in research — was 1,850 at the beginning of 1970.

In 1969, 1,538 students entered veterinary colleges. Almost 30 per cent had acquired academic degrees prior to entering the professional school. Today, nearly 800 veterinarians are taking post doctoral courses at schools of veterinary medicine.

Veterinary student enrollment for the 1969-70 academic year reached a record high of 5,471, including 490 women students.

The Veterinary Medical Curriculum. All veterinary schools require a minimum of two years of pre-veterinary college study for entrance, and four additional years of professional study for graduation and the conferring of the degree of doctor of veterinary medicine (D.V.M. or V.M.D.). However, the average number of years spent in college prior to entering a veterinary school is three and one-third years. Therefore, the typical student graduating as a doctor of veterinary medicine has spent just over seven years in college. Before a veterinarian can practice in a state he must obtain that state's license by passing an examination given by its board of veterinary examiners.

The curriculum at a veterinary medical school is in many respects similar to that offered in medical schools. In fact, in some of the basic courses such as bacteriology, immunology, histology, and others the material is virtually identical in all fields of medicine. Only in the advanced courses do medical concepts and applications begin to be more specifically confined to the various species of domestic animals.

Classroom Subjects

Veterinary students devote some 5,000 class hours, including clinical experience, to subjects such as anatomy, physiology, pharmacology, pathology, microbiology, biochemistry, surgery, medicine, public health, preventive medicine, and parasitology.

Consequently, today's graduate veterinarian is a medically trained, scientifically oriented professional person capable of rendering many services and accepting wide responsibilities in all areas of animal health and in many areas of public health.

Typical Curriculum of a Veterinary Medical College
FIRST YEAR

Gross Anatomy of Domestic Animals
Neuroanatomy
Histology and Embryology
Animal Husbandry
Physiological Chemistry
Physiology
Animal Genetics
Botany

SECOND YEAR

Radiobiology
Physiology
Experimental Physiology
Bacteriology and Immunology Laboratory
General Pathology

Today's veterinarian is highly trained to give his patients the best possible care.

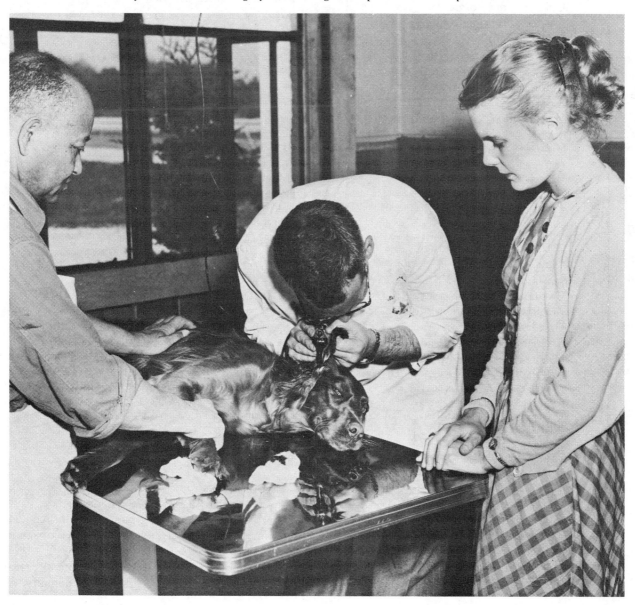

249

General Pathology Laboratory
Special Pathology
Special Pathology Laboratory
Parasitology
Animal Husbandry
Pharmacology
Public Health

THIRD YEAR

Public Health and Preventive Medicine

General Surgery
Surgical Exercises
Non-Infectious Diseases
Infectious Diseases of Large Animals
Small Animal Medicine
Small Animal Surgery
Applied Anatomy
Obstetrics
Clinical Pathology
Special Surgery
Diseases of Poultry
Roentgenology

FOURTH YEAR

Large Animal Surgery
Small Animal Surgery
Special Pathology
Jurisprudence, Ethics, and Business Methods
Clinical Conferences
Clinics
Laboratory Animal Medicine
Toxicology
Nutrition

Colleges of Veterinary Medicine are located at the following institutions:

Auburn University
Auburn, Alabama 36830

University of California
Davis, California 95616

Colorado State University
Fort Collins, Colorado 80621

University of Georgia
Athens, Georgia 30601

University of Illinois
Urbana, Illinois 61801

Iowa State University
Ames, Iowa 50010

Kansas State University
Manhattan, Kansas 66502

Michigan State University
East Lansing, Michigan 48823

University of Minnesota
St. Paul, Minnesota 55101

University of Missouri
Columbia, Missouri 65202

Cornell University
Ithaca, New York 14850

Ohio State University
Columbus, Ohio 43210

Oklahoma State University
Stillwater, Oklahoma 74074

University of Guelph
Guelph, Ontario, Canada

University of Pennsylvania
Philadelphia, Pennsylvania 19104

L'Ecole de Medicine Veterinaire
St. Hyacinthe, Quebec, Canada

Purdue University
Lafayette, Indiana 47907

University of Saskatchewan
Saskatoon, Saskatchewan, Canada

Texas A&M University
College Station, Texas 77843

Tuskegee Institute
Tuskegee Institute, Ala. 36088

Washington State University
Pullman, Washington 99163

The Activities of Veterinary Medicine

Special Interests of AVMA's Members

From the 1970 Directory

	Number	Per Cent
Large Animal Practice	1,422	6.4
Mixed Practice	7,435	33.6
Small Animal Practice	5,766	26.2
Other Specialized Practices	3,801	17.3
Public Health	363	1.7
Regulatory Veterinary Medicine	1,452	6.6
Military Veterinary Service	833	3.8
Unknown	974	4.4
TOTAL	22,046	100.0

U.S. Animal Population

The United States Department of Agriculture and other reliable sources estimate the animal population of the United States as follows:

Livestock

Cattle	109 million
Hogs	55 million
Sheep	22 million
Horses	7 million

Pets

Dogs	32.6 million
Cats	22 million
Pet Birds	20 million

Approximately 31 million families in the United States own either one or more dogs, or one or more cats, or both.

Many veterinarians are engaged in general practice. The general veterinary practitioner administers to the needs of practically every species of domestic livestock and poultry, as well as those of pet animals.

Of the approximately 4,000 animal hospitals in the United States, some 3,000 either include or specialize in the treatment of small animals such as cats, dogs and pet birds.

Veterinarians in Agriculture

The major responsibility of the large animal practitioner is to prevent, control, and eradicate diseases of livestock and poultry, and to insure that meat and meat products — as well as milk and milk products — are wholesome and disease free.

Veterinarians working in cooperation with the U.S. Department of Agriculture and State Departments of Agriculture are also responsible for organized animal disease eradication and control programs.

According to the U.S. Department of Agriculture, the combined inventory and production value of the nation's livestock was above an annual rate of $43 billion on January 1, 1970.

The per capita consumption of meat from poultry and livestock in the United States for 1969 was as follows: 42 pounds of poultry including broilers, turkeys and other fowl; and 181 pounds of red meat which includes beef, veal, pork and lamb.

The same source estimated losses from some of the major livestock diseases as follows: Mastitis - $500 million; bloat - $105 million; vibriosis - $104 million, and leptospirosis - $12 million.

Hog cholera can be controlled by vaccination, but each year prior to the current eradication program, hog farmers lost over $50 million to this disease. Today's losses are estimated to be one half of this amount.

Today's losses due to brucellosis are estimated at one tenth of the $90 million in losses reported for 1947. Tuberculosis affects only one animal in 3,000 head of cattle in today's reports on the disease's incidence. Fifty years ago five per cent of the cattle in the United States were reported to have the disease.

In the United States, livestock diseases once present that have been eradicated or drastically reduced include pleuropneumonia, cattle tick fever, foot-and-mouth disease, screwworm infection, vesicular exanthema, tuberculosis, and brucellosis.

Veterinary Medicine and Public Health

The primary objective of public health veterinary medicine is the prevention of human illness from animal sources. Over 100 diseases of animals have been recorded as being transmissible from animal to man. Over 80 of these have been reported in the United States, but less than 30 are of major concern. Anthrax, brucellosis, tuberculosis of bones and glands, parrot fever, erysipelas, rabies, and leptospirosis are

---

SOME STATISTICS

Pet Population Estimates

32,600,000 dogs
22,000,000 cats
20,000,000 birds
500,000,000 fish

---

some of the more commonly known.

**Some Veterinary Accomplishments
Benefitting Human Health:**

Dr. Maurice Hall, a U.S.D.A. veterinarian, showed that carbon tetrachloride — a compound used in dry cleaning — was a practical treatment for hookworn in man as well as animal.

Dr. Cooper Curtice, also a U.S.D.A. veterinarian, discovered that insects transmit infection between animals or from animals to man. It was this discovery which led to the conquest of yellow fever, malaria, and tick-borne typhus.

Dr. Karl Meyer, a veterinarian doing research for the Hooper Foundation, solved the mystery of botulism, a kind of food poisoning, thus helping create the canned food industry.

Dr. Otto Stader, a small animal practitioner developed one of the fracture immobilizing devices now widely used by bone specialists.

A veterinarian's—Dr. Frank Schofield—research on the cause of sweet clover poisoning in cattle led to the isolation of a potent anticoagulant. The drug, dicumarol, is now being used in treating heart disease in humans.

Dr. Alfred E. Earl, a New Jersey veterinarian caring for laboratory animals in a drug research firm,

---

Today's veterinarian is found in one of almost 30 special interest fields among these classifications:

- General practice, specializing in either large or small animals or both
- Research in government, in industry, or at a university
- Teaching at a university
- Public Health at the local, state or federal level
- Regulatory affairs at the local, state, or federal level
- Laboratory animal medicine
- Zoo animal medicine
- Military service, in the field, in regulatory affairs, or in public health

discovered the tranquilizing effect of reserpine and established a research project which uncovered, and is still uncovering, new tranquilizers for application in veterinary medical and human medical fields.

Col. Harry A. Gorman, U.S. Air Force veterinarian, developed an artificial hip joint for dogs and, working with medical orthopedists, successfully adapted the prosthesis to man.

Meat Inspection

To protect the public from diseases transmissible through food from animals to man, meat and meat products receive a thorough inspection from veterinarians employed by the Consumer and Marketing Service of the U.S. Department of Agriculture. This federal service inspects about 80 per cent of meat and meat products consumed in the United States, for safety and wholesomeness. Every working day federal meat inspectors condemn approximately one million pounds of meat or meat products as unsafe or diseased.

When the Wholesome Meat Act of 1967 is fully implemented, all meat sold in the United States will be inspected for wholesomeness.

Federal food inspection, under the provisions of the Wholesome Meat Act of 1967, is performed in 3224 meat processing plants in 1211 cities and towns, and in 1004 poultry plants in 717 cities and towns.

The act provides for a Consumer and Marketing Service which at the beginning of 1970 had 1437 veterinarians and 6069 food inspectors on its staff.

Inspection of Imported Animals

Veterinary inspectors at U.S. ports of entry prevent the introduction of animal diseases from imported animals or animal products. They also help enforce health regulations in the traffic in animals, both intrastate and interstate.

Veterinarians annually inspect about 1 million animals presented for importation at all major U.S. air and ocean ports.

The Case of Rabies

Rabies is transmitted through infected saliva by contact with open wounds or bite of animals. Preventive measures include vaccination of dogs, elimination of stray dogs, and control of wild animal hosts.

The rabies problem in the United States is measured not so much by the number of human deaths as by the number of persons who require treatment—more than 30,000 persons each year are bitten by suspected rabid animals and are required to take treatment.

According to the U.S. Public Health Service, 1967 was the first year free of human deaths from rabies originating within the borders of the United States. Rabies in humans has been on the decline for a number of years, with only one death reported in each of the four years prior to 1967. The highest number in recent years was nine deaths in 1956. Large numbers of laboratory confirmed cases of animal rabies are reported each year. The 1966 total was 4,198 and was a two per cent increase over the previous five year average. Skunks and foxes accounted for 57 per cent of the animal rabies in the United States in 1966, with only 412 rabid dogs reported.

The significant decrease of rabies is generally attributed to the successful development of rabies control programs conducted throughout the United States under the direction of veterinarians.

Veterinarians in Research

Veterinarians in government agencies, educational institutions, private industry — including packing houses, animal feed producers, and drug manufacturers — and in non-profit research institutions are continuously engaged in research projects designed to advance animal as well as human health.

Veterinarians are engaged in the care of experimental animals used in medical research. They also participate in the development and testing of biological products, such as vaccines and serums, which require the use of laboratory animals.

The laboratory animal industry is valued at a figure in excess of $500 million. An estimated 60 million small animals, including poultry and other birds, are used in the United States each year for research, laboratory instruction and testing of drugs and biologics.

Veterinary medical research is carried on by such governmental departments and agencies as the U.S. Department of Agriculture, the Department of Health, Education and Welfare, and the Atomic Energy Commission.

The Animal Disease and Parasite Research Division of the Consumer and Marketing Service of the U.S.D.A. conducts the nation's most extensive veterinary research program. Its laboratories investigate many phases of diseases of domestic animals. Their research projects are being expanded at the National Animal Disease Laboratory at Ames, Iowa, which began operation in 1961. The new laboratory investigates animal diseases now present in the United States.

Facilities at the Plum Island, New York, Animal Disease Laboratory represents a large-scale attempt by the United States to provide research protection against those animal diseases which do not exist in this country, but may be introduced. The Communicable Disease Center of the U.S. Public Health Service has within its organization a rabies research laboratory, a veterinary public health laboratory to study bacterial diseases, and special units which are concerned with animal-borne encephalitis, ring-worm, and parasites.

Veterinarians in Industry

Veterinarians employed by private pharmaceutical

manufacturing firms supervise the development, production, and testing of biological products and drugs for use with animal and man. As members of packing companies they strive to improve meat quality and find new uses for animal by-products. In many non-profit institutions they apply their knowledge of bacteriology, parasitology, animal diseases and hygiene to the development of new food products and the improvement of quality, sanitation, packaging, and shelf-life of current products.

The USDA's Veterinary Biologics Division has the responsibility of licensing both the veterinary biologicals and the establishments which produce them. At the beginning of 1970 there were 280 types of veterinary biologics produced at 55 establishments. There were 42 veterinarians on the biological control program's staff of 125.

Veterinarians in the FDA

The basic objectives of the FDA veterinarian are to protect the health of animals and to safe-guard the wholesomeness of foods of animal origin. Manufacturers of veterinary drugs are required to submit data to prove that the use of the drug by food-producing animals is safe for the ultimate human consumer. Then, veterinarians decide by tests and other criteria whether the product will result in residues, or metabolites of questionable safety, in the edible tissues of a treated animal, or its milk or eggs.

In a typical year, FDA's Bureau of Veterinary Medicine reviews over 1,000 new drug applications and processes about 8,000 applications for the use of new drugs in the manufacture of medicated feeds.

Veterinarians in the Armed Forces

Veterinarians serving as officers in the Armed Forces fulfill the function of veterinary public health officials for troops at home and overseas. They supervise inspection of food prepared and served to troops at home and abroad; are engaged in research in such special military fields as bacteriological warfare, effects of space flight on living beings, diet development, and food packaging, and guard the nation against foreign livestock diseases. They also provide medical care for all animals under military supervision.

Approximately 800 veterinarians serve as officers in the Army Veterinary Corps and the Air Force Veterinary Service.

Veterinary Medical Research

Military veterinarians are involved in such studies as:

• High altitude problems. The problems man will face at high altitudes are being solved by using animals in vehicles projected into space.

• Problems of acceleration and deceleration. Prob-

NATIONAL DOG WEEK

The official slogan of National Dog Week is "Deserve to be your dog's best friend." The objectives are:

1. To educate dog owners in the basics of good dog care.

2. To help every dog find a good home.

3. To increase participation in dog clubs, obedience training classes or animal welfare organizations.

4. To pay tribute to the dog's role as companion and protector.

5. To achieve fair and effective legislation for dogs and dog owners.

6. To encourage dog owners to be considerate of others and to observe laws regarding licensing, leashing and curbing.

---

lems of acceleration and deceleration have been brought closer to solution by extrapolating physiological results obtained by the use of animals. Data obtained from animals made it possible to use human volunteers in this project.

• Space flight and space travel. Lower animals have been projected to phenomenal heights and have lived to return and furnish invaluable scientific data. Veterinary participation in the "animal in space" program is an indispensable supplement to the "man in space" program, it extends to the care and training of the animals used and to the interpretation of data they furnish.

• Nuclear energy. Veterinary officers are engaged in radiation experiments to determine the effects of ionizing radiation upon animals and, by extrapolation, upon man. Exposed animals and plants are also being studied as possible sources of food in the event of nuclear warfare. Acceptable tolerances for food are being investigated, and standards and instruments for field trials are being developed.

• Flight and ground feeding research. Military veterinarians with operational knowledge of military transport, feeding requirements, physiological limitations of personnel, and scientific knowledge of foods are assisting food technologists and other research personnel in research in flight and ground feeding. Their work has produced the world's safest and most modern in-flight and ground feeding rations, such as combat rations, dehydrated foods, precooked frozen meals, precooked hot meals, survival food packets, special box and sandwich lunches, and food in liquid and tablet form for high altitude jet pilots.

Reprinted by permission of the
American Veterinary Medical Association

FULL-AND PART-TIME CAREERS

Handler

EXTENSIVE training, studying, and experience are the prerequisites for this career. Love of dogs, excitement, hard work, and travel are also needed. A handler must build his reputation slowly and carefully. Careful selection of dogs that you will handle can help you attain success. Merely handling for the "fee" can damage a reputation.

To be a successful handler, it is helpful to have a personality which is pleasing to clients as well as to their dogs.

When handling is combined with other lucrative projects, such as grooming and boarding, it is possible to earn a comfortable living. However, the work is hard and demanding, the hours long and erratic, and the stresses and strains continuous. Winning is a great thrill and the competitions are always challenging, which makes this a great field for the dedicated.

To be a successful handler, it is helpful to have a personality which is pleasing to clients as well as to their dogs. (Handler Annemarie Moore showing Airedale Terrier owned by Mr. and Mrs. Frederick Kipp.)

Dog Breeder

This is a most difficult field in which to start an exclusive career. So much depends on luck and timing as well as reputation and the public's changing tastes; as a result, it is best to combine breeding with another doggy enterprise. By so doing, it is possible to develop good stock, and a reputation without being totally dependent on early success.

Breeding is truly hard work. A knowledge of all the factors that go into producing fine dogs must be acquired; this demands study as well as experience. Then follows the actual physical work—caring for the brood bitches, feeding, keeping the kennels clean, assisting during whelping, giving up sleep whenever necessary, caring for puppies, etc. Then, selling the puppies often involves correspondence, phone calls, and visitors—all time-consuming work.

Selecting a breed of dog which will sell and prove to be popular over the years is the first step in this business venture. Secondly, it is wise to use a breed that has a fairly good-sized litter and that whelps easily. A good breeding program requires using the

Dog Breeding is a difficult, time consuming and sometimes very frustrating career. However, for those who love dogs, the pleasure of a beautiful litter of puppies outweighs many of the negative aspects. (Photo courtesy of Ruth Klein, Highland Park, Ill.)

254

best stock; thus, building up an outstanding group of bitches is essential. Growing slowly and weeding out those dogs which are not adding to the kennel are good practices.

It may take years before one sees any real return on an investment in breeding; that is why combining it with another enterprise is suggested.

Boarding

Starting a boarding kennel involves a major investment since land and an attractive building are needed in order to make this a successful business venture. A proper site must be located which is convenient for clients and which is sufficiently isolated so that neighbors will not be annoyed by barking. Operating a boarding kennel is hard work; however, it usually makes an excellent return on the investment.

If you wish to combine a boarding kennel with a breeding kennel, the two sections must be separated. Boarding rates should be sufficiently high so that they

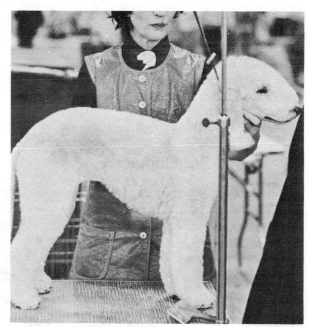

A grooming shop requires clean and attractive facilities and the ability to properly groom a variety of breeds.

A boarding kennel requires a substantial investment in land and facilities.

cover the cost of feeding and caring for the dog as well as allowing for a good profit. A wise business practice is to request board payment in advance, if possible.

While being boarded, the dogs must be fed a good quality diet, their living facilities must be kept clean, and they must be groomed regularly. Employees to perform these functions must be found, unless the kennel owner is willing and able to undertake all these chores himself.

Grooming Shops

A well-located grooming establishment can be a most lucrative enterprise since most dog owners today

want to keep their pets looking their best and are willing to pay well for this service. To begin, advertising is needed in order to acquire clients. Once a reputation is made and there is a following of satisfied customers, word of mouth will create more than enough business. Clean, neat, and attractive facilities, kindness and consideration to the dogs, and competent work will insure success. Of vital importance is the ability and knowledge in grooming the dog in the correct manner as prescribed by the standard for that breed.

A grooming business can be the exclusive business of a shop or it can be in conjunction with other related activities. This is a vocation which requires you to be on your feet most of the day; it involves physical labor and stamina.

Sales

Retail—The Pet Store

Selling puppies can be a profitable business, but it should be conducted honestly and carefully. Puppies should be sold at a fair price; they should be in good health, and, if pure bred, the pedigree and registration papers should be available at the time of the sale. Keeping the puppies clean, healthy, and sweet smelling until they are sold is quite a job. Handling puppies means that both facilities and care must be available. An important aspect of this puppy trade is to have a good source of supply from breeders.

Dog supplies can be sold in conjunction with the sale of puppies, in a grooming or boarding establishment, or as the exclusive purpose of a shop. When a good line of products, well displayed, is offered, business can be quite good. A wide variety of dog products in addition to dog books, make it possible to provide customers with everything they could possibly need for their pet's care. Of course, intelligent business practices are needed in this field as in any other business venture.

Wholesale

A wholesaler who supplies local pet stores with all their needs is another good business enterprise. Ingenuity and wise and prudent management can spell success.

Pet Cemetery

Providing a burial spot and all the necessary services can be a most lucrative business and certainly a service to the bereaved pet owner. Many communities do not have pet cemeteries, thus, an intelligent business man can find ample opportunity to start a profitable enterprise.

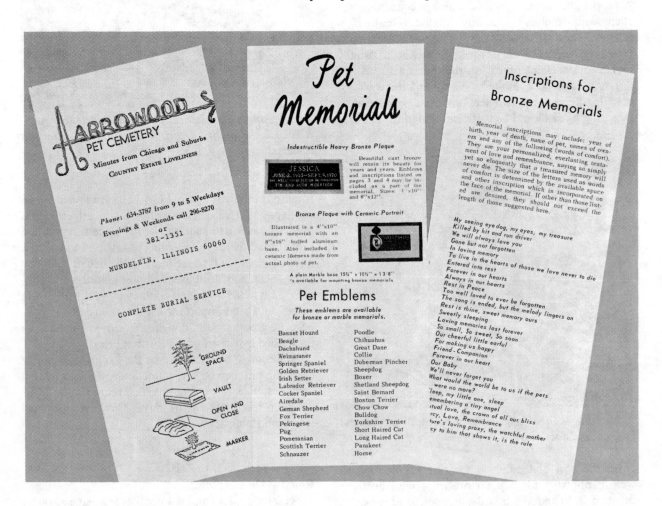

Writing

People are always interested in reading about dogs. Fiction and non-fiction material about our four-footed friends is one of the more popular fields of writing. Most newspapers have a regular column devoted to information and advice on dog care. Many magazines maintain a dog section; there are numerous magazines devoted exclusively to dogs and there are always new dog books. Thus, a good writer who is knowledgeable in the dog field can usually find an outlet for his creative endeavor.

Photography

Dog ownership is, in itself, a luxury, and most dog owners will indulge themselves in much, much more than the mere possession of a dog. Many dog owners desire pictures of their dogs, either for advertising purposes or merely for pleasure. The talented photographer, who is able to truly capture a dog with expression and good form, will rapidly make a reputation for himself. Taking fine pictures of show dogs can, in itself, be a full-time occupation.

Advertising in the dog journals, displaying work at

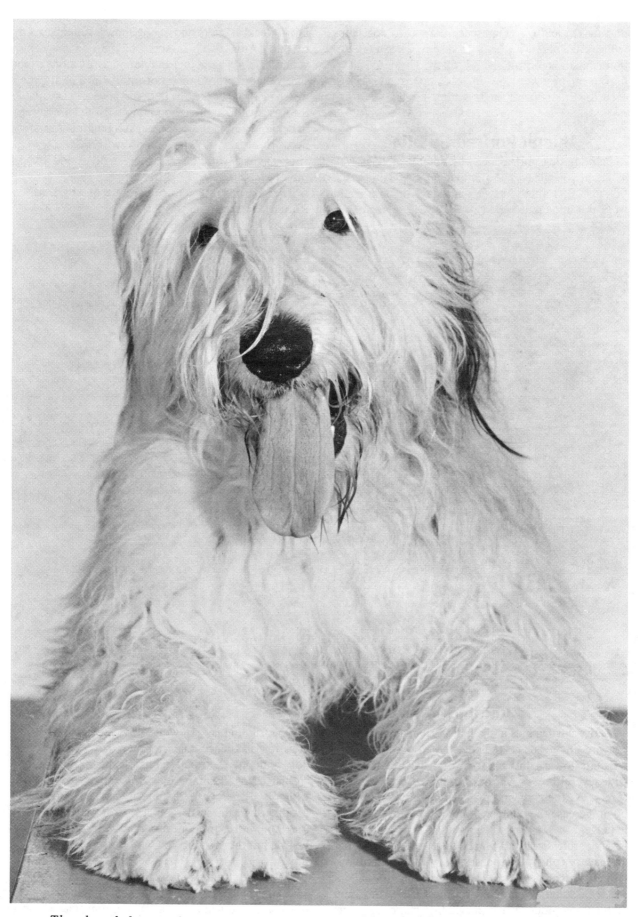

The talented photographer who is able to capture a dog with expression will build a fine reputation.

257

dog shows, and offering "special rates" to dog clubs will give the photographer a good start. Once a reputation is made, referrals should follow. However, starting out can be a very slow process, and instant success, even for the most talented, is rare.

Animal Portrait Painting

Painting dog portraits can be an enjoyable as well as lucrative endeavor. An individual possessing artistic talent and ability, as well as a love of dogs could work this into quite a good business. Displaying paintings at local art fairs and at dog shows would be a way to start. Advertising in some of the dog magazines would also aid in giving the young artist more exposure. Some artists do their portraits from a photograph which means that the dog does not have to be available for a "special" sitting. Good dog portraits are always in demand and in the dog fancy a reputation can grow by word of mouth. So if you do work of merit, keep your charges within reason and a long and happy career is assured.

The dog portraits shown here are oils by Barbara Ruisch of Barrington, Illinois.

Judging

Active participants in the dog world may eventually become involved in judging. Often handlers will gravitate toward this line of work. Their familiarity with several breeds will have prepared them for this career. As their judging proficiency grows, they will often increase the number of breeds they are licensed to judge.

The professional all-breed judge gets a good per day salary, plus all expenses. The work is arduous though; it involves a great deal of traveling throughout the year, standing on one's feet most of the day, and making decisions which inevitably make someone unhappy.

Training

Dog training is a growing field. Trainers may train dogs for obedience contests; they may take problem dogs and cure their bad habits, or they train dogs for special needs. Training may be conducted in classes with the owner participating, it may be "privately" conducted in the owner's home, or it may be in conjunction with a training program with the dog being boarded at the training kennel for a specific period of time.

Obedience training classes exist nearly everywhere. Many such classes are offered in conjunction with other adult education programs. Group classes normally have 25 to 30 dogs and owners present; they

meet once a week for about ten weeks, and the owner is generally charged a fee for this instruction.

In addition to obedience training, there are many other specialized fields. Dogs are being trained as guards, watch dogs, police dogs, army dogs, messengers, guide dogs, trackers, hunting dogs, for bench shows and for field trials. These specialized areas require a trainer who is experienced and competent. Becoming a professional requires years of apprenticeship and a great deal of dedication and hard work.

Manufacturing

There is a fantastic number of products manufactured for the use and consumption of the canine population. This is a multi-million dollar field which ranges from dog food, dog equipment, dog medicine, to dog toys. It is big business which offers well-paying jobs for people in all areas—sales, production, research, advertising, and management.

Dog Walking

Don't laugh, this is good temporary type work for an individual desiring extra income in his free time. Dog-owning apartment dwellers who work make excellent clients; in a large building, there may be more than enough dogs to keep one dog walker busy. An enterprising person might even hire others to handle other buildings and develop a thriving enterprise. In New York, for a variety of reasons, dog walking has become quite a successful business. Other metropolitan areas should also present such a business opportunity. Requirements for such an occupation: enjoyment of outdoor work in all weather conditions, a liking for dogs, reliability, and honesty. Here is a career that could be handled by a capable person of any age, teenager to senior citizen.

Typing Pedigrees

Here we have a career that makes very few demands as far as commitment to dogs. For the person who can type neatly and accurately, typing pedigrees can be a profitable sideline. Virtually all breeders present their puppies to their new owners with a nicely completed pedigree, and most breeders don't have the time to do this laborious chore themselves. By advertising in magazines such as *Dog World* or *Popular Dogs,* you may be able to start a modest endeavor.

Dog walking is a way of earning extra money. Busy city dwellers make good clients.

CONVERSATION WITH A HANDLER

WHAT services does a handler provide for the client?
Handlers provide a gamut of services to those who want to have their dogs shown by a professional. A handler may be asked to condition, train, groom, board, and show a dog. Some handlers may even help with stud service, whelping of puppies, and selling puppies. These other services are usually done as special favors. Their main job is *showing*.

Is it advantageous to have a handler?
If you want to make a top dog into a champion, the handler can be valuable in helping you attain this end.

Is it possible for an owner to show his dog well?
Yes, of course! But, an owner should realize that, to show a dog well, a dog needs to be properly groomed, trained to walk and stand, and to be in top condition. The owner who knows how to prepare and show his dog can certainly do so. However, the novice shouldn't expect to win top honors until he has acquired experience and know-how. Anyone can take a dog in the ring, but the handlers are there, not for a hobby, but to win those ribbons.

Does a handler have any "extra" advantages when in the show ring?
Frankly, yes. A good handler, with a reputation of handling only top quality dogs, has a distinct advantage. The judges get to know the handler, and they will often automatically feel that the dog being shown by this handler has merit. Thus, the handler's reputation casts favorably on the dogs he shows.

On the other hand, some handlers do not have such good reputations. It is generally known that these handlers show any dog for the handling fee. Thus, such a handler does not give your dog any special advantage.

If one wants to win, what are the tricks of the trade?
First of all, you need to have an outstanding dog, one that is as close to the breed standards as possible. Your dog should be in top condition for the show. He should be trained to walk and stand correctly. His coat should be in fine shape—well groomed, clean, and with all the necessary furnishings. Nothing should interfere with the dog's showing. Whoever is handling him should, through their dress and behavior, allow the dog to have his day—nothing should compete for the judge's attention with the dog.

Do you ever refuse to handle a dog?
Quite frequently. I will only handle a dog that I feel can be a winner and has potential. I never accept a dog that I believe cannot make an acceptable showing.

Are there any breeds that you feel are more difficult to prepare for showing than others?
Yes, the Terriers require extensive work on their coats in order to get them into show condition. Terriers that are to be shown must never be clipped. Hand stripping is the only way to get their coats into the correct condition. Most Terriers have a double coat — a hard outer coat and a soft inner coat. Stripping well in advance of a show and then regular brushing and combing will get it into shape.

People who do not show their dog often wonder why their dog looks different from those in the ring. Often this difference is due to the grooming. Terriers that are clipped will have an entirely different coat than those that are stripped.

Why is winning so important?
Many of my clients have diverse reasons for wanting to win blue ribbons. For some, it is just needing to be a winner. This type of individual will often pay great amounts of money and buy a champion. If they can afford it, this type will try to own or make many champions. Often they are not even interested in the breed. They just want winners and will buy any number of dogs of all breeds just to own champions. Here the dogs serve as ego boosters and as little else.

Other clients see winning at shows as essential, perhaps to their business interests. If they are breeding dogs, this is important. Stud fees and puppies demand a higher price if the word "champion" is there. Then, of course, there is the dog lover and hobbyist who owns a fine quality dog and wants to see it become a champion, just for pure, unselfish pleasure.

Do you think being a professional handler is a good career for a person to choose who loves dogs?
Naturally loving dogs is essential, but, more than that, you have to be willing to put in a tremendous amount of hard work. Dogs have to be prepared for the show; this involves training, grooming, and conditioning. Thus, you're on your feet all day long. Then, you have to load the dog crates in your car, drive for hours to the show and then spend the day on your feet again —grooming and showing. Loading your car back up again, more driving, motels at night, cold dinners, and this is the life of a handler on the show circuit. There is money to be made, but the hours are long and the work exhausting. Only a strong back and a strong heart can enjoy this type of routine.

CHAPTER XI
ALL ABOUT THE BREEDS

Mary Houghton

ALL ABOUT THE BREEDS

THERE are so many breeds from which to choose that to find the ideal one may seem like an overwhelming task. On the following pages you will find breed histories and traits which will be of assistance in making a selection. Each of the breeds recognized by the American Kennel Club is listed with a brief history and a description of the traits that distinguish that particular dog. For fuller information, consult your library for books about any specific breed. Before making a final decision, it is strongly recommended that you consult breeders and owners and attend local dog shows or field trials.

GROUP I: SPORTING DOGS

THERE are three basic types of sporting dogs, classified according to their use. These are the pointing breeds, the spaniel or flushing breeds, and those used primarily for retrieving and used often in the water. However, there are exceptions, such as the Brittany Spaniel that points and the Irish and American Water Spaniels which are used mainly as retrievers.

In many ways the pointing breeds have similarities. They normally weight between 50 and 85 pounds and are basically bird hunters.

WIRE-HAIRED POINTING GRIFFON

Created by E. K. Korthals of the Netherlands, the Wire-haired Pointing Griffon is an outstanding sporting dog. Korthals set out to produce a truly versatile gun dog that could work in land and water. Today, he is a strong swimmer, thus this makes him a good water retriever. Because he is quite heavy-set, he is slow, but he proves useful in areas where his harsh coat gives protection.

This breed is quite intelligent and easily trained, but it is not as popular as other pointing dogs.

POINTER

The Pointers of today descend from stocks in France, Spain, and England. Brockton's Bounce, Satter's Major, Garth's Drake and Whitehouse Hamlet are names of famous Pointers who have made this breed what it is.

The Pointer is a fine upland dog which has speed and wide range. The National Field Trial Champion Association Stake held its first running in 1896. The first nine years the Setters won. Finally, the Pointers

The Pointer.

came into their own, and now the winners are divided between these two breeds.

Pointers are known to mature and develop faster than Setters, and they are also more independent and competitive. Since they do mature early, they should be trained young; thus, either devote the time to this training or have a professional do the job. This must be attended to or a good hunter could be lost.

The Pointer is a dog that loves hunting and is really more interested in the sport than in the man. Thus, he is not overly affectionate. His short-haired coat makes grooming easy. The Pointer is primarily a gun dog and is not content to be merely a family pet.

GERMAN SHORTHAIRED POINTER

In the German Shorthaired Pointer, we find a sporting dog of amazing versatility. He is a dog that points, retrieves on land and water; he can cold trail, flush quarry from heavy cover, and he is a good family pet.

Crossing the Spanish Pointer with the Bloodhound and the Foxhound and possibly even the Greyhound

The German Wirehaired Pointer.

The German Shorthaired Pointer.

(for speed), the German Shorthair is a breeding achievement.

Today, the popularity of this breed is growing tremendously. His breeding is perfect for the hunting conditions that now exist. The German Shorthair is also perfect for the man who can own only one dog. For the hunter on foot, this is the ideal dog since it does not range far, hunts to the gun, points his game, retrieves, and has all day hunting endurance.

Training can be started when the pup is quite young, and, since he is an early developer, he can do a good job of hunting by the age of one year.

GERMAN WIREHAIRED POINTER

Still a rare dog on the hunting scene, the German Wirehaired Pointer won American Kennel Club recognition in 1959. For hunting purposes, they are quick, have good endurance, a keen nose. They are easily trained and perform well in the field. This breed

is good for upland bird hunting. They point and retrieve both on land and water.

This dog is quite affectionate and enjoys being a one man dog.

CHESAPEAKE BAY RETRIEVER

This retriever is truly an American breed from the Chesapeake Bay area. The story told is that two puppies rescued from a sinking ship became the founders of this line of rugged water retriever.

Amazing toughness, endurance, stamina, and adaptability make this a popular dog. It is probably the Chesapeake's coat, which is water and weather proof, that allows it to face the cold and wet undauntingly. Thus, this gives him an advantage over other breeds. His red-tan color matches the marshland, giving him fine cover.

Chesapeakes are known for their stubbornness. They make fine watch dogs and take good care of their "family." They are serious, quiet, and very good companions.

CURLY-COATED RETRIEVER

Surprisingly, this handsome dog is not very popular. His name is derived from the curls which adorn his body. It is believed that the Curly-Coated Retriever resulted from crosses among the St. John's Newfoundland, the Irish Water Spaniel, and the Poodle.

Thanks to his protective coat, he is able to endure cold, water, and rough terrain. The curls do get tangled with underbrush, and, thus, the coat requires constant attention.

This is an affectionate pet as well as an outstanding water retriever. He trains easily, has a gentle disposition, and a wonderful nose.

FLAT-COATED RETRIEVER

Not very popular in America, the Flat-Coated Retriever is well-known abroad as a good shooting dog and retriever. The ancestry suggests the St. John's Newfoundland, Labrador, Gordon Setter, and even the Irish Setter. The Flat-Coated Retriever made his first show appearance in Birmingham, England, in 1860. Originally, these dogs were the gamekeepers' dogs in Great Britain.

Flat-Coated Retrievers are very strong swimmers, and they are able to withstand icy water for long duration. They love their work and retrieve exceedingly well. Being rugged and stubborn, they require training of a firm yet kind nature. Their coats are thick, smooth, and fine-haired.

As a house pet, the Flat-Coated Retriever is quiet, clean, obedient, affectionate, and most devoted to the family and children. He is a fine watch dog.

GOLDEN RETRIEVER

A true retriever type of sporting dog, the Golden Retriever's job is to find and retrieve game shot down either on water or land. They are most helpful in finding wounded birds and retrieving them. The Golden's appearance is what distinguishes it from the other retrieving breeds. Their beautiful gold coat, dark brown eyes, aristocratic carriage, feathering, cleanliness, and water-proof coat make them a most desirable hunting companion and family pet.

The origins of this breed are not completely certain.

It is generally accepted that in England during the 1860's, cross breeding resulted in the Golden Retriever. They appeared in America during the early 1900's. Since their first entry, their performance in field trials has been quite fine. In 1932, the Golden Retriever was registered by the American Kennel Club under its own classification and has done well in shows ever since. Taking to obedience work easily, they are popular entries in obedience trials. The popularity of this breed has grown continually since 1932, undoubtedly because of its good looks, fine personality, and performance as a hunting companion.

As pets, they are superb—affectionate, obedient, easily trained, good with children, and most attractive. Moderate grooming will keep them sharp in appearance. As a sporting dog, a good daily walk is essential to keep them fit. They make good watch dogs too.

LABRADOR RETRIEVER

Field trial records prove that the Labrador has outstanding ability as a hunting dog. Labradors have placed first more than any other breed.

The history of this fine sporting dog is not completely clear. Coming from Newfoundland, the Labrador was known as the St. John's dog, and he was bred in England from about 1800. Today's Labrador

The Labrador Retriever.

is a strong swimmer, has astounding scenting ability, withstands cold and icy water, and is a foremost retriever on land and water. He is also a fast dog on land or water; and, he has a tender mouth.

Most dog authorities recommend the Labrador as

a good all-around hunting dog as well as an outstanding companion. They are incredibly even-tempered, good-natured, stable, intelligent, and full of real stamina. As an outstanding house pet and real friend who loves his master and children, this breed cannot be surpassed. He is easily trained and takes great pride in his work.

The Labrador is usually black but golden Labs are also popular. These golden-colored Labs should not be confused with another breed, the Golden Retriever.

ENGLISH SETTER

The English Setter is a hunting dog of great beauty and grace. Its beauty has made this breed popular at conformation shows as well as at field trials.

Considered to be America's oldest sporting dog,

The English Setter.

this attractive breed gave the pointers quite a time in the popularity race. Their hunting method is quite similar to the Pointer's. English Setters are fast, able to range widely, and can retrieve with a tender mouth. They also have a keen nose and fine sense of direction. They work well under all conditions. Possessing a long coat that helps them to cope with the lower temperatures, they are most popular in the North. In the South, they may be seen clipped in order to withstand the higher temperatures and the brush.

Although they train easily, care must be exercised that they are not forced. Their development is slower than a Pointer's. Kindness and true affection will result in a lifelong friend. They are real companions, and they make fine family pets—being loyal, a "one man dog," gentle, well-behaved, and most affectionate.

These dogs are of English ancestry. Two names are mentioned whenever their background is discussed —Edward Laverack of Shropshire, England, and R. L. Purcell Llewellin of Pembrokeshire, South Wales. These men played an outstanding role in developing

the breeds. Laverack emphasized the beauty for show standards in his breeding program, and Llewellin favored breeding for hunting ability. The Llewellin strain is still recognized today.

Since this is such an attractive and capable gun dog, it is not surprising that he is one of America's most popular sporting dogs.

GORDON SETTERS

Although the Gordon is not seen to any great extent, he is an ideal dog for the man who owns only one dog and wants to enjoy a full day of shooting. Here we have a dog that has been bred primarily for hunting rather than for show. This is a hardy breed that can be trained for any kind of upland game. Enjoying water, he is a good waterfowl retriever.

Due to incorrect breeding, shyness developed, and the Gordons did not function well when kept in a kennel. These problems resulted in a decline in interest in the breed. Serious attempts were made to correct these faults. As a result, we are now finding dogs that are well-built, active, strong, aristocratic in appearance, intelligent, and with no signs of shyness.

Desiring companionship, the Gordons still do not enjoy being kenneled. They develop late both physically and emotionally. Training should not be started too early. Since they are natural hunters, very little training is actually required.

The Gordon Setter.

The Gordon hails from Scotland where, as early as the 1600's, they established themselves as grouse hunters. Brought to America in 1842 by George Blunt, one was given to Daniel Webster and another to Henry Clay.

Devotion to master, family, and children make him a good dog to have around the house. He is a fine watch dog; he needs a moderate amount of grooming to keep his soft and silky coat looking well.

The Irish Setter.

IRISH SETTER

Because of this dog's beauty, he has lost ground as a sporting dog and gained ground as a show dog and pet. Only a few are seen competing in field trials today. However, when bred from hunting stock and properly trained, they make excellent shooting companions. For the hunter desiring only one dog, the Irish Setter is ideal since he can point quail, grouse, woodcock, or pheasant.

Today's Irish Setter is a descendant of Elcho, who was imported from Ireland in 1875. At first, the primary use of this breed was for hunting and field trials. However, once he became popular as a show dog, the "hunting qualities" began to suffer.

The Irish hunts and works in a manner quite like the English Setter—with average speed, medium range, excellent nose, and staunchness on point.

Irish Setters are sensitive dogs, and, if not handled correctly, they can become quite headstrong. Kindness and patience are essential elements in their training, and they should not be forced or punished harshly.

Most Irish Setters can be recommended as house pets since they are affectionate, jolly, intelligent, and most lovable. Caution should be exercised when purchasing an Irish Setter because their breeding for beauty has resulted in too many animals that are prone to illness, neurosis, and depression. They require only a daily walk, but they do need regular grooming.

AMERICAN WATER SPANIEL

The American Water Spaniel was recognized by the American Kennel Club in 1940; however, he was known long before that as a fine sporting dog. First appearing in the Midwest, the American Water Spaniel served well as an all-around "meat hunter."

He hunted duck, grouse, chickens, squirrels, or rabbits.

Due to his tightly-curled, waterproof coat, he is able to endure the iciest water and the coldest temperature. Keen scent and high intelligence have provided him with spectacular adaptability. Sturdiness, compact size, and courage have prepared him to play his role well.

The exact origins of this breed are unclear. It seems that crosses here in the Midwest in the Fox and Wolf River areas among the English and Irish Water Spaniel and the Curly-Coated Retriever finally resulted in the American Water Spaniel.

Admirers of the breed feel that the American Water Spaniel is an outstanding swimmer, has abundant endurance, and that he is most responsive to commands.

Thanks to his sharp intelligence, the American Water Spaniel trains easily. Early training is recommended. Although a natural retriever, he should learn retrieving by the force method in order to develop control.

The American Water Spaniel's lack of popularity today is due to the fact that he is not very attractive and has never been a show dog. He's a good choice for the hunter who isn't concerned about competition with larger or faster breeds.

BRITTANY SPANIEL

The only Spaniel that points its game is the Brittany. The Brittany is a Spaniel in size and in temperament, and it shares the Spaniel's natural ability to retrieve.

Hailing from France where they were raised for centuries, the Brittany may have originally appeared in Spain. The real development of the breed took place in Britain. After they were imported into America, they were used as a "dual" dog—in other words, as a "bench" type and "field" type. Breeders are

The Brittany Spaniel.

striving to have dogs that can win at both types of shows.

In the field, the Brittany can be compared to the Setter; however, it does not range quite as far. An experienced dog will range depending on the cover—wide in open cover and restricted in deep cover. Since the Brittany has a well-protected body and no tail to injure, he prefers deep cover once he has learned that birds are likely to be found in such spots.

The Brittany thrives in cold weather, and some of the breed have difficulty in very hot weather. The largest number of Brittanies are used to hunt pheasant, but they can hunt all types of game birds. Since they do well in water, they can also retrieve ducks. The Brittany has been criticized for not having a "classy" point since it does not have a tail to set him off. Also, the Brittany points with a lower head than the larger pointing breeds. Otherwise, there is little difference; they point their game at about the same distance, and they are just as staunch and intense.

The Brittany, as stated, has only a stub of a tail, and he has a dense white coat with orange or liver markings. His hair is not as silky as that of other Spaniels and his loose skin prevents injury from thorns and underbrush.

Being quite sensitive is another important characteristic of this breed. The average Brittany is not timid, but he does have to be handled more gently than the average Pointer or Setter. He responds best to kindness rather than rough orders, and, therefore, he trains easily. Simple yard training can be started at six months, but most handlers don't try to break them to steady to shot and wing until they are two years old.

Because of his size, he makes a good pet as well as a good hunting companion. Moderate grooming and exercise will keep the Brittany fit.

CLUMBER SPANIEL

The origin of the Clumber is open to speculation since he is heavier and slower than many of the Spaniels. Conjecture is that the breed is a result of crosses with Basset Hounds and possibly St. Bernards. The name is derived from Clumber Park, the estate of the Duke of Newcastle in England. In any case, the Clumber Spaniel has never become popular in America, mainly because its heaviness and slow movement have not endeared it to hunters. This breed enjoyed much more attention in England on estates with an abundance of game. Their speed was not important, and they could flush game and retrieve quite leisurely.

In appearance, the Clumber is a real beauty—coloring is basically white with occasional lemon spot or splotches. They are large dogs with large heads and silky, dense coats. They weigh up to 65 pounds.

The Clumber is an old breed and has been registered here since 1883. As a quiet, sedate, attractive pet, the Clumber may be just the thing. They are most dignified, well-tempered, and easily trained. They *do* need regular grooming of their straight silky coat, but they require only moderate exercise.

COCKER SPANIEL

Of such great popularity in America, the American Cocker Spaniel led the dog registrations in this country for 17 years. Because of its beauty and sparkling personality, the Cocker gained as a family pet and show dog rather than continuing as primarily a hunting dog. Since so few are used for hunting, it is difficult to purchase one with a "hunting heritage." Breeding today has been more concerned with "show," thus, the Cocker is now a compact, richer coated dog than most hunters desire. Their large eyes are vulnerable when hunting in heavy underbrush, and their coats are quite a chore to keep up for the typical sportsmen.

Out in the field, the Cocker stays close within gun range, quartering the ground well. The Cocker works by scent, and, when he nears his prey, his tail moves gaily and his pace and drive become cautious. When scenting game, he flushes the bird or rabbit and, then, drops (sit or lay) until the shot is fired. Then, the Cocker can follow hand and whistle signals to retrieve.

The American Cocker Spaniel has a rounded skull, short legs, and a body which is short with a broad chest. This breed is divided into three varieties, based mainly on their color differences. The divisions are black, any other solid color (including black and tan), and parti-colors.

Although the Cocker has so many appealing features—a beautiful coat which is soft and silky, lovable

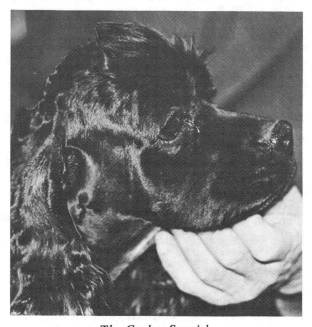

The Cocker Spaniel.

expressive eyes, and intelligence and affection—great caution should be exercised in purchasing a puppy. Their popularity resulted in over-breeding, and many Cockers seen today are neurotic, have eye and ear troubles, feet and skin problems, are shy, nervous, and snappy. This snappy tendency makes him a difficult pet to have if there are children in the family. They require only moderate exercise, but, they do need regular combing and brushing.

ENGLISH COCKER SPANIEL

First recognized by the American Kennel Club in 1946, the English Cocker Spaniel has already won fame in field trials as a truly hard-working sporting dog. This was Elizabeth Barrett Browning's dear "Flush" about whom she wrote so lovingly.

Very similar in appearance to the American Cocker Spaniel, the English Cocker has longer legs and a longer muzzle. They are described as being unusually merry animals that display their gaiety and cheerfulness continually. Devotion, intelligence, affection, and sensitivity are more of their attributes. In the field, they are quick and sturdy with fine endurance. As pets, they are lovable, devoted, loyal, and a pleasure to be with. Regular grooming is necessary to keep up their beautiful coat. Ear care is important to prevent infection.

ENGLISH SPRINGER SPANIEL

Another outstanding candidate for the all-around shooting dog is the English Springer Spaniel. These dogs will pursue their prey, quartering the ground thoroughly and flushing out the game—both furred and feathered. Unlike the pointing breeds, the Spaniel (except for the Brittany) *does not point*. The Springer is the top pheasant dog of all the hunting breeds. It is the most popular since its size and strength give it more speed and endurance than the other Spaniel breeds. Retrieving is one of the outstanding feats performed by the Springers. Thanks to their webbed toes, they are able to handle all types of water, and their thick coat allows them to endure the coldest weather.

Originating in Spain early in the 13th century, they were later spread through Europe and Britain; they were used by sportsmen as hunting dogs. Although brought to America in the 1600's, they were not approved by the American Kennel Club until 1924.

This breed is quite unusual in its fondness for children and its affection for all. Since they mature late, they are quite playful and childish for a longer period. They are sensitive and require an immense amount of love and affection. A Springer owner has described them as "love sponges"—they need to sop it up. Moderate grooming and exercise are required to maintain health and appearance. Because of their long ears, they are prone to ear infections. Some Springers

The English Springer Spaniel.

have "nervous stomachs" and are prone to colitis. Care in purchasing from healthy breeding stock is recommended.

FIELD SPANIEL

Fashion caused the development of this heavy-boned, long dog. Breeders finally became aware of the unfortunate results of their endeavors, and today the Field Spaniel is better proportioned and more appropriate as a sporting dog. However, Field Spaniels

The Field Spaniel.

have rarely been seen at dog shows until very recently. Importation of stock from England has helped to revive this breed.

The Field Spaniel is quite similar to the Cocker except that he is taller and larger. Usually black, he is agile, speedy, and easily trained. He also possesses endurance, perseverance, and intelligence.

IRISH WATER SPANIEL

Reputed to be a hard worker that could withstand icy water and retrieve in heavy cover, the Irish Water Spaniel was imported from Ireland to this country as a water retriever. The dog has been used in the Middle West since the 1870's for duck hunting. This Spaniel is a very old breed that hailed from the Iberian Peninsula prior to its appearance in Ireland. They were among the first retrievers to be registered by the American Kennel Club.

Justin McCarthy, a sportsman of Dublin, Ireland, was the earliest known breeder and exhibitor of the Irish Water Spaniels. His dog, Boatswain, is the forefather of today's dogs of this breed.

The Irish Water Spaniel is used today mainly to retrieve waterfowl. However, they are quite able to retrieve upland game. Their noses are excellent, and they will track a cripple until found. They work well in rough water, heavy cover, and even in mud. Usually, it is best to trim their coats to avoid picking up burrs and to prevent their fur from icing up in cold weather. Being powerful swimmers, they have amazing endurance.

In appearance, he is often called the "clown of the Spaniel family." His fur is densely curled with a characteristic top knot. He is the tallest of the Spaniels, with liver coloring and a well-developed and strong head.

The Irish Water Spaniel matures very slowly and does not truly become adult until the age of two. Training should not be started until they are at least six months of age. They do love water, and they can begin swimming at three months. Most authorities feel that they train easily with firmness and patience, but that force retrieving must be taught for control.

This Spaniel is a loyal, peaceful, light-hearted dog that will fit in well as a pet. Keeping them well-groomed prevents shedding in the house. They are very good with children, but they are quiet and do not make good watch dogs. Since they are happiest when swimming, running, and retrieving, they should not be kept confined without an opportunity to indulge in their specialty.

SUSSEX SPANIEL

Being a "slow poke" has limited the popularity of this golden, liver-colored dog. Stockiness and massiveness make hunting difficult for him, but his kind disposition makes him a lovable pet.

Developed in England, the Sussex worked the ground carefully and stayed close to the gun. The dog was one of the first breeds to be recognized by the American Kennel Club.

An unusual trait of this breed is that they "give tongue," or speak when on the scent of game. This bark informs the hunter where the action is, but most judges consider the bark a serious fault.

WELSH SPRINGER SPANIEL

Closely resembling his Spaniel relatives, the Welsh is larger than the Cocker but smaller than the Springer. In coloring, he is red and white only. Today, he is not as popular nor as well-known as his "cousins."

In the Welsh Springer Spaniel, we find a hunting dog of excellent qualities—a keen nose, impervious to weather, outstanding endurance, a retriever on land and water, and, when properly trained, a joy of a hunting companion.

Perhaps his limited popularity is due to an independent nature which makes training somewhat difficult. However, Welsh Springers make fine pets since they have an even disposition, a compact size, a way with children. They also make fine watch dogs.

VIZSLA

First admitted to the American Kennel Club registry in 1960, the Vizsla is an old European breed. Primitive stone etchings show a Hungarian dog strongly similar to today's Vizsla. The Hungarian terrain was the site of this hunting dog's escapades as a fine pointer. Against great odds and difficult circumstances, this breed has survived wars and occupations. Fanciers of the breed have persevered, and, today, the Vizsla has a growing following of admirers. He is an attractive, stately, efficient, rusty and gold colored sporting dog. A smooth coat makes grooming easy. Like most hunting dogs, the Vizsla loves to run and needs room.

WEIMARANER

A new addition to the sporting dogs in this country was made when the first Weimaraners were brought here from Germany in 1929. Sponsored in Germany by nobility in Weimar, their breeding was most carefully controlled, as well as their sales. The number of Weimaraners has been limited to 1500 in Germany.

Originally, Weimaraners were selectively bred in order to combine the attributes of an all around hunting dog—pointing, retrieving, trailing, and working in all kinds of terrain and weather.

When considering the Weimaraner as a family dog, remember that this is a large dog that enjoys room to run. Its smooth coat makes grooming easy. He makes a good companion, is loyal, and can be used as a watch dog. Training is accomplished easily, and the Weimaraner is exceedingly obedient.

GROUP II: HOUNDS

THIS group consists of two very different types of hounds—the scent followers and the sight hunter.

The Beagle is the best known scent follower tracking dog and is the most popular hound in America. The Harriers, Foxhounds, Dachshunds, Bassets, and Bloodhounds are also of the scent following group.

The Greyhounds, Wolfhounds, and Whippets are in the sight-hunter group. Constructed in a streamlined design, these dogs run in huge leaps, driving their hind legs ahead of their front ones.

Afghans and Borzois have dense coats, and the Borzoi and Irish Wolfhound are among the tallest of the dog breeds.

AFGHAN HOUND

The Afghan Hound originated in the area of Afghanistan and what was Ancient Egypt, probably between 3,000 and 4,000 B.C. The name means "baboon" or "monkey-faced hound." These hounds were kept by the aristocracy and were used as royal gifts. It is felt that this breed would not have survived had it not been protected and maintained by royalty and the wealthy. Coming from a locale that has extremely cold Winters and boiling Summers, the Afghan Hound has developed great adaptability. They were used to guard flocks and to hunt deer and other animals.

Their body is built to maneuver on hilly, uneven terrain; they make excellent hurdle racers. Afghans are beautiful, elegant, proud dogs who carry themselves with regal bearing. They are one-man dogs and are very reserved with strangers. They do not require any clipping, but they do need regular grooming. Afghans need regular exercise to stay in top physical condition.

BASENJI

Although much of the history of the Basenji is unknown, he is one of the oldest breeds of dogs still in existence known to mankind. Professor Thomas Noack reported in his writings for the Zoological Society about Central African dogs . . . . "That the gen-

The Afghan Hound.

The Basenji.

eral form of these dogs is the same as those of old Egypt, that is, a small dog with upright ears and a ringer tail. The color is yellow, reddish-yellow and white, black and white, or brown. The skulls are highly interesting, especially the profile, in proportion and dimension so similar to that of the Canus Palustris that they may be taken for living fossils."

The Basenji's earliest record of existences goes back to 3600 B.C. where, from Egyptian engravings, it was learned that a Basenji type was the favorite companion and hunting dog of the IV Dynasty Egyptians. It was not until engravings from 2300 B.C. were found that it was conclusive that this type of dog was a Basenji. Many of the engravings found showed exact markings and colors of Basenjis.

From these engravings it was determined that the Basenji came from the Upper Nile region. As tribute, Basenjis were given to the Pharoahs, high ranking nobility, and priests of early Egypt, along with gems and objects of art from the primitive natives that lived in that era. A photo of an engraving in the Journal of Egyptian Archaeology shows a raft with a pair of beautiful red and white Basenjis standing on the deck. They have gold collars encrusted with gems and stones on golden leashes, held by a native who is covered with animal skins and brilliant colored bird plumes.

The Basenji was held in such high esteem that they took part in religious and other elaborate ceremonies. If one was killed in the field or died, the entire household would shave their heads in mourning of a lost friend. They were also embalmed and buried in the family tomb.

It is also inferred by the Bible in Exodus 11:7, approximately 1491 B.C., that the reason the Basenji doesn't bark was in accordance with God's prophesy concerning the first born of the Egyptians when Moses was trying to release the Jews from bondage, "But against any of the children of Israel shall not a dog move his tongue against man or beast."

With the fall of the Egyptian Dynasty the Basenji faded into complete obscurity until 1861 A.D. when explorers of the Dark Continent mentioned dogs described as Congo Terriers, Bongo, Nyam-Nyam, and Zande dogs. In 1868, Dr. Schweinforth described the poultry and dogs of the Central African natives of Nyam-Nyam, which is located south of Sudan. Several other explorers of this time also wrote about a barkless dog describing the Basenji in great detail.

From 1895 attempts were made to bring the Basenji into Europe but, due to killing distemper, it was not until 1937 that he was successfully brought to England and there able to survive and reproduce. Basenjis were brought into the United States in 1937, but ill fortune and distemper seemed to plague them and it was not until 1940 that they got a real start. With the present day perfected vaccines the Basenjis, as other breeds, have been able to survive the onslaught

of the dreaded diseases of hepatitis, distemper, and leptospirosis.

The Basenji is a very versatile creature, being able to adapt himself to almost any climate and is now raised in all corners of the globe.

Their exceptional cleanliness, ease of house-training, and total lack of doggy smell makes them hard to beat as house pets. They have a beautiful short, satiny coat which requires little attention.

Although known as the "barkless breed," the Basenji is definitely not mute and does possess vocal cords, uttering all sounds common to other breeds with the exception of the usual bark. They make excellent watch dogs, warning their owners of approaching newcomers or danger by deep growling or shrill whining. Some are known to utter a one-syllable woofy bark, but this only when greatly disturbed. Their own particular noise is best described as a mixture between a chortle and a yodel, and is not unlike a young cockerel's first attempts at crowing, having a "Brr-r-r-r-r" sound. Basenjis use this unique gift as a form of speech, and as one owner puts it, "They do not bark, they talk," using different intonations to express different reactions. Otherwise they are quiet, preferring to listen and observe, and what a blessing this is today in our noisy suburbs and cities.

The Basset Hound.

BASSET HOUND

The Basset Hound was another dog considered to be of ancient breeding and was developed originally in France and Belgium. They were used for slow trailing of game, such as deer, rabbits, raccoon, and to find wounded birds. Except for the Bloodhound, they have the best scenting ability. The sound of their voice is another Basset characteristic.

The Basset is a one-man dog who will be a good hunting companion and a fine family pet. Affectionate and fairly easy to train, the Basset can be a fine addition to the family. They are awkward and rather docile, but their sad expression endears them to many. They are easy to groom and require a moderate amount of exercise. Since they are lethargic, it is important that they are not allowed to get fat.

BEAGLE

An ancient hunting dog, the Beagle's origin is somewhat unclear. It is known that they were used on fox hunts, usually in packs, and they were noted for their tracking ability. The Beagle's voice has been compared to a bugle or a wail. Today, they are very popular in field trials as well as family pets.

The Beagle's popularity in the United States has been phenomenal. They were the most popular dog in 1953. This tremendous popularity is due to the fact that they adjust well to virtually any type of living accomodation. They are lovable and playful with grown-ups and children; they are clean and neat, and they do not bark excessively indoors. Their smooth coat is easy to groom.

BLOODHOUND

The Bloodhound is considered to be perhaps the most ancient of the scent-type hounds. Carefully bred through the ages, they were maintained even by the dignitaries of the church for riding to the hounds.

Although bred in England for centuries, it is the United States that has developed their usefulness. Here, they have been used for tracking both lost persons and criminals. They have been credited with locating hundreds of escaped convicts, pursuing criminals, and they have exhibited amazing determination, endurance, and perseverance.

BORZOI

Called by its common name—Russian Wolfhound —until 1936, the Borzoi has been used since the 17th Century to hunt wolves and other game in his native Russia. Although the exact origin of this breed is not certain, it is believed that the Borzoi descended from various crosses, including the Greyhound.

Borzois were first brought to the United States around 1889. However, because of the many crossings which had occurred, breeding beautiful, true, well-proportioned Borzois has often been difficult. Very few kennels have produced properly conformed Borzois.

Borzois should be given an opportunity to exercise extensively and should not be raised in confinement. Good grooming is essential.

BLACK AND TAN COONHOUND

Believed to be a descendant of the extinct English Talbot Hound, Bloodhound, and Foxhound, the Black and Tan Coonhound is still relatively new on the scene. They are favorites here in the United States for hunting coon and possum, particularly at night. Black and Tans hunt by scent and keep their noses close to the ground. They acclimate well to any weather and terrain.

DACHSHUND

Used as a hunter of badger for centuries, the Dachshund now comes in three coat varieties—smooth, wire, and long-haired—and standard and miniature sizes. At first, German breeders kept stud books, recording only those dogs of known hunting ability. In time, coat identification was also included.

The Dachshund was registered in the American

The Long Haired Dachshund.

Kennel Club in 1885, however, it is certain that the breed came to our shores long before that.

Although used primarily as a pet today, many Dachshunds participate in field trials here and in Europe hunting rabbit. As house pets, they are noted for the cleanliness of their habits, their loving, cheerful, and loyal disposition, and the ease of grooming. They should not be allowed to get too fat; daily exercise and a well-balanced diet should control this.

SCOTTISH DEERHOUND

Described by some as being a rough-coated Greyhound, the Scottish Deerhound was identified as early as the 16th Century. Their size made them perfect for hunting deer. Always having great worth, the Scottish Deerhound could be owned only by Knights and Earls during the Middle Ages. A nobleman could obtain freedom from a death sentence by offering a leash of these large dogs.

Today, in the United States, it is illegal to hunt antlered game with dogs, so the Scottish Deerhound is used to hunt other game. They make fine pets, companions, and watchdogs. Their personalities make them ideal one-man dogs. They train easily, are dependable, loyal, and devoted. Because of their size, they are happiest when not too closely confined.

FOXHOUND, AMERICAN

The Spanish explorer, Hernando De Soto, brought the first hounds to this country, and they were used to hunt Indians rather than foxes. Later, in the mid 1600's, Robert Brooke brought a pack of hounds to this country which became the foundation of the present breed.

The American Kennel Club identifies four different types of hunting activity, each one requiring hounds possessing special characteristics.

1. Field trial hound—speed and jealous nature important.

2. Fox hunting with a gun—slow trailer with good voice needed.

3. "Trail" or "Drag" hounds—speed alone counts.

4. Hunting in packs—accustomed to other dogs.

Fox hunting has increased tremendously in popularity, and the American Foxhound's popularity is bound to increase along with this sport.

FOXHOUND, ENGLISH

The English Foxhound was used in England for fox hunting, in which upper class Englishmen indulged. They were imported to the United States in 1738, and they have been used in this country for the same purpose.

The English Foxhound differs from the American version mainly in that it is a somewhat stouter dog.

The Greyhound.

GREYHOUND

Carvings in the Tomb of Amten in the Valley of the Nile depict the Greyhound. This would indicate that the Greyhound breed has been in existence since 2900 B.C.

Ownership of these dogs was restricted to Egyptian royalty; the Pharaohs owned large kennels of them for the royal sports of racing and hunting.

Greyhound coursing became a sport in Britain in 1576. Dog racing with a mechanical rabbit has grown in popularity in this country since 1920.

HARRIER

In appearance, the Harrier gives the impression of being a small version of the English Foxhound. Records suggest that Harriers were brought to England by the Normans and were used to hunt hares there. They have been used to hunt since colonial times in the United States.

IRISH WOLFHOUND

The Irish Wolfhound is believed to be the tallest dog. This breed is an ancient one known since Roman days. Originally, they were used to hunt wolves and elk; today, they still are used in the West to hunt wolves and coyotes. Because of its size and strength, the Irish Wolfhound makes a fine guard dog.

273

Their huge size, however, does limit their popularity as a pet. It is recommended that only those persons having spacious accommodations consider adopting this breed of dog. The Irish Wolfhound is very loyal, gentle, affectionate, and even-tempered.

NORWEIGIAN ELKHOUND

A companion to the Vikings, the Norwegian Elkhound is a noble and ancient breed. Developed to hunt in the Norwegian countryside, we find here a dog that is strong, fast, compact, and possessing fine scenting power and real beauty.

The hunting versatility of this breed is shown by their ability to hunt mountain lion, raccoon, fox, lynx, as well as elk.

They are still not very well known in this country, but more and more people are hearing about this breed's intelligence, dependability, and fearlessness. For those in need of such a hunting dog, the Norwegian Elkhound is one to consider.

OTTERHOUND

The Otterhound is very rare in the United States. Its ancestry is quite vague, and it is thought that the Harrier, Bloodhound, Water Spaniel, Airedale, and Bulldog may all have been involved in the formation of this breed.

They are outstanding swimmers. They have an oily undercoat to protect them; they also have webbed feet.

Most Otterhounds seen in this country have been imported—not to hunt—but as something "different."

RHODESIAN RIDGEBACK

The Rhodesian Ridgeback is characterized by a ridge of dorsal hair which grows from hip to shoulder in a direction opposite that of the rest of his short, glossy coat. This breed is a native of South Africa where it is known as the African Lion Hound. Their origin can be traced back to the Dutch, Germans, and Huguenots, who emigrated to South Africa during the 16th and 17th Centuries and brought their dogs with them. These dogs were subsequently bred with the native dogs owned by the Hottentots. The resulting sturdy, vigorous dog which could hunt big game, tolerate the African Bush, withstand the daily drastic temperature changes, and protect his master and family was the Rhodesian Ridgeback. In 1955, they were the 112th breed to receive recognition by the American Kennel Club.

Although they are used occasionally in this country for hunting, they are mostly kept as pets. They train easily, are good with children, adapt well to all surroundings and climates, and are loyal to their master and family.

SALUKI

The Saluki is undoubtedly the oldest pure bred domesticated dog in the world. The primitive carvings

The Saluki.

of ancient man show hounds which resemble the Saluki. The Moslems called the dog "the noble one" and believed it to be a gift from Allah. They were never sold but only given as gifts. The Crusaders brought some of these dogs back to Europe with them; yet, they were relatively unknown in Europe until the end of the 19th Century, and, in 1927, the American Kennel Club added them to their list.

The Saluki is cherished for his beauty, elegance, grace, gentleness, and speed. He is loyal, affectionate, and serves well as a watchdog.

WHIPPET

Only between 75 and 100 years of age, the Whippet is a young breed. It is an "English Greyhound in miniature" and exceptionally fast. Originally they were used for rabbit coursing in an enclosure. Their name is believed to come from "snap-dog" as the sport was called "snap dog coursing" (the dog that snapped up the most rabbits during a race was the winner). English miners called him the "poor man's race horse." His speed is up to 35 miles per hour. The Whippet is gaining in popularity as a house pet because of his slender beauty, elegance, quiet and gentle nature, and small size.

The Whippet.

GROUP III: WORKING DOGS

THESE dogs were bred to work at such duties as pulling milk carts, doing police work, carrying messages, or guarding animals or property.

ALASKAN MALAMUTE

An ancient breed from the Arctic, the Alaskan Malamute's origins are obscure just as those of the people of that area. The Malamute is considered the native dog of Alaska, and he has been used as a working dog—pulling sleds and carrying heavy loads.

In recent times Byrd's Antarctic expeditions used Malamutes for hauling, and they did exceedingly well. Sled-dog racing has become a popular sport, and, naturally, the Alaskan Malamute holds many racing records.

The Alaskan Malamute is being shown at dog shows here in the United States, and they are quite popular in areas where they can be enjoyed with Winter sports. They make large pets; they are good with children; and, they take most to cold climates.

BELGIAN MALINOIS

This breed is one of the three types of Belgian sheepherding dogs. The Malinois' coat and color are the only differences from the Belgian Sheepdog and the Belgian Tervuren. The coat of the Malinois is short, and its color is rich fawn to mahogany with black overlay. The dog was first registered as a separate breed for show classification by the American Kennel Club in 1965. The Malinois, named for the town of Malines in Belgium, is sometimes mistaken for the German Shepherd.

BELGIAN SHEEPDOG

Serving in Belgium as sheep herding dogs, the Belgian Sheepdog (Groenendael) came into prominence during World War I. In the war, they served heroically on the battlefield—finding the wounded and delivering messages. Today, they are used extensively in police work and are shown regularly at obedience trials.

Groenendaels make fine watch dogs, are good workers, and are devoted companions. Being a large dog, they do best when allowed room in which to romp.

BELGIAN TERVUREN

Differing from the Belgian Sheepdog only in color, the Belgian Tervuren has a common origin. Being light fawn at birth, it matures into a rich mahogany color overlaid with black whereas the Groenendael is always solid black. Having originally been bred for working as a herding animal, the Belgian Tervuren is excellent in obedience work. It has been registered as a separate breed since 1959.

BERNESE MOUNTAIN DOG

One of the four varieties of Swiss Mountain Dogs, the Bernese is a long-haired dog of large size. These dogs were brought to Switzerland by the Roman invaders 2,000 years ago. At that time, they were used as draught dogs, pulling wagons to and from the market.

The Bernese is a handsome, hardy dog which can live outside in an unheated kennel. He requires a minimum amount of grooming, and he is most faithful and loyal.

DIFFERENCES BETWEEN THE ALASKAN MALAMUTE AND THE SIBERIAN HUSKY

Often mistaken for each other, they are similar in appearance, but there are distinct differences between the two breeds.

1. **Size**—The Alaskan Malamute is by far the larger. They are designed for hauling cargo over rough terrain. Males—25 inches at the shoulders—85 pounds. Females—23 inches at the shoulders—75 pounds. The Siberian Husky is smaller. Males—21 to 23½ inches at the shoulders—45 to 60 pounds. Females—20 to 22 inches at the shoulders—35 to 50 pounds.

2. **Head**—The Malamute's skull is broad, and the spacing between the ears is wide. The Siberian Husky skull is medium, and the spacing between the ears is narrow.

3. **Eye Color**—Malamute must have brown, almond-shaped eyes. Husky's eyes may be either brown or blue, with one eye brown and one blue.

4. **Coat**—Malamute—should have a coarse coat. Husky—a soft coat is desirable.

The Bouvier des Flandres.

The Briard.

BOUVIER DES FLANDRES

The background of this ancient breed is that of a working dog used in Belgium to drive cattle. They were used during World War I as army dogs, and the breed was nearly lost because of the extensive damage to the area of its origin. Fortunately, a few were saved, and, because of careful breeding, the Bouvier des Flandres is popular today—both as a show dog and as a police, army, defense, or obedience trial dog.

In appearance, we find a bushy-faced dog with a hard, wavy coat which is truly water-proof. Their color possibilities range from fawn to black, gray, salt and pepper, and brindle. Remember, this is a working dog, and he is happiest with responsibility.

BOXER

Known in Europe since the 16th century, the Boxer was "modernized" in Germany during the last 100 years. One can see Bulldog-type features in today's Boxer, and it is also suggested that there have been terriers in their bloodlines as well. Some authorities have found evidence that the Boxer originated from Tibetian fighting dogs. They were used in Germany for dog fighting and bull-baiting until these sports were outlawed. Perhaps that is how they acquired their name.

During World War I, the Boxer was used in the German Army as an army dog, and he was subsequently used for police work.

The Boxer has gained popularity in this country because of his intelligence, strength, affection, loyalty, protectiveness toward family, and elegance.

Easy to groom, good with children, requiring a good daily walk—the Boxer makes a fine pet for those desiring a larger dog.

BRIARD

Used originally in the French countryside to herd, guide flocks, and guard property, this is a most an-

cient breed. Today they are still the sheep dogs of France.

Briards were used during World War I by the French army, and they distinguished themselves by finding wounded soldiers, hauling war material, and serving on guard duty. Their big feet, water-proof coat, endurance, and desire to please make them adept for many types of work.

Briards are serious, quiet (only barking when necessary), and easy to raise and train. This is a large dog and he should not be confined in close quarters. The Briard adjusts well to all temperatures. It can live comfortably outdoors in the coldest weather but also in warmer Southern climates. Because the Briard does not shed, it is a clean dog to have around the house. Combing once a day keeps it neat. Requiring no clipping or bathing, it is an easily maintained dog.

In temperament, the Briard is rather serious. He has a frightening bark, makes a good watch dog, and loves to romp and play with children.

BULLMASTIFF

Known as the "Gamekeeper's Night Dog," this breed was the result of a cross between the Bulldog and the Mastiff in order to obtain a top notch guard dog that could protect large English estates from poachers. This cross produced the perfect dog for the job—dark brindle in color, strong enough to knock a man down, fearless, with enough self-control not to maul the victim, and trainable. The Bullmastiff is growing in popularity in this country as more people are seeking powerful guard dogs. Their short coats are easy to maintain, and they are comfortable in cold or warm weather. They have been recognized by the American Kennel Club since 1933.

COLLIE

Known to Americans of all ages as that incredible "Lassie," the star of movies and television, the Collie is still the shepherd worker in Scotland, England, and Wales. Two varieties of this breed exist—the rough-coated and the smooth-coated. Since sheepherding is an old occupation, it seems reasonable to speculate that the Collie has been man's helper for several centuries. Official records show the Collie first entered the Birmingham Dog Show in 1860. Today's Collie is the product of selective breeding, and he is more beautiful than the Collie of former days. They were registered by the American Kennel Club in 1885, and they have been popular ever since. It is believed that the first Collies were brought to our shores as working dogs in colonial days.

The Collie is beautiful, gentle, most affectionate, strong, speedy, easily trained, loyal and a good watch dog. He requires a great deal of exercise and the rough-coated Collie requires extensive daily brushing. The smooth-coated Collie is much easier to groom. Probably due to its popularity and the desire to keep perfecting the breed, problems did develop. Too many beautiful specimens with deafness, blindness, or lack of intelligence were appearing. Careless breeding practices were the cause. Today, there is a growing realization that narrowing the head is not producing as bright a dog as the Collie should be. Before buying a Collie, check to be sure that there is no blindness or deafness in the parents. Select a dog not purely on appearance but one that is tops in temperament as well.

DOBERMAN PINSCHER

Aristocratic in appearance, the "Dobe" is a foremost guard dog. Today, the breed is used by factories, stores, estates, and the armed service to protect territory and property. Surprisingly, the Doberman Pinscher is a fairly new breed, developed in Germany during the 1870's by Louis Doberman. It was his desire to breed a dog that was lithe, alert, fearless, and extremely powerful. The Doberman Pinscher proves that he succeeded!

The "Dobe" is a clean-cut, compact dog that belies his weight and strength. The adult male weighs between 65 and 70 pounds, but he does not appear to be that heavy. He is amazingly muscular and has tremendous power.

For those desiring a watch dog or guard dog, the Doberman qualifies well. Being alert, agile, highly trainable, and speedy, he has proven himself capable through police work, army work, and as a guide dog for the blind. He is known to be devoted and affectionate to his owner and family.

GERMAN SHEPHERD

Bred and developed as a working dog, the German Shepherd has received tremendous popularity due to its phenomenal success as a war dog, guard dog, and guide to the blind. Originally a herding and farm dog in Germany, the Shepherd spread all over the world after World War I.

Undoubtedly, it is the Shepherd's character which has resulted in its popularity. They are distinguished for their loyalty, courage, ability to be trained for special services, lifetime friendship, and protection. They have predominated as aids to the blind.

Being able to endure all climates, they live successfully all over the world. A good brushing will keep their double coat looking neat and clean. They do love to run, and they need daily exercise. Some authorities suggest that they need some work or else they may tend to stray. German Shepherds seem to be particularly susceptible to chronic diarrhea. Researchers are now trying to determine the cause of this affliction. Hip dysplasia has appeared in this breed and the potential purchaser should make sure that his dog has been certified by the Orthopedic Foundation Association.

This is a tough, noble dog that will take the playfulness of your children.

GIANT SCHNAUZER

Developed in Germany, the Giant Schnauzer is the largest of this breed which comes in three sizes—Giant, Standard, and Miniature. Produced as a herding dog to drive sheep and cattle to market, the Giant Schnauzer remained exclusively a German dog until after World War I (the Germans used them as war dogs and in police work). Since they made their appearance in the United States at the same time that the German Shepherd was enjoying immense popularity, the Giant Schnauzer never made a great impression. They are affectionate and devoted, make good watch dogs, and are amazingly resistant to illness.

GREAT DANE

The name of this dog is of uncertain origin, for the Great Dane is another dog of German breeding. This dog was originally used by the Germans as a boar hound; however, there is evidence that dogs very similar to the Great Dane existed as long ago as 3000 B.C. in Egypt.

The Great Dane is an elegant and beautiful giant-type dog. The ones bred today are gentle and, amazingly enough, make good house pets. They are easy to groom and adjust well, even to apartment living. Gentle with children, quiet, and fearless, they also serve as fine guard dogs. As with most Giant Breeds, the Great Dane has a short life span and is prone to diabetes, heart conditions, and arthritis. They require warm, soft living quarters and lots of exercise.

GREAT PYRENEES

The Great Pyrenees first appeared in Europe between 1800 and 1000 B.C. and is believed to have

The Great Pyrenees.

The Komondor.

come from Central Asia or Siberia. French writers wrote of their service as guardians of the Chateau of Lourdes back in the 1400's. In France, they served as assistants to the shepherds guarding and patrolling the flocks. Then, in 1675, the Great Pyrenees became a "Royal Dog" when adopted by the Dauphin, the future Louis XIV. The breed was then desired by all nobility.

Recognized by the American Kennel Club in 1933, the Great Pyrenees has been in America since 1824 when brought to this country by General Lafayette.

The role of this dog is a varied one. Primarily a watch dog, they are also used by the sportsmen to pull sleds and to do guide work on ski trips. During World War I, they were used for pack work, and they have been used to smuggle contraband over the Pyrenees, between the French-Spanish border, for many years.

Beauty, intelligence, loyalty, devotion, love of children, quiet, requiring only moderate exercise and grooming make them an ideal pet for those desiring a large dog.

KOMONDOR

Bred by Hungarian shepherds for ten centuries, the Komondor was used as a guard dog against wolves and thieves. Their thick, wooly coats served as protective barriers and their keen intelligence helped them against strong adversaries.

Recognized by the American Kennel Club in 1937, the breed is not very popular here. This is probably due to its unkempt appearance, resulting from its

usually matted long-haired coat. When properly groomed, they are quite attractive—always all white —immense in size, strong, and highly protective. Very devoted to their master and family, they are suspicious of strangers and they make ideal guard dogs.

KUVASZ

In Hungary, the Kuvasz was bred into the form of dog that we know today. However, this is truly an ancient breed, probably coming from Tibet and believed to have been used by Sumerian herdsmen seven or eight thousand years ago.

They were guard dogs of kings, as well as of shepherds, since the 1400's. First brought to this country in the 1920's, the Kuvasz made slow strides. Today, as throughout their history, this breed is valued as a guardian. They are devoted, loyal, intelligent, fearless, acclimate well to all climates, are quiet, strong, and speedy. Playing with children is one of their preferences, and they are a one family dog. They require a great deal of exercise. Their coat, because of its texture, is dirt resistant, even though it is white. Only infrequent bathing is recommended. A thorough brushing daily will keep them well-groomed. Their coats should never be cut, but they do shed.

MASTIFF

The exact origins of this breed are open to conjecture. Perhaps originating in Asia, the Mastiff has been bred in England for at least 2,000 years. Records show that they fought against the Roman invaders in 55 B.C. Later, they were used in dog fights, for bullbaiting, and for bear-baiting. Their greatest service was as tie dogs (tied by day and freed at night) to protect against wolves and other savage animals. They also served in the nobles' hunting packs.

Today, they have a reputation of being a most courageous dog, and they are selected by those desiring a strong, alert guard dog.

NEWFOUNDLAND

A breed which developed in Newfoundland, this dog is believed to have some Great Pyrenees ancestry; however, most of the Newfoundland's exact origins are hazy and unknown. The Newfoundland is a large dog, well-suited to working on that island. Their heavy coats and large webbed feet have made them most successful there. In England, the breed was refined to be as we know it today.

Although still used as a working dog in many parts of the world, the Newfoundland is gaining in popularity here in America because of his sweet disposition. As a companion and playmate to children, the Newfoundland is tops. His size makes him an outstanding guard and watch dog. In addition, he is noted for his life saving ability in water.

OLD ENGLISH SHEEPDOG

Records of this breed go back about 150 years. Bred originally in England, its ancestors are not clearly known. Originally used to drive sheep and cattle to market, today they are popular as pets and in the show ring. Perhaps, they would be even more popular if so many people were not afraid of the grooming job required by their heavy, dense coat. They do need brushing and combing, but they require little trimming.

PULI

Used by the Hungarian sheepherders, the Puli has driven and herded sheep for more than 1,000 years. His technique of controlling the herd by jumping up on them or running over their backs is quite characteristic.

The Puli is a solid-colored dog—either a dull black, gray, or even white. His coat is unusual, consisting of a soft undercoat with profuse, long outercoat. In its natural habitat, the Puli gives a very unkempt appearance with its coat matted and corded.

Recognized by the American Kennel Club in 1937, the Puli is used here as a guard and companion. Being a medium-sized dog, he is peppy and bouncy. This helps to increase his popularity in this country.

ROTTWEILER

A working dog used by the Roman armies to drive their cattle, the Rottweiler also became a companion, guard, and even a draft animal. Having spread to Europe by means of invaders, most of the dogs became located in Germany. Probably, the dog's name comes from the town of Rottweil. Therefore, this breed must be at least 1,900 years old.

The Rottweiler is related to the Doberman Pinscher, but the Rottweiler is a heavier and slower dog. Since 1910, when it was used for police training, the breed has witnessed a slight revival. Recognized by the American Kennel Club in 1935, the Rottweiler has never enjoyed a large following. This dog is courageous, dignified, powerful, self-reliant, active, obedient, and faithful. Having a short, coarse flat coat makes grooming easy.

SAMOYED

Considered perhaps to be the most beautiful breed, the Samoyed has been bred pure for hundreds of years. Living in the snowy and icy lands between the White Sea and the Yenisei River, the Samoyed and their masters have a nomadic existence. Here they worked faithfully as sledge dogs and as reindeer shepherds.

For the last 100 years, they have appeared at dog shows in England. Today, the Samoyed is found all over the world. They make fine companions, good watchdogs, are of high intelligence, strong and sturdy. A good brushing and combing will keep them beautiful. They require little trimming, merely keeping the ears neat. Their thick white coat helps them adapt to all types of climates.

STANDARD SCHNAUZER

The Standard Schnauzer is the oldest of the three types of Schnauzer—Giant, Standard, and Miniature. It is believed that the Schnauzer breed is a quite old German breed since he appears in paintings by Dürer painted between 1492 and 1504. Rembrandt and Sir Joshua Reynolds and others of that period have portrayed this breed as well.

Exactly how this dog was produced is conjecture, but some authorities suggest that Poodle, Spitz, and possibly Shepherds were used in its creation.

At first, the Standard Schnauzer was classified as a terrier, but, in 1945, he was placed in the Working Group. In Germany, the Schnauzer has always been a working dog—he was a rat catcher, a guard, an army dog, and a police dog. Because of his sharp intelligence, he has proved most successful in obedience trials. He makes a good medium-sized pet; he is devoted, clean, does not shed, is easy to groom. In order to look proper, he does require regular clipping. Standard Schnauzers make good watch dogs, too!

SHETLAND SHEEPDOG

Actually a miniature Collie, this is still a working dog. Their history is obscure since there are no written records. It would seem that they developed a small stature because it was advantageous in order to survive in this rocky, barren locale of the Shetland Islands. Due to their isolation, this breed was not "discovered" until the 20th century. The Sheltie was recognized by the English in 1909. Setting standards proved to be difficult, but today the Sheltie should be from 13 to 16 inches in height.

Breeders today desire to produce dogs that, except for size, resemble the Rough Collie in appearance, expression, and character. Undoubtedly because of their background, they make willing workers, train easily, make excellent guard and watch dogs, as well as fine companions.

SIBERIAN HUSKY

Kept as a pure breed for hundreds of years in north-eastern Siberia, the Siberian Husky was used by the natives as sled dogs, guards and companions. Their talent for sled-dog racing was discovered, and they were taken to Alaska, Canada, and the United States, where they set records. Many consider the Siberian Husky to be the strongest draft animal.

They are striking in appearance. They have a soft double coat with color from white to black. Growing numbers are finding that the Siberian Husky makes a fine pet since he is gentle and friendly, alert, easily trained, clean, free of body odor, and adapts well to all climates.

ST. BERNARD

Although records are non-existent as to the exact origin of this breed, it seems probable that they appeared in Switzerland as a result of Roman invasions. Their name comes from St. Bernard de Menthon, the founder of the Hospice in the Swiss Alps or possibly from the St. Bernard Pass in the Swiss Alps. Used at first as watch dogs, they soon proved themselves proficient as path finders, and they were capable of locating helplessly lost or snowbound people. For several hundred years, the monks and the St. Bernards carried out their rescue work. Stories of their exploits have become legendary.

Because of large losses in the breed, crosses with the Newfoundland were made and proved successful in revitalizing the St. Bernard. This cross also accounts for their long coat.

The St. Bernards have witnessed growing popularity here in the United States. They are marvelous with children, make fine guard dogs, and are placid, calm dogs to have around the house. Because of their great size and weight, they are prone to structural problems. Hip dysplasia should always be ruled out prior to purchase. They have large appetites, enjoy lots of exercise, and need regular grooming.

WELSH CORGI

Welsh Corgis (the name is derived from the Welsh "cor," dwarf, "gi," dog) have been used for centuries

The Welsh Corgi.

in Wales for cattle herding. There are two kinds, the Pembroke and the Cardigan, which are recognized as two separate breeds. The Cardigan is possibly the original Corgi and may belong to the same group as the Dachshund. The Pembroke, some writers claim, is the offshoot of a crossing of this dog with the Spitz and then with Schipperkes brought to Pembrokeshire by a colony of Flemish weavers in Norman times.

The popular conception that the only difference between a Pembroke and a Cardigan is that the latter has a long bushy tail and the former is tailless is wrong. The Cardigan is a longer, heavier dog than the Pembroke, with larger, more rounded ears, heavier bone, and round feet rather than oval ones with a slightly bowed front and a distinct crook to the forelegs. The Cardigan should be less fine in foreface than the Pembroke. Its coat is short or medium as against the medium coat of the Pembroke. There is a variety of Cardigan, though not of Pembroke, known as the "Blue Merle," which in fact is not really blue but a mixture of blueish-grey and black, with white and red markings. The same coloration is present in Shetland Sheep Dogs and Collies, and some writers postulate that it may have been the original coloration of these breeds.

Pembrokes have generally far outnumbered Cardigans both in England and in the U.S. In 1969, 4,165 Pembrokes were registered in England as opposed to 192 Cardigans, while in 1970 in the U.S.A. 2,446 Pembrokes were registered and 294 Cardigans. This may be due to two reasons: 1) that the British Royal Family has had Pembrokes 2) the fact that Cardigan breeders in England for years squabbled among themselves and did not agree on a standard as readily as did the Pembroke breeders.

GROUP IV: TERRIERS

THIS group consists of the dogs which go into the earth after game. They were bred to go into holes and do battle with and bring out or kill the quarry. Farmers have used them to control rats and vermin, while hunters have used them to hunt game. Their courage, ability, and style have won the admiration of dog lovers everywhere.

AIREDALE TERRIER

The extinct Old English Terrier is thought to be an ancestor of the Irish, Fox, Welsh and Airedale Terrier. Crosses among the Otterhound, Scotch Terriers, and the Bull Terrier were used to develop this breed. The Airedale is the largest of the terrier group and has been used by sporting Yorkshiremen to hunt fox, badger, weasels, etc. Originally, they were called Waterside Terriers, Working Terriers, and Bingley Terriers.

Airedales have been shown in England since the 1860's and are now Germany's favorite terrier. Popular at dog shows, they are still quite working dogs—used to hunt game in Africa, India, and Canada while they also are used for police work in Germany and Great Britain. Their records as messengers and for their sentry work during World War I is outstanding.

Even though quite ferocious when working, the Airedale Terrier is always a puppy at heart—with a sweet, playful disposition. Airedales make fine pets, particularly with children. However, their puppy-like qualities must be controlled early or they can become a destructive nuisance. They enjoy hearty daily walks, and their coats need to be trimmed.

AUSTRALIAN TERRIER

Hailing from Australia, this terrier's form was developed by crossing the now extinct Broken-hair Terrier with other terriers—possibly the Dandie Dinmonts, Sky Terriers, Cairnes, and Scotties—in order to improve the breed. First shown in Australia in 1885, they became increasingly popular undoubtedly because of their usefulness as small hunters in the Australian bushland. The breed was first admitted to the American Kennel Club in 1960.

The Australian Terrier is one of the smallest working terriers, weighing from 12 to 14 pounds and standing only ten inches shoulder height. This breed makes a fine pet—apartment-sized! Their coats are water resistant, require little grooming and no clipping or stripping. They are affectionate, spirited, good watchdogs, and yet they are quieter than most terriers.

BEDLINGTON TERRIER

Lamb-like in appearance, the Bedlington is far from a lamb in personality. Originally a favorite of the English coal miners and nail makers, the Bedlington served as a ratter and entertained by racing and dog

The Bedlington Terrier.

fighting. Although believed to be one of the oldest terrier breeds, the Bedlington was first shown in 1871.

The Bedlington is a very strong and healthy dog and makes a fine pet. His appearance is quite distinctive; he is lovable and loving, but he gets jealous easily. Trimming is necessary to keep him looking as he should.

BORDER TERRIER

Here we have a terrier that was developed purely as a working dog. Shepherds, farmers and sportsmen of the Cheviat Hills of Great Britain maintained the Border Terrier because of its strength, endurance, and pluck. The breed was useful in protecting livestock against foxes which they could track and kill.

Although not well known in this country, the Border Terrier makes a good pet. He has a waterproof coat, requires little grooming, acclimates to a variety of climates, and makes a spunky companion.

The Bull Terrier.

BULL TERRIER

Bull Terriers come in two varieties—the white and the colored. The breed was established in 1835 by crossing a Bulldog with a White English Terrier.

The Bull Terrier was originally bred as a sporting dog for fighting. This was a permissible sport in England in the 1800's, and the Bull Terrier was well-suited for it because of great strength, agility, and courage. Today, the Bull Terrier is a companion dog. His keen intelligence, almost uncanny sense of judgment, and sincere craving for affection make him a fine pet. If raised with children, he generally is very good with them and has amazing patience. However, the Bull Terrier puppy is a most energetic and vigorous dog, and, in playing with a very young child or toddler, he might unintentionally frighten or hurt him.

Bull Terriers make good watchdogs because of their formidable appearance and their poised dignity. Rarely barkers, they seem to sense when a situation calls for action. As with any active dog, the Bull Terrier likes to be exercised and to be played with. Since they are natural pugilists and fighting was the original use of these dogs, caution must be taken to prevent them from becoming involved in a dispute.

CAIRN TERRIER

Originally a working terrier, the Cairn Terrier hunted otter, foxes, and other vermin on the Isle of Skye. The Cairn is believed to be one of the oldest of the British terrier breed.

The Cairn is a hardy, active, small terrier. Their spirit and alertness make them good watchdogs. Those bothered by an active dog that likes to bark at strangers, cars, and other dogs should beware. Affectionate, loving and loyal, they make fine apartment-sized pets. They love taking good walks with their masters each day, but they are content even if they can't have one. Easy to groom, they require only the merest tidying

up around the ears, feet, and tail. They have no doggy odor, and, if combed and brushed daily, they do not shed.

DANDIE DINMONT TERRIER

The clown-like Dandie Dinmont Terrier is an old breed portrayed by Gainsborough in 1770 in a portrait of Henry, third Duke of Buccleuch. Used as a hunter of rodents, foxes, badgers, and otters, this low slung dog also makes a fine house pet. Intelligent, good with children, a good watchdog with a sturdy double coat, the Dandie Dinmont is a most affectionate companion. With its double coat, the dog requires only a daily grooming and no clipping or stripping.

FOX TERRIER

The Fox Terrier is an ancient English breed; it is available in two varieties—smooth and wire. The smooth terrier was first shown in 1862, 15 to 20 years prior to the wire. Amazingly, the original standard, drawn up in 1876, of the Fox Terrier Club of England has been barely changed. They were very popular in England for fox hunts as they would seek and unearth any reluctant fox.

The Fox Terrier has won the Best in Show at the Westminster Show more than any other breed. He

The Smooth Fox Terrier.

has ranked in the top ten of the American Kennel Club's most popular breeds for 23 years.

The Fox Terrier is a bouncing, active, constantly on the go, gay, responsive dog. He can be enjoyed by those with a similar personality. For the more sedate type of individual, the Fox Terrier may be too active, busy, and mischievous.

IRISH TERRIER

Bred originally as a working dog, the Irish Terrier is believed to be one of the oldest terrier breeds. He can be trained to hunt small and even large game, and he can retrieve on land or water. During World War I, he served as a messenger and sentinel.

Considered to be a real "daredevil," the Irish makes a fine pet. He is hardy, loyal, adaptable to all climates, affectionate, frolicsome, extremely healthy and long lived. The Irish makes a fine watchdog and serves well as a protector of children.

KERRY BLUE TERRIER

This terrier breed originated in Ireland where they were bred pure for hundreds of years. Its role was that of a working and sporting dog—herding sheep and cattle, hunting small game, retrieving from land and water, and ratting.

The Kerry's coat must be the characteristic "Kerry blue." In Ireland, they are shown untrimmed (in the rough) whereas, in the United States, they have neatly trimmed coats for show purposes.

A good companion, watchdog, and friend, the Kerry adapts to city or country living. To look properly groomed, clipping or stripping is required. They enjoy good daily walks.

LAKELAND TERRIER

The Lakeland Terrier originated in the Fell district

The Lakeland Terrier.

of Cumberland, England near the Scottish border. Related to the Welsh, Airedale, and probably the Bedlington, the Lakeland is one of the oldest working terriers used to exterminate foxes.

Like the other terriers of his type, the Lakeland has a hard, wiry body coat and a soft undercoat which helped him to survive hard work in all weathers.

In the household, the Lakeland is a guardian and an entertainer. They are gay and cheerful, alert, courageous, and intelligent. Hardy and sturdy, they are small dogs with big hearts. They thrive with sev-

eral daily walks, and they are adaptable to all climates. The Lakeland is a lean dog and should never be allowed to get too heavy. Lakelands look best when stripped several times a year, and then they are easy to keep well-groomed by a brushing a few times a week. They are suited to apartment living if necessary.

MANCHESTER TERRIER

Bred as a true ratter, the Manchester was intended for the poor man's sport of rat killing and rabbit coursing. They were first produced from a cross between a Whippet and a mixed terrier; possibly the Greyhound or Dachshund entered into the cross as well.

The Manchester is a sleek, clean, glossy-coated dog. There are two sizes—toy, weighing 12 pounds and under, and a medium-sized version, weighing over 12 pounds. They make fine house pets and good companions, as they are intelligent, easy to groom, and they have very clean habits.

NORWICH TERRIER

These terriers appeared in England around 1880, They were quickly adopted by Cambridge University students, who called them Cantab Terriers. This hardy, active dog was most helpful during fox hunts.

Today, they make nice house pets as their hard coats are easy to keep clean and do not require any trimming. They make good watchdogs, and they are loyal, one master dogs.

MINIATURE SCHNAUZER

This breed is of German origin and, except for size, it is identical to the Standard Schnauzer. Crosses with Pinschers, Spitz, Poodles and Affenpinschers possibly created this smaller sized Schnauzer.

A working dog, the Miniature Schnauzer was originally used to kill vermin and rats. Although in the United States he is classed with the terriers, this is not true in England or Germany.

The Miniature Schnauzer is an ideal pet for town or country. They are hardy, active, and intelligent, thus, they are easily trained. They also love children. They should be stripped or clipped several times a year to keep them looking smart. They do enjoy barking which may be annoying to some. Only a moderate amount of daily exercise is required.

SCOTTISH TERRIER

Many stories exist concerning the antiquity of the Scottish Terrier. However, there is no conclusive proof, and the only certainty is that they were first shown in their own class in Birmingham, England in 1860. The first pair of Scotties were brought to the United States in 1883. Some authorities claim that the Scottish Terrier descended from the original Skye Terrier of the Isle of Skye.

Originally used by professional fox hunters, the

The Scottish Terrier.

hounds trailed fox, and then the terriers went to ground. The Scottie was considered invaluable for baiting the fox. He is built low and small with great digging strength.

For many years, the Scottie was extremely popular and fashionable. For nearly 15 years he was among the first ten breeds in American Kennel Club registrations. Artists and advertisements served to bring the Scottie before the public eye. President Roosevelt's Fala also helped its rise in popularity.

The Scottie has a character all his own. He is aloof, reserved, dignified and very independent. Coolness to strangers and loyalty to his own master are well-known Scottie traits. He has a keen nose, good vision, acute hearing, and he truly loves to hunt and dig for vermin. A very playful dog, the Scottie will keep this trait until old age. He looks best when stripped or clipped. His coat is easy to keep clean and he should be bathed only rarely. He is happy with a combing and brushing several times a week. Training must be handled with firmness and kindness.

SEALYHAM TERRIER

Bred originally to hunt fox, badger, and otter, the

The Sealyham Terrier.

Sealyham Terrier was named after the Sealyham estate near Haverfordwest in Wales. Here, in the middle 1800's, they were bred by Captain John Edwardes who tried to perfect the dogs' endurance and gameness for hunting. They were first shown in Wales in 1903, in England in 1910, and they were registered by the American Kennel Club in 1911.

An even-tempered dog with a sweet disposition, the Sealyham makes a fine pet and companion. A stripping or clipping several times a year will keep him in "show condition." Moderate daily grooming and exercise are all that he requires.

SKYE TERRIER

Over 400 years old, this breed has changed very little. The motto of the Skye Club of Scotland and which certainly fits the Skye is, "Wha dour meddle wi' me." Their flowing coats cover the eyes and sweep to the floor; it undoubtedly served them well as protection, but it is considered as quite a chore by many dog owners. Hailing from the Northwestern islands of Scotland, the Skye served well hunting foxes, weasels and otters in the rough rocks and burrows of his misty homeland.

Quickly discovered by the nobility, the Skye became a favorite of Queen Elizabeth I and Queen Victoria.

Two varieties of Skyes are recognized—the prick-eared and the drop-eared. They make beautiful pets, showing elegance and dignity, but only those willing to devote a great deal of time daily to grooming them should consider owning one. It is said that they are fighters and snap readily at strangers. Thus, they are good as guard dogs. They like children and they are quite intelligent.

STAFFORDSHIRE TERRIER

The Staffordshire Terrier was created by crossing a terrier with a Bulldog. The development of this breed was to create a dog that was well-suited for the sports of pit fighting and bull baiting. Long associated with these bloody sports, the Staffordshire takes his name from Staffordshire, England, where miners continued the sport of dog fighting long after it became illegal.

Today, these terriers are used as guard dogs. They are intelligent and easily trained. Their smooth coats make grooming an easy job.

WELSH TERRIER

In their native land of Wales, the Welsh Terriers have been used for hundreds of years to hunt otter, fox, and badger. This rough-haired, black and tan terrier, is considered to be one of the oldest terrier breeds. They were first shown in England in 1884 and brought to the United States in 1888.

In appearance, they look like miniature versions

The Welsh Terrier.

Today the double-coated (hard and dense outer coat and soft undercoat), pure White Westie has a growing following. This is an unpampered dog in appearance—rough and ready for a run or walk in the snow or the sun. They acclimate themselves well to most localities and most situations. Their beautiful coat requires a stripping at least twice a year to look really tops, and they must never be trimmed like a Scottie. Even though they are white, they are easy to keep clean and need only a daily combing and brushing to look tip top. When groomed daily, they do not shed and they have no doggy odors. In fact, they should rarely be bathed since a bath softens their characteristic hard coat.

Westies make delightful pets. Their compact size makes them appropriate for a city apartment or for any sized home. They are affectionate dogs with lovable, charming personalities. Amazingly hardy, the Westie is a spunky dog that puts on a very fearless act. They like to bark at every moving object outside of their houses, and, thus, they make fairly good watchdogs. They are good with children when raised with them. Their tolerance level is limited and they will retire to a quiet corner under the couch rather than be annoyed by a toddler. Loyal to master and family, the Westie is very attached to his own hearth.

It seems that, as with other white dogs, they tend to be prone to skin problems. Their litters are often small and whelping may be difficult. This playful, happy dog has won many admirers.

The West Highland White Terrier.

of the Airedale. Serving as a companion and a watchdog, the Welsh Terrier is also an intelligent and most affectionate pet. They are considered by many to be the calmest of the terriers. They are easy to groom and to keep clean. Naturally, they love a daily walk.

WEST HIGHLAND WHITE TERRIER

Undoubtedly the Westie is from the same terrier family as the Cairns, Scotties, and the Dandie Dinmonts. They were called Rosenearth Terriers and Poltalloch Terriers originally because they were first bred at Poltalloch, Scotland. It is told that Colonel Malcolm of Poltalloch bred these white terriers because he had accidentally shot and killed one of his rust colored terriers during a hunt; as a result, he wanted a white breed so that a similar accident wouldn't occur. Thus, the occasional white puppies from the Scottie, Cairn, and Dandie Dinmont Terriers were bred together, and they created the West Highland White Terrier breed. Interbreeding of the Cairn and the Westie continued until 1917 when the American Kennel Club ruled that no Cairn could be registered if its pedigree carried a West Highland White ancestor in three generations. This decree ended the interbreeding and resulted in today's pure bred Westies.

GROUP V: TOYS

THE dogs of this type are those weighing between one and one-half and 18 pounds. Because of their small size, the toy breeds are very popular as house pets and companions.

AFFENPINSCHER

Known in Europe since the 17th century and nick-named the "Monkey Dog," they served as rat catchers. The Affenpinscher is probably the progenitor of the Brussels Griffon. Although far from popular, the Affenpinscher does make a good pet and companion. Since 1936, they have been recognized by the American Kennel Club.

In appearance, they are quite unusual. They look like a "handful of bristles." Their ears and tail are docked. Mostly a quiet dog, they will bark if they sense any danger.

BRUSSELS GRIFFON

Bred to hunt and to kill rats and stable vermin, the Brussels Griffon is a humorous looking dog with an extremely rough, wiry coat, pricked cropped ears and superb intelligence. He is very easily trained. It is suggested that training be started at an early age as he can be stubborn and overly sensitive.

CHIHUAHUA

There are two varieties of this tiny dog—the long-coated and the smooth-coated. They are the world's smallest dogs, sometimes weighing as little as one pound.

Some authorities believe that today's Chihuahua is a descendant of the dogs owned by the Toltecs and Aztec tribes of Mexico. In any case, they are now very popular because of their compact size, grace, intelligence, and saucy expression.

ENGLISH TOY SPANIEL

Cherished by King Charles II of England and thus also known as the King Charles Spaniel (black and tan), this breed undoubtedly made its way to England from the East—possibly Japan. Later other varieties developed—Blenheim (white and red), Prince Charles (white, black, and tan), and Ruby (chestnut red). These varieties differ only in color.

Diminutive in size, the English Toy Spaniel makes a perfect apartment size pet. Its long silky coat enjoys a good combing and brushing. Still having some hunting instinct in its blood, this breed enjoys a romp in the outdoors.

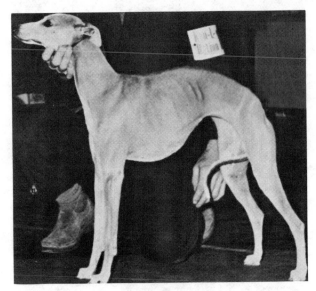

The Italian Greyhound.

ITALIAN GREYHOUND

Believed to have been in existence in its present form for over 2,000 years, the Italian Greyhound is a dwarfed version of the large Greyhound. Evidence indicates that they were popular in upper class Roman society. Although the breed has not changed, it has undergone refinement. It is now one of the smallest and fastest dogs. He is very graceful and dainty, being described as looking like a fine piece of porcelain.

The Italian Greyhound's coat is short-haired and glossy, making it easy to maintain. Calm, affectionate, and sensitive, yet with plenty of pep, he is a fine house pet. He chills easily and must be protected during cold weather.

JAPANESE SPANIEL

Appearing on old Chinese temples, pottery, and embroidery, the Japanese Spaniel probably originated in China and later appeared in Japan. Commodore Perry received some as gifts when he opened Japan to Western trade in 1853. Japanese breeding kennels supplied the world until problems forced breeders in other parts of the world to take up the slack.

Japanese Spaniels are Oriental in appearance, aristocratic, stylish and have full coats. They are bright and alert; they thrive in any climate. Strangers are not favored, thus making them good watchdogs. Due to their size, they make an ideal apartment-living pet.

MALTESE

A dainty toy and one of the oldest breeds, the Maltese is from the island of Malta. Possibly, they have been in existence over 2,800 years. It is believed that the Maltese was worshipped by the Egyptians. Now, it is primarily a lady's lap dog and household pet. If you are planning on a toy dog, remember that Maltese dogs:

- have long silky hair which requires much grooming.
- are spirited and independent.
- make smart and affectionate pets.
- are healthy and strong.
- are clean in their habits.

MINIATURE PINSCHER

Believed to have originated in Germany several centuries ago, this tiny dog has attained surprising popularity. Actually, he is small only in size. Otherwise, he has the personality of a much larger dog.

In appearance, one finds a dog that is sleek, trim, and muscular. He makes a fine watchdog thanks to an acute hearing sense. Used on the stage, he also seems to be a natural show dog. The Miniature Pinscher is a fine apartment size pet since it requires little exercise. Grooming is minimal and he makes a faithful companion.

The Miniature Pinscher.

The Papillon.

PAPILLON

Represented in the paintings of Rubens, Boucher, and other old masters, the Papillon was long popular with the noble ladies. It is told that one followed Marie Antoinette to the guillotine and died of a broken heart. The dogs had ardent admirers throughout Western Europe. Interestingly enough, some have droop ears like Spaniels, and others have butterfly ears (accounting for the name).

Possessing a lovable personality, they are hardy, attractive, intelligent, lively, adore children, adapt to all climates, and are apartment size. They look and feel best when combed and brushed regularly.

PEKINGESE

At one time in China, the theft of one of these sacred dogs was punishable by death. Truly an ancient breed, records trace the Pekingese to the Tang Dynasty of the Eighth Century. They were first introduced to the West after the looting of the Peking Imperial Palace by the British in 1860.

Still displaying a regal bearing today, the Pekingese is dignified, affectionate, loyal, full of pep and stam-

The Pekingese.

The Pug.

ina. He is virtually fearless but never aggressive and loves a playful romp.

POMERANIAN

The Pomeranian is a descendant of the sled dogs of Iceland and Lapland. Probably, it is a scaled down version of the Spitz variety. It is said that the Pomeranian had been a favorite of Queen Victoria; this helped their popularity in England. It made its first appearance in the United States in 1899 and has become one of the most popular toy breeds.

Weighing no more than seven pounds, the Pomeranian is intelligent, has a docile disposition, a vivacious personality, and makes a fine companion.

PUG

A short-faced dog with a tightly-curled tail, the Pug is probably Chinese in origin. Imported by the Dutch East India Company, the Pug soon became a favorite

of English, French, Dutch, and Italian nobility. However, other breeds gained pre-eminence, and the Pug lost favor. Surprisingly, since the 1930's the Pug has returned in popularity.

The Pug makes an ideal apartment-size pet. He requires little care and makes a clean, alert companion.

SHIH TZU

Believed to be a cross between the Pekingese and the Lhasa Apso, the Shih Tzu is thought to have orig-

The Shih Tzu.

The Pomeranian.

inated in the Tibet and China area. Because of his mane, he is known as the "Lion Dog." This breed is growing increasingly popular in this country because of its compact size and unusual appearance. In 1957 the Shih Tzu Club of America was started, and in 1969 the breed was recognized by the American Kennel Club.

288

SILKY TERRIER

A native of Australia, the Silky is believed to be derived from a cross between the Australian Terrier and Yorkshire Terrier. They were exhibited for the first time in 1907 and admitted to the American Kennel Club in 1959.

The Silky is a toy with true terrier character and spirit. Although primarily a pet, the Silky is a good rat and snake chaser. Proper grooming is essential to keep his lovely coat in order. He is intelligent, loyal, and makes a fine apartment-size pet.

TOY POODLE

The Toy is the smallest of the Poodles. Long a favorite of royalty and nobility, they were favorites of Louis XVI of France, and they have been represented in paintings by Dürer, the German artist, and Goya, a Spanish painter.

Their prime function has been as a sleeve dog or lap dog, although some were used to hunt truffles.

They are clean, intelligent, perky, excellent pets, and "nearly human" according to their owners. Cautious selection is necessary. Since the Poodle is this country's most popular breed, it has suffered. Beware of nervous, snappy, barking, and anxious dogs. Veterinarians claim to see more and more Poodles (the products of improper breeding) that have ear and eye problems, weak knee joints, and fussy stomachs. Be certain to purchase from only the most reputable breeder.

The Toy Poodle.

YORKSHIRE TERRIER

A relative newcomer to the dog world, the Yorkshire was developed in Lancashire and Yorkshire. Believed to be a descendant of the Skye Terrier and other terriers, the Yorkshire was used by weavers as a ratter. Then, the dog became quite fashionable with the wealthy women of the late-Victorian era. Selective

The Yorkshire Terrier.

breeding has scaled them down to their present size—not to exceed seven pounds.

Their personality is lively like a terrier's, but their coats present problems to their owners. Combing and brushing is a constant chore. To protect their coat, they are usually not allowed to frolic; they often wear ribbons to keep their hair from tangling.

GROUP VI: NON-SPORTING DOGS

IN this group, we find a miscellaneous collection of breeds with a variety of characteristics, sizes and backgrounds.

BOSTON TERRIER

As a result of a cross between a White English Terrier and an English Bulldog, the Boston Terrier became a native American breed. Since the development of this breed occurred in Boston, the name Boston Terrier was adopted.

Since 1893, the Boston Terrier has been recognized

The Boston Terrier.

by the American Kennel Club. Today, this is one of America's popular breeds due to their even temper, gentle disposition, keen mind, and compact size. The smooth coat is easy to maintain and their size makes them suitable for apartment living.

BULLDOG

The Bulldog is considered by many to be a grotesque deformity because of its ugly face, short legs, short life span, and reproductive problems. The Bulldog has an interesting history. Originating from ancient stock and developed in England, the Bulldog earned his name because of his participation in the sport of bull baiting. This was a cruel sport enjoyed by all levels of English society from 1209 until it became illegal in 1835. Generally, bull baiting entailed catching the bull by the ear or the nose and then pin-

The Bulldog.

ning or throwing it. To succeed, these dogs had to be courageous, fierce, and powerful.

Since the demise of bull baiting, the Bulldog has changed; no longer ferocious, he is the mascot of the U.S. Marines and Yale University. Breeding is quite difficult. Sterility in bitches is common and whelping is usually a problem resulting in Caesarean sections. They are good-natured, but they tend to be short-tempered and stubborn. Bulldogs need little grooming or exercise. Don't be surprised when they snore!

The Chow Chow.

CHOW CHOW

The Chow Chow is believed to be a Chinese breed of hunting dog of Chinese emperors and used as a guard, sled dog and pet. Imported by Queen Victoria in 1880, general interest developed in the breed in England and subsequently in the United States.

Interestingly, this is the only breed with a blue-black tongue. They are loyal to their master and to no one else. Basically, they are not emotional dogs and don't bark, although some have been known to be sensitive. They are happiest in areas having a cool temperature. The Chow Chow needs little trimming but enjoys a good brushing and combing. Because of their massive size, they make good guard dogs around the house.

DALMATIAN

The Dalmatian is one of the most unusual and distinctive of all dogs in appearance. Clean-limbed with his clearly defined spots of black or liver standing boldly against a pure white background, he makes an imposing sight, whether in a show ring or out for a stroll with his owner.

An ancient dog for sure, but with an unclear background, the Dalmatian was often found with wandering gypsies. His role has been a varied one; he has been used as a draft dog, a sentry, army dog, coach dog, fire house dog, shepherding dog and used for tracking, retrieving, hunting vermin and many other field sports. Because of his appearance and memory, he has been used in the circus, on the stage, in television and in the movies.

Best known as a coach dog, the Dalmatian seems particularly suited for this role because of a love of horses. He has the title of the only "recognized carriage dog" in the world.

An aristocratic dog in appearance, the Dalmatian is affectionate, faithful, a good watchdog, good with children, and he is loyal to his master and family. Grooming is easy since he requires no stripping or clipping but only brushing to keep his coat clean and gleaming. He adapts well to all climates and is a neat, clean dog. Born all white, the spots develop quickly giving the Dalmatian his own distinctive appearance.

FRENCH BULLDOG

Actually a toy Bulldog, the French Bulldog probably originated through special crosses of the English Bulldog. Not popular in England, they were received with favor in France.

Bat ears are the distinctive characteristic of this breed as well as the flat shape of the skull.

It was the French Bulldog Club of America which standardized the breed that enjoyed remarkable popularity in the early 1900's.

The "Frenchie" makes a frolicsome pet. He is quiet, intelligent, clean, easy to groom, and a good watchdog. He requires little exercise and he makes a perfect apartment-size dog.

KEESHOND

The Keeshond's appearance suggests that its origin is Arctic and of the same strain as the Samoyed, the Chow Chow, the Norwegian Elkhound and the Pomeranian.

The favorite dog of the Dutch people for hundreds of years, the Keeshond was once the symbol of one of their political parties. They served mainly as a "barge dog" on the small vessels that were used on the canals and rivers.

The Dalmatian.

The Keeshond.

Considered by the Dutch to be an ideal pet and companion, the Keeshond is alert, adaptable, and good with children. The beautiful coat is easy to care for since it does not mat, is water proof, and requires little brushing.

The Lhasa Apso.

LHASA APSO

Hailing from the land of Tibet, this breed, which is over 800 years old, was the special dog of the Dalai Lama and was often given as gifts to dignitaries. These lovely little dogs were kept indoors as watchdogs. They are well-suited to this job since they have acute hearing and will bark in warning of any approach.

Lhasa Apsos have a very hardy nature, beautiful heavy coats, are easily trained and make happy pets. Their coats do require a great deal of daily care or they will become matted, tangled, and unsightly. Since they have "watchdog" instincts, they do bark at any disturbance and should not be selected by persons annoyed by such behavior.

POODLE

Poodles in the United States come in three sizes— Standard, Miniature, and Toy. Except for size, there is no difference between them. Ranking tops in popularity all over the world the Poodles are acclaimed for their intelligence, versatility and nearly human-like qualities. They have served as hunting dogs, circus dogs and watch dogs. Probably originating as a water dog, the Poodle does resemble the Irish Water Spaniel and the Curly-Coated Retriever and he still loves to swim. The Standard Poodle is believed to be the oldest of the three varieties.

The Standard Poodle (large) must be over 15 inches at the shoulder; the Miniature must be between ten and 15 inches; and, the Toy must be ten inches at the shoulder or less.

Their coats come in a great variety of colors and their coats may be trimmed in a variety of ways. A poodle needs to be clipped regularly otherwise the coat mats. This is a regular expense which should be considered (unless you can do it yourself). They are a hardy breed, but their reputation has suffered from being over bred and over pampered. Many poor specimens have been produced for profit and this has resulted in the temperamental, high strung, neurotic, sickly poodles often seen today. If carefully selected from a discriminating breeder, a Poodle is certainly an outstanding pet and companion.

SCHIPPERKE

A dog of Belgian ancestry, the Schipperke was originally used as a watchdog to guard the canal boats and the Guilds. Their small size was perfect as they did not take up much room on the barges. Until 1888, they were called "Spits" but received their present name when a specialty club was formed at that time. The name Schipperke is Flemish and means "Little Captain."

Their docked (cut) tail is characteristic. They make an ideal house pet, have a water proof coat which requires little grooming, a peppy personality, and like children.

The Poodle.

The Schipperke.

MISCELLANEOUS CLASS

THE miscellaneous class is composed of pure bred dogs recognized by the American Kennel Club. However, because of their small numbers, they are shown together. The following breeds may be exhibited in the miscellaneous category:

- Akita
- Australian Cattle Dog
- Australian Kelpie
- Bichon Frises
- Border Collie
- Cavalier King Charles Spaniel
- Ibizan Hound
- Miniature Bull Terrier
- Soft-Coated Wheaten Terrier
- Tibetan Terrier

AKITA

The Akita is a dog of ancient Japanese origin. In the northern provinces of Japan, the Akita was used to hunt such game as deer, wild boar, and bear. Today, he is used as a working dog and for police and army duties.

The Akitas are active dogs with large frames. They are very affectionate to their masters, have good natures, and are extremely alert. Thus, they make fine watch dogs and good pets.

The Akita Club of America has been trying to attain recognition of this breed by the American Kennel Club. Currently, there are over 1,300 Akitas listed in the Akita Stud Book.

AUSTRALIAN CATTLE DOG

The Australian Cattle Dog is a working dog that has won the respect of his master by protecting and herding his flock. He is believed to be part Collie, Kelpie, and Dingo. His job entails silently circling the herd and nipping the heels of any strays. This breed is still very rare in the United States.

AUSTRALIAN KELPIE

The Australian Kelpie is a new breed which originated in the 1870's. Their job was to herd sheep in their native Australia. The Kelpies are hard working dogs with outstanding scenting and hearing abilities.

BICHON FRISES

Le Bichon Frises is an ancient breed from Teneriffe, the largest of the Canary Islands, where they were known originally as "The Teneriffe." They were brought to France after the war with Italy and gained favor in the royal court; Henry III was particularly charmed by them. However, the breed lost favor and in the 20th Century became a dog of the streets or a circus entertainer.

Its name means cute or lovable curly. During the World Wars, the development of the breed suffered but has now been revived. France officially recognized "Le Bichon Frise" in 1933, and other European countries have since recognized them. In 1956, two Bichons arrived in the United States and, since that time, the number has grown steadily.

The Bichon Frise Club of America was organized in 1964. Since these are gay, joyful little dogs with an adorable appearance and fine temperament, they will continue to win the hearts of all who meet them. (The Bichon Frises has been eligible to compete in the Miscellaneous Class of A.K.C. shows since September 1, 1971.)

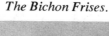

The Bichon Frises.

BORDER COLLIE

At present, the Border is recognized as a distinct breed only in Australia. The Border Collie is a working sheepdog and has been bred for its abilities rather than appearance.

CAVALIER KING CHARLES SPANIEL

Today's Cavalier King Charles Spaniel looks exactly like the small Toy Spaniels one can see in the canvasses of the Old Masters. The Cavalier King Charles Spaniel differs from the breed known as the English Toy Spaniel in the construction of the muzzle. The English Toy Spaniel has a very short face and virtually no muzzle whereas the original King Charles (today's Cavalier King Charles Spaniel) has a much longer fore-face.

It is believed that the Cavalier King Charles Spaniel (longer face) developed during the 13th Century in Italy. From the 15th Century, this breed was represented in the paintings of Titian, Clouet, and Sir Joshua Reynolds.

In 1945, the Kennel Club in England recognized the Cavalier whereas, in the United States, it is shown only in the miscellaneous class.

This breed makes a perfect small pet. The dogs are compact in size, are easy to groom (they don't need any special trimming), and they have an even temperament.

IBIZAN HOUND

This dog is designed for speed and can be distinguished from the Greyhound by his large upright ears. They have smooth coats, and their color is chestnut and white.

SOFT-COATED WHEATEN TERRIER

The Soft-Coated Wheaten Terrier is a versatile and adaptable companion and pet, sound in temperament, and quietly devoted to his work and his owner. He is one of the oldest of the terriers of Ireland, where, for generations, he has been used for herding, hunting, and guarding.

The Soft-Coated Wheaten's popularity has increased steadily since he was officially recognized in Ireland in the late 1930's.

In the United States, the Soft-Coated Wheaten can be shown in the Miscellaneous Class at American Kennel Club approved shows and sanctioned matches.

The number of Soft-Coated Wheatens in the United States has grown from 13 in 1961 to at least 400. Now, there are more than 300 registered with the Soft-Coated Wheaten Terrier Club of America.

TIBETAN TERRIER

Two thousand years ago, the Tibetan Terrier guarded the monasteries of Tibet. Even today, he serves well as a guard dog just as he did then. He has been accepted by the English Kennel Club, but he is still rare in this country. The first Tibetan Terrier came here in 1956.

This breed makes a fine watch dog, has a good temperament, is very intelligent and amazingly clean. He adapts well to any climate.

VARIETY GROUPS

THESE are pure bred dogs which are still so rare in the United States that the American Kennel Club has not recognized them at all. They cannot be shown at officially sanctioned shows. However, breed clubs have their own shows and they may be displayed at fun matches. When their numbers grow and they become better known, many of these breeds will gain the official recognition they are seeking.

Here are a few of these ultra-rare breeds:
- Australian Shepherd
- American Eskimo
- Bearded Collie
- Canaan Dog
- Chinese Crested Dog
- Japanese Shiba
- Mexican Hairless
- Toy Fox Terriers
- Tibetan Spaniel

AUSTRALIAN SHEPHERD

The Australian Shepherd came to the United States with Australian sheep imported in the 1800's. Originally, these dogs were crossbred members of the working collie family. Stockmen of the West further developed the breed while maintaining their versatility, keen intelligence, strong herding instinct, and eye-catching appearance.

Australian Shepherds are easily trained, have good dispositions, are gentle with children, and make fine companions.

At present, the International Australian Shepherd Association is seeking American Kennel Club Miscellaneous Class status.

AMERICAN ESKIMO

The American Eskimo originated in cold, snowy, and rugged climate and performs well in these conditions. As a breed, the American Eskimo is healthy, hardy, and adapts well to changes of climate. It is an intelligent, sturdy, and dependable dog that has been bred down in size and, thus, is suitable for virtually any home.

Their beautiful white coat is practically "self cleaning" and requires only a good regular brushing. They make fine watch dogs, are good with children, and are loving and devoted to their owners.

Although the American Eskimo is not recognized by the American Kennel Club, it is recognized by the United Kennel Club.

BEARDED COLLIE

Virtually extinct until a recent revival of interest saved it from disappearance, the Bearded Collie is an old working breed.

For hundreds of years Beardies have been used as hard workers in the sheep and cattle country that lies on both sides of the border between Scotland and England. Even today the dogs drive sheep or cattle from pasture to barnyard, or stand guard over the flock. Some believe that the Beardie is the ancestor of the Old English Sheepdog.

CANAAN DOG

The first four Canaan Dogs were imported in 1965 from Israel by Mrs. Jack Berkowitz. According to legends, this ancient breed of dog, more than 3,000 years old, was attached to the throne of Queen Jezebel with a golden collar and chain.

The Hebrew people knew them as "Kelef Kanani," or Canaan Dog, and used them as cattle and guard dogs. Then, when the Hebrew population was dispersed, the dogs fled into the Negev Desert and became wild. The Bedouin and Druze kept some as guard dogs, and so the breed survived.

Dr. Rudolphina Menzel of Israel was requested by the Haganah (the Israeli underground) to find a dog suitable for guarding the rural Israeli settlements and for training as war dogs. Dr. Menzel, who had studied in Vienna under Professor Hauck, one of the world's foremost authorities on the origin of dogs, thought of the Canaan dogs and set out catching, re-domesticating and breeding them.

The Canaan's studbook exists in Israel kept by the Israel Kennel Club.

The official Israel Standard of the breed aims at retaining the wild dog characteristics of the breed in appearance, in frugality in feeding, care, and their resistance to disease. They are a hardy breed, adjust to all climates, have a lovable disposition, and a great desire to please.

CHINESE CRESTED DOG

The Chinese Crested is of such ancient vintage that its exact origin has been lost. Their unusual appearance and rarity makes them quite distinctive.

Their temperament is even; they are affectionate, and very protective. The Chinese Crested is extremely clean, odor free, intelligent, very hardy, and healthy. Small in size, he makes a perfect pet for apartments.

JAPANESE SHIBA

The Japanese Shiba gives the impression of being a miniature German Shepherd. The Shiba dog is of Japanese ancestry, having a soft, short coat in colors ranging from pure white to fawn, buff; and tri-color. Those with experience with the Shiba state that it is an affectionate, easily trained, intelligent breed, thus making it an excellent house pet.

MEXICAN HAIRLESS

The Mexican Hairless ranges in size from three to 15 pounds. Their body is absolutely hairless with only a coarse tuft of hair on top of the skull.

It is necessary to earn the affection of the Mexican Hairless; they are stubborn and therefore difficult to train, and they easily become angry. Their normal body temperature is 104 degrees; they perspire through their pores, and their skin must be greased in order to keep it soft.

The Mexican Hairless was recognized years ago by the American Kennel Club but was later dropped due to the small number of registrants.

TOY FOX TERRIER

The Fox Terrier comes in three sizes. The toy is the smallest, ranging from three and a half to seven pounds. Though it is still not recognized by the American Kennel Club, the toy is growing in popularity because of its versatility—an ideal house pet and a good hunting companion. The coat is short and satiny, requiring little grooming. They are easily housebroken, clean, trim, little rascals and make fun pets. The Toy Fox Terrier is recognized by the United Kennel Club.

TIBETAN SPANIEL

The Tibetan Spaniel is a recognized breed in England, Finland, Sweden, and West Germany, but is still rare in the United States.

This is a small breed, ranging in weight from nine to 15 pounds. Originally, they were bred by the Monks in the Monasteries of Tibet. Gay and independent, they are most loving to their owners but aloof with strangers. Their coat is double, silky in texture, and set off with a richly plumed tail which curls over the back. Their face is flat like the Pekingese.

UNITED KENNEL CLUB BREEDS

**Breeds recognized and registered
by the U.K.C.:**

American Bull Terrier
American Eskimo
American Toy Terrier
Airdale Terrier
American Water Spaniel
Alaskan Malamute
Arctic Huskie
Basset Hound
Beagle
Bloodhound
Boston Terrier
Boxer
Miniature Boxer
Chihuahua
Chow Chow
Collie
Collie, Columbian
Collie, Smooth
Dachshund, Smooth
Dachshund, Longhaired
Dalmatian
English Shepherd
Fox Terrier, Smooth
Fox Terrier, Wire
Toy Fox Terrier
German Shepherd
Great Dane
Greyhound
Pekingese
Pomeranian
Poodle
St. Bernard
Scottish Terrier
Spaniel, Cocker
Whippet

Coonhound Breeds

American Black and Tan Coonhound
Bluetick Coonhound
English Coonhound
Plott Hound
Redbone Coonhound
Walker Coonhound
American Black and Tan Fox
    and Coonhound

The American Black and Tan Coonhound.

The Bluetick Coonhound.

The English Coonhound.

CHAPTER XII
DOG HEROES

THE DOG HERO AWARDS PROGRAM

THE Quaker Oats Company first presented the Ken-L Ration gold medal award to America's Dog Hero of the Year in 1954. The gold medal has since become the leading canine award of its kind in the nation.

The medal is presented each year to the dog who, in the opinion of a panel of noted judges, performs most heroically in saving human lives or property. Presentations are made in August or September for the competition period which begins during the same month of the preceding year.

Only pets are considered, and such professionally-trained canines as bloodhounds, seeing-eye dogs, and police dogs are not eligible, unless the deed they performed was outside their normal sphere of activity. In order to be eligible for national honors, a dog must first have been awarded a Ken-L Ration bronze medal locally.

These local awards are given to dogs whose heroic feats are brought to the selection committee's attention through newspaper stories and communications from interested people. The veracity of the story and worth of the deed are evaluated by a coordinating committee, and the awards are presented locally by company representatives. An average of 70 such local awards are made during a given competition period.

At the end of the competition period, a panel of three judges evaluate the deeds of all the local winners and select America's Dog Hero and four runners-up among them. The judges, representing different facets of the dog world, rate the runners-up in order of merit. Once the judges reach a decision, the coordinating committee begins accepting candidates for the following year's competition.

In addition to the gold medal, America's Dog Hero receives a $1,000 bond in its owner's name, a gold-plated leash and collar, a custom-made dog blanket, a gold plaque, and a year's supply of dog food. These prizes are awarded to the winning dog and its owners at a banquet held in the dog's honor in a large American city.

Runners-up are awarded silver-plated leashes and collars, silver plaques, custom-made dog blankets, and a six-months' supply of dog food at ceremonies in their local areas. Their owners receive bonds ranging in value from $100 to $500.

The Ken-L Ration Dog Hero Awards program has brought great credit and public attention to the many dogs who have displayed their devotion to mankind by performing courageous and intelligent acts of heroism. Many Americans have learned through the awards that dogs make devoted pets and companions as well as good neighbors.

TANG

1954 DOG HERO OF THE YEAR

Winner of the first annual gold medal award as America's Dog Hero of the Year was Tang, a huge, friendly collie from Denison, Texas. Owned by Air Force Capt. and Mrs. Maurice Dyer, this dog, possessing a protective instinct to a remarkable degree, saved no fewer than five children from death or severe injury.

Four times he leaped in front of fast-moving automobiles and pushed children to safety just split seconds before tragedy could strike. On another occasion, he planted himself squarely in front of a parked milk delivery truck and refused to budge, barking loudly all the while. When the puzzled driver alighted to ascertain the cause of the strange behavior of the normally friendly dog, he found that a two-year-old girl had clambered into the back of his truck,

from which she would almost certainly have fallen. The moment she was removed, Tang ceased his barking and returned placidly to the sidewalk.

Tang, without any training whatsoever, had originally established himself as the protector of children at the air base in Alaska at which Capt. Dyer was stationed. As speeding army trucks rumbled past the homes of the military personnel, Tang would herd his charges back from the road, and twice he actually pushed tiny tots from directly in front of the automobiles.

Transferred to Perrin Air Force Base, Capt. Dyer took up residence in nearby Denison, Texas. There, the Dyers and their neighbors were witnesses to the sight of Tang saving two more children in similar fashion. This great-hearted dog passed away in 1958.

TAFFY

1955 DOG HERO OF THE YEAR

An appealing, honey-colored cocker spaniel from Coeur d'Alene, Idaho, named Taffy, was the second winner. Owned by Mr. and Mrs. Ken Wilson of that city, Taffy was instrumental in saving her little master, Stevie Wilson, three, from a watery grave at the bottom of icy Fernan Lake.

Taffy's exploit began when Stevie's father, wishing to try out a saddle horse, went to a corral at the edge of the lake. Stevie and Taffy were placed in a spot from which they could not get into trouble. One of the neighbors, however, let the child and dog out, and the two proceeded to roam about.

Wilson, riding the horse about the corral, was surprised to see Taffy suddenly come bounding into the enclosure, barking excitedly and racing about the horse. Although puzzled by the dog's unusual actions, Wilson at first did not pay particular attention, thinking that the boy was in a place where he was safe from harm.

Taffy, realizing that her antics were not succeeding in getting Wilson to understand, suddenly broke away and dashed toward the lake. A moment or two later, she reappeared, dripping wet, barking at the top of her lungs, and nipping at the horse's legs until Wilson was almost thrown from his mount.

Suddenly realizing that the dog would never leap into the cold lake water unless something were amiss, Wilson stopped and shouted to the neighbor to ask if Stevie were safe. When the neighbor replied that he had let the child out, Wilson leaped off the horse and set out after the racing Taffy. The excited dog led him to the lake edge, where he saw Stevie's bright red mackinaw floating on the surface.

Jumping into the four-foot-deep water, Wilson lifted his unconscious son from the bottom of the clear lake. While neighbors summoned a pulmotor, he worked over the tot with artificial respiration. The youngster hovered between life and death for six hours before regaining consciousness.

An attending physician, shaking his head in wonderment at the child's recovery, said that undoubtedly just a few more moments at the bottom of the icy lake would have proved fatal.

LASSIE

1956 DOG HERO OF THE YEAR

Because his dog was deliberately disobedient, Gary Gustafson, 6, of San Carlos, Calif., is alive today. The deed that prevented a tragedy was responsible for the selection of his dog, Lassie, a Shetland sheepdog, as Dog Hero of the Year in 1956.

At night, Lassie would settle herself near Gary's door and never budge from that spot until the morning. Around midnight one night, the elder Gustafsons were roused from deep sleep by Lassie, who rushed into their bedroom, barking and whining, and even pulling at their bedclothes. Astounded by the dog's strange actions, for she had been taught never to enter their room, they at first attempted to order her back to Gary's room at the other end of the house.

Lassie stubbornly refused to leave, and even increased her whining and barking and pulling at their bedclothes. They finally decided that she must want to go outside. But when Mr. Gustafson took her to the door, she retreated, and began racing back and forth between the door and Gary's room, indicating that she wished to be followed. With a sigh of resignation, Mr. Gustafson followed her into Gary's bedroom, there to find Gary lying on the floor in a pool of blood, having suffered a hemorrhage as an aftermath of a tonsillectomy the week previous.

Rushed to a hospital, Gary was given emergency treatment, and physicians there said that another 15 minutes' delay would have cost the youngster his life. Lassie, the puppy that Gary insisted on choosing, had proven herself the prize of the litter.

BLAZE

1957 DOG HERO OF THE YEAR

A beautiful, white-faced collie named Blaze became the second of his breed to capture the annual gold medal and earn the 1957 award for his owners, Mr. and Mrs. Duane Hecox of Timewell, Illinois.

One day, while little Dawn Hecox, 2½, was playing in the yard on the Hecox farm, the child decided to get a better look at some baby pigs which were in a fenced-in enclosure nearby. She crawled through the fence, infuriating the mother sow, who charged her, knocked her to the ground, and was severely mauling and biting the child when Blaze, a short distance away, went into action.

Despite an ever-present fear he had of this massive sow, Blaze never hesitated. With a single bound, he cleared the fence and attacked the sow so savagely that she gave ground. The badly injured child, shocked and bleeding, was given enough time to crawl back through the fence to safety.

Hearing the commotion, the parents rushed to the scene, picked up their stunned and bleeding child, and hurried her to the hospital. There it was found that four teeth had been knocked out, numerous severe bites had been sustained, and she was in a state of shock. For two days, she was on the critical list, and was under the constant care of physicians for three weeks before recovering.

DUTCHESS

1958 DOG HERO OF THE YEAR

The 1958 gold medal was captured by Dutchess, a German shepherd, owned by Mr. and Mrs. Donald Phillippi of Excelsior, Minnesota. Dutchess saved Linda Phillippi, 10, from death by drowning, in a stirring display of courage and stamina.

The story began when Mr. Phillippi took three of his children for a ride on Lake William in his boat. Dutchess watched idly from the shore, since the Lake adjoins the Phillippi property.

Suddenly, as they neared the middle of the lake, the boat capsized while making a turn, and all occupants were thrown into the deep water. In addition to Mr. Phillippi, only one of the group, Johnny, 11, could swim. The other children, Matthew, 6, and Linda, 10, hung on desperately to the side of the overturned craft, with their father striving to keep their heads above water. The younger children were on the verge of panic, and were fast losing their grip on the boat.

Dutchess, 150 yards away on shore, sensed immediately what had happened. Without an instant's hesitation, she leaped into the water and swam to the scene with powerful strokes. As she reached the boat, Mr. Phillippi made a sudden and daring decision, for the boat was sinking rapidly and catastrophe was staring him in the face. He ordered Linda to grasp Dutchess' collar, As she did so, the dog, without a word of command, turned abruptly and struck out for shore, towing the almost dead weight of the 10-year-old girl behind her.

As Dutchess stumbled ashore after finishing the 150-yard swim, Linda collapsed exhausted on the bank. Dutchess now turned and was about to strike out for the boat again, when she saw that a neighbor had reached the scene in his own boat and was taking the other survivors to safety.

LADY

1959 DOG HERO OF THE YEAR

The first mongrel, or mixed breed, ever to capture a gold medal was the 1959 winner, Lady, a collie-shepherd. Lady's owners were Mr. and Mrs. Walter Abel of Mehlville, Mo., whose son, Tommy, 3, is alive today only because of the intelligence and persistence of this "curbstone setter."

It was a dark, cold February afternoon when Tommy wandered away from his suburban home near St. Louis. As he roamed about, accompanied by Lady, he failed to realize that he was getting farther and farther away from familiar territory. As dusk approached and the afternoon grew chill, Tommy suddenly found himself mired in a swamp, far from any human habitation.

A searching party, organized after the parents discovered his absence, had given up after failing to come anywhere near the place where Tommy was caught. The child, hysterical and exhausted, was so spent he could no longer even cry for help. At this point, Lady, who had been watching his unsuccessful efforts to free himself, hurried away—but this was no abandonment of her little master.

Racing through the woods and barking at the top of her lungs, Lady happened upon two telephone linemen. The unusual actions of the dog, for Lady was rushing back and forth and whining, indicated that she wished them to follow her. Finally convinced that something was wrong, they followed her.

After traveling a long distance and almost abandoning the whole idea as foolish, they reached the crest of a hill and found below them the exhausted child.

KEG

1960 DOG HERO OF THE YEAR

The second German shepherd to reign as National Dog Hero of the Year was the 1960 winner, Keg, owned by Mr. and Mrs. William McMannis of Bozeman, Montana.

Mr. McMannis, a professor of geology at Montana State College, had left for the school one morning, and Mrs. McMannis, who was doing some shopping, had left little Karen, their 18-month-old daughter, in the care of a neighbor.

Playing with her inseparable companion, Keg, the child wandered to the edge of the backyard, then suddenly decided that she would cross a footbridge that spanned Kelly Creek, normally a quiet little stream but at this time at flood stage. As she toddled along the bridge, Karen suddenly lost her balance and fell backward into the torrent.

Before the neighbor could act, Keg, a powerful dog, leaped into the water after the child. As he reached her side, he attempted to seize her dress, but could not manage to get a secure grip. Unable to hold Karen otherwise, he clamped his teeth into her shoulder, and with powerful strokes, began moving steadily toward the shore as they were swept downstream.

Battling the current with a furious determination, he managed to reach a spot where the stream widened, and pulled the unconscious child part way up the bank to where the pursuing neighbor could reach them.

DUKE

1961 DOG HERO OF THE YEAR

Fire, perhaps the most dreaded of all dangers to a dog, was responsible for the near-tragedy that won for Duke, a rollicking collie from Niles, Ohio, the gold medal as dog hero of 1961.

It was a blustery March afternoon when Penny Grantz, 10, daughter of Mr. and Mrs. John Grantz of Niles, went to the backyard to burn some papers. The wind caused the child's skirt to billow and suddenly burst into flames as flying ashes caught it. The terrified girl, panic-stricken, began to race toward the house 25 yards away.

Duke, playing nearby, took in the situation with a glance. Barking loudly, he overtook the child and, although possessing the average animal's dread of fire, seized her flaming skirt in his teeth and tore and pawed the garment off her to the ground, sustaining burns to his mouth in the process.

Penny's father, a night worker who was asleep at the time, heard the commotion and dashed from the house. By this time the flames had spread to her blouse and other clothing, and he ripped these off and rushed her to a hospital.

BEGGAR

1962 DOG HERO OF THE YEAR

One of the largest dogs ever to capture the annual gold medal as Dog Hero of the Year was a 165-pound female St. Bernard named Beggar, owned by Mr. and Mrs. Robert D. Mitchell of Sacramento, California.

Beggar's heroic action followed the disappearance of her little master, Bobby Mitchell, three years old, from his home in Carmichael, Calif., where the family resided at the time. By the time that his mother, busy with housework, discovered his absence, Bobby had wandered far from home, and was hopelessly lost. A search party failed to find any trace of him.

A Boy Scout troop, however, encamped along the rain-swollen American River, came across the child and Beggar, both soaking wet, a few feet from the river's edge and more than a mile from their home. Leading the shivering tot by the sleeve, and with her protective instincts fully aroused, the massive dog at first refused to surrender her little charge to the scouts.

When a family friend was brought to the scene, however, she gave him up docilely and trotted home after them. There the child's wet clothing was removed, and teeth marks on his body confirmed his story of how he had fallen into the river and Beggar had seized him in her huge jaws and swam to the bank.

DUTCH

1963 DOG HERO OF THE YEAR

Dutch, a fun-loving German shepherd from Troy, Pa., who leaped into icy water to rescue a four-year-old boy and thereby save the life of his three-year-old brother as well, was the winner of the tenth annual gold medal in 1963 as America's Dog Hero of the Year.

Hugh Hawthorne, four, and his little brother, Gordon, three, were playing on a pier which extends into the water of a pond near their home on the outskirts of Troy. As they scuffled on the pier, Gordon suddenly lost his balance and tumbled into the water, at this point approximately 12 feet deep. Horror-stricken, Hugh plunged in to save him. Neither child could swim a stroke.

Taking in the situation at a glance, Dutch, who had been looking on, raced onto the pier and leaped into the water, then standing at a cold 34 degrees. With powerful strokes, he made his way to Hugh and grabbed the lad by the ankle. Paddling swiftly, he

towed the spluttering lad to shore. Gordon, floating face downward, still remained in the water.

The clamor set up by Dutch and Hugh brought the boys' mother, Mrs. Gerald Hawthorne, to the scene on the run. Although nearly nine months pregnant, she dived into the water and was able to tow her unconscious son to shore.

Having watched a demonstration of mouth-to-mouth resuscitation on a television station five months earlier, she began efforts to revive Gordon who was "blue in the face, almost rigid, and with eyes open as though dead." Long minutes later, he gave a gurgle, and she rushed to the telephone and summoned aid.

A policeman arriving on the scene shortly afterward helped with the mouth-to-mouth resuscitation efforts, and a doctor then put his respiratory machine to work. Although apparently "dead" three times, the lad was finally revived at Troy Memorial Hospital and was allowed to return home at noon the next day.

BUDDY

1964 DOG HERO OF THE YEAR

Buddy, a 20-month-old purebred collie from Budd Lake, N.J., who saved nearly 300 goats in a raging fire that leveled most of his master's goat dairy farm, was named winner of the 11th annual gold medal in 1964.

In the early hours of a cold January morning, a fire had been roaring in the farm's maternity barn for some time before Buddy's frantic barks of warning were heard by his masters, Mr. and Mrs. Matthew S. Crinkley, Jr. Awakened by the commotion, the Crinkleys rushed to the windows only to see the walls and roof of the barn tumbling into a flaming pile of ruin.

Racing to the yard, they were astonished and elated to see Buddy marching back and forth with the effi-ciency of a Prussian general, watching over the entire flock of 70 expectant mother goats he had herded out of the barn. Despite severe burns on his paws and nasal damage from smoke inhalation, Buddy had maneuvered to safety an entire herd of animals that are notoriously stubborn, by pushing them and nip-ping at their feet.

The warning of this dedicated farm dog allowed the Crinkleys just enough time to save a second barn, which housed their remaining 30 goats, by wetting down a roof where sparks were beginning to ignite the structure. The 100 goats, together with those since born of the expectant mothers, later constituted a flock of nearly 300 goats that would surely have been lost had it not been for this devoted collie.

PATCHES

1965 DOG HERO OF THE YEAR

One of the most incredible rescues in all canine history earned for a Spanaway, Wash., mongrel the 12th annual gold medal, emblematic of "America's Dog Hero of the Year for 1965."

He was Patches, a Collie-Malemute, and the second mixed-breed in the history of the award to capture the top spot.

The amazing exploit, or series of exploits, that earned for Patches the first place rating in the eyes of the judges, took place on a near zero December night at Lake Spanaway, just south of Tacoma. Patches' owner, Marvin Scott, went down to a small pier below his lake home to check on possible ice damage to a patrol boat moored there. Patches "tagged along", a circumstances for which Scott would ever after be thankful.

Noting that a film of ice was beginning to form around the boat, Scott attempted to push on the stern line with a piece of timber. As he pushed with the timber he slipped from the icy pier and struck a floating dock causing him to tear virtually all of the tendons and muscles in both legs. He rolled off into the icy, 15-foot-deep water and went under.

Suddenly, while still below the surface, he felt something grasp him by the hair. It was Patches, who had leaped into the frigid water and was holding him firmly. Patches pulled the dazed and shivering man to the surface, then towed him nearly 20 feet to where he could seize the edge of the floating dock. Dimly aware that the dog, too, was by now nearly drowning and was almost exhausted from his rescue efforts,

Scott managed to push him onto the dock.

But as Scott, his legs immobile and useless, vainly attempted to climb onto the dock himself, the combination of the frigid water, his injuries, and the water he had swallowed caused him to virtually "black out" and his grip on the dock loosened. He fell back into the water and again went under.

But again it was Patches to the rescue. The courageous dog leaped in instantly, again seized him by the hair, and this time pulled him about four feet to the dock. After Scott had recovered enough to push Patches onto the dock, the man hung on grimly to the dock and screamed for help, but with the late hour and the wind against him, his cries could not be heard. At this critical moment, when Scott was certain each moment would be his last, Patches once more proved to be the difference between life and death.

Bracing his four feet firmly on the dock boards, Patches grasped Scott's overcoat collar and tugged. Encouraged by this unexpected assistance, Scott struggled with every ounce of strength he had left, and somehow, between the two of them, the gasping man was able to pull his body up onto the dock.

After he had regained his breath, Scott began crawling toward the house, with Patches in front of him holding tenaciously to his collar and using every bit of strength he possessed to help pull the shivering and agonized man along. The two laboriously made their way in this fashion up a rock-studded, 300-foot slope to a point near the back door, where Scott was able to throw a stone against the door and alert his wife.

HERO

A stout-hearted collie from Priest River, Idaho, with the amazingly appropriate name of "Hero," was the winner of the 13th annual gold medal as America's Dog Hero of the Year for 1966.

The first "show dog" ever to capture the honor, Hero, owned by Mr. and Mrs. George Jolley, gave an exhibition of courage, stamina, and intelligence that has seldom been exceeded.

Mrs. Jolley and her son, Shawn, three, were atop a haystack in the barn, and Mrs. Jolley was pitching hay down to horses coming in from the pasture through the open barn door. The first inkling she had that Shawn was not beside her was when she heard the child scream, and she saw Shawn racing across the floor to the end of the barn, with a maddened horse racing after him.

Mrs. Jolley shouted for Hero, although she hadn't the slightest idea where the dog was. At this moment, Shawn attempted to slide under a tractor at the end of the barn, but his clothing caught on a projecting piece of the vehicle. He was completely at the mercy of the raging horse, which raised its front feet to stamp the life out of the boy.

At this desperate and climactic moment Hero appeared and, before the horse's hooves could descend on the helpless child, Hero had seized the animal by the nose and was hanging on grimly.

The enraged horse swung the dog furiously to one side and then the other, and finally succeeded in hurling him against a tractor wheel, where Hero sank in a heap. But, amazingly, he was up an instant later and flying back at the horse before the latter could bring its feet down on the child.

Battling an adversary 15 times his size, Hero managed to give Mrs. Jolley time to drag Shawn to safety under the tractor. Now she joined the fray, poking at the horse with a stick while the latter continued to pound Hero viciously. Suddenly, the animal decided to break off the fight, and raced out the door toward the pasture, with Hero in close pursuit. Only after he saw it disappear into the distance did Hero sink to the ground, with blood pouring from his nose and mouth.

Mrs. Jolley rushed him to a veterinarian in Spokane, Washington, 45 miles away, where it was found that Hero had suffered crushed forefeet, had had five teeth either broken or knocked out, and four ribs broken. But it was typical of this dog's fighting heart that, just six weeks later, he lined up with other collies in a dog show and won three more points toward the coveted rating of "champion."

MIJO

1967 DOG HERO OF THE YEAR

A powerful, 180-pound St. Bernard named Mijo, from Anchorage, Alaska, was the winner of the 14th annual gold medal as America's Dog Hero of the Year in 1967.

Mijo saved the life of her 13-year-old mistress, Philiciann Bennett, after the girl had become mired in a water-filled gravel pit and, unable to free herself, was up to her chin in water and was about to drown. Mijo swam to her rescue, pulled her free of the mire, and towed her to safety. Mijo's heroic deed also probably saved the life of Philiciann's brother, Mitchell, 11, who was scrambling to reach his sister and would have been similarly trapped himself.

The amazing exploit of Mijo, owned by Mr. and Mrs. Jake Bennett of Anchorage, began on a September day, when Philiciann and Mitchell took the dog for a walk. Freed of her leash but wearing a neck chain, Mijo was romping on the edge of a water-filled gravel pit with the children when suddenly the ground, softened by rain, slid beneath them. Philiciann found herself in water up to her neck, with Mitchell some distance away but safely high and dry for the moment.

A competent swimmer, the girl attempted to "push off," but discovered that the effort only made her sink deeper. At this point, realizing that she could not free her feet, and with the water now up to her chin, the panic-stricken girl screamed for help. Mitchell, a short distance away, began to scramble down the deep embankment to reach her side, totally unaware that a similar fate might befall him.

At this moment of crisis, the girl saw Mijo making her way toward her. After making an apparently aimless circle in front of Philiciann, the dog suddenly lowered her head and came up directly beneath her. She made a desperate grab for the dog's chain collar and hung on grimly.

With the first of her powerful strokes, Mijo yanked the girl's feet free of the clinging mud, and headed for open water. Once away from the treacherous mud, she turned and, towing the almost dead weight of the 105-pound girl along, swam to a nearby bank and pulled her part-way up the bank to safety. Mitchell, watching the scene in amazement, now managed to make his way safely out of danger also.

RINGO

Ringo, a "part St. Bernard" mixed breed from Euless, Texas, was the 15th annual gold medal winner as America's Dog Hero of the Year in 1968.

Ringo's great exploit began on a day when his little master, 2½-year-old Randy Saleh, wandered away from home just 15 minutes before a gate was to be installed to stop the child's constant roaming. A two-hour police search failed to locate the child.

But about this time, Harley Jones, a school maintenance employee, driving along busy and dangerous Pipeline Road three-quarters of a mile from the Saleh home, found himself halted by a long line of cars ahead of him as he crossed a hill and approached a blind curve. Motorists in the line of 40 cars warned Jones that there was a "mad dog in the road ahead." He parked his car and went to the head of the line to investigate.

As he walked around the curve, he saw Ringo, resolutely stationed in the center of the road, blocking cars and even leaping against their fenders to halt the vehicles. Just a few feet ahead, and unseen, was little Randy, playing in the center of the heavily traveled roadway, as he had been doing for nearly 15 minutes.

Jones looked on in wonder as the dog, after stopping a car, would rush back to the child and nudge him to the side of the roadway. But the little fellow, apparently thinking it was some sort of game, would immediately scurry back to the center of the highway and sit there, laughing. The dog, almost exhausted from nearly a quarter of an hour of this, was almost frantic, but he continued to race toward every oncoming car to halt it before his little charge could be hit.

Approaching cautiously because of the dog's highly aroused protective instinct, Jones talked soothingly to Ringo, and finally calmed him enough to permit the man to pick up the child. With Ringo's teeth menacingly at the calf of his leg every step of the way, Jones managed to gain the side of the road. The dog now relaxed, and allowed the automobiles to pass without incident.

TOP

1969 DOG HERO OF THE YEAR

A courageous, child-loving Great Dane named Top, from Los Angeles, California, who saved two children from death or severe injury by two heroic deeds within eight weeks, was the winner of the gold medal in 1959.

Owned by a young German immigrant actor, Axel Patzwaldt, 25, the harlequin-type dog will always limp noticeably on his right rear leg, which was shattered when he was struck by a truck as he pushed a young girl from the path of the swift-moving vehicle. But the injury failed to prevent Top from initiating the rescue of a two-year-old child from drowning just eight weeks later.

The huge dog's exploits began on an April day when an 11-year-old neighbor girl was allowed to take him for a walk. A short distance from home, she started across the street, not noticing that a large truck was swiftly approaching. Suddenly realizing that the child was unaware of her danger, Top barked loudly, jumped in front of her, and pushed her backwards out of the way. She was unhurt, but Top was not so lucky—the truck hit him, breaking his right rear leg.

He was rushed to an animal hospital, where the leg was set and placed in a cast. His master took him home, and for seven weeks Top limped about painfully. Then, one week after the cast was removed, Patzwaldt let him out into the apartment house backyard, which contained a swimming pool. Just a few seconds later, Top came bounding back to the door, soaking wet and barking at the top of his lungs.

Patzwaldt and other residents ran to find out the reason for his noisemaking. They followed the excited and wildly-barking dog to the pool, and looked down to see the apparently lifeless body of two-year-old Christopher Conley, of the same address, lying on the bottom in six feet of water. Obviously, Top had leaped into the pool in an attempt to aid the tot, and failing in that, had summoned help by his loud and continuous barking.

Patzwaldt dove into the pool and brought the child out. Although the boy was apparently dead, the man began mouth-to-mouth resuscitation efforts while others called a fire rescue squad. By the time the firemen arrived, Patzwaldt had managed to arouse a spark of life in the tot. Rushed to Citizens Emergency Hospital in West Hollywood, the child began to show signs of improvement, and eight hours later was pronounced out of danger.

GRIZZLY BEAR

1970 DOG HERO OF THE YEAR

"Grizzly Bear," an extremely gentle St. Bernard from Denali, Alaska, which battled and finally routed a real grizzly bear that had attacked and was mauling his mistress, was selected as winner of the gold medal in 1970.

The 180-pound, 20-month-old dog, amazingly enough, had always been called "Grizzly Bear" rather than by its long, officially registered name of Polar Blu Samaritan von Barri. He is owned by Mr. and Mrs. David Gratias of Denali, who own and operate a lodge, and live in a cabin behind the main building.

Around noon one cold Spring day, Mrs. Gratias heard a noise in the backyard and went to investigate. She went out the front door, the only entrance to the cabin, leaving it open with her two-year-old daughter, Theresa, sleeping just inside. She also unleashed Grizzly Bear, thinking to give him some exercise while she was outside. But as she reached the backyard, she discovered a young grizzly bear cub there. Assuming that its mother must be near, she raced back toward the open front door. As she rounded the corner of the house, she came face to face with the mother grizzly.

The huge beast raised itself up to its eight-foot height and grabbed at her. Mrs. Gratias, conscious only of the fact that she must get to the open door and protect her daughter, attempted to side-step the animal. But her feet slipped on the icy ground. She fell, and lay stunned by the force of her fall.

In a flash, the grizzly was upon her, raking her cheek with one paw while it sank the other deep into her shoulder. But as it bent down to inflict a possibly fatal bite, the bear was suddenly staggered backwards as Grizzly Bear crashed into it with every ounce of his 180 pounds. Roaring with rage, the bear came back at her, but the dog, maneuvering smartly and slashing at the bear with his teeth and paws, managed to keep himself constantly between the animal and his helpless mistress.

At this moment, Mrs. Gratias, overcome with terror and loss of blood, lapsed into unconsciousness. When she came to, the dog was licking her face in an attempt to revive her. Sitting up dazedly, she suddenly remembered what had happened. She raced to the open door, to find Theresa inside, sleeping soundly. The bear had vanished.

Mrs. Gratias's wounds eventually healed, and fortunately, the claw marks on her face was not so deep as to cause disfiguration. Although Grizzly Bear was spotted with blood, no wounds were found, and it was assumed that the blood had come either from Mrs. Gratias or the bear itself.

TRIXIE

1971 DOG HERO OF THE YEAR

Trixie, a mixed breed dog from Lynn, Massachusetts, who raced for help and brought rescuers to her two-year-old master when he was drowning in icy water, was the 18th winner of the gold medal as America's Dog Hero of the Year for 1971.

Trixie, a "part beagle," was instrumental in saving the life of little Richard "Ricky" Sherry, when the tot tumbled into Buchanan Bridge Pond near his home. Medical history was made when the child was miraculously restored to life with no mental or physical damage after approximately 20 minutes without a heart beat.

The story of Trixie's exploit began around 11 a.m. on a cold April day when little Ricky somehow managed to squirm through a tiny space in the fence that enclosed the Sherry's backyard. His absence was quickly discovered, and a next door neighbor, Mrs. Felix Manna, volunteered to help search for him. She was only a few steps from the house when Trixie, sopping wet and barking at the top of her lungs, rushed up to her. Racing back and forth and looking over her shoulder as dogs do when they wish to be followed, Trixie set off for nearby Buchanan Bridge Pond, about 100 yards from the Sherry home, with Mrs. Manna hurrying behind her.

At the water's edge, Trixie halted, looked up at Mrs. Manna, and barked continuously. The woman peered out into the water but could see nothing. Trixie, seeing that her "message" could not be understood, leaped into the 35-degree water, paddled out a short distance, and began swimming in a small circle, barking all the while. Looking closely at the center of the circle, Mrs. Manna finally perceived what turned out to be the tip of the child's jacket, which had blended perfectly with the water. She plunged into the frigid five-foot-deep water and brought the child out.

Firemen responding quickly to the distress call could find no sign of life in the boy, although "unbelievable amounts of water" were forced out of the child's lungs. He was rushed to Lynn Hospital, where a team of physicians waited. With his body temperature standing at only 60 degrees, they were virtually certain that the child was beyond hope, but nevertheless used every known method of medical science to try to save him. By noon the next day, his temperature had returned to normal, and a week later he was permitted to go home.

316

GLOSSARY

Almond eye—the tissue surrounding the eye is almond shaped.
Angulation—angles formed where bones meet at joints—hindquarters and forequarters.
Apple head—the irregular roundness of the top skull—frequently humped toward center.
Apron—the longer hair found below the neck and on the chest—also known as frill.
A. K. C.—American Kennel Club.

Babbler—hound that barks when not on the trail.
Balanced—well-proportioned, symmetrical, all body parts in balance.
Bandog—a dog tied during the day and released at night.
Bandy legs—hocks turned outward—a serious fault which can be caused by rickets.
Barrel—rounded rib section.
Bat ear—ears erect and broad at the base and rounded at the top.
Bay—the sound or bark of a hunting hound.
Beard—bushy, thick hair appearing under the jaw.
Beefy—over development of the hind quarters.
Belton—color description signifying a blend of white and colored hairs, such as orange belton, blue belton, liver belton.
Bench show—type of dog show where dogs being shown must be on display (on the bench) during the time they are not in the ring.
Best in Show—the dog judged to be the best of all the breeds in a specific dog show.
Bird dog—a sporting dog that has been trained to hunt birds.
Bitch—a female dog.
Bite—the position of the upper and lower teeth when the mouth is closed.
Blaze—marking or white stripe which runs up the center of the face between the eyes.
Blinker—a hunting dog that points at a bird and leaves it or finds a bird and doesn't point.
Blocky—formation of the head which is square or cube-like.
Bloom—the sheen of a dog's coat when it is in top condition.
Blue—color term which may vary from light blue gray to slate—a steel blue-blue gray.
Blue merle—a color term—blue and gray mixed with black—a marbled tone.
Bobtail—either a dog that is naturally without a tail or one with the tail docked extremely short—usually an Old English Sheepdog.
Bossy—over-development of the shoulder muscles.
Brace—two dogs—a pair.
Breed—pure-bred dogs basically equal in size and structure.
Breeder—the individual who owns the dam at the time of breeding.
Breeding particulars—sire, dam, date of breeding, whelping date, sex, color, etc.
Brindle—a color term—a blending of black hairs with those of a lighter color—such as gray, tan, or brown.
Brisket—the forepart of the body below the chest, between the forelegs, closest to the ribs.
Broken color—the self color broken by white or another color.
Broken-haired—a rough wire coat.
Broken-up face—the nose receded, a deep stop, wrinkle, and undershot jaw (example—Bulldog, Pekingese).
Brood bitch—the female dog used for breeding purposes.
Brush—a tail well covered with hair, bushy.
Bullbaiting—a sport of ancient times where the dog was used to tease and torment the bull.

Burr—the inside of the ear—the irregular formations which can be seen.
Butterfly nose—a dark nose with flesh colored spots.
Buttocks—the rump or hips.
Button ear—the ear flap folded forward in such a way as to cover the opening and with the tip close to the skull.
Bye—at field trials, the dog remaining after the other dogs entered in a stake have been paired in braces by drawing.

Canine—the group of animals, including dogs, foxes, wolves, jackals.
Canines—the two upper and two lower sharp pointed teeth next to the incisors.
Castrate—the removal of the male dog's testicles.
Cat-foot—a compact, rounded, short foot like that of a cat.
Catch dog—dog used by sportsmen to hold a hunted animal so that it can be taken alive.
C. D. (Companion Dog)—a suffix which signifies that the dog has made a passing score in the novice class at the required number of obedience trials.
C. D. X. (Companion Dog Excellent)—suffix signifying that the dog has passed in Open Class at the required number of shows in obedience competition.
Champion—prefix granted by the A. K. C. to a dog who has defeated a specified number of dogs in the required number of show competitions.
Character—the expression, appearance, individuality, and deportment considered typical of a breed.
Cheeky—rounded, full thick cheeks.
Chest—section of the body enclosed by the ribs.
China Eye—a clear, blue eye.
Choke collar—a chain or leather collar which can be tightened or loosened by the trainer's control of the lead.
Chops—the joints or very pendulous flesh of the lips and jaw.
Clip—method used to trim the coats of certain breeds.
Cloddy—rather heavy, low, thick.
Coat—hair covering on the dog.
Cobby—short-bodied, compact.
Condition—general appearance of the dog or health as displayed by the coat, behavior, and body development.
Conformation—dog's form and structure; proportion and arrangement of the body parts in accordance with the breed standard. Term used to distinguish breed judging from obedience or field trials.
Corky—active, alert, lively, responsive.
Couple—two hounds.
Coupling—the part of the body between the ribs and pelvis.
Coursing—sport of chasing the hare by Greyhounds.
Cow-hocked—the hocks turn inward.
Crank tail—tail carried down and resembling a crank in shape.
Crest—upper, arched portion of the neck.
Cropping—cutting or trimming of the ear leather so that the ears stand erect.
Crossbred—dog whose sire and dam are representatives of two different breeds.
Croup—back part of the back, above the hind legs.
Crown—highest part of the head; the topskull.
Cry—baying or "music" of the hounds.
Cryptorchid—the adult whose testicles are retained in the abdominal cavity. Bilateral cryptorchidism involves both sides; that is, neither testicle has descended into the scrotum. Unilateral crytorchidism involves one side only; that is, one testicle is retained or hidden, and one descended.
Culotte—longer hair on the back of the thighs.

Cur—mongrel.
Cushion—fullness or thickness of the upper lips. (Pekingese.)

Dam—female parent.
Dappled—mottled marking of different colors, no one predominating.
Deadgrass—tan or dull straw color.
Derby—field-trial competition for young, novice sporting dogs usually between one and two years of age.
Dewclaw—extra claw or digit on the inside of the leg; a fifth toe.
Dewlap—loose, pendulous skin under the chin.
Diehard—nickname of the Scottish Terrier.
Dish-faced—the nasal bone is formed in such a way that the nose is higher at the tip than at the stop.
Disqualification—decision made by a judge or by a bench show committee following a determination that a dog has a condition that makes it ineligible for any further competition under the dog show rules or under the standard for its breed.
Distemper teeth—discolored or pitted teeth as a result of distemper or other disease or deficiency.
Dock—to shorten the tail by cutting.
Dog—a male dog; also used collectively to designate both male and female.
Dog show—competitive exhibition for dogs at which the dogs are judged in accordance with an established standard of perfection for each breed.
Domed—evenly rounded in topskull; convex instead of flat.
Double coat—outer coat resistant to weather and protective against brush and brambles, together with an undercoat of softer hair for warmth and waterproofing.
Down-faced—muzzle inclining downwards from the skull to the tip of the nose.
Down in pastern—weak or faulty pastern (metacarpus) set at a pronounced angle from the vertical.
Drag—trail prepared by dragging a bag impregnated usually with animal scent along the ground.
Drawing—selection by lot of dogs to be run, and in which pairs, in a field-trial stake.
Drop ear—the ends of the ear folded or drooping forward.
Dropper—cross between bird dogs.
Dry neck—skin taut; neither loose nor wrinkled.
Dual champion—a dog that has won both a bench show and a field trial championship.
Dudley nose—flesh-colored nose, often having eyerims of same shade.

Elbows out—elbows turning out or off from the body; not held close.
Ewe neck—concave curvature of the top neckline.
Expression—general appearance of all features of the head as viewed from the front and as typical of the breed.
Eyeteeth—upper canines.

Fall—hair hanging over the face.
Fancier—a person especially interested and usually active in some phase of the sport of pure-bred dogs.
Fangs—the canine teeth.
Feathering—longer fringe of hair on ears, legs, tail, or body.
Feet East and West—the toes turned out.
Fetch—retrieving of game by the dog; also the command.
Fiddle front—forelegs out at elbows, pasterns close, and feet turned out. French front.
Field Champion (Field Ch.)—prefix used with the name of a dog that has been recorded a Field Champion by A.K.C. as a result of defeating a specified number of dogs in specified competition at a series of A.K.C. licensed or member field trials.
Field trial—a competition for certain hound or sporting breeds in which dogs are judged on ability and style in finding or retrieving game or following a game trail.
Flag—long tail carried high; frequently referring to one of the pointing breeds.
Flank—side of the body between the last rib and the hip.
Flare—blaze that widens as it approaches the topskull.

Flat bone—leg bone whose girth is elliptical rather than round.
Flat-sided—ribs insufficiently rounded as they approach the sternum or breastbone.
Flews—upper lips pendulous particularly at their inner corners.
Flush—to drive birds from cover, to force them to take flight. To spring.
Flying ears—drop ears or semi-prick ears that stand or "fly."
Forearm—bone of the foreleg between the elbow and the pastern.
Foreface—front part of the head, before the eyes. Muzzle.
Foster mother—bitch or other animal, such as a cat, used to nurse whelps not her own.
Foul color—color or marking not characteristic.
Frill—hair under neck and on chest.
Fringes—longer hair on ears, tail, or body.
Frogface—extending nose accompanied by a receding jaw, usually overshot.
Front—forepart of the body as viewed head on; i.e., forelegs, chest, brisket, and shoulder line.
Furnishings—the long hair on the foreface of certain breeds.
Furrow—a slight indentation or median line down the center of the skull to the stop.
Futurity stake—class at dog shows or field trials for young dogs which have been nominated at or before birth.

Gait—manner in which dog walks, trots, or runs.
Game—hunted wild birds or animals.
Gay tail—tail carried up above back line.
Gazehound—Greyhound or other sight-hunting hound.
Geld—castrate.
Genealogy—recorded family descent.
Goose rump—too steep or sloping rump with tail set too low.
Grizzle—bluish-gray color.
Groom—to brush, comb, trim, or otherwise beautify the coat.
Groups—the breeds as grouped in size divisions to facilitate judging.
Gun dog—a dog trained to work with his master to find live game and retrieve game that has been shot.
Guns—sportsmen who do the shooting at field trials.
Gun-shy—a dog that fears the sight or sound of a gun.

Hackles—hair on neck and back raised involuntarily in fright or anger.
Ham—muscular development of the hind leg just above the stifle.
Handler—person who handles a dog in the show ring or at a field trial.
Hard-mouthed—dog that bites or marks with his teeth the game he retrieves.
Harefoot—a foot whose third digits are longer; a narrow foot.
Harlequin—patched or mottled coloration, usually black on white. (Great Danes.)
Harness—leather strap shaped around the shoulders and chest, with a ring at its top over the withers.
Haw—third eyelid or membrane in the inside corner of the eye.
Heat—seasonal period of the female. Estrum.
Heel—see Hock; also a command to the dog to keep close beside its handler.
Height—vertical measurement from the withers to the ground; referred to usually as shoulder height.
Hie on—command to urge the dog on; used in hunting or in field trials.
Hock—tarsus or collection of bones of the hind leg forming the joint between the second thigh and the metatarsus; the dog's true heel.
Honorable scars—scars from injuries suffered as a result of work.
Hound—dog commonly used for hunting by scent or sight.
Hound-marked—coloration composed of white, tan, and black. The ground color, usually white, may be marked with tan and/or black patches on the head, back, legs, and tail. The extent and the location of such markings, however, differ in breeds and individuals.

Hound jog—normal pace of the hound.
Hucklebones—top of the hipbones.

Inbreeding—mating of closely related dogs of the same standard breed.
Incisors—upper and lower front teeth between the canines.
Interbreeding—breeding together of dogs of different varieties.
Isabella—fawn or light bay color.

Judge—the arbiter in the dog show ring, obedience trial, or field trial.

Kennel—building where dogs are kept.
Kink tail—sharply bent tail.
Kiss marks—tan spots on the cheeks and over the eyes.
Knuckling over—faulty structure of carpus (wrist) joint allowing it to double forward under the weight of the standing dog; double-jointed wrist often with slight swelling of the bones.

Layback—angle of the shoulder blade as compared with the vertical.
Lead—a strap, cord, or chain attached to the collar or harness for the purpose of restraining or leading the dog. Leash.
Leather—flap of the ear.
Level bite—when the front teeth (incisors) of the upper and lower jaws meet exactly edge to edge. Pincer bite.
License—formal permission granted by A.K.C. to a non-member club to hold a dog show, obedience trial, or field trial; or to a person to handle dogs in the show ring for pay.
Line breeding—mating of related dogs of the same standard breed, within the line or family, to a common ancestor.
Lippy—pendulous lips or lips that do not fit tightly.
Litter—the puppy or puppies of one whelping.
Liver—a color term; i.e., deep, reddish brown.
Loaded shoulders—when the shoulder blades are shoved out from the body by over-development of the muscles.
Loin—region of the body on either side of the vertebral column between the last ribs and the hindquarters.
Lumber—superfluous flesh.
Lumbering—an awkward gait.
Lurcher—crossbred hound.

Mad dog—rabid dog.
Mane—long and profuse hair on top and sides of the neck.
Mantle—dark-shaded portion of the coat on shoulders, back, and sides.
Mask—dark muzzle.
Match show—usually an informal dog show at which no championship points are awarded.
Mate—to breed a dog and bitch.
Merle—color term, usually blue-gray with touches of black.
Miscellaneous Class—competitive class at dog shows for dogs of certain specified breeds for which no regular dog show classification is provided.
Molera—incomplete, imperfect or abnormal ossification of the skull.
Mongrel—dog whose parents are of mixed-breed origin.
Monorchid—a unilateral cryptorchid.
Music—the baying of the hounds.
Mute—to run mute, to be silent on the trail; i.e., to trail without baying or barking.
Muzzle—the head in front of the eyes—nasal bone, nostrils, and jaws. Also, a strap or cage attached to the foreface to prevent the dog from biting or from picking up food.
Muzzle band—white marking around the muzzle.

Non-slip Retriever—the dog that walks at heel, marks the fall, and retrieves game on command; not expected to find or flush.
Nose—organ of smell; also, the ability to detect by means of scent.

Occiput—upper, back point of the skull.
Occipital protuberance—a prominently raised occiput characteristic of some gun-dog breeds.
Open bitch—bitch that can be bred.
Open class—class at dog shows in which all dogs of a breed, champions and imported dogs included, may compete.
Otter tail—thick at the root, round, and tapering, with the hair parted or divided on the underside.
Out at elbow—elbows turning out from the body as opposed to being held close.
Outcrossing—mating of unrelated individuals of the same breed.
Overhand—heavy or pronounced brow.
Overshot—front teeth (incisors) of the upper jaw overlap and do not touch the front teeth of the lower jaw when the mouth is closed.

Pace—gait which tends to promote a rolling motion of the body. The left foreleg and left hind leg advance in unison, then the right foreleg and right hind leg.
Pack—several hounds kept together in one kennel. Mixed pack is composed of dogs and bitches.
Paddling—moving with forefeet wide.
Pads—soles of the feet.
Paper foot—a flat foot with thin pads.
Parti-color—marks or patches of two or more colors.
Pastern—leg below knee of front leg or below hock of hind leg.
Pedigree—written record of a dog's descent of three generations or more.
Penciling—black lines dividing the tan on the toes.
Pica—craving for un-natural food.
Pied—large patches of two or more colors. Piebald, parti-colored.
Pigeon breast—chest with a short protruding breastbone.
Pile—dense undercoat of soft hair.
Plume—long fringe of hair hanging from the tail as in the Pomeranian.
Poach—when hunting, to trespass on private property.
Point—the immobile stance of the hunting dog taken to show the presence and position of game.
Points—color on face, ears, legs, and tail when correlated—usually white, black, or tan.
Police dog—dog trained for police work.
Pompon—rounded tuft of hair left on the end of the tail when the coat is clipped. (Poodle)
Premium List—advance-notice brochure sent to prospective exhibitors and containing details regarding a forthcoming show.
Prick ear—erect and usually pointed at the tip.
Professional handler—a person licensed by the A.K.C. to show dogs for their owners, for a fee.
Put down—to prepare a dog for the show ring; also used to denote a dog unplaced in competition.
Puppy—dog under 12 months of age.
Pure-bred—dog whose sire and dam belong to the same breed, and are themselves of unmixed descent since recognition of the breed.

Quality—refinement, fineness.

Racy—long legged and slight.
Rat tail—the root thick and covered with soft curls; at the tip devoid of hair, or having the appearance of being clipped. (Irish Water Spaniel.)
Register—to record a dog's breeding particulars.
Retrieve—hunting term. The act of bringing back shot game to the handler.
Ring tail—carried up and almost in a circle.
Roach back—a convex curvature of the back toward the loin. Carp back.
Roan—a fine mixture of colored hairs with white hairs; blue roan, orange roan, lemon roan. (English Cocker Spaniel.)
Roman nose—a nose whose bridge is so high as to form a slightly convex line from forehead to nose tip.

Rose ear—small drop ear which folds over and back so as to reveal the burr.

Rounding—cutting or trimming the ends of the ear leather. (English Foxhounds.)

Rudder—tail.

Ruff—thick, longer hair growth around the neck.

Runt—under-sized puppy.

Sable—lacing of black hairs over a lighter ground color.

Saddle—a black marking over the back, like a saddle.

Scent—the odor left by an animal on the trail (ground scent), or wafted through the air (air-borne scent).

Scissors bite—a bite in which the outer side of the lower incisors touches the inner side of the upper incisors.

Scout—the handler's assistant.

Screw tail—short tail twisted in more or less spiral formation.

Second thigh—that part of the hindquarter from the stifle to the hock, corresponding to the human shin and calf. Lower thigh.

Seeing Eye dog—a dog trained by the institution, The Seeing Eye, as guide for the blind.

Self color—one color or whole color except for lighter shadings.

Semi-prick ears—ears carried erect with just the tips leaning forward.

Septum—line extending vertically between the nostrils.

Shelly—narrow body, lacking the correct amount of bone, weedy.

Shoulder height—height of dog's body as measured from the withers to the ground.

Sickle tail—carried out and up in a curve.

Sire—male parent.

Sled dogs—dogs worked often in teams to draw sleds.

Smooth coat—short hair, close-lying.

Snipy—pointed, weak muzzle.

Soundness—state of mental and physical health when all organs and faculties are complete and functioning normally, each in its rightful relation to the other.

Spay—to perform a surgical operation on the bitch's reproductive organs to prevent conception.

Speak—to bark.

Spectacles—shadings or dark markings over or around the eyes or from eyes to ears.

Splashed—irregularly patched, color on white or white on color.

Splayfoot—flat foot with toes spreading. Open-toed.

Spread—accentuated width between the forelegs.

Spring of ribs—curvature of ribs for heart and lung capacity.

Squirrel tail—carried up and curving more or less forward.

Stake—designation of a class, used in field trial competition.

Stance—manner of standing.

Standard—description of the ideal dog of each recognized breed, to serve as a word pattern by which dogs are judged at shows.

Standoff coat—long or heavy coat that stands off from the body.

Staring coat—hair dry, harsh, and sometimes curling at the tips.

Station—comparative height from the ground, as high-stationed, low-stationed.

Staunch (or stanch)—to remain still on point until the birds are flushed.

Stern—tail of a sporting dog or hound.

Sternum—breastbone.

Stifle—joint of the hind leg between the thigh and the second thigh. The dog's knee.

Stilted—choppy, up-and-down gait of a straight-hocked dog.

Stop—step up from muzzle to skull; indentation between the eyes where the nasal bone and skull meet.

Straight hocked—no significant angulation at the hock joints. Straight behind.

Straight shoulders—the shoulder blades rather straight up and down, as opposed to sloping or "well laid back."

Stud book—record of the breeding particulars of dogs of recognized breeds.

Stud dog—male dog used for breeding purposes.

Style—term used to describe dogs movement, action and point.

Substance—bone.

Superciliary arches—prominence of the frontal bone of the skull over the eye; the brow.

Swayback—concave curvature of the back line between the withers and the hipbones.

T.D. (Tracking Dog)—suffix used with the name of a dog that has been recorded a Tracking Dog as a result of having passed an A.K.C. licensed or member tracking test. The title may be combined with the U.D. title and shown as U.D.T.

Team—usually four dogs of one breed.

Terrier—a group of dogs used originally for hunting vermin.

Thigh—the hindquarters from hip to stifle.

Throatiness—loose skin under the throat in excess.

Thumb marks—black spots on the forelegs.

Ticked—small, isolated areas of black or colored hairs on a white ground.

Timber—bone, especially of the legs.

Tongue—baying or voice of hounds on the trail or on scent.

Topknot—a tuft of longer hair on top of the head of some breeds.

Toy dog—one of a group of dogs characterized by very small size.

Trace—a dark stripe down the back of the Pug.

Trail—dog hunting by following ground scent.

Triangular eye—eye set in surrounding tissue of triangular shape; three-cornered eye.

Tricolor—three-color: white, black, and tan.

Trim—to groom the coat by plucking, stripping, or clipping.

Trumpet—slight depression or hollow on either side of the skull just behind the orbit or eye socket, the region comparable with the temple in man.

Tucked up—characterized by markedly shallower body depth at the loin. Small-waisted.

Tulip ear—ears carried erect with a slight forward curvature.

Turnup—uptilted foreface.

Type—characteristic qualities distinguishing a breed; the embodiment of a standard's essentials.

U.D. (Utility Dog)—a suffix used with the name of a dog that has been recorded a Utility Dog by A.K.C. as a result of having won certain minimum scores in Utility Classes at a specified number of A.K.C. licensed or member obedience trials. The title may be combined with the T.D. title and shown as U.D.T.

Undershot—front teeth (incisors) of the lower jaw overlapping or projecting beyond the front teeth of the upper jaw.

Varminty—keen, very bright or piercing expression.

Vent—anal opening.

Walleye—eye with a whitish iris; a blue eye, fisheye, pearl eye.

Weaving—when in motion, the crossing of the forefeet or the hind feet. Traveling "in and out."

Weedy—light-boned, too lightly formed.

Wheaten—pale yellowish color.

Wheel back—the back line arched markedly over the loin. Roached.

Whelping—act of giving birth to puppies.

Whelps—unweaned puppies.

Whip tail—carried out stiffly straight, and pointed.

Whisker—longer hairs on muzzle sides and underjaw.

Wind—catching the scent of game.

Winners—award given at dog shows to the best dog (Winners Dogs) and best bitch (Winners Bitches) competing in regular classes.

Wirehair—crisp, wiry, harsh coat.

Withers—highest point of the shoulders, immediately behind the neck.

Wrinkle—loosely, folded skin on sides of face and forehead.

320